China and Democracy

China and Democracy

The Prospect for a
Democratic China

EDITED BY
SUISHENG ZHAO

Routledge
New York   London

Published in 2000 by
Routledge
29 West 35th Street
New York, NY 10001

Published in Great Britain by
Routledge
11 New Fetter Lane
London EC4P 4EE

10   9   8   7   6   5   4   3   2   1

Library of Congress Cataloging-in-Publication Data

China and democracy : the prospect for a democratic China / edited by Suisheng Zhao.
    p.   cm.
   Includes bibliographical references.
   ISBN 0-415-92693-9 — ISBN 0-415-92694-7 (pbk.)
    1. Democracy—China.   2. Democratization—China   3. China—Politics and government—1976–   4. China—Politics and government—20th century.
   I. Zhao, Suisheng.
   JQ1516.C4525   2000
   320.951—dc21   00-032310

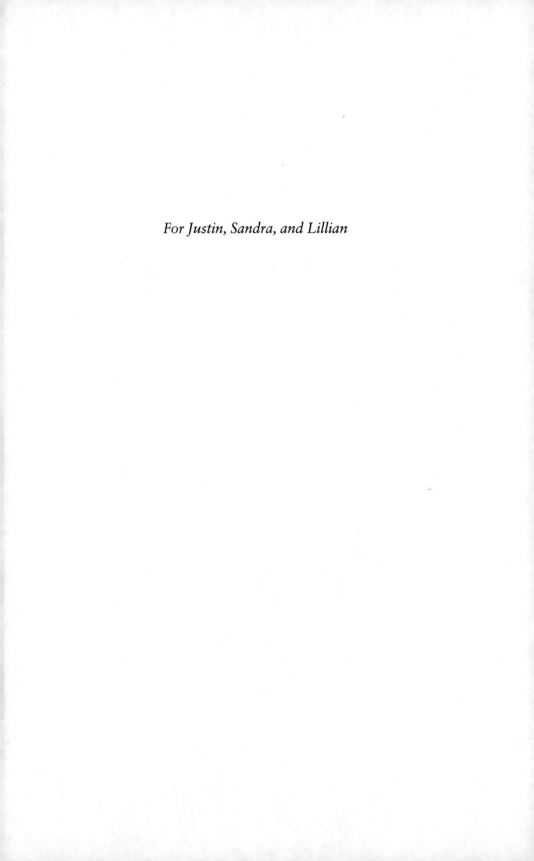

For Justin, Sandra, and Lillian

Contents

III Chinese State-Society Relations and Democracy

IV The Prospects for Democracy in China at the Dawn of the Twenty-First Century

Foreword

LARRY DIAMOND

For the long-term future of democracy there is no more important country than China. This is true simply by virtue of China's size. It is a nearly continental country, and its population is one-fifth of all humanity. It is the cultural, if no longer national, homeland of millions of Chinese immigrants to other countries. If its economic development continues without a catastrophic interruption, its commercial, scientific, intellectual, cultural, and (potentially less benign) military dynamism is bound to be felt increasingly throughout Asia and the rest of the world. Barring an economic and ecological implosion, China is the emerging superpower of the twenty-first century. If, on the other hand, there is an implosion, the consequences will be destabilizing for all of Asia, and indeed the world.

One need not subscribe simplistically to the theory—some call it "doctrine"—of a democratic peace to appreciate how the democratization of China could contribute to regional and international peace and security. A China governed by open and transparent politics, constitutionalism, a rule of law, and the deliberative procedures of democracy would be a China more likely to resolve its conflict with Taiwan through peaceful accommodation. Indeed, the Republic of China on Taiwan has declared a democratic constitutional system on the mainland to be a precondition for unification. Practically, it is difficult to imagine a political formula for unification that would not heavily rely on a federal or confederal constitutional framework, and this could only be credible and meaningful politically within the larger context of democracy, buttressed by an independent judiciary.

Beyond the Taiwan problem, a China governed by the more comprehensive architecture of democracy—not just competitive, free, and fair elections at all levels of power, but a pluralistic civil society, a free press and intellectual life, institutions of horizontal accountability, and a rigorous, independent judicial system—would be a more responsible regional neighbor and global actor. It would be better able to control the corruption and organized crime that otherwise threaten to undermine the security and legal orders of many countries. By controlling corruption, redressing social grievances, removing unpopular rulers, managing political conflict, negotiating new political bargains with regional and ethnic minorities, and compelling the state to respond to severe and growing ecological problems, a genuinely democratic system would refurbish political legitimacy and thus enhance the long-run political stability of China. Even within the Chinese Communist Party (CCP) there is growing recognition that China must evolve more open, responsive, accountable, and participatory political structures, or else risk rising political instability, even turmoil.

This is not to say that the *process* of democratization will be without its own perils. Between the current reality of incipient but still extremely limited pluralism, with widespread repression and arbitrary rule, and the long-term goal of constitutional democracy in China, lies a formidable process of institutional change. Many CCP leaders appear to have some sense of the direction in which China must move politically, but no strategic clarity or confidence in how to get there. No one—least of all Jiang Zemin—wants to be the Chinese version of Mikhail Gorbachev. None of the top leadership of the CCP seems willing to see the party risk losing control in the process of opening up. There is also the danger, for China's neighbors and for the West, that rising nationalism, which Suisheng Zhao analyzes in the concluding chapter of this volume, could be aggravated by the process of democratization as competing political parties and candidates search for some basis on which to mobilize and capture a majority of the electorate—or as a besieged ruling party seeks to divert attention from its own domestic failures.

If Chinese communist leaders decide to look around for a model of controlled, gradual, phased democratization led from above, they need look no further than to the island across the strait that they claim as a part of China: Taiwan. There, a decadent Kuomintang (KMT), which had suffered the traumatic loss of political control over the mainland in 1949, began to defend and reconstruct its rule on the foundation of more limited government (what Thomas Metzger has called an "inhibited center"), with local electoral competition taking place under the overall control of the single, ruling party. There, elections gradually became more competitive over time, as the ruling party slowly gained in self-confidence and political capacity, and as a diverse assortment of independent candidates gradually cohered into an opposition network, the *dangwai*, and then, in 1987, into an opposition party, the Democratic Party. Gradually, the Republic of China evolved from a failed state that had to flee the mainland, to an inhibited and increasingly pluralistic—albeit still autocratic and repressive—political center, eventually to what Metzger calls a "subordinated" political center, giving extensive freedom and autonomy to its citizens and allowing for many arenas of decision making.[1] In somewhat different language, one could say that Taiwan gradually shifted (and South Korea more rapidly) to democracy from what Robert Scalapino calls an "authoritarian pluralist" system "wherein political life remains under the unchallenged control of a dominant-party or single-party regime; strict limits are placed on liberty . . . ; and military or national security organs keep a close eye on things," but there exists a civil society with some autonomy from the state and some capacity to express diverse interests, as well as a mixed or increasingly market-oriented economy.[2]

The Taiwan case bears significant implications for China's future, not only because of the national and cultural connections, but because China has begun to follow the path of Taiwan's evolution.[3] Although the political regime of the KMT on Taiwan was never totalitarian, it did evolve from an early period of terror and severe domination by a quasi-Leninist ruling party to a much more limited and pluralistic, less ideological form of authoritarianism. Since Deng Xiaoping's rise to power, China has treaded a path of political change that bears some intriguing similarities to that in Taiwan. From an *uninhibited political center* that obtains (whether through revolutionary fervor or terror and coercion) the society's total compliance with its ideology, policies, and commands, China has been evolving since 1978 toward an *inhibited* center, a more conventional authoritarian (if not authoritarian-pluralist) system.[4] The Chinese Communist Party has lost its revolutionary zeal, even its commitment to socialism, as it has increasingly sanctioned market principles and incentives. With economic reform, the relationship between state and society has altered significantly over the past two decades, as several of the essays in this volume show. Ineluctably, the emergence of the market has brought with it diverse economic interests and a loosening of central state control. This has nurtured increasing pluralism in intellectual life, challenging socialist dogma with increasing boldness, and a growing diversity of associations autonomous from the state. As Suisheng Zhao notes in his introduction, this has led as well to "a reduction in the scope and arbitrariness of political intervention in daily life," and to greater political participation that is not centrally mobilized. To be sure, there is one huge dimension of pluralism that remains off-limits, as the 1999 crackdown on the Falun Gong religious movement shows, and that is any challenge, however implicit, to the political hegemony of the Communist Party. Nevertheless, evolution toward a liberalizing, authoritarian-pluralist system always begins with pluralism in arenas outside politics. If this evolution is allowed to continue, it will (as it did in Taiwan, and before that in Spain) transform politics as well, when changes in leadership, the economy and society, or other national conditions open the opportunity for systemic political change.

The literature on regime transitions has lacked an adequate appreciation of the degree to which fairly rapid and bounded transitions to democracy have often been preceded and facilitated by longer periods of struggle, pressure, transformation of the political culture, and weakening of state control by an increasingly pluralistic, vibrant, and pro-democratic civil society.[5] This tilling of the democratic soil and pressure from below occurred even in Taiwan, a classic instance (or so it has generally been depicted) of democratization from above.[6] If China is ever to democratize, even by reforms from above, it will certainly require pressure from an increasingly organized and assertive civil society that pushes the Communist Party, or whatever authority is then in control of the state, to liberalize further than it would otherwise do.

In this regard, some readers might draw a pessimistic conclusion from the chapters in this volume dealing with mass political culture, which find little evidence of mass public pressure for democracy in China today. But that is today; as the century turns, Chinese students may be absorbed in a materialist pragmatism, concerned with their own careers. When political consciousness does sweep the campuses, it now seems more likely to take a nationalist rather than democratic turn. The strong undercurrent of nationalism in both ruling party and opposition politics will not likely abate any time soon, and could easily be inflamed again and again by overt hostility from or conflicts with the West. However, no one can predict how mass public attitudes will evolve in ten or even five years' time. Certainly, as several chapters in this book argue convincingly, the Confucian cultural inheritance does not present an insurmountable obstacle to democratization, and in any case culture is not fixed and unchanging. As China increasingly opens up to the world, it is likely that a growing body of Chinese political thinkers and activists will argue for democracy on something like the universalistic normative principles Baogang He espouses in chapter 5. Already this type of thinking is growing among Chinese intellectuals, and this elite (or more appropriately, counterelite) phenomenon could be the harbinger of a broader political movement.

If China succeeds in integrating more and more with the global flow of goods, services, culture, and information, it will be transformed in ways that we can only dimly imagine now. Ordinary Chinese people will have much more access to independent information, and to a wide range of alternative ideas, not only through books but through music, television, movies, and the dizzying range of other information flows and sites on the Internet. Some of these flows may appear threatening, inducing a nationalist backlash, but on balance integration is likely to be broadening, pluralizing, and subversive of the existing authoritarian political order. Even in its flows of investment and technology, globalization will likely have a politically liberalizing impact, as global investors demand a more secure and predictable institutional environment that can only be obtained by strengthening the rule of law, and hence by augmenting the independence and capacity of the judicial system.[7]

A number of institutional changes in the 1990s suggest a more optimistic view of the prospects for democratic change in China. In a loose parallel to Taiwan, a key early element of political change lies in the increasing autonomy of local-level authority and the introduction of at least partially competitive and free elections for local governing bodies at the village level. Although competitive elections for the positions of village head and committee member are now in place for probably no more than a third of China's nearly one million villages, the process has been mandated by national law for more than a decade, and some villages have now experienced four rounds of such contests. In some regions the nomination process is becoming distinctly fairer and more open, and the procedures and values of a secret-ballot election, with political competition and choice, appear to be improving and taking root. Gradually, authority relations at the microlevel are being transformed, and the Communist Party monopoly on village administration is loosening. China's central government is actively working to improve and standardize competitive village elections—and even seeking international assistance in the process—for the same reason it initiated them in 1987: it needs this democratic vehicle to control corruption, channel peasant frustrations, generate greater efficiency and legitimacy at the local level, and thus maintain political stability.[8]

Political decompression in China has other dimensions as well. Modest competition has been introduced for election to the party congress. The National People's Congress, and especially some provincial and local people's congresses, are evolving from rubber stamps into more autonomous, professional, and inquisitive bodies, and delegates at all levels are pressing for further reform. The decentralization of economic and political responsibility to provincial and lower-level governments is giving rise to a "nascent federalist structure." Rule is becoming more institutionalized, less personalized, with the enforcement of mandatory retirement ages and two-term limits on officials. A "system of law" is beginning to emerge, partly through a law on administrative litigation (implemented in 1990) that enables citizens to sue government agencies and officials for abuse of state power. By the mid-1990s, the number of lawsuits continued to rise, and more than a third led to relief for the plaintiffs, either through a favorable court decision or through an out-of-court settlement.

Chinese citizens are becoming more aware of their political and economic rights and more assertive in defending them. Access to independent information is expanding, and so is the number of semiofficial and private (as opposed to state or party-controlled) associations—such as those of lawyers, private entrepreneurs, consumers, and environmentalists—that are "civic" in their concerns to articulate interests and affect public policy as well as in their creation of social capital through the horizontal organization of individuals as self-motivated citizens. Finally, as Michel Oksenberg tells us, in the 1990s "China's elite political culture has begun to change. Democracy has begun to be enshrined as an ultimate goal for China."[9]

To be sure, China remains an authoritarian, one-party state with strong corporatist controls over civil society and appalling human rights violations.[10] But early steps toward liberalization are discernible even within the political system. As it enters the new century, the key question confronting the CCP is whether it has the nerve, the imagination, and the self-confidence to accelerate the process of liberalizing political change. As Oksenberg has written, the core challenge has yet to be addressed even partially: reforming—by constraining—the Chinese Communist Party's institutional hegemony over all aspects of politics and government. With its legitimacy waning and society and the economy rapidly changing, the CCP cannot stand still. It must either move forward toward democracy (however gradually) or risk losing control over the process of political change. Moving forward need not entail for some time—as it did not for many years in Taiwan—the toleration of an explicitly oppositional political party, but it would require competitive elections to move up to the township and county levels, and ultimately to the provincial level (where the scale of politics would make meaningful choice inconceivable without alternative parties). And it would necessitate such other changes as separation of the party from the government; detachment of the judiciary from party control; "transferring the military from party to government command"; allowing much more space for formation of independent interest groups and voluntary associations; and "subjecting the party to greater external scrutiny by a vigorous press and more assertive parliaments."[11]

If China can negotiate these treacherous steps of political liberalization in the next decade, it will be poised for a peaceful transition to democracy a decade or two later, when its greater levels of economic development, societal pluralism, and international engagement will make such a transition both more viable and more necessary. If the Chinese Communist Party balks at such changes (and at crafting *a more general strategy of political reform*), the prospect of a political rupture will significantly increase, and along with it, the possibility that political change will be violent, even chaotic, and seriously destabilizing for China's neighbors and the world beyond.

With their rich insights into China's difficult history and conflicted present, the essays in this volume will prove an important guide to understanding China's choices and dilemmas in the years to come.

Notes

1. The three ideal types of political centers—uninhibited, inhibited, and subordinated—were first developed by Thomas A. Metzger and further refined through discussions with Ramon H. Myers. Metzger introduced these concepts in Ramon H. Myers, ed., *Two Societies in Opposition: The Republic of China and the People's Republic of China after Forty Years* (Stanford, Calif.: Hoover Institution Press, 1991), xvii. These ideal types are also explained in Linda Chao and Ramon H. Myers, *The First Chinese Democracy: Political Life in the Republic of China on Taiwan* (Baltimore, Md.: Johns Hopkins University Press, 1998), 7–9. That book provides a comprehensive history of Taiwan's evolution from authoritarian rule to democracy.
2. Robert A. Scalapino, "Will China Democratize? Current Trends and Future Prospects," *Journal of Democracy* 9, no. 1 (1998), 38–39.
3. For a more explicit consideration of whether limited elections, as in Taiwan, may provide a model for the democratization of China, see *China Quarterly* 162 (2000), "Elections and Democracy in Greater China," edited by Ramon Myers and Larry Diamond.
4. Thomas A. Metzger, "Will China Democratize? Sources of Resistance," *Journal of Democracy* 9, no. 1 (1998), 20.
5. Ruth Berins Collier and James Mahoney, "Adding Collective Actors to Collective Outcomes: Labor and Recent Democratization in South America and Southern Europe," *Comparative Politics* 29, no. 2 (1997), and Larry Diamond, *Developing Democracy: Toward Consolidation* (Baltimore: Johns Hopkins University Press, 1999), 233–39.
6. Yun-han Chu, *Crafting Democratization in Taiwan* (Taipei: Institute for National Policy Research, 1992).

7. On these political implications of globalization, see Thomas L. Friedman, *The Lexus and the Olive Tree: Understanding Globalization* (New York: Farrar, Straus and Giroux, 1999).

8. Kevin J. O'Brien, "Implementing Political Reform in China's Villages," *Australian Journal of Chinese Affairs* 32 (1994), 33–60; Lianjiang Li and Kevin J. O'Brien, "The Struggle over Village Elections," Department of Political Science, University of California, Berkeley, October 21, 1997; Melanie Manion, "The Electoral Connection in the Chinese Countryside," *American Political Science Review* 90, no. 4 (1996), 736–48; Jean C. Oi, "Economic Development, Stability, and Democratic Village Self-Governance," in Maurice Brace, Suzanne Pepper, and Shu-I Tang, eds., *China Review* (Hong Kong: Chinese University Press, 1997), 125–44; Carter Center, "Village Elections in China, March 2–15, 1998," Carter Center Delegation Report, Atlanta, Georgia, March 25, 1998; International Republican Institute (IRI), "Village Committee Elections in the People's Republic of China," Washington, D.C., January 1997; IRI, "Election Observation Report: Fujian, People's Republic of China," May 1997.

9. Michel Oksenberg, "Will China Democratize? Confronting a Classic Dilemma," *Journal of Democracy* 9, no. 1 (1998), 27–40, quotation on 30; see also Minxin Pei, "'Creeping Democratization' in China," *Journal of Democracy* 6, no. 4 (1995), 65–79; Minxin Pei, "Is China Democratizing?" *Foreign Affairs* 77, no. 1 (1998), 68–82; Minxin Pei, "Citizens versus Mandarins: Administrative Litigation in China," *China Quarterly* 152 (1997), 832–62; Minxin Pei, "Chinese Civic Associations: An Empirical Analysis," *Modern China* 24, no. 3 (1998), 285–318; Minxin Pei, *From Reform to Revolution: The Demise of Communism in China and the Soviet Union* (Cambridge, Mass.: Harvard University Press, 1994), chap. 5; Chih-yu Shih, "The Institutionalization of China's People's Congress System: The Views of People's Deputies," *International Politics* 33 (1996), 145–62; Yingyi Quian and Barry R. Weingast, *China's Transtition to Markets: Market-Preserving Federalism, Chinese Style* (Stanford, Calif.: Hoover Institution Press, 1995).

10. In addition to the annual human rights report of Amnesty International, Human Rights Watch, and the U.S. Department of State, see Amnesty International, *China: No One Is Safe* (New York: Amnesty International, 1996); Martin King Whyte, "Social Trends and the Human Rights Situation in the PRC," paper presented to the twenty-seventh Sino-American Conference on Contemporary China, Institute of International Relations, Taipei, 1998.

11. Michel Oksenberg, "The Long March Ahead," *South China Morning Post,* 1 October 1999, 1.

Introduction

China's Democratization Reconsidered

SUISHENG ZHAO

Observation on China's democratization has often oscillated between two extremes of optimism and pessimism in the past decade. Optimistic observers believe that the end of the Cold War started a great expansion of democracy and a new period in modern world history, or in the words of Samuel Huntington, a third wave of "global democratic revolution, which is "the most important political trend in the late twentieth century."[1] In this case, China had no other choice but to follow the tide and democratize soon. Indeed, immediately after the Tiananmen Square crackdown on democratic protests in June 1989, many commentators looked to the demise of the communist regimes in the Soviet Union and Eastern Europe to predict an imminent collapse of the communist authoritarian regime in China. Ruan Ming, a prominent political dissident from China, used the phrase "last days of the empire" to describe the communist authoritarian regime shortly after the Tiananmen massacre and asserted that "the June Fourth slaughter destroyed the Deng Xiaoping empire."[2] Lucian Pye, a prominent China watcher in the United States, also declared, in his presidential address at the 1989 annual meeting of the American Political Science Association, that "we are today confronted with a unifying challenge in the crisis of authoritarianism that is undermining the legitimacy of all types of authoritarian systems throughout the world, including the Marxist-Leninist regimes. Authoritarian governments are about to pass from this earth."[3]

However, instead of the imminent collapse of Deng Xiaoping's authoritarian regime, China experienced astonishing economic growth after Deng took a historical southern China tour to push for continuing market-oriented economic reforms.[4] The communist government rebuilt its authority based upon the surging economic achievement after the Tiananmen crackdown. Although it is arguable if rapid economic growth indeed enhanced the legitimacy of the

1

communist regime, there is no doubt that economic modernization did not ensure the transformation of China into a liberal democracy. The change in the former Soviet Union and Eastern Europe, for many Western observers, demonstrated the victory of democratic values and systems. The same change, however, for the leaders and many people in China demonstrated the necessity of maintaining political stability and holding an undivided national sovereignty, as they were frightened by economic drift, political instability, ethnic fragmentation, and violence in the former Soviet Union and Eastern Europe. In the meantime, the success of China's economic development opened new opportunities for a good portion of Chinese people to pursue nonpolitical careers and become prosperous. As a result, many Chinese people previously active in pursuing political ideals became more and more pragmatic toward democratic ideals and focused their attentions on economic and other nonpolitical endeavors in the 1990s.

On the tenth anniversary of the 1989 crackdown on the pro-democracy movement, a *New York Times* reporter in Beijing observed, "Young Chinese, in particular, say they are more concerned with pursuing careers than multiparty democracy, which they see as a distant prospect. Many students and other Chinese now view 1989 protests as naive and its leaders as uncompromising."[5] An *Asiaweek* reporter in Beijing also found that "[w]hile the world fixates on Tiananmen, in Beijing citizens and cadres alike are far too busy building a modern China to dwell on the T [Tiananmen] word."[6] Standing next to a busy intersection about eight miles west of Beijing's Tiananmen Square at the eve of the tenth anniversary of the 1989 crackdown, another *New York Times* reporter found that "hundreds of retirees were practicing a traditional flag-waving dance to the pounding of drums." Happily pursuing a popular hobby, the dancers seemed unaware that exactly ten years ago that night, "this same intersection was the scene of the first major bloodshed as troops moved to crush student-led demonstrations in Tiananmen Square."[7]

This development has led some scholars to doubt if China can establish a liberal democracy any time soon. The speculation thus inclined toward another extreme: pessimism. In his 1996 prediction of post-Deng political development in China, Richard Baum listed only two among the ten scenarios as democratic. Both of the democratic scenarios were characterized as "unlikely" (one "less likely" and the other "least likely").[8] In his 1999 discussion of political reform in China, John Burns argued that the regime was more resilient than we were led to believe by those who thought it would fall or must democratize as the Chinese Communist Party (CCP) adapted to the social and political changes in China.[9] This pessimistic view seems in line with many empirical studies of Chinese politics that demonstrate that Chinese authoritarianism has endured for millennia and communist China has repeatedly moved against shifting tides of recent world history.[10]

Given the fact that Taiwan, with a similar historical and cultural connection, has successfully transited toward a democratic polity in the last decade of the twentieth century, is the pessimistic view about mainland China really sustainable? What really happened in the People's Republic of China (PRC) during the last decade of the twentieth century? Will the PRC democratize any time soon in the twenty-first century? To find answers to these questions, we have to take a step back to examine the historical record of China's search for democracy and bridge what Baogang He has called "a gap between Western normative theories of democracy and empirical studies of China's political developments and democratization."[11] This book represents a modest effort to reconsider China's democratization from the historical perspective, and combining normative explorations and empirical investigations, it tries to find answers to certain questions. What are the lessons from the failure of the democratization efforts in mainland China during the twentieth century? What are the major barriers for the successful transition toward democracy in the PRC? What are the major political trends in China toward the beginning of the twenty-first century? And will the PRC adopt a democratic polity any time soon?

Finding answers to these questions is critically important not only for understanding the political development of China but also for any assessment of global politics in the future. China's dramatic economic growth in the last two decades of the twentieth century, and the prospect of its rise as a great power in the twenty-first, has greatly increased its weight and importance in world affairs. Consequently, the progress, or lack thereof, in China's transition to democracy has became a central concern of the international community.

The Historical Record of the Chinese Search for Democracy

China's search for democracy started with its intellectuals' soul-searching for a national salvation after the decline of the Chinese Empire in the nineteenth century. Seeing Western countries as powerful and prosperous, they yearned to find recipes from the West. Marxism and democracy were two such recipes that were borrowed and experimented with in China during the twentieth century.

Inspired by Marxism, a group of radical intellectuals launched a communist revolution and founded the CCP in 1921. Mao Zedong led the CCP and established the PRC in 1949. Although Mao won China's national independence and gave rise to Chinese international status, his communist transformation did not bring prosperity to the Chinese people. After Mao's death, Deng Xiaoping launched a market-oriented economic reform in 1978. The reform produced rapid economic growth while at the same time resulting in the eradication of communism and the profound "three-belief crises" (*sanxin weiji*): crisis of faith in socialism (*xinxin weiji*), crisis of belief in Marxism (*xinyang weiji*), and crisis of trust in the party (*xinren weiji*).[12] Many intellectuals, particularly the younger generation of intellectuals, turned to Western liberal ideas and called for Western-style democratic reform. The democracy movement quickly gained momentum in China's urban areas and eventually led to the large-scale Tiananmen demonstrations in spring 1989.

Democracy is not new to the Chinese intellectual and has been experimented with in China since the turn of the twentieth century. However, as the first two chapters of this book—by Andrew Nathan and myself, respectively—indicate, the results of democracy experiments in mainland China during the twentieth century were a series of tragedies. The very early experiments with democratic reforms in the later Qing period, including abolishing the Confucian examination system, sending students to the West, and establishing provincial and national assemblies, destroyed the reforming government and accelerated the final collapse of the Qing dynasty. The first attempt to erect a democratic republic, San Yat-sen's 1911 revolution, lay at the mercy of a militarist, Yuan Shikai, who turned the new form of constitutional government into a personal dictatorship. The first modern political party in Chinese history, the Nationalist Party (Kuomintang, or KMT), while wholeheartedly espousing Western-style parliamentarianism in its early years, established a one-party dictatorship led by Chiang Kai-shek after the victory of the military expedition in 1927.[13] The CCP promised a new "democratic state" in its struggle against the KMT but allowed no freedom of expression nor opposition of any political forces after it took power in 1949. While the post-Mao democratic activists appealed to the ideals of democracy and were brutally repressed by the communist regime, an obvious gap between their democratic ideals and their political practice was revealed even during the period of their confrontation with the communist regime in Tiananmen Square in 1989.[14]

China introduced many institutions of Western democratic government, including various forms of legislature, such as national assembly and the people's congress. China also promulgated numerous constitutions that promised the freedom of speech and organization. However, as indicated by Nathan, leaving aside Taiwan since the late 1980s, China's legislatures were never able to exercise the authority they were supposed to enjoy under the constitution and the laws. The freedoms of organization and expression prescribed in constitutions were always subject to such severe limits that they could not be used with much effect in political competition. Democratic experiments in the twentieth century of mainland China, therefore, repeatedly proved to be failures.

This historical record compelled Lloyd E. Eastman to state, "Because of the nature of Chinese society and of its political traditions, it is perhaps one of China's tragedies during the twentieth century that, in the quest for a viable political system, attempts had been made to erect democratic institutions. In a profound sense, Anglo-American democracy was not suited to China. . . . In China, an authoritarian system of rule is perhaps better able to produce the greatest happiness of the greatest number."[15] This statement was an echo to Frank J. Goodnow's infamous assertion in the very beginning of the twentieth century that "a monarchy is better suited than a republic to China."[16]

From the vantagepoint of the post–Cold War world, it is impossible for most scholars to agree with Eastman and Goodnow that democracy is not applicable to China. Although the failed experiments of Chinese democracy in the twentieth century seem to justify their pessimistic statements, the lessons of the past, as Nathan suggests, are more ambiguous than they seem on the surface.

Nobody can promise that democracy will work if tried; neither can anyone conclude that past failure proves China to be unsuited for democracy. Therefore, it is important to investigate the causes for the failure of Chinese democratic experiments in the mainland and look for favorable changes for the successful transition toward democracy.

In chapter 2, I will attribute the failure of these experiments to the shortsighted and instrumentalist attitude of Chinese political leaders and intellectuals toward democracy. It is my feeling that democracy in the Chinese political and intellectual discourse was never regarded as an *end*, but merely a *means* for gaining national power and wealth under wise and enlightened rulers. Chinese intellectuals looked around the world to find modern political means to build a rich nation and a strong military; it didn't seem to matter if the method used was liberal democracy or Marxist communism. In this narrow prism, Chinese intellectuals introduced democracy when they found that it had brought power and prosperity to Western countries and turned to communism when they saw that it had made the Soviet Union strong. The political leaders of both the CCP and the KMT borrowed the democratic form of governmental institutions, such as a constitution, a national assembly, and a people's congress, as a means to mask their autocratic rule. Chinese intellectuals' overanxiousness to get results out of democracy and Chinese political leaders' cynicism toward democracy were equally responsible for the tragic failure of democratic experiments on mainland China.

In a broader sense, Andrew Nathan in chapter 1 identifies nine sets of causes that were cited widely by scholars to explain the failure of China's democratic experiments. As an example, democracy as it is defined in the Western democracies did not constitute the mainstream of modern Chinese political ideology. Almost every political movement tried to garb itself in the mystique of democracy, but what was usually in mind as democracy was a mystical solidarity of state and people—in fact a kind of authoritarianism. The more powerful a political movement became, the less it looked to democracy for solutions to China's problems. Nathan also describes other important reasons for the failure of Chinese democracy, such as internal or external war, which was not conducive to building democratic institutions; military intervention in politics, which undercut democracy by undermining civilian authority; and political and cultural barriers.

Unlike the pessimists, Nathan views these causes for the failure of China's democratic experiments with an eye on the lessons for the future success of democratic transition. Different from extreme optimists, Nathan looks for positive changes in China's political and economic landscape that may eventually create sufficient conditions for democracy to develop in the long run. Nathan points out that more and more Chinese intellectuals began rethinking the reasons for China's political misfortunes and groped their way toward a belief in pluralistic democracy as the kind of political system that could provide responsible and effective government. This belief, in however vague a form, had spread to a wide section of Chinese society. In addition, China faced the most peaceful, unthreatening international and domestic environment in the twentieth century. As a result of market-oriented economic reform, China was pushing into the ranks of newly industrialized countries. It was not only a politically independent nation, but was also recognized as a rising regional, and potentially global, power. Facing these changes, more and more Chinese intellectuals had to reconsider democratic values and systems as ultimate ends instead of a means for something else. Nathan concludes that history gives Chinese democrats reasons for courage because the situation is different and more favorable to democracy today.

Chinese Political Culture and Democracy

One of the most controversial issues in the study of China's potential democratization is whether or not Chinese political culture in general and Confucianism in particular stand in the way of China's transition to democracy. One side of the debate argues that Chinese political culture is the ideological underpinning of "oriental despotism," and hence antidemocratic. Lucian Pye, for example, argues that Chinese political culture embodies an intolerance of conflict and a yearning for authority, and therefore is inhospitable to democracy.[17] The other side holds that Chinese political culture, particularly Confucianism, was full of humanism and was conducive to democracy. Thomas A. Metzger, for example, argues that "very different from the Arab-Muslim world's much weaker interest in democracy, this Chinese enthusiasm for the democratic ideals is rooted . . . in the Confucian way of defining proper governance. . . . This tradition-rooted enthusiasm for democracy has remained central to Chinese political discourse, and fuels contemporary Chinese demands for democracy."[18]

In an effort to bridge the two opposing views on whether or not Chinese political culture is an obstacle to democracy, Shaohua Hu in chapter 3 argues that Chinese political culture in general and Confucianism in particular is neither pro-democratic nor antidemocratic, but "a-democratic." In its opposition to despotism, defense of the people's rights and interests, support of participation, and emphasis on civic virtue and egalitarian tendency, Confucianism is not an insurmountable obstacle to democratization. Yet this humanistic spirit does not provide legitimate reasons to believe that Confucianism is democratic. The fact that Confucianism does not advocate popular sovereignty and individual liberty excludes the possibility that Confucianism is democratic. In its view of human nature, emphasis on filial piety, deference to authority, the rule of men, and lack of mechanism against despotism, Confucianism offers little help to the process of democratization. Yet these characteristics evince no evidence that Confucianism is antidemocratic. Hu therefore labels Confucianism "a-democratic" and argues that Confucian doctrine is less political theory than ethical teaching. As an idealistic doctrine preaching morality, Confucianism is more applicable to traditional society than to modern society and, therefore, one should not expect it to help in democratization. It is also unjustifiable, however, to exaggerate the negative influence of Confucian tradition, which has done little in arresting the democratic movement. The success of democracy in Taiwan suggests that while Confucianism offers little help and even creates some problems in the democratization process, its negative impact on the process is not overwhelming. It is wrong to blame Chinese authoritarianism solely on Confucianism, although Confucianism may play a very important role in maintaining the status quo.

In chapter 4, the comparative study of Chinese political culture and Western democracy by Enbao Wang and Regina F. Titunik confirms Shaohua Hu's observation. This chapter focuses on a traditional Chinese concept, *minben*, which means that the people are the primary sources of state power. In a comparison between the ideas of minben and Western democratic ideas, they find that while the concept of minben promotes accountable government, it does not necessarily point to a democratic system as the solution to achieving accountability and public welfare. Its emphasis is on "the good of the people," which serves both democracy and authoritarianism. The basic ideas of minben share some aspirations of Western democracy, as both give priority to the well-being of the people, and assert that the people should not be abused by those in power and that they themselves have the power to bring down despotic government. However, minben differs from democracy in significant aspects. Democracy requires not simply a political system that maximizes the public good, but a system that balances individual freedom and the collective good. The emphasis on the good of the people by the concept of minben may reinforce the juxtaposition between the common good, on the one hand, and the threat of chaos (*luan*) on the other, a juxtaposition sustaining authoritarianism.

In chapter 5, Baogang He takes a normative approach and goes beyond the debate on whether or not Chinese political culture is compatible to democracy. He argues against cultural relativism and advocates the universalistic notion of democratic morality and justice discoverable by reason. According to He, traditional Chinese political culture has a sage's conception of morality, which demands that Chinese people be altruists and wise men who are the first to be concerned with the world's troubles and the last to rejoice in their own happiness. This kind of morality maximizes seeking for the highest ideal of the moral state. It was easily used by the CCP to develop a goal-based morality, which takes the communist society as a primary goal and demands that individuals should be sacrificed for the well-being of collective interests, denying even the right to complain about making such a sacrifice. The official goal-based morality has become a tool of the CCP to deprive people of their rights.

He believes that China's transition to democracy or, in his words, China's democratic institutional design, does not require a sage's conception of morality, or goal-based morality. Yet it would be wrong to take this further and argue that no form of morality constitutes a normative basis for democratic politics. He argues that China's democratic transition should be based on a morality characterized by urgent recognition of some universal principles such as equal liberties, institutional protection of rights, and fair procedures for democratic institutional design. The universal idea of rights should provide a right-based foundation for a moral critique of Chinese authoritarianism as well as constructive guidance to China's democratic transition. Democratization in China should be developed in light of a universal doctrine of right-based morality.

The studies of Chinese political culture in these three chapters find no strong evidence to support the argument that Chinese people are culturally unable to organize self-interested action in an open, competitive public sphere. As indicated by Nathan in chapter 1, the failure of Chinese democracy cannot be attributed to culture, which is in good part the product of institutions. When institutions do not work, they produce a culture of despair. Working to change culture, then, is not necessarily the most cost-efficient way to institutionalize democracy, and may even be the wrong way. In addition, China's political culture today is different from what it was earlier in this century. Thanks to economic and social development, the spread of mass education and the mass media, the deep social penetration of Chinese political institutions during the Cultural Revolution, and the broad social impact of government policies, the attitudes of the average Chinese citizen toward political authority has changed dramatically. Easy acceptance of authority is less widespread than it was before. Some of the characteristics of a democratic political culture—perception of the salience of government, belief in one's own ability to understand and affect government, tolerance of different opinions—are more widespread in China today than they have been historically. Nobody can make precise predictions for tomorrow's development. Yet with new means of communication, such as the Internet and other information technology, and the trend of globalization, particularly after China's accession into the World Trade Organization (WTO), Chinese political culture will certainly change further in the twentieth-first century.

Chinese State-Society Relationship and Democracy

Another controversial issue in the study of China's democratization regards the changing relationship between society and the state, and particularly the strength and nature of the emerging civil society and its impact on China's democratic transition.[19]

Civil society is a Western concept and the meaning attached to it in the West is various. One brief and straightforward definition of civil society is the "existence of institutionalized autonomy for social relationships and associational life, autonomy vis-à-via the state."[20] Many scholars have seen the weakness of civil society in China as one of major barriers to the effective development of democratic institutions. As Andrew Nathan indicates in chapter 1, democracy depends on the existence of autonomous social forces and groups that demand access to policy making, and that have enough financial and other power to force the state to respect the rules that grant them this access. In his view, the Chinese search for democracy failed in the twentieth century partly because there were no social forces that had a strong interest in defending democratic procedures. Before the communists took over state power in China, civil society was not absent, but it was too weak to keep the state power in check. After the PRC was founded, the communist regime invented the so-called socialist democracy by emphasizing the unity of interests between the people and the communist state. The CCP claimed that it did not have special interests of its own, that it ruled China solely in the fundamental and unified interest of the people. Thus, the communist regime left no room for the development of individual interest and the institutional base of civil society. All institutional instruments of social-interest articulation, including newspapers and magazines, were under the complete control of the communist state.

This is the typical state-society relationship described in the literature of totalitarianism.[21] Obviously, the totalitarian model is no longer sufficient to explain the state-society relationship in China today. In chapter 6, Yijiang Ding finds that China's state-society relationship has undertaken a dramatic change since economic reform was implemented in the 1980s. Some liberal intellectuals challenged the socialist democracy and the unity of interests between state and society. As a result, emphasis on the difference rather than the unity of interests as the foundation of democracy became well known among Chinese intellectuals and even gained some official acceptance. Ding provides a detailed documentation on the conceptual changes in Chinese intellectuals' rethinking of the state-society relationship before and after the Tiananmen incident in 1989.

According to Ding, the development of market-oriented economic reform was characterized by the recognition of diverse economic interests and rights. In the name of improving socialist democracy and promoting economic reform, liberal intellectuals criticized the unity of interest for ignoring the important reality of social and economic diversity and accused the overemphasis on the unity of interests of obstructing social and economic development in the 1980s. They called for recognizing the difference of interests between the state and society and for allowing society to protect itself from the state. In a challenge to the concept of socialist democracy, pluralism was said to be a precondition for democratic politics because the purpose of democracy was to allow articulation of various social interests by people of different social groups. The concept of *civil society* was introduced to justify a degree of separation of society from the state. It was argued that the state should abandon part of its power over society in order to allow members of civil society to enjoy a degree of freedom in social and economic life.

While the intellectual discussion was going on, the relationship between the communist state and society came to be more and more complicated due to deepening of economic reforms and the loosening of ideological control brought about by such reforms in the 1980s. There were many subtle advances in the separation of the state from society. For example, the communist state reduced the scope and arbitrariness of political intervention in daily life. Ordinary citizens began to enjoy much greater freedom of belief, expression, and consumption. In addition, the CCP expanded the opportunities for popular participation in political affairs by introducing competitive elections to local legislatures and expanding the role of the people's congresses. Although the political participation that was allowed and the views that could be safely expressed were subject to important restrictions, these changes greatly reduced the degree of state control over society. Moreover, due to the repudiation of the ideological concepts associated with Mao's later years, the responsibility of the state was increasingly defined as expanding democracy rather than exercising dictatorship.[22]

Did these changes result in the emergence of a civil society pitted against the political state in China? Ding's chapter does not answer this question directly, but it does reveal that the meaning of *civil society* as understood by Chinese intellectuals in the 1980s was a rather passive one. Instead of the well-organized civil society confronting the political state, as was the case in the West, it was no more than a depoliticized sphere of social and economic life in China. The focus was not on the right of society to participate in the political process, but on limiting state power to the political sphere. The emphasis was on separation rather than participation. In this sense, the autonomy of society as it was argued for was still quite limited.

In chapter 7, Edward X. Gu confirms Ding's observations on the passivity of Chinese society in relation to the communist state with a case study of four intellectual groups that were organized independent of the communist state during the 1989 Tiananmen pro-democracy movements. Gu argues that the thesis of the "civil society against the state" is very misleading in this case. He proposes a concept of plural institutionalism to approach the relationship between intellectuals and the state in the 1980s. Gu's case study reveals that Chinese intellectuals as a whole were a highly segmented faction, linking in different ways with the state. The institutional base for intellectuals' opposition to the party-state was weak, and the confrontation of Chinese intellectuals with the communist state was neither a coherent nor a mainstream phenomenon. Gu believes that the Chinese civil society was only a phantom in the air and that it cannot be conceptualized in terms of the balance between the strength of the communist state on the one side and of society on the other. Citing Tang Tsou, Gu asserts that the Chinese state still shaped society even as society labored to reemerge from its control.[23]

Was this situation changed in the 1990s? Did the Chinese state still have such strength in shaping its relationship with the society? In chapter 8, Dawn Einwalter challenges what she calls the *undue emphasis* given to the state by a case study of the Xu Honggang campaign in promoting the public morality of self-sacrifice in 1994. Einwalter finds that after nearly two decades of dismantling the mechanisms of collective production in favor of market-oriented reform in the creation of the socialist market economy, the CCP diluted the relevance of socialist morality and made it appear antithetical to the new demands of the market. Although the communist state still claimed to embody socialist morality and retained the right to propagate this morality throughout society, it had to fight against the concepts of competition, profit, and the satisfaction of self-interest that were introduced by market reforms. Although the state tried to restrict self-interest to the economic realm and continued to provide models of selfless behavior such as soldier-heroes Lei Feng and Xu Honggang to guide noneconomic behavior, the leaking of self-interest action into areas of life out-side the economic realm proved unavoidable. Socialist moral imperatives con-tinued to fray. Despite its ostensible encouragement of public morality, the Xu Honggang campaign failed to provide models of citizen action.

Indeed, the deepening of economic reform seriously limited state power in the 1990s. To facilitate economic reform, the CCP had to refrain from interven-ing in socioeconomic activities and concern itself largely with political supervi-sion and coordination. The party-state became a network of the bureaucratic elite, with the training and connections used to hold on to power. The commu-nist regime based its survival largely on the success of economic performance in the reform era rather than on ideological correctness and mass-mobilization.[24]

In the second part of chapter 6, Yijiang Ding confirms this empirical observa-tion through a study of a Chinese intellectual's rethinking of the state-society relationship in the post-Tiananmen years. Ding indicates that the brief period of post-Tiananmen political backlash failed to inhibit further development and widening acceptance of the new ideas on democracy and the state-society rela-tionship among a new generation of Chinese intellectuals. Discussion on the role of the state, societal freedom and independence, and social and political plural-ism continued. He notes that during the intellectual exploration of democracy in the 1990s, the issue of civil society attracted much greater attention. Civil soci-ety was redefined as a private sphere of autonomous economic and social activi-ties based on the principle of voluntary contract and a public sphere of political participation. The inclusion of participation in politics marked the difference between Chinese intellectuals' understanding of the civil society in the 1990s and the economically free but politically passive one of the 1980s. Based on this more active definition, Chinese liberal intellectuals proposed a relationship of "positive interaction" between the state and society. In this relationship, civil society would play an active role in protecting societal freedom, opposing state domination, developing social pluralism, and promoting democracy. Ding points to strong evidence that Chinese scholars participating in the discussions of civil society were well aware of one another, and that the regime tolerated them in the 1990s. According to Ding, as a result of the decline of communist ideology, the communist regime lost much of its radicalism and became selec-tively repressive, targeting only those who directly challenged its rule while leav-ing others alone so long as they did not present a direct threat. Meanwhile, the post-Tiananmen political alienation, combined with unprecedented opportuni-ties in the market economy, increased the independence of intellectuals and their distance from the regime. These intellectuals were moving away from their tra-ditional dependency on the state, and toward increasing autonomy.

Prospects for Democracy in China at the Dawn of the Twenty-First Century

The changing state-society relationship clearly shows that political liberaliza-tion has taken place in China. It is still uncertain, however, whether China will

move toward democracy any time soon. Political liberalization and democratization are two analytically distinct processes. Liberalization involves reducing
state control over the society, and democratization entails an institutionalization of political participation from below.[25] Although most scholars agree that
"the era of Deng Xiaoping (1978–97) can be characterized as a period of liberalization,"[26] analyzing the prospects for democracy in China is inherently a
controversial issue. While normative theorists may draw a positive picture of
the inevitable triumph of democracy in China, empirical investigation calls for
prudence in making predictions. The scholarly study of democratization in
other parts of the world has demonstrated that the transition to democracy is a
complicated, frustrating, often uncertain and protracted process.[27] If China is to
become democratic, the Chinese people must actively press for it, and the
Chinese government must feel the pressure to change its authoritarian rule. The
concluding section of the book includes four chapters of empirical investigation
that give prudent analyses on Chinese people's demands for democracy and the
conditions for a successful transition in China.

Chapters 9, 10, and 11 investigate the prospects for democracy by use of survey data gathered in China during the 1990s. Survey research and systematic
data gathering is a new development in the study of Chinese politics because
until very recently it had been very difficult for any observers, particularly foreign observers, to collect valid public opinion data or undertake serious field
surveys in China. This situation is changing along with the widening of reform
and the general opening up of China. When the government felt the need for
more and more survey information on public opinion for policy making and
sometimes for propaganda purposes, many Chinese academic and research
institutions began to conduct public opinion surveys. In the meantime, some
foreign scholars were allowed, with certain restrictions, to collect their own survey data in recent years. With precaution in survey design, and often in collaboration with Chinese scholars, foreign researchers have been able to collect
meaningful survey data or selectively use Chinese survey data to make valid
analyses.[28]

Chapter 9, the outcome of a collaboration between two American scholars,
Daniel V. Dowd and Allen Carlson, and their Chinese colleague, Mingming
Shen, investigates the prospect for democracy in China using survey data from
Beijing residents in the mid-1990s. This chapter focuses on public opinion and
its implications for a democratic transition. It assumes that a public opinion climate favorable to a transition toward democracy is a necessary condition for
the emergence of a democratic polity. This research finds that although the
future was likely to bring pressure for a more liberal society with more "private
space" for the individual, there was little apparent public opinion pressure for
democracy, especially in comparison to other values, in the 1990s. It also finds
that income had no effect on the respondents' preferences for political democracy or individual freedom. These findings call into question to what extent
citizens in Beijing at the end of the twentieth century possess political values

supportive of democracy, and what the likely future trends will be in public opinion related to democracy.

The findings in chapter 9 are confirmed by Che-po Chan in chapter 10, an investigation on the political orientation of Chinese university students after the 1989 crackdown on the democratic movement. By careful analysis and reinterpretation of the raw survey data collected by Chinese academies and research institutes, Chan finds that although students' political beliefs remained the same before and after 1989, their involvement in politics changed from idealism to the pragmatism of a down-to-earth approach to China's problems. Utility, efficiency, and feasibility were major considerations of the pragmatic attitude. Skepticism, experimentation, and reform were the pragmatic keys to social progress. Whether reality fit with the normative political principles was no longer the ultimate consideration; rather, whether the principles could solve existing problems became the main concern. Chan suggests two sources that contributed to the political pragmatism of the university students. One was the setback of the 1989 movement, and the other was the change in opportunities on campus in the 1990s. Before 1989, the general underdevelopment of China's economy had channeled student interests almost exclusively to the political arena. After the failure of the Tiananmen demonstrations, university campuses were under close political surveillance. Any challenge to the political authority might result in great sacrifice. On the other hand, university campuses were abundant with economic possibilities, which provided an alternative way for students to express themselves. Restricted political opportunity and the opening up of economic channels led Chinese university students to pursue nonpolitical careers. Based on this empirical investigation, Chan concludes that although 1990s university students were still concerned for the future of China and wanted to contribute to China's progress, they had taken the opportunity to pursue their professional careers and their own advancement in China's booming economy.

Chan's chapter touches on a theoretical issue about the causal relationship between economic development and democratization. The observation that authoritarian rule is prevalent among low-income countries while democracy is more commonly found among wealthy countries has prompted some political scientists to argue that "a high level of economic development has stronger democracy-promoting effect."[29] However, Chan's research shows that the success of market-oriented economic reform did not bring immediate positive impact upon the transition toward democracy in China.

In chapter 11, Tianjian Shi takes on this controversial issue and examines whether economic development is associated with successful elections in Chinese villages. Shi's chapter focuses on semicompetitive elections of village committees in rural China using empirical data gathered from a 1993 nationwide survey. The direct election of village committees started as a national policy in 1987 and continued after the 1989 Tiananmen incident. The introduction of direct elections into rural villages is the most significant political reform implemented by the Chinese government. These elections may be a training ground for democracy as, increasingly, villagers have voted more responsive and talented leaders into office, many of them young entrepreneurs who may or may not be members of the Communist Party.[30] Shi's analysis reveals that there is not a linear correlation between economic development and democratic transition, as social mobilization theory suggests. Specifically, he finds that the relationship between economic development and village elections appears to lie on a curve. Economic wealth increases the likelihood that a village will hold semicompetitive elections in which villagers choose their leaders, but that likelihood diminishes as economic wealth increases further. Rapid economic development may even delay the process of competitive elections because incumbent leaders can use newly acquired economic resources to consolidate their power. Development causes this to happen in the following three ways: first, it makes peasants more dependent on the village authority; second, it provides incumbent leaders with the resources to co-opt peasants; third, it provides incumbent leaders with resources to bribe their superiors into ignoring the decision of the central government to introduce competitive elections to Chinese villages.

While economic development did not immediately bring democracy, some other political values, notably nationalism, have gained ground in China. In chapter 12, I discuss how nationalism moved quickly to fill the void left by the decline of communism, and how it became one of the driving forces for China's modernization in the 1990s. Nationalism, rather than democracy, was the only bedrock of political belief shared by both the communist regime and its critics. It is ironic that pro-democracy demonstrators in Tiananmen Square, when confronting the government, claimed that patriotism drove them to demonstrating in the streets; most people involved in the demonstration equated promoting democracy with patriotism. The sanctions against China by the Western countries after the Tiananmen incident provided a good opportunity for the communist regime to position itself as the representative of the Chinese nation to defend China's national interests. Taking this opportunity, the communist state launched a patriotic education campaign in the early 1990s, which fanned nationalistic flames to create a sense of commonalty among citizens when the regime faced a threat to its legitimacy. Chinese intellectuals accepted this nationalist appeal because they wanted to help build a prosperous and strong nation so that nobody would dare bully China again. Under these circumstances, nationalism became an important political value that competed with the value of liberal democracy in China, in spite of the fact that nationalism and liberal democracy have reinforced each other in many other societies. Although most Chinese intellectuals did not say that democracy was less appealing to them, many of them emphasized that they were patriots first and democrats second in the 1990s. In this case, the rise of nationalism in China was associated largely with authoritarianism rather than democracy.

These prudent analyses on the prospects for democracy in this concluding section resonate in some ways through all chapters of this book. Contributors find no simple answers, but a complicated picture in their reconsideration of China's democratization. On the one hand, this volume reconfirms the normative assertion that the dominant trends in China, just as elsewhere, are toward political liberalization and democratization. Chinese political culture and Confucianism are not a particular obstacle to democratic transition. The authoritarian rule of the communist state and its capacity to control Chinese society has been greatly undermined by the success of market-oriented economic reform. The society has become increasingly autonomous.

On the other hand, empirical investigations in this book suggest that political liberalization and the weakening of authoritarian rule do not guarantee the success of democratic transition. Thomas A. Metzger is right when he asserts that "it is doubtful that China will adopt the Western liberal model of democracy any time soon."[31] There are many reasons to be skeptical about the short-term prospects for democratization in China in view of the lessons of historical failure, the general underdevelopment of civil society, the emerging Chinese pragmatism toward democratic ideals, political apathy among university students, and the strong undercurrents of competing political values. Although Chinese political culture is not particularly antidemocratic, neither is it particularly pro-democratic. Notwithstanding the long-term impact of economic development on the progress of democratic transition, its immediate consequences have not been particularly favorable to the success of democratization. Larry Diamond and Marc F. Plattner have said that "sound political institutions, capable and democratically committed leaders, and responsible citizens" are crucial in creating a democratic political culture and society.[32] We have yet to see these conditions fully develop in China.

This book is divided into four sections. The first section analyzes the historical record of the Chinese search for democracy in the twentieth century. The second section addresses the debate over whether Chinese political culture is a barrier or facilitator in the transition to democracy. The third section tries to examine the changing relationship between the Chinese communist state and the society. The concluding section uses empirical survey data to explore the prospects for democracy in China. Most of chapters in this book, except chapters 4 and 12, were previously published in different issues of the *Journal of Contemporary China*, which I edited. Some of them were thoroughly revised or updated for this book. The editor and most contributors to this book are Chinese scholars who have participated in the Chinese search for democracy in different stages of their personal lives and who later received systematic academic training in the West. These analyses are drawn on their personal experiences and also from their recent field research in China. The contributions by a number of distinguished American scholars enrich this book significantly. In particular, I would like to express my sincere appreciation to Larry Diamond of Hoover Institution for taking time to write the foreword for this book.

The last touch on this book was made when I was a 1999–2000 Campbell

National Fellow at Hoover Institution of Stanford University. I would like to thank the National Fellows Program of Hoover Institution for providing me with such a wonderful opportunity and comfortable environment to conduct my research and writing.

Notes

1. Samuel P. Huntington, "How Countries Democratize," *Political Science Quarterly* 106, no. 4 (1991–92), 579. For a more complete discussion, see Samuel P. Huntington, *Third Wave: Democratization in the Late Twentieth Century* (Norman: University of Oklahoma Press, 1993).
2. Ruan Ming, *Deng Xiaoping Diguo* (Deng Xiaoping: Chronicle of an Empire) (Taipei, Taiwan: Shibao Chuban Gonshi, 1992), 258.
3. Lucian W. Pye, "Political Science and the Crisis of Authoritarianism," *American Political Science Review* 84, no 1 (1990), 3.
4. For one study of the southern China tour and its consequences, see Suisheng Zhao, "Deng Xiaoping's Southern Tour: Elite Politics in Post-Tiananmen China," *Asian Survey* 33, no. 8 (1993), 739–56.
5. Elizabeth Rosenthal, "Memories of Tiananmen Fade, Stunted by Public Silence," *New York Times*, June 4, 1999, electronic edition.
6. Ron Gluckman, "Ten Years On," *Asiaweek*, May 28, 1999, electronic edition.
7. Erik Eckholm, "In Beijing, Reminders of '89 Protest are Few," *New York Times*, June 4, 1999, electronic edition.
8. Richard Baum, "China after Deng: Ten Scenarios in Search of Reality," *China Quarterly* 145 (1996), 169–72.
9. John Burns, "The People's Republic of China at 50: National Political Reform," *China Quarterly* 159 (1999), 580–94.
10. It is interesting to note that Marc Blecher uses the notion of "China against tides" to title his textbook. See *China against the Tides: Restructuring through Revolution, Radicalism, and Reform* (London: Pinter, 1997).
11. Baogang He, *The Democratization of China* (London: Routledge, 1996), 5.
12. For one study of the impact of reform on the official ideology, see Jie Chen, "The Impact of Reform on the Party and Ideology in China," *Journal of Contemporary China* 9 (1995), 22–34.
13. For a study of the authoritarian regimes of the KMT in the mask of constitutional forms of government, see Suisheng Zhao, *Power by Design: Constitution-Making in Nationalist China* (Honolulu: University of Hawaii Press, 1996).
14. Joseph W. Esherick and Jeffrey N. Wasserstrom gave a good example in their study of the Tiananmen Square demonstration, which I will quote in chapter 2 of this book.
15. Lloyd E. Eastman, *The Abortive Revolution: China under Nationalist Rule, 1927–1937* (Cambridge, Mass.: Harvard University Press, 1974), 179–80.
16. Ernest P. Young, *The Presidency of Yuan Shih-k'ai: Liberalism and Dictatorship in Early Republican China* (Ann Arbor: University of Michigan Press, 1977), 221.
17. Lucian Pye, *The Dynamics of Chinese Politics* (Cambridge, Mass.: Oelgeschlager, Gunn and Hain, 1981); Lucian Pye, *The Spirit of Chinese Politics* (Cambridge, Mass.: Harvard University Press, 1992).
18. Thomas A. Metzger, "Sources of Resistance," *Journal of Democracy* 6, no. 1 (1999), 19.
19. See, for example, Timothy Brook and B. Michael Frolic, eds., *Civil Society in China* (Armonk, N.Y.: M. E. Sharpe, 1997); Arthur Lewis Rosenbaum, ed., *State and Society in China: The Consequences of Reform* (Boulder, Colo.: Westview Press, 1992); Philip C. C. Huang, "'Public Sphere' and 'Civil Society' in China," *Modern China* 19, no. 2 (1993), 216–17; and Heath B. Chamberlain, "On the Search for Civil Society in China," *Modern China* 19, no. 2 (1993), 199–215.

20. Martin King Whyte, "Urban China: A Civil Society in the Making?" in Arthur Lewis Rosenbaum, ed., *State and Society in China*, 77. For a detailed study of the concept of civil society, see Thomas A. Metzger, "The Western Concept of the Civil Society in the Context of Chinese History," *Hoover Essays* no. 21, 1998.

21. For a systematic discussion of totalitarianism, see Juan J. Linz, "Totalitarian and Authoritarian Regimes," in Fred I. Grenstein and Nelson W. Polsby, eds., *Macropolitical Theory* (Reading, Mass.: Addison-Wesley, 1975). In an article published in the early 1990s, Roderick MacFarquhar still used the term *totalitarian triangle* to describe the tight control of the communist state over society in China. See MacFarquhar, "The Anatomy of Collapse," *New York Review of Books*, September 26, 1991, 5–9.

22. For one empirical study of these changes, see Suisheng Zhao, "Three Scenarios," *Journal of Democracy* 9, no. 1 (1998), 54–59.

23. Tang Tsou, "The Tiananmen Tragedy: The State-Society Relationship, Choices, and Mechanisms in Historical Perspective," in Brantly Womack, ed., *Contemporary Chinese Politics in Historical Perspective* (Cambridge: Cambridge University Press, 1991), 302.

24. For a detailed study of political reform and the resulting dual structure of leadership, see Suisheng Zhao, "Political Reform and Changing One-Party Rule in Deng's China," *Problems of Post-Communism* 44, no. 5 (1997), 12–21.

25. For one theoretical perspective on the distinction of these two processes, see Guilmermo O'Donnell and Philippe Schmitter, "Tentative Conclusions about Uncertain Democracies," in O'Donnell, Schmitter, and Lawrence Whitehead, eds., *Transitions from Authoritarian Rule* (Baltimore: Johns Hopkins University Press, 1986).

26. Andrew Scobell, "After Deng, What? Reconsidering the Prospects for a Democratic Transition in China," *Problems of Post-Communism* 44, no. 5 (1997), 23.

27. See, for example, Juan J. Linz and Alfred Stephan, *Problems of Democratic Transition and Consolidation: Southern Europe, South America, and Post-Communist Europe* (Baltimore: John Hopkins University Press, 1996); Arend Lijphart, "The Southern European Example of Democratization: Six Lessons for Latin America," *Government and Opposition* 25, no, 1 (1990), 65–83.

28. One excellent example of this undertaking is Tianjian Shi's book *Political Participation in Beijing* (Cambridge, Mass.: Harvard University Press, 1997).

29. John B. Londregan and Keith T. Poole, "Does High Income Promote Democracy?" *World Politics* 49, no. 1 (1996), 1–30.

30. For one study of village elections in China, see Anne F. Thurston, *Muddling Toward Democracy: Political Change in Grassroots China*, Peacework 23 (Washington D.C.: United States Institute of Peace, 1998).

31. Thomas A. Metzger, "Sources of Resistance," *Journal of Democracy* 6, no. 1 (1999), 19.

32. Larry Diamond and Marc F. Platter, Introduction to Diamond and Platter, eds., *Democracy in East Asia* (Baltimore: Johns Hopkins University Press, 1998), xxvii.

Part I

China's Search for Democracy in the Twentieth Century

Chinese Democracy

The Lessons of Failure

ANDREW J. NATHAN

In the summer of 1915 former Columbia University political science professor Frank J. Goodnow wrote an essay for Chinese president Yuan Shikai exploring what kind of political system was best suited to Chinese conditions. "It is of course not susceptible of doubt that a monarchy is better suited than a republic to China," Goodnow wrote. "China's history and traditions, her social and economic conditions, her relations with foreign powers all make it probable that the country would develop ... constitutional government ... more easily as a monarchy than as a republic."[1] Goodnow's advice proved disastrous. Yuan made an abortive, and for him personally fatal, bid for the throne; Goodnow went down in history as a reactionary. Yet on their face, the failed experiments of the next eighty years showed Goodnow's concerns to be justified. I shall, however, argue that the lessons of the past are more ambiguous than they seem on the surface. Although my analytical categories are similar to Goodnow's, my conclusions are different.

Democracy in its most generally accepted sense has never actually been tried in China. Minimally, democracy means open, competitive elections under universal franchise for occupants of those posts where actual policy decisions are made, together with the enjoyment of the freedoms of organization and speech (including publication) needed to enable self-generated political groups to compete effectively in these elections.[2] China has never had a chief executive elected by direct popular vote. Until 1992 in Taiwan, it never had a national legislature elected by direct, universal franchise. Except for Taiwan since 1989, there has never been more than one strong political party running in an election. And, again with the exception of Taiwan since 1992, speech and organization have never been free of serious restriction.[3]

When we speak of democratic experiments in modern China we have in mind two things: efforts to establish legislatures that were chosen in relatively open, competitive elections and that tried to exercise their constitutional powers; and efforts to establish freedoms of speech and organization. We can refer to these two kinds of efforts as the *electoral* and the *liberal* dimensions of democracy. When we speak of democratic failures, we mean that elected legislatures were unable to exercise the authority they were supposed to enjoy under a constitution and laws, and that freedoms of organization and expression were subject to such severe limits, either legally or extralegally, that they could not be used with much effect in political competition.

Specifically, China's main democratic experiments (leaving aside Taiwan) and their failures have been as follows:

- In 1909, provincial assemblies were elected in all Chinese provinces, and in 1910 the government of the Qing dynasty convened a National Assembly, half of whose two hundred members were appointed by the court and half of whom were elected from the provincial assemblies. The franchise was limited to less than one-half of 1 percent of the population. The freedoms of organization and speech were limited in law, although they were fairly extensive in practice. Only the legislatures were elected, not the executive branches, and the legislatures were granted limited, essentially advisory, powers. These institutions were ineffective while in office and lasted for a short time, falling with the dynasty.

- In 1912 and 1913 a Parliament was elected, consisting of a Senate elected by the provincial assemblies and a House directly elected by an all-male, economically elite franchise consisting of about 10.5 percent of the population. The election was attended with much corruption. The parliament had considerable powers on paper, including those of electing the president and confirming the cabinet. However, in practice the parliament was weak; the entire central government exercised little power. The constitutional system was interrupted twice by coups aimed at restoring the empire.

- In 1918, a new parliament was elected that lasted until 1923. Again the election—based on a limited franchise—was marked by corruption, and the powers of parliament were exercised weakly and intermittently, also with much corruption.

- The May Fourth Movement era of relative freedom of the press, political organization, and academic investigation and debate, dating roughly from 1912 to 1937, constituted another phase of democratic experimentation in the early republic, aside from the elections just mentioned. This era of liberalism occurred more because of the weakness of government repression than because of a firm legal and customary basis for political freedoms, although these freedoms were listed in Chinese constitutions at the time.

- In 1947 and 1948, the national government held elections, in those areas it controlled, for National Assembly, Legislative Yuan, and Control Yuan. Suffrage was universal, but due to wartime conditions and Kuomintang dominance of politics, the elections were neither complete nor competitive. Under the quasi-Leninist system of one-party dominance, these institutions did not begin to exercise their constitutional powers until recent years, in Taiwan.

- The People's Congress system of the People's Republic of China, which was put into effect in 1954, has democratic elements on paper, including universal suffrage, direct election since 1979 of the lower two levels of the four-level hierarchy of congresses, and constitutional powers for the legislature amounting to parliamentary supremacy. Yet the people's congresses have never exercised their powers in practice.

In sum, the democratic experiments were few in number, short in duration, and limited in their democratic characteristics. They were not robust on the electoral dimension after 1918, nor on the liberalism dimension after 1937.

Democratic institutions malfunctioned in numerous ways. Elections were corrupt, parliaments were factionalized, the free press was irresponsible, political groups were unprincipled. Political actors outside these institutions refused to accept the outcomes of elections, did not obey laws passed by legislatures, and did not respect the legal freedoms of the free press or the organizational rights of legally constituted organizations. At base, the failure of democracy consisted in a failure of democratic institutions to acquire authority, or in Samuel Huntington's phrase, to become institutionalized.

To draw lessons from failure, we need to know its causes. This is difficult, as causes were numerous and interactive. The saying "failure is an orphan, success has many fathers" applies well enough to political practice, but it often has to be reversed in political analysis. In politics as in biology, psychology, and engineering, failure is often overdetermined. It is impossible to identify distinct effects of each cause or to measure the relative importance of interacting causes. Moreover, the causes of failure exist on at least three analytical levels and thus potentially provide lessons of three types. Some involve conditions that democratic activists can do little to change; others concern institutional arrangements that democrats might have a hand in affecting; still others concern the democrats' strategy and tactics.

What follows are nine sets of causes for the failure of modern Chinese democracy that have been or can be suggested, each with its own possible lessons.

Ideology

Democracy in the sense in which we have defined it has not constituted the mainstream of modern Chinese political ideology. Almost every political movement has tried to cloak itself in the mystique of democracy, but what most had in mind as *democracy* was a mystical solidarity of state and people—in fact, a kind of authoritarianism. The more powerful a political movement was, the less it looked to democracy for solutions to China's problems. One reason, then, for democracy's failure was that most Chinese were not convinced democracy was the answer for China.

The implications of this lesson today are not necessarily discouraging. The ideological landscape has changed enormously in the last twenty years. Since the Lin Biao incident of 1971, more and more Chinese have been rethinking the reasons for China's political misfortunes. By the time of the democracy movement in 1978 and 1979, a small minority had groped its way toward a belief in pluralistic democracy as the kind of political system that could provide responsible and effective government. By the spring of 1989, this belief, in however vague a form, had spread to a wide section of at least the urban public.

Since its beginnings in the Tiananmen demonstration of April 5, 1976 (later known as the April Fifth Movement), the contemporary democratic movement has been rhetorically effective in deploying the regime's democratic pretensions against it. Although this may have helped mobilize some support in society, it has proven a thin shield against repression. Strong voices within the ruling party have used Marxism and Leninism as a framework for arguing for freedom of the press and political competition. Many of these advocates have been expelled from the party during periods of repression, but it appears that many who remain in the party have been influenced by their arguments. Meanwhile, members of the democratic movement overseas are now exploring the relevance of human rights and political pluralism to China's cultural tradition and developmental needs. In Taiwan, democratic elements in the official ideology have proven robust and expandable when called upon by both the opposition and the ruling party to justify and to some extent shape the transition toward democracy. A similar development of ideology might be possible in mainland China.

However, ideology alone cannot make democracy succeed. Democratic institutions have to prove themselves effective in solving China's problems in order to survive, or their attractiveness will remain only theoretical. In this sense, ideology today provides a permissive environment for democratic institutionalization, but it does not guarantee success.

National Security Problems

Democratic institutions repeatedly failed in the face of internal or external war. Even when China was not actually fighting a war, its leaders and people perceived national security as severely threatened, by all powers in the 1910s and 1920s, by Japan in the late 1920s through the 1940s, by the U.S. in the 1950s, by the two nuclear-armed superpowers in the 1960s, and by the Soviet Union until the mid-1980s. Democracies seem able to wage foreign wars effectively, and can sometimes survive civil wars, but the Chinese experience confirms the often-drawn conclusion that war is not a conducive environment in which to build democratic institutions.

The implications of this lesson for Chinese democrats today are encouraging. China faces the most peaceful, unthreatening international environment in a century and a half, with little prospect that it will be disrupted. Civil disorder is a possibility and a succession struggle among leadership factions is a near certainty, but civil war is unlikely to occur. No group can mount a civil war so long as the military remains united, and military breakdown is unlikely for a number of reasons to be discussed below.

Chinese democrats, however, can do little to affect the international or domestic security environments, at least until they take power and establish strong democratic institutions. So the lesson of the past in this respect, while encouraging, is not particularly practical.

Militarism

The Chinese experience at several points supports the widely accepted view that military intervention in politics undercuts democracy by undermining civilian authority. The failures of several of the early democratic experiments were linked to military coups and warlordism. The failure of democracy under the Kuomintang coincided with Chiang Kai-shek's increasing reliance on the military as the basis of his regime. The lesson is less obvious in the case of post-1949 China, where the conventional wisdom has it that "the party controlled the gun." In fact, Mao's power was based to an important degree on his exclusive control of the Chinese military machine through his chairmanship of the Central Military Affairs Commission, so that his was also a sort of quasi-military regime.

Many believe that a military coup or a recurrence of regional militarism is a possibility today. My reading of the tea leaves is different. First, China lacks a Latin American–type tradition of military rule or "guaranteeism" that would make a coup legitimate in the eyes of the people, the civilian leaders and bureaucrats, or the military itself. Second, Chinese military people appear reluctant to take responsibility for solving China's political and economic problems since they do not believe they have solutions for these problems. Third, the enormous size of the Chinese officer's corps would make it difficult to coordinate a coup without leaks and intramilitary opposition. A military coup would benefit some commanders—probably certain department heads in the Central Military Affairs Commission, and the Beijing garrison commander and Beijing military region commander—more than others, creating jealousy among those left out, those who might even be more senior and command larger forces than the members of the coup coalition.

Fourth, one of the factors historically facilitating regional militarism was the existence of foreign spheres of interest. Contrary to popular images, the Western powers were not opposed to democratic institutions in republican China, did not take direct steps to frustrate them, and gave but slight support to the warlords. In fact, the foreign powers offered consistent diplomatic recognition to China's successive central governments and provided important financial support through loans, and customs and salt revenues. Still, the foreign presence helped warlords, even if only marginally, through arms sales, by providing the occasional haven of the foreign concessions, and with whatever it contributed to the weakness of the central government. This historical element, of course, is absent today.

Finally, the most important factor working against a coup is that the People's Liberation Army already exercises strong influence on central party politics through its direct representatives among the Elders and in the Politburo. In the past, the military's interests were represented by leaders like Mao Zedong, Lin Biao, and Ye Jianying, whose roots were as much in the military as in the party. In this way, the military was able to have its say without directly taking power, as in the arrest of the Gang of Four and the fall of Hu Yaobang and Zhao Ziyang. This tradition is carried on today by Deng Xiaoping and Yang Shangkun. After the death of Deng and Yang, the military will no longer have senior leaders whose careers have followed a dual military and civilian track, who can wear two hats as central party leaders and representatives of military interests. Yet instead of directly taking power, future military and party leaders will probably agree on some senior officers who can formally or informally enter the highest levels of government to represent military interests.

What are those interests? Given its national security mission and the increasing professionalization of the military, the officer corps appears to give priority to political stability, economic development, and the technical upgrading of the economy. The officers probably disagree about how to achieve these goals, but younger officers seem to favor following reform wherever it leads, even if it involves abandoning traditional ideas of socialism. If democratization could promote stability and reform, they would have no reason to oppose it.

The lesson of history, then, is that democrats must find ways to keep the military out of politics. But the strongest force for achieving this will be the vigor and legitimacy of civilian political institutions, whether democratic or not. This again is a lesson that provides no direct guide to action but also offers no reason to be discouraged.

Political Culture

It is often argued that Chinese political culture is inhospitable to democracy. Lucian Pye, for example, has argued that Chinese political culture embodies an intolerance for conflict, a yearning for authority, and a stress on personal loyalty that leads to factionalism, which in turn destroys the functioning of democratic institutions.[4] It is a view widely held among Chinese democrats themselves.

This is a difficult argument to evaluate historically. Without direct data to tell us what the political culture of the past was, we can only infer culture from historical behavior (including written texts). Yet this makes the argument that culture causes action circular, because culture and action are measured by the same evidence.

The more we learn about late-nineteenth and early-twentieth-century Chinese political behavior, the less warranted seems the argument that Chinese of any class were culturally unable to organize self-interested action in an open, competitive public sphere.[5] It is true that democracy failed, but it is fallacious to attribute the failure to culture. One could equally well argue that culture is in good part the product of institutions.[6] When institutions do not work, they produce a culture of despair. If elections do not count because important issues are not raised or because elected officials have no power, people will not go to the trouble of voting seriously. If a legislature has no power, legislators will not treat their jobs seriously. If earlier democrats had been able to institutionalize democracy, a more democratic political culture would have been engendered. Working to change culture, then, is not necessarily the most cost-efficient way to institutionalize democracy, and may even be the wrong way.

In any case, China's political culture today is different from what it was earlier in this century. Thanks to economic and social development (discussed further below), the spread of mass education and the mass media, the deep social penetration of Chinese political institutions and the broad social impact of government policies in China, politics have become more salient to the average Chinese citizen than they were before, and citizens are better informed and more interested. Because of the experiences of the cultural revolution, which affected virtually every Chinese family, easy acceptance of authority is less widespread than it was before. Circumstantial evidence and preliminary survey data suggest that at least some of the characteristics of a democratic political culture—perception of the salience of government, belief in one's own ability to understand and affect government, tolerance of different opinions—are more widespread in China today than they seem to have been historically.[7]

Until they take power, it is difficult for democrats to do much about culture except talk about it. Thus we confront another lesson that offers little guidance for practical action, although it also gives democrats no reason to be discouraged.

Underdevelopment

It is well-established that the level of development affects a country's ability to practice democracy. The theory is disputed, the minimum level of development needed for democracy is ill-defined and probably not very high, and the development-democracy relationship may not be a direct or linear one. Until recently, however, China was so poor and underdeveloped that the democratic theory in its most brutal form probably did explain much of China's difficulty in establishing democratic institutions, but its explanatory power for the past is limited, and its predictive power for the future is negligible.

The most obvious relationship between development and democracy is that the majority of the population was too ill-educated and poverty stricken to taken an interest in politics. Whatever democracy existed was thus elite democracy. Yet this consideration cannot explain the failure of the early republic's limited-franchise institutions to function well or to become institutionalized. Historically, elite democracy in many countries was a step toward full democracy because it allowed competitive institutions to become established before mass participation began.

A second argument involving underdevelopment is that an underdeveloped country faces urgent developmental problems that do not brook the disunity and slowness of democratic policy making. The argument for developmental dictatorship was used as an ideological rationale, and may have been to some extent a real motive, for both the nationalist and the communist regimes in limiting democracy, but in fact, dictatorships cost more in famines and ecological disasters than they gain in development. The estimated fifty million Chinese dead at the hands of their own governments in this century (not counting the twenty-seven million killed by the government-caused famine of 1958 to 1961) testify to this fact.[8]

A third argument relates underdevelopment to the weakness of civil society. To some extent democracy depends on the existence of independent social forces and groups that demand access to policy making and have enough financial and other power to force the state to respect the rules that grant them this access. In this view, democracy gets institutionalized when there are social forces that have an interest in defending democratic procedures. In a backward society these forces are weak. This argument applies well to late Qing and republican China. Civil society was not absent in those years, but it was relatively weak compared to the countries where democracy established itself.

Whatever the force of these three developmental arguments in explaining past problems, socioeconomic development in China is far more advanced today. China's per capita gross national product (GNP) places it already above the minimum level at which democracy has been practiced with reasonable success in some other nations. And because of low prices of housing, basic foods, and medical care, per capita GNP figures understate the average level of welfare in China. A more meaningful measure of development is the human development index developed by the U.N. Development Program. According to this index, China ranks in the middle level of countries, along with many that practice democracy.[9] Since development is thought to affect democracy via such mediating factors as geographic mobility; mass media reach; organizational and economic participation; and political information, interest, and other public attitudes, this measure of development is more relevant to political analysis than straightforward per capita GNP figures.

Here is still another lesson from the past that offers little guidance to practical action by democrats, since they, like other Chinese, are already committed to development as a goal, aside from whatever impetus it may lend to democratization. Our reflections on this variable once again suggest, however, that at least the failures of the past are not a premonition of what will happen in the future.

Peasant Mass

Some Chinese argue that it is difficult or impossible to build democracy in a society with a large peasant mass. This argument is often simply a restatement of theories we have already considered: either the theory that Chinese political culture, here seen as a peasant culture, is inhospitable to democracy; or the argument that developmental backwardness, seen as a feature of a peasant society, is adverse to democracy. Sometimes, however, the peasant society argument has a distinct meaning—that peasants as a majority social group, if given the chance to vote, will vote against liberalism, cosmopolitanism, and competitive institutions and will use their democratic access to reinstall dictatorship. The argument is that the peasants are anti-urban, antiforeign, anti-intellectual, and authoritarian.

This argument is difficult to defend. Several functioning democracies have large peasant populations. In modern Chinese history, the peasant masses had little to do with the failure of democracy.

Moreover, Chinese peasants today are more modernized, literate, urbanized, mobile, industrialized, and cosmopolitan than the proponents of this theory give them credit for being. It is more appropriate to call them *farmers* than *peasants*.[10] Chinese farmers have proven capable of operating simple democratic institutions at the village and township levels. They have considerable access to mass media, are sophisticated about market opportunities nationwide, and understand well the impact of national policies on their immediate interests. It seems likely that if Chinese farmers had the chance to vote in meaningful elections, they would vote a well-informed version of their interests.

There are, to be sure, contradictions between rural and urban Chinese residents in their economic and political interests. The impact of democratizing the system so that peasants can affect policy will be adverse to some urban interests. Chinese democrats, who are overwhelmingly urbanites, may fear this. But the fact that farmers have strong policy interests constitutes a favorable condition for institutionalizing democracy, not an unfavorable one. The lesson of these reflections is that democrats must be prepared to see other social groups benefit from the opening of the political system that they alone are currently pushing.[11] Democratization will not hand over control of policy to the proponents of democracy.

Flaws in the Constitutions/Institutions

One might argue that earlier Chinese constitutions failed because they were ill-designed. I do not reject this argument in principle, but for most Chinese constitutions it is impossible to sustain it on the basis of historical record. Political conflicts that ended in the failure of democratic experiments usually took one of two forms: struggles among parliament, cabinet and president, or subversion of constitutional principles by military- or party-based dictatorship.

The provisional constitution of 1912, under which most government business was conducted from that year until 1923, was criticized for ambiguity that permitted conflicts among the branches of government to develop. Other failures did not seem to arise from constitutionally engendered paralysis, however, but from politicians ignoring and circumventing the constitution.

In fact, China's major constitutions all seem to have been fairly good ones, though quite different from one another. The constitutions of 1923 and 1946 have been especially praised by legal scholars. The 1923 constitution was never really put into effect because the government that promulgated it was almost immediately overthrown. The 1946 constitution has proven to have some remarkable strengths in Taiwan; the reform so far has done away with the temporary provisions that were added to it rather than changing the constitution itself, though discussions have been initiated regarding altering the five-yuan structure, the method of presidential election, and clarifying the relationship of presidential and cabinet power. The People's Republic constitutions of 1954 and 1982, which are quite different from the 1923 and 1946 constitutions but similar to one another, offer on paper a workable set of institutions for moving China toward democracy: a series of four levels of people's congresses from the local to the national level, exercising popular sovereignty. What has undermined the democratic potential of these constitutions is domination by the Chinese Community Party.

The lesson for democrats today is that China's constitutional tradition offers as good a starting point as any for building democratic institutions. No conspicuous mistake made in the past stands as a guidepost to what should be avoided. Since none of the previous Chinese constitutions experimented with federalism or with judicial review, we have no reason to conclude either that these institutions would not work or that they are needed. As a practical matter, it may be most realistic to build democracy on the existing People's Republic constitution, with its provisions for National People's Congress (NPC) supremacy and its strong rights articles. Yet history offers no lessons as to what kind of constitution is definitely unsuited to China, or what constitutional arrangements are most suited to China in the abstract. Constitutionalism of any sort has not yet really been tried.

Moral Failures of the Democrats

Many Chinese historians write as if China's democratic experiments failed because the participants abused the process. Analogously, many democrats argue today that the democratic movement is weak because of the failure of its members to unite, to handle funds well, to establish an attractive image, and so on. This moral argument is like the political culture argument on a smaller scale: it is hard to distinguish preexisting moral weakness from the behavior induced by being placed in institutions that do not work. In fact, some of the behavior deemed to be moral failure would be good, competitive, democratic behavior within working democratic institutions.

In reflecting on this purported lesson of history, one is caught between two irreconcilable truths. On the one hand, to paraphrase Jean-Jacques Rousseau, if democratic institutions are to function well, they have to take human beings as they are and not as they ought to be. On the other hand, pervasive moral degeneration can undermine any system of political institutions. The mystery is that when institutions work, they work morally as well as in other ways, and when they fail, they fail in many ways at once, including morally. The fact that moral failure is part of general failure does not mean that moral exhortation is an effective avenue to institution building.

Not only is this lesson of history ambiguous, but its practical implications are once again unactionable. Moral behavior can be wished for, asked for, and encouraged by mechanisms of reward and oversight, but it hardly seems a viable point of access to the problem of democratic institution-building.

Elite Transactions Theory

The theory of elite transactions works at a different level of analysis from those discussed so far. [12] It concerns not the conditions for democracy, but the ways in which the success or failure of institutions come about through the interactions of political elites, operating in pursuit of what we assume they perceive as their political interests. This approach leads us to look at faction leaders, and militarists, Yuan Shikai, Chiang Kai-shek, Mao Zedong and other major actors, to see where they thought their political interests lay, and try to figure out why they behaved as they did.

This line of thought leads to something like the following formulation: China was an empire that broke up, leaving in place military elites and civilian elites with power bases in the relatively weak, localized, civil society; since the empire did not evolve but broke down, there were no rules of the game in place; democratic experiments represented an initial consensus that seemed attractive because of the prestige of the Western model, which military elites thought they could adopt to legitimate their rule, and which civilian elites hoped to use to gain a greater share of power; once these institutions were in place, however, military-based elites did not see benefit in sharing power with electorally based elites, who lacked sufficient financial or other resources to compel such power sharing.

The lessons of this line of analysis are familiar from the literature on democratic regime transitions. Democracy will be firmer if it evolves from the current system rather than being set up on the shards of a broken system; it will be better established if it evolves gradually. It can become institutionalized if it serves the interests of all or most of the powerful social and political forces in the society, and its survival will be helped by moderate, compromise-oriented leadership. Once again, these lessons are hard for democrats to put to use in practical politics for the time being, because for now and in the foreseeable future the fate of Chinese politics depends on many large forces that they do not control.

Our investigation has proven inconclusive; democracy has not worked thus far, but it is hard to disentangle specific reasons for its failure. We have explored a list of possible lessons. Were the earlier failures due to wrong institutions, to wrong leadership, to insufficient civil society, to foreign intervention, to problems of political culture? The nature of history is so complex that it does not permit us to identify a single or a small number of key causes of democracy's failure. Democracy failed across a broad front.

History does, however, give Chinese democrats reasons for courage. In the past, few Chinese really wanted democracy; today many of them do. In earlier years, authoritarianism seemed more likely to solve China's pressing problems— weakness and division; today democracy seems more likely to solve the pressing problems—dictatorship and stagnation. In the past, political institutions lacked authority and administrative capability; today the Chinese bureaucracy is large and strong. The regime's legitimacy is compromised, but many of its institutional procedures seem well-accepted. The situation, then, is different, and more favorable to democracy. History does not promise that democracy will work if tried, but neither does it warrant the conclusion that past failures prove China to be unsuited for democracy. Unfortunately, however, the historical record is not generous with practical guidance to democrats on how to bring about a transition to democracy or how to make it work once it begins to take shape.

Notes

1. Ernest P. Young, *The Presidency of Yuan Shih-k'ai: Liberalism and Dictatorship in Early Republican China* (Ann Arbor: University of Michigan Press, 1977), 221.
2. The definition follows Joseph A. Schumpeter, *Capitalism, Socialism and Democracy*, 3rd ed. (New York: Harper Torchbooks, 1962). The sense in which it is minimal has been discussed by Carole Pateman, *Participation and Democratic Theory* (Cambridge: Cambridge University Press, 1970).
3. On restrictions of political rights, see Andrew J. Nathan, "Political Rights in Chinese Constitutions," and "Sources of Chinese Rights Thinking," in R. Randle Edwards, Louis Henkin, and Andrew J. Nathan, eds., *Human Rights in Contemporary China* (New York: Columbia University Press, 1986).
4. Lucian W. Pye, *The Dynamics of Chinese Politics* (Cambridge, Mass.: Oelgeschlager, Gunn and Hain, 1981).
5. See, e.g., William T. Rowe, *Hankow: Conflict and Community in a Chinese City, 1796–1895* (Stanford: Stanford University Press, 1989); David Strand, *Rickshaw Beijing: City People and Politics in the 1920s* (Berkeley and Los Angeles: University of California Press, 1989).
6. See, e.g., Susan Shirk, *Competitive Comrades* (Berkeley and Los Angeles: University of California Press, 1982); Andrew G. Walder, *Communist Neo-Traditionalism: Work and Authority in Chinese Industry* (Berkeley and Los Angeles: University of California Press, 1986).
7. Andrew J. Nathan and Tianjian Shi, "Cultural Requisites for Democracy in China: Findings from a Survey," *Daedalus* 122, no. 2 (1993), 95–123.
8. R. J. Rummel, *China's Bloody Century: Genocide and Mass Murder Since 1900* (New Brunswick, N.J.: Transaction, 1991); R. J. Rummel, *Indivisible Human Rights: The Relationship of Political and Civil Rights to Survival, Subsistence and Poverty* (New York: Human Rights Watch, 1992).
9. U.N. Development Program, *Human Development Report 1990* (New York: Oxford University Press, 1990), 128.
10. Myron Cohen, "Cultural and Political Inventions in Modern China: The Case of the Chinese 'Peasant,'" *Daedalus* 122, no. 2 (1993), 150–70.
11. James D. Seymour, "What the Agenda Has Been Missing," in Susan Whitfield, ed., *After the Event: Human Rights and Their Future in China* (London: Wellsweep, 1993).
12. Donald Share, "Transitions to Democracy and Transition through Transaction," *Comparative Political Studies* 19, no. 4 (1987), 525–48; Adam Przeworski, "Some Problems in the Study of the Transition to Democracy," in Guillermo O'Donnell, Philippe C. Schmitter, and Lawrence Whitehead, eds., *Transitions from Authoritarian Rule: Comparative Perspectives* (Baltimore: Johns Hopkins University Press, 1986).

2

A Tragedy of History

China's Search for Democracy in the Twentieth Century

SUISHENG ZHAO

Democracy, as one set of normative values, is an important component of Chinese political discourse in the twentieth century. The democratic form of political institutions has also prevailed since the collapse of the old imperial institutions in the early twentieth century. As a matter of fact, China has experimented with almost all forms of democratic institutions, including the presidential system, the parliamentary system, federalism, and constitutional monarchy. China has also established an "old republic," a "new republic," and a "people's republic," as well as the National Assembly and the People's Congress. Numerous constitutions have been promulgated. Nevertheless, these democratic forms of government have never taken root on mainland China. Chinese intellectuals, burning with righteous indignation at the failure of democratic experimentation, went to the streets repeatedly to protest the dictatorship and to appeal for democracy. Nevertheless, all popular democratic movements, from the May Fourth Movement in 1919 to the Tiananmen demonstrations in the spring of 1989, have ended without instilling a democratic system on mainland China. It is no wonder that Lloyd E. Eastman has said, "Because of the nature of Chinese society and of its political traditions, it is perhaps one of China's tragedies during the twentieth century that, in the quest for a viable political system, attempts had been made to erect democratic institutions. In a profound sense, Anglo-American democracy was not suited to China. . . . In China, an authoritarian system of rule is perhaps better able to produce the greatest happiness of the greatest number."[1]

Eastman's statement is obviously too pessimistic. Chinese democrats have firmly rejected his assertion and continued their calls for democracy in China. Nevertheless, it is undeniable that numerous tragedies characterize the historical record of various efforts to introduce democracy into China in the twentieth century. If the historical reality is not recognized and the causes for the failure are not explored, it would be hard to prevent the recurrence of tragedy in China. It is from this perspective that this chapter examines the historical record of the Chinese search for democracy in the twentieth century and explores the causes for the failure of Chinese democracy.

Democracy in the West

Democracy originated in the West and was introduced to China in the early twentieth century. Democracy in the West is first a value system that emphasizes individual freedom and liberty. John Locke's argument for natural rights and John Stuart Mill's statement on the limits to the authority of society and government over the individual have long been the normative foundations of Western democracy. Yet democracy in the West is, more important, a set of political institutions that constitute what Aristotle called "the rule of many." A modern theorist, Seymour Martin Lipset, indicates that a democratic system is one that makes possible regular and institutionalized or constitutionalized opportunities for changing the set of officials who are responsible for governing the political system.[2] Deane Neubauer emphasizes electoral competition in which all adults should be free to participate under the principle of "one man, one vote."[3] Robert Dahl refers to democracy as *polyarchy,* in which government shows continual responsiveness to the preferences of its citizens, who are viewed as political equals. He shows that a reasonably responsive democracy can exist only if at least eight institutional guarantees are present: (1) freedom to form and join organizations; (2) freedom of expression; (3) the right to vote; (4) eligibility for public office; (5) the right of political leaders to compete for support and votes; (6) alternative sources of information; (7) free and fair elections; and (8) institutions for making governmental and policies dependent on votes and other expressions of preferences.[4] Although similar in principles, a variety of democratic institutions have been adopted in different countries. Arend Lijphart groups them into two diametrically opposite models: the *majoritarian* model and the *consensus* model. British democracy is an original example of the majoritarian model, and Switzerland and Belgium serve as examples of the consensus model. The U.S. system has combined several institutional features of the two, and therefore is considered another pattern of democracy.[5] In spite of the institutional variety, the core ideal of all democratic governments is the same: to preserve the principles of individual rights and competitive political institutions.

Western Expansion and Reforms of the Qing Court

In China prior to the late Qing dynasty, individual rights were never recognized; nor were competitive political institutions. The mandate of the emperors came from "heaven" and could not be challenged by political oppositions. Confucian doctrine assumed a natural harmony between the rulers and the ruled (*tianren heyi*) and a strict hierarchy in the political order. It was the economic expansion of the Western powers into China, and the worldwide emergence of modern democratic regimes in the nineteenth century, that began to challenge the traditional natural harmony of political order and made it possible for democratic ideas to be introduced into the Middle Kingdom.

China was economically self-sufficient and politically isolated from the outside world before the Opium War in 1842. China's defeat in the Opium Wars was not only a source of national humiliation, but also led to the first of many unequal treaties forced on the country by Western powers to open over a dozen ports along the southeast coast and the Yangtze River to foreign trade. Facing the challenge of Western economic expansion, the Qing government had to made a choice of either driving out Westerners or adapting itself to the new developments. Because it did not have the capacity to drive Westerners away, the Qing government had to make the choice to adapt itself to the new development. As a result, the Self-Strengthening Movement (*Ziqiang Yundong*) and the Westernization Movement (*Yangwu Yundong*), led by comprador bureaucrats in the latter half of the nineteenth century, were aimed at introducing Western technologies to preserve the rule of the Qing government. The overriding concern in these movements was to build a strong Chinese state that could survive and prosper in a hostile international arena. As a by-product of this movement, Western ideas and institutions were also introduced by some Chinese intellectuals who had the chance to observe the emergence of Western democratic systems in the nineteenth century.[6] For example, Yan Fu and Liang Qichao, who visited the West and later became the major spokesmen for the first generation of the modern Chinese intelligentsia that emerged at the turn of century, arrived at the conclusion that the countries in the world that were powerful were also democratic. China would thus need to borrow not only technologies from abroad, but also Western liberal ideas and values that had given rise to these technologies.[7]

As a result, in January 1898, Kang Yuowei and Liang Qichao, two reform-minded modern intellectuals at the turn of the century, proposed to the Guangxu Emperor to stimulate capitalist ethics and industrialism in China in order to produce strength and prosperity. They also proposed a parliamentary system to secure popular participation and bind the ruled to the rulers actively rather than passively. They believed that constitutional reform (*bianfa*) was the secret of Meiji Japan's success. This effort of modern intellectuals culminated in the heroic but ill-fated Hundred Days Reform (*baire weixing*), led by the Guangxu Emperor from June to September 1898—the famous coup that attempted to change China from the top.

Although the Hundred Days Reform was aborted by a countercoup, China could not be placed back where it had been. Three years after the Hundred Days Reform, the Qing court issued an imperial edict to reform bureaucratic structures. The major contents of the reform as declared were the same as those that would have been carried out by the Hundred Days Reform. These included establishment of the Ministry of Foreign Affairs as the first of six ministries, modification of the Confucian examination system, establishment of new schools, granting scholarships for students studying abroad, and establishing military academies to train a modern officer corps. The peak of the reform by the Qing court was the "preparing the constitution" (*yubei lixian*) movement in 1908. According to the plan of the movement, local assemblies would be immediately established in 1908, elections for provincial assemblies would be held in 1909, and a national assembly would be elected in 1910. Finally a constitution would be promulgated in 1917.[8]

The Tragedy of Republic

The reforms of the Qing court aimed at mobilizing local gentry and intelligentsia in an advisory role to maintain the imperial government. Albeit moderate, this was the first attempt in Chinese history to define imperial power through political institutions—namely, the constitution and assemblies rather than the mandate of heaven.

Unfortunately, reform destroyed the reforming government, for the reform further undermined the already tenuous imperial government and exacerbated tensions between the local gentry and the Manchu autocracy. Modern educated students and military officers developed radical nationalist views that synthesized provincial loyalties with ethnic hostility to the alien Manchu dynasty. Local provincial gentry and merchants rapidly transformed the newly established representative assemblies into formal platforms to advocate constitutional programs of political decentralization. These developments led to a radical republican revolution in 1911, when constitutional gentry and merchants, former officials, new army officers, and youthful radicals led by Sun Yat-sen, a Western educated nationalist leader, launched a revolutionary uprising, which eventually overthrew the Qing dynasty.

The outcome of the revolution was the declaration of the first Chinese republic. But it soon became apparent that the real accomplishment of the revolution had been simply to deliver the coup de grace to the imperial administrative and political institutions that had already been eroded from within by the usurpation of provincial officials, military officers, and nonofficial gentry. The alternative republican form of political institutions that emerged to replace the shattered imperial system soon fell into a new type of autocratic rule in China.

The republican government, established on New Year's Day, 1912, adopted a presidential system with Sun Yat-sen as the provisional president. Three months later, Sun Yat-sen yielded his presidency to Yuan Shikai according to an earlier agreement. Yuan was the chief military modernizer among the imperial forces; he had used his position to double-cross both the monarchy and the republican leaders during the revolutionary period. On the one hand, Yuan forced the emperor to issue an imperial edict allowing the revolutionaries to set up the republic. On the other hand, he obtained from Sun Yat-sen the assurance that the republic would survive only if he were made the first president of the republic.

After resigning the presidency, Sun Yat-sen sought to check Yuan's personal ambitions by means of a parliamentary majority and a responsible cabinet. Sun thus insisted on a cabinet system of collective leadership, which was prescribed in the Provisional Constitution of the Republic of China, and worked hard to build his own political party.[9] Sun declared the establishment of the Kuomintang (KMT) on August 25, 1912. The KMT controlled the majority in both houses of the parliament in the elections of the winter of 1912 to 1913. The parliamentary leader of the KMT, Song Jiaoren, prepared to lead a KMT cabinet, to "put the president in a position of no responsibility," and to peacefully regain the power that had been seized by Yuan Shikai.[10] In order to assure his personal power and prevent the KMT from establishing the majority government, Yuan Shikai plotted the assassination of Song Jiaoren at the railway station in Shanghai on March 10, 1913. He then declared the dissolution of the KMT and the unseating of its members in the parliament on November 4, 1913. Yuan promulgated a new constitution on February 18, in which a presidential system was prescribed.[11] According to the new constitution, Yuan Shikai's presidential power would not be checked by any other political institutions.

In this case, the republic, a supposedly democratic form of government that had been introduced from the West, was thoroughly distorted in China. The Republic of China (ROC) under Yuan Shikai became the first regime in Chinese history that carried out a personal dictatorship in the name of a constitutional form of government.

Encouraged by his success, Yuan went further with an attempt to cast away the republic. In October 1915, he suddenly announced that he would accept "the overwhelming popular demand" for the reestablishment of imperial rule. Yuan fixed the date for his own enthronement as January 1, 1916. To his surprise, however, resistance to the monarchical restoration came strongly from all over China. Under heavy pressure, Yuan was forced to cancel all his monarchical plans and to restore the republic on March 22, 1916. The reign of a dynasty, which was to be called *Hongxian* (The Dynasty of Glorious Constitutionalism), lasted less than three months, "leaving behind nothing more than some extremely rare proof coins for the delectation of numismatists."[12]

Yuan's failure demonstrated that the Chinese people had abandoned the traditional monarchical system. Indeed, no attempt to restore the monarchical system in China has since succeeded . The surviving Chinese republic, however, did not mean that China would be able to establish a representative government any time soon. The conflict between borrowed Western political systems and indigenous political and social structures was one of the most complex and fascinating problems confronting Chinese elites. The first response to the West by those elites representing the high culture of traditional China was essentially one of rejection. Subsequently, democratic political values and institutions conceived and developed in the West were gradually accepted and even championed by avant-garde elements, and became an essential part of the inevitable development and an article of faith of Chinese intellectuals in the twentieth century. Nevertheless, it must be pointed out that these Western values and institutions were taken largely at face value and distorted in China's practice.

By any account, the failure of the monarchical restoration by Yuan Shikai suggested that the authoritative position of constitutional government was established and the dominant strand of Chinese political thinking in the early twentieth century was democratic. In these circumstances, all autocracies and forms of authoritarian rule later in China had to mask themselves with a constitutional form of government. This was the case with the new cabinet form of government led by Duan Qirei after Yuan's abortive monarchical restoration. Duan was a warlord. Relying on his military power, he not only made the president (Ni Yuanhong) a puppet under his control, but also totally ignored the National Assembly. However, because he suppressed an attempt to restore the monarchy by Zhang Xun in June 1917, Duan became a hero for remaking the republic at the time. In 1920, another warlord, Chao Kun, defeated Duan Qirei and established another republican government. Chao also boosted himself as a hero for remaking the new republic. It was indeed a historical irony that the republic was made and remade time and time again by warlords. Thus, in the "republic," constitutional forms of institutions, including the presidency, cabinet, and parliament, all became the instruments of warlords' rules and had nothing to do with democratic values. Thereafter, the name and content of constitutional government fell apart.

The Establishment of One-Party Dictatorship

Party politics is an important institution in modern democracy. Before the time of the late Qing dynasty, China had never had political parties (*zhengdang*) except cliques or cabals (*pengdang*), which were prohibited by the emperor and therefore often took the form of secret societies.[13] After the 1911 revolution, political parties began to emerge and party politics were experimented with in China. A historical irony was that although China's party politics started with multiparty competition, it ended up with the establishment of one-party dictatorship.

According to a study of early republican history by Zhang Yufa, a leading republican historian in Taiwan, 682 parties or associations emerged from 1911 to 1913. More than thirty of them could be called political parties with relatively complete political platforms.[14] The most important of these was the Kuomintang, or KMT, which evolved from the Xingzhonghui (Revive China Society), China's first political party, organized in 1894. Xingzhonghui's name was changed to Tongmenghui (Common Alliance Society) in 1905 and finally into the KMT (the Nationalist Party) after the 1911 revolution. The KMT had a hybrid nature, combining a Western parliamentary party and a Leninist style revolutionary movement in its early years. Inspired by Western democratic ideas, it had a genuine inclination to practice parliamentary politics. The party was dedicated to two basic political principles: nationalism and republicanism.

Yet, born of and organized as a revolutionary movement, the KMT and its leaders were also committed to military rule and one-party dictatorship before a constitutional government was to be established.

In the early years after the 1911 revolution, the KMT wholeheartedly espoused Western-style parliamentarism, strongly supported the immediate installment of a constitutional government, and willingly competed with other parties in the political marketplace.[15] Nevertheless, corruption, military intervention, and the chaotic factionalism and division within and among all political groups after the founding of the Republic of China in 1912 crippled Chinese parliamentarism and made a mockery of constitutionalism.[16] The KMT, without military strength or a mass political base, lay at the mercy of strong military men like Yuan Shikai.

It was in this historical context that Sun Yat-sen conducted a thorough reorganization of the KMT in 1924.[17] The reorganization owed its beginning to the spreading influence of the Soviet Revolution and the rise of the Communist Party in China. Since its inception in 1894, the revolutionary movement led by Sun Yat-sen had always sought foreign assistance. While Sun appealed to the president of the United States for help in recognizing his Guangzhou government in 1921, the United States, as well as other Western countries, all turned a deaf ear to his requests.[18] It was therefore a relief when the newly founded Soviet Union extended the hand of friendship to Sun and the KMT. Sun quickly turned to Soviet aid for reorganizing the party and reconstructing China. The first Soviet advisor, Michael Borodin, arrived in Guangzhou in August 1923. By October, he had convinced Sun and the KMT leaders that "party reforms must be undertaken immediately."[19] With the help of the representatives from the Soviet Union, Sun held the First National Congress of the KMT at Guangdong in January 1924. Many prominent members of the Chinese Communist Party (CCP) participated in the congress, which enacted a party statute, set up an organization at both central and local levels, and issued a manifesto that looked forward to working closely with the Soviet Union and the CCP.[20]

While the reorganization marked the emergence of the KMT as a much more effective political force, it was influenced strongly by communist organizational skills and the Leninist line of a revolutionary party. The emphasis of the reorganization was on party discipline and the role of the military. The KMT organization was now closely modeled after the Soviet Communist Party with a hierarchical structure. The Huangpu (Whampoa) Military Academy was set up in May 1924. It was modeled on the academy for Red Army officers in the Soviet Union. The party's commissar in the academy was to have sole charge of the political training of the cadres, and to share the general administration with the president of the academy. Chiang Kai-shek, who had been in Moscow in the summer of 1923 to study the organization of the Red Army, was appointed as the president of the academy, and Liao Zhongkai, another man who had intimate dealings with the Communists, became the party commissar. When Liao Zhongkai was assassinated in August 1925, Chiang Kai-shek became the supreme leader in the academy.

Thus, when the KMT established its dominant position in China through military expeditions in 1927, its hybrid nature was seriously skewed toward a one-party dictatorship. The nationalist regimes led by Chiang Kai-shek in Nanjing abandoned party competition by declaring the Communist Party illegal in April 1927. There was a very severe purge of Communists from the ranks of the Nanjing regime and large-scale murders and persecutions took place in the lower Yangtze Valley.[21] A few months later, the Nationalist government in Wuhan led by Wang Jingwei also conducted a severe purge of the Communists from its own ranks in August 1927.[22]

Following the suppression of the Communists, in 1928 the KMT regime formally declared the beginning of a political tutelage (*xunzheng*) period, which was described in Sun Yat-sen's "Fundamentals of National Reconstruction" (*jianguo fanglue*). The principal aim of political tutelage, according to Sun Yatsen, was to enable the KMT "to instruct the people in the pursuit of constructive work of a revolutionary nature."[23] This principle was interpreted by the "Essentials of Political Tutelage" (*xunzheng yuefa*), adopted by the Standing Committee of the KMT's Central Executive Committee on October 3, 1928, to mean that the KMT should possess supreme authority in the regime during the period of political tutelage. The chief point of the "Essentials" was to proclaim that the KMT, through its Congress or the Central Executive Committee (CEC) or the Central Political Council (CPC), on behalf of the National Assembly, was to exercise the sovereign power of the nation during the period of tutelage.[24] The beginning of this period of political tutelage marked the establishment of the first one-party dictatorship in China. It was the rule of the one-party system that set the KMT as the supreme authority of the nationalist regime and as a monopoly of political power in China.

Disillusionment over Democracy

The establishment of the KMT one-party dictatorship in China coincided with the decline of democracies throughout the world. While democratic development reached a peak in many respects among the independent nations of the world in the 1920s, democracy or democratic trends were snuffed out during the following two decades in Germany, Italy, Austria, Poland, the Baltic states, Spain, Portugal, Greece, Argentina, Brazil, and Japan. As Samuel P. Huntington explains, "The war fought to make the world safe for democracy seemed instead to have brought its progress to an abrupt halt and to have unleashed social movements from the Right and the Left intent on destroying it."[25] In the meantime, the economic successes of fascism in Germany and communism in the Soviet Union were impressive to some Chinese elites.

China's experience with democratic institutions, coupled with the change in political trends in the world, brought to many Chinese intellectuals a sense of disillusionment about democracy. Five constitutions had been formulated during the period from 1912 to 1926, but they did little to fortify public confidence in democratic institutions. Members of the Representative Assembly were more responsive to the guns of Yuan Shikai and Duan Qirei than to the will and needs of the people. The Chinese republic had made a mockery of its Western models. Many Chinese intellectuals, therefore, reached the sad conclusion that "China had attempted to institute democratic government before the Chinese people had been prepared for the responsibilities of democracy."[26] Although this conclusion supported the KMT's political tutelage theory, not all intellectuals who agreed with this argument were supporters of the KMT. A discussion on whether China needed a democracy or a dictatorship was thus provoked in the 1930s. This debate illuminated the disillusionment of those Chinese intellectuals with democracy.

The criticisms of democracy by Chinese intellectuals were cast mostly from a utilitarian point of view. Under the slogan "rich nation, strong army" (*fuguo qiangbing*), what these people sought was an effective government. They feared that the inauguration of democratic rule at that time would weaken the nation and worsen the conditions of instability. From this perspective, these Chinese intellectuals demanded an enlightened despotism. It is notable that most of the intellectuals who were disillusioned with democracy were highly intelligent and Western-educated. For example, Hu Shi, one of the best-known Chinese intellectuals in the twentieth century, argued that despotism was a necessary preparatory stage of nationhood.[27] Chien Tuan-sheng, a Harvard University graduate of political science who had returned to China wrote, "[W]hat I call a totalitarian state must have a dictator . . . who has ideals, who plans for the real benefit of the people."[28]

By the 1930s, democracy as a system of government had come under attack for its seeming inability to cope with the mounting economic and political crises in many parts of the world. As a result, Chinese intellectuals turned to dictatorship and found that a totalitarian state might be a useful means for China's national salvation. It was argued that democratic government functioned only when the sole demand for the government was to police the society. The development of modern economic systems had, however, transformed the responsibilities of government when economic production had to be planned and rationalized. In this case, only a totalitarian government could coordinate the complex operations of a modern economy.

It is ironic that the advocates of dictatorship in the 1930s were motivated by the same goal as that of the advocates of democracy in the earlier part of the century: namely, to build an economically strong and militarily powerful China. In the earlier part of the century many Chinese intellectuals, including those most Westernized, such as Yan Fu and Liang Qichao, embraced democracy not because democracy contributed to the individual fulfillment of Chinese people, but because democracy presumably contributed to a more vigorous society and in turn to a stronger nation. If democracy could not serve this end, these Chinese intellectuals then felt it easy or even necessary to turn to other Western ideas and institutions, including fascism and Marxism, that might better serve this end.

When it was perceived that Russia, Italy, and Germany had devised seemingly more effective methods of dictatorship in strengthening their nations in the 1930s, Chinese intellectuals shifted their focus to an enlightened dictatorship.

The Politics of the KMT Government Design

Chinese intellectuals were instrumental in the moves toward democracy because they searched for democracy as a means to promote national prosperity. They lost confidence in democracy when democracy was found to not serve their needs effectively. Chinese political leaders were even more instrumental toward democracy because they used democracy largely as an instrument in their aspiration for political power. The political rivalry among major leaders of the KMT—namely, Chiang Kai-shek, Wang Jingwei, Hu Hanmin, and Sun Ke—over the institutional design of the nationalist government during its formative period from 1925 to 1937 clearly revealed this utilitarian attitude toward democracy. Seven versions of the Chinese nationalist government's Organic Law (guomin zhengfu zuzhi fa) and two constitutions were promulgated to design a nationalist government during this period. Rather than using the opportunity to design a democratic government, each KMT leader tried to establish a set of governmental institutions that would help enhance his personal power.[29]

The power struggle over institutional design focused on the choice between the presidential and cabinet systems. When the nationalist government was first established in Guangzhou in 1925, it was designed as a cabinet form of government in which the president was a figurehead and several members of the National Government Council shared ultimate authority. However, when the Organic Law of October 3, 1928 set up the five-power government according to the doctrine of Sun Yat-sen, a presidential system was introduced in which the president was to be the Commander-in-Chief of the armed forces and conferred the power of issuing executive orders.[30] The cabinet system was restored according to a revised Organic Law promulgated on December 30, 1931, in which executive power was almost exclusively vested in the hands of a lower organ, the Executive Yuan. The cabinet system remained until 1936, when a constitution was promulgated; according to that constitution, the president became a single executive and possessed the centralized power of the government.

The alternative design of governmental institutions was to a great extent related to the outcome of power struggles among major political leaders of the KMT regime. The cabinet system from 1925 to 1928 was designed as a result of the balance of power among the competing leaders for succession to Sun Yat-sen. When Sun died on March 12, 1925, he gave no indication as to who should be his successor, while his four outstanding lieutenants (namely, Chiang Kai-shek, Hu Hanmin, Wang Jingwei, and Liao Zhongkai) were potential successors for his position. After Liao Zhongkai was assassinated on August 20, 1925, Chiang Kai-shek, Hu Hanmin, and Wang Jingwei were left in a bitter, even bloody struggle for leadership of the KMT and the nationalist government. Wang Jingwei was regarded as the leader of the KMT's left wing.[31] The right wing of the party was led by Hu Hanmin. Chiang Kai-shek, as an ambitious latecomer in politics, cautiously maintained a central position. No single leader could prevail during these years. It was due to this balance of power situation that the first Organic Law approved by the CEC of the KMT on July 1, 1925 designed a cabinet form of government. The chairman of the national government was merely a presiding officer elected by and from the members of the National Government Council. Although Wang Jingwei assumed the chairmanship of the council, six influential members of the Standing Committee of the council, including his leading rival, Hu Hanmin, sat at his side, and the military was under the control of his other rival, Chiang Kai-shek. This balance of power sustained the collective leadership of the cabinet system.

The balance of power, nevertheless, was tilted to the advantage of Chiang Kai-shek by 1928. Implicated in the assassination of Liao Zhongkai,[32] Hu Hanmin was forced to leave China for Europe in the end of 1925 and thereby temporarily dropped out of KMT politics. Relying on his military capacity, Chiang Kai-shek openly challenged Wang Jingwei by setting up a rival nationalist government in Nanjing in 1927. After about one year of repeated trials of strength, including bloody military battles, Chiang finally defeated Wang and established a unified nationalist government in Nanjing. At the Fourth Plenary Session of the Second CEC in February 1928, Wang Jingwei was expelled from the party on the charge of supporting a communist uprising in Guangzhou on December 11, 1927. Chiang Kai-shek, as the chairman of the military commission and the commander-in-chief of the Nationalist Army, took over the chairmanship of the CEC Standing Committee at the Fifth Plenary Session of the CEC in August 1928. From this powerful position, he requested a revision of the Organic Law in order to adopt a presidential system.

The presidential form of government lasted for about three years. Starting in 1930, Chiang's dominant position was challenged by a grand anti-Chiang coalition composed of leading figures in the KMT, including Wang Jingwei, Hu Hanmin, and Sun Ke, and backed by several powerful regional militarists. While none of these political leaders was able to challenge Chiang Kai-shek alone, a combination of their forces was strong enough to block Chiang's ambitions. A balance of power between Chiang Kai-shek and the anti-Chiang coalition was thereby established. Under these circumstances, Chiang Kai-shek was forced to accept the cabinet form of government, which was designed by Wang Jingwei at the Peace Conference held in Shanghai in October 1931. The First Plenary Session of the Fourth CEC of the KMT revised the Organic Law and restored cabinet system in December 1931.

This cabinet form of government lasted about five years and was replaced once again by the presidential system in 1936 when Chiang Kai-shek eliminated his leading rivals, including Wang Jingwei, Hu Hanmin, and Sun Ke. Wang Jingwei, although made the president of the Executive Yuan in the cabinet form of government established in the end of 1931, was more and more closely associated in the public mind with the policy of appeasing Japanese aggression. He survived an assassination attempt on November 1, 1935 and was forced to resign from the government and leave Nanjing to go abroad to seek medical treatment.[33] Hu Hanmin took up residence in Hong Kong in October 1932 and in effect cast all his fortune with Guangdong provincial militarists thereafter. He died at his home on May 12, 1936.[34] Sun Ke took the presidency of the Legislative Yuan in 1932 and was in charge of formulating a permanent constitution during the years 1932 to 1936. While he made a great effort to insert a cabinet government in the constitution, he had to give in to Chiang Kai-shek's demand for the presidential system finally after both Wang Jingwei and Hu Hanmin had disappeared from the competition.[35] Chiang Kai-shek was left as the sole victor in the power contest. The presidential system was thus written into the constitution promulgated on May 5, 1936. Chang Kai-shek, as the president, became China's new dictator until he was forced to flee to Taiwan in 1949.

The "Socialist Democracy"

The establishment of a "People's Republic" by the victory of the Communists in 1949 did not change the fate of democracy in China. The Communist regime claimed that its system was a socialist democracy, with the so-called democratic procedure of democratic centralism and mass line (*qunzhong luxian*). Democratic centralism meant discussion of an issue within the party (or among the people) followed by unified implementation of whatever decision was reached at the top. The mass line involved gathering information from the masses before making a decision, then persuading the masses to accept the decision. In no case were these "democratic procedures" designed to encourage pursuit of competing individual or group interests or to achieve compromises among such interests. In principle, their purpose was to maintain the unity of interest between the party and the people and to guarantee the wholehearted implementation of the party policy and line.

Just like the political leaders of the KMT, Chinese communist leaders also took an instrumental attitude toward democracy, which was used to justify the communist dictatorship. Chinese communist leaders claimed that the CCP did not have special interests of its own and ruled China solely in the fundamental interests of the society as a whole. It also claimed that the individuals' interests were inseparable from those of society and the CCP was the trustee of the social interest. Individual interests therefore were subordinate to the social interest represented by the CCP. The socialist democracy thus justified the nondemocratic power of the communist state to restrict individual rights and the monopoly of the CCP over political authorities in the name of the Chinese people as a whole.

In another similarity with the KMT regime, the CCP government was totally at ease in making numerous constitutions; four "new" constitutions were promulgated in 1954, 1975, 1978, and 1982. Yet these constitutions did not produce a democratic form of government and were not to be used by individuals to protect their rights. Rather, they served only to justify communist rule. As Andrew Nathan's study of Chinese constitutional tradition has indicated, the democratic rights of citizens in these constitutions were not derived from human personhood but were consistently regarded as a grant given by the communist state to the citizens, to enable the citizens to contribute their energies to the needs of the nation. Communist leaders thus were able to add and withdraw rights casually. They could also write laws to restrict constitutional rights. In this situation, although some democratic rights were written in these constitutions, the Chinese people could hardly exercise the democratic rights prescribed there.

For example, while the 1992 constitution prescribed freedom of speech and expression, the constitution also established an obligation for each citizen to uphold the four "basic principles" of party leadership, socialism, dictatorship of the proletariat, and Marxist-Leninist-Maoist thought. In the meantime, the state-secrets regulations prohibit the revelation of matters that are classified as secrets of state or that "ought not to be revealed." The criminal code prohibits "counterrevolutionary" (this clause was later changed to "national-security harming") incitement and propaganda. If an act of speech is held to constitute counterrevolutionary or national-security harming incitement, it becomes a crime that may draw a penalty of imprisonment of no less than five years.[36]

In this case, democracy was only an instrument with which the CCP ruled China. It was never seen as an ultimate value system or embodied in a set of political institutions to protect the individual rights of Chinese people. Although the Communist leaders of China criticized the KMT's one-party dictatorship before 1949, it also established a one-party dictatorship of the CCP to replace the one-party dictatorship of the KMT.

Democracy Pursued by the Post-Mao Democrats

The tragedy of the Cultural Revolution (1966–1976) revealed the weakness of the Chinese Communist system and discredited China's socialist democracy. As a result, the next generation of Chinese intellectuals launched a new search for democracy in the post-Mao era, beginning with the Beijing Democracy Wall Movement in the winter of 1978. This new search was characterized by wave after wave of student demonstrations and protests in defiance of the Communist dictatorship, culminating in the massive popular protest of 1989, which was brutally cracked down on by the Communist regime.

The search for democracy in post-Mao China was led by several prominent intellectuals, and its participants were mostly college students and educated urban residents. The questions that these democrats asked were a hundred years old: Why was China still so backward? How could the rulers tap the people's energy to invigorate the nation? Similar to their predecessors in the earlier half of the century, they viewed democracy still as an instrument that would bring to bear the collective wisdom of the people for modernization. An examination of the views of the Democracy Wall activists and the leaders of the 1989 pro-democracy demonstrations may reveal this instrumental attitude and some other features of the democracy movement in post-Mao China.

The Democracy Wall Movement started as a popular action denouncing the tragic Cultural Revolution. Most participants in the movement were former Red Guard members. Wei Jingsheng, the best-known leader of the movement, had been a high school student when the Cultural Revolution was launched in 1966 and became one of the old Red Guard members who, at the end of 1966, formed the famous Committee for United Action in Beijing. Wei's father was a former People's Liberation Army (PLA) veteran and later a high-ranking cadre in the central government. Wei spent four years in the PLA (1969–1973) and then worked as an electrician at the Peking Zoo. Wei Jingsheng was the founder of the dissident journal *Tansuo* (Exploration), which was the most militant of all nongovernmental publications during the Democracy Wall period. It ran many articles that were highly critical of Marxist ideology and of the Chinese communist government; it also dealt with the subjects of democracy and modernization.

Although the Democracy Wall activists challenged party dictatorship and Marxist ideology, the participants in the Democracy Wall Movement held an instrumental attitude toward democracy, which was treated often in simplistic and even idealistic ways. During the Democracy Wall period, one of the most famous ideas was that China needed democracy as a "fifth modernization" in addition to Deng Xiaoping's "four modernizations" of agriculture, industry, science and technology, and defense. This theme was put forward by Wei Jingsheng in an article in *Tansuo*. Wei listed three reasons for demanding democracy. The first was that democracy was the opposite of the autocracy of the Chinese system and protected human rights; Wei believed that democracy was a cooperative system that recognized the equal rights of all human beings and resolved all social problems on the basis of cooperation. The second reason was that democracy brought about prosperity; Wei claimed that democracy was the prerequisite for rapid economic modernization. Autocrats were engaged in conspiracy and violence in their struggle for power, causing great social upheavals and irreparable damage to production and living conditions. In contrast, democracy provided the most favorable conditions for economic development. The third reason was that democracy provided freedom. Wei stated that democracy, because it promoted prosperity, created optimal opportunities for the pursuit of freedom. Like the Chinese democrats in the early part of the century, Wei emphasized that, as a system of harmony and cooperation, democracy was the form of government that protected the rights of all. Founded on the recognition of everyone's right to preserve his life, democracy would provide everyone with an equal opportunity to realize their rights and freedoms. Democracy regarded harmony with individuality as the basic condition of its existence. In essence, it was a form of cooperation.[37]

These appeals for democracy were obviously based on instrumental considerations. They were simplistic and idealistic. Perhaps the main reason that the Democracy Wall activists presented a simplistic and idealized image of democracy was because it enabled them to use it as a forceful polemical instrument in their criticism of the Chinese autocratic system.[38] However, due to the fact that this view of democracy did not go much beyond that of the Chinese democrats in the early part of the twentieth century, it may be argued that the Chinese search for democracy had not made real progress by the end of the 1970s.

The activists of the democracy movement in the late 1980s were somehow different. Most of participants in the movement were college students. Their leaders were well-established intellectuals, but most of them were well-trained natural scientists rather than social scientists. For example, Fang Lizhi was a physicist and academic administrator. He was expelled from the CCP in 1987 because his campus speeches in favor of academic freedom were deemed largely responsible for the student demonstrations in the winter of 1986. Fang's continued criticism of the regime helped create the atmosphere for the spring 1989 movement. Another leader, Yan Jiaqi, was trained as an applied mathematician. As the founder and former head of the Institute of Political Science at the Chinese Academy of Social Sciences in Beijing, he served as a high-level political advisor to the former party general secretary Zhao Ziyang prior to the democracy movement's breaking out.

The leaders of the late 1980s democracy movement were apparently more sophisticated than their counterparts in the late 1970s. They advocated the establishment of democratic institutions and procedures as a means of curbing power. For example, Yan Jiaqi believed that both traditional and modern Chinese systems were "nonnormative" as they lacked rules for power transfer. In contrast, "normative" political systems possessed basic rules and procedures for power transfer, such as those laid down in the U.S. Constitution. Yan stated that power transfers in the history of the People's Republic of China had taken place through internal power struggles without any procedural framework. Yan regarded the Cultural Revolution as a direct result of the lack of procedures for power transfer.[39] While Yan and his colleagues discovered the importance of democratic institutions and procedures, they still saw democracy as an instrument for China's prosperity; they focused most of their attention on arguing what democratic institutions and procedures could *do* for China than discussing what those institutions and procedures would *be*.[40]

One important feature of the late-1980s democracy movement was that it focused its attack on Chinese culture. Fang Lizhi blamed China's "feudal culture" for the country's absolutism, narrow-mindedness, and love of authority. Yan Jiaqi blamed what he called China's "dragon culture" for the persistence of autocracy and personalized authority. As Andrew Nathan has pointed out, "the obsession with culture has been characteristic not only of the Deng era, but of democratic discourse in China throughout the century."[41] Liang Qichao, for example, argued that the trouble with the Chinese was that they were slavish, ignorant, selfish, dishonest, cowardly, and passive. Nathan indicates that the democrats' criticism of Chinese culture ironically aligned themselves with the official view that the Chinese people were too backward to deserve the democracy that the democrats were demanding. After all, democracy would entail the exercise of power by peasants and workers who might turn out to be "anti-Western, anti-scientific, and anti-intellectual," according to cultural critiques.[42]

The instrumental attitude toward democracy was to a certain extent responsible for creating a gap between the democratic ideals and the political practice of the Chinese democrats in the post-Mao era. Democratic principles were easily abandoned when they did not work to their advantage. For example, during the period of the Tiananmen hunger strike in 1989, a student leader, Wuer Kaixi, told premier Li Peng, "If one fasting classmate refuses to leave the square, the thousands of other fasting students on the square will not leave." Two Western observers indicated that Wuer was explicit about the principle behind this decision: "On the square, it is not a matter of the minority obeying the majority, but of 99.9 percent obeying 0.1 percent."[43] These Western observers pointed out that while this might have been good politics, it was not democracy. Democracy in this case was not only linked to a vision in which people would "share the same views" and have "identical ideals," but also served as an instrument of a few leaders against the will of the majority people. That way these scholars complained that "it is thus difficult to analyze the events of China's 1989 spring as a democratic movement in the pluralist sense of the term."[44]

Conclusion

Ever since the Western impact on China was felt, Chinese intellectuals have yearned to find recipes from the West for the country's national salvation. Democracy is only one of the recipes that Chinese intellectuals have found and experimented with in the twentieth century. In the quest for a viable political system, attempts have been made time and again to erect democratic institutions. Nevertheless, the outcome has been one tragedy after another on mainland China. Why does the tragedy persist? Apart from the nature of Chinese society and of its political traditions, Chinese political leaders' cynicism toward democracy and Chinese intellectuals' overanxiousness to get the results of economic modernization and social harmony from democracy are also responsible for the tragic outcome, as we have demonstrated in this chapter.

It is indeed an important fact that the term *democracy* has acquired a strong positive connotation for most educated Chinese and has become a shibboleth in the political discourse since the beginning of the twentieth century. Therefore, Chinese political leaders had to make use of the democratic form of government and institutions even though they were to establish an autocratic rule. The notions of republic, constitution, presidential system, cabinet system, National Assembly, and People's Congress were only instruments in the eyes of many cynical Chinese political leaders. In a different fashion, Chinese intellectuals were so anxious to restore China's powerful position in the world that they also treated democracy as an instrument. They accepted the values and institutions of democracy when they saw that democracy brought prosperity to Western countries. In the same fashion, they also turned to communism and fascism when they found that these nondemocratic systems made Russia and Germany strong.

The Chinese search for democracy was closely related to a history of violent revolution. Impatient Chinese intellectuals launched the revolutions of 1911, 1927, 1949, and 1989. Although these revolutions mobilized massive popular participation, their outcomes at best were "majority despotism" rather than liberal democracy. Chinese history after the fall of the Qing dynasty was a revolutionary history characterized by life-or-death struggles. These revolutions created revolutionary heroes like Yuan Shikai, Chang Kai-shek, and Mao Zedong, but did not produce founders of democratic polity like George Washington.

It is really a tragedy that Chinese political history in the twentieth century can be characterized by a fantastic cycle of revolution-dictatorship-revolution-dictatorship. The indignant grave diggers of the dictatorship have always established new dictatorships and thus produced new indignant grave diggers. All revolutionary opponents of authoritarian regimes have claimed to be democrats, yet once they achieve power, they all turn to be authoritarian themselves. How to stop the vicious circle in China and how to end the tragedy in the Chinese search for democracy are both theoretical and practical questions that should be further explored by scholars of Chinese studies as well as the practitioners of Chinese democracy.

Notes

1. Lloyd E. Eastman, *The Abortive Revolution: China under Nationalist Rule, 1927–1937* (Cambridge, Mass.: Harvard University Press, 1974), 179–180.
2. Seymour Martin Lipset, "Some Social Requisites of Democracy: Economic Development and Political Legitimacy," *American Political Science Review* 53 (1959), 69–105.
3. Deane E. Neubauer, "Some Conditions of Democracy," *American Political Science Review* 61 (1967), 1002–09.
4. Robert A. Dahl, *Polyarchy: Participation and Opposition* (New Haven: Yale University Press, 1971), 3.
5. Arend Lijphart, *Democracies: Patterns of Majoritarian and Consensus Government in Twenty-One Countries* (New Haven: Yale University Press, 1984).
6. Samuel P. Huntington indicated that what could be reasonably called a democratic political system at the national level of government first appeared in the United States in the early nineteenth century and then gradually emerged in northern and western Europe, in the British domains, and in a few countries in Latin America. See Huntington, "Will More Countries Become Democratic?" in Roy C. Macridis and Bernard E. Brown, eds., *Comparative Politics: Notes and Readings* (Chicago: Dorsey Press, 1986), 68.
7. Maurice Meisner, *Mao's China and After: A History of the People's Republic* (New York: The Free Press, 1986), 13.
8. Zhao Xiaolie, "Wuanqing zhengzhi tizi biange lunxi" (An Analysis of the Political System in the Late Qing Dynasty), *Shixue Yuekan (History Studies Monthly)*, March 1988, 114.
9. Chien Tuan-sheng, *The Government and Politics of China* (Cambridge, Mass.: Harvard University Press, 1961), 71.
10. Ibid.

11. For a chronological description of these events, see Lei Feilong, *Zhonghua Minguo Kaiguo Qishi nain lai de Zhengzhi (Politics of the Republic of China in its Seventy Years of History)* (Taipei: Guangwen Shuju, 1981), 281–371.

12. Paul M. A. Linebarger, et al., *Far Eastern Governments and Politics: China and Japan* (Princeton, N.J.: Van Nostrand, 1956), 132.

13. Generally speaking, political parties are organized around political ideas, whereas cliques are organized around individual leaders.

14. Zhang Yufa, *Minguochunian de Zhengdang (Political Parties in the Early Republican Years)* (Taipei: Institute of Modern History, 1985), 32.

15. For an excellent discussion of the early history of the KMT party politics in English, see George T. Yu, *Party Politics in Republican China: The Kuomintang, 1912–1924* (Berkeley and Los Angeles: University of California Press, 1966).

16. For a description of the early factional competition, see Jerome Chen, "Defining Chinese Warlords and Their Factions," *Bulletin of the School of Oriental and African Studies* (University of London) 31, no. 3 (1968), 563–600.

17. For an excellent study of this development, see George T. Yu, *Party Politics in Republican China,* 183.

18. Ibid., 160.

19. Ibid., 172.

20. For an overall review of the historical documents and facts on the reorganization of the KMT, see Chongguo Dier Lishi Dangan Guan (China Second Archive Library), ed., *Zhongguo Kuomintang Di Yi, Er Ci Quanguo Daibiaodahui Huiyi Shiliao (Collection of the Archives and Documents of the KMT First and Second National Congresses)* two vols. (Nanjing: Jiangshu Guji Chuban She, 1986). This book provides all (available) proceedings of meetings and documents on the principles and the process of the KMT reorganization.

21. Mainland China has published numerous articles and books criticizing the brutal purge of communists by Chiang Kai-shek in 1927. They call this incident the "April Twelfth Counterrevolutionary Coup." Taiwan also has published many articles and books to justify the purge. They call this the *qingdang* (cleaning the party). One of the books published in Taiwan is Li Yunhan's *Chonggong dao Qingdang (From Tolerating Communists to Cleaning the Party)* (Taipei: Zhongguo Xueshu Zhuzuo Jiangzhu Weiyuanhui, 1966).

22. For a detailed description of the purge of communists in Wuhan, see Liu Jizheng et al., *Wuhan Guomin Zhengfu Shi (A History of Nationalist Government in Wuhan)* (Wuhan, China: Hubei Remin Chuban She, 1986), 372–433.

23. Sun Yat-sen, "Fundamentals of National Reconstruction," article 8, in *Geming Wenxian (A Collection of Revolutionary Documents)*, vol. 70 (Taipei: The KMT Party History Commission, 1976), 386.

24. This document was important because before the promulgation in 1931 of the Provisional Constitution there was a tutelage constitutionalism, in fact, if not in name. For a text of the "Essentials of Political Tutelage," see *Geming Wenxian*, vol. 70, 388–389.

25. Samuel P. Huntington, 68.

26. Lloyd Eastman, *The Abortive Revolution,* 142.

27. Ibid., 144.

28. Ibid., 147.

29. For a detailed analysis of the KMT's government institutional design during this period, see Suisheng Zhao, *Power by Design: Constitution-Making in Nationalist China* (Honolulu: The University of Hawaii Press, 1996).

30. Article 13 of the revised Organic Law of October 3, 1928.

31. Sun Yat-sen's collaboration with the Communists and the reorganization of the KMT in 1924 on the Leninist model generated a severe left-right antagonism within the KMT. The left-right alignments among the party leaders and their rank-and-file supporters reflected a pro-and-con stand on the KMT-Communist rapprochement that divided them right

down to the lowest level of the party organization. The left wing of the party took a line in favor of allying with the Communists; the right wing distrusted the Communists.

32. Liao Zhongkai was a radical leader of the left wing of the KMT. He openly advocated close cooperation with the Communists after the death of Sun Yat-sen. Liao hence became a major target attacked by the right wing of the party. Hu Hanmin, as the leader of the right wing, led the attack on Liao. Ten days before the assassination, Hu Hanmin held a meeting of the rightist members of the CEC, who planned to oust Liao from the government. In the meantime, a younger brother of Hu Hanmin, Hu Yisheng, allowed his zeal to outrun his discretion to the extent of urging in print that Liao should be "removed." Hu Hanmin thus became one of the suspects in the assassination of Liao Zhongkai.

33. The assassination of Wang Jingwei was a historical myth in China. It was recorded by many eyewitnesses who made contradictory statements. Some people said that the assassination was incited by the Communists and anti-Japanese activists, and others believed that it was done at Chiang Kai-shek's instigation. For a collection of the eyewitness records, see Qiang Jiangzhong, ed., *Ci Wang Neimu* (Inside Stories about the Assassination of Wang) (Jilin, China: Jilin Wenshi Chuban She, 1986).

34. For one analysis of Hu Hanmin's last years in Hong Kong, see Zhou Binwo and Chen Hongmin, *Hu Hanmin Pinzhuan* (*A Study of Hu Hanmin's Life*) (Guangzhou, China: Guangdong Renmin Chuban She, 1990), 238–90.

35. Lloyd E. Eastman describes the constitutional dispute between Sun Ke and Chiang Kai-shek from 1932 to 1936 in his *The Abortive Revolution*, 163–80.

36. Andrew J. Nathan, *Chinese Democracy* (New York: Alfred A. Knopf, 1985).

37. Baogang He, "Democracy Viewed by Three Chinese Liberals," *China Information* 6, no. 2 (1991), 25–28.

38. Ibid.

39. Yan Jiaqi, *Shounao lun* (*On the Head of State*) (Hong Kong: Zhonghua shuju, 1987), 18–19.

40. Andrew J. Nathan, "Tiananmen and the Cosmos," *New Republic*, July 29, 1991, 32.

41. Ibid., 35.

42. Ibid.

43. Joseph W. Esherick and Jeffrey N. Wasserstrom, "Acting Out Democracy: Political Theater in Modern China," in Jeffrey N. Wasserstrom and Elizabeth J. Perry, eds., *Popular Protest and Political Culture in Modern China* (Boulder, Colo.: Westview Press, 1992), 30.

44. Ibid.

Part II

Chinese Political Culture
and Democracy

3

Confucianism and
Western Democracy

SHAOHUA HU

At the beginning of the third millennium, democracy has made great strides all over the world, yet has not taken root in mainland China, a country established as Asia's first democratic republic in 1911, and which accounts for more than one-fifth of the world's population. Many explanations have been offered as to why China fails in its efforts toward democracy.[1] Not the least of these explanations is that Confucianism stands in the way of China's democratization.

The debate over whether Confucianism is compatible with Western democracy has a long history.[2] Generally speaking, one side of the debate has regarded Confucianism as the ideological underpinning of "oriental despotism," hence dismissing it as antidemocratic.[3] The other side has held that Confucianism was full of humanism and was far from undemocratic.[4] Useful as the debate may be, it suffers methodological problems. An obvious problem is that both Confucianism and Western democracy are barely defined. This may result from a wrong assumption that the two definitions are unproblematic, or from the fact that both Confucianism and Western democracy defy easy definition. Derived from this major problem are three minor ones. First, both factions are one-sided in choosing different aspects of Confucianism and China's political traditions to support their own arguments, but neither challenges the facts supporting their opponents' arguments. Second, in enlisting support from Confucian theory and Chinese reality, both sides have done little to analyze the relationship between those factors. And third, both sides tend to ask if Confucianism facilitates or obstructs Chinese democratization, but do not focus on examining in which aspects, or to what extent, Confucianism affects democratization.

The purpose of this chapter is not to deliver a final verdict on this debate, but to clarify some problems, hence making further debates more fruitful. At the beginning of this four-section chapter, I will attempt to define Confucianism and Western democracy. In the second section, I will show how Confucian doctrine is similar to and different from Western democracy. Having examined the relations between Confucian doctrine and Western democracy, I will then turn to the relationship between Confucianism as a state ideology and China's political traditions. In the last section, I will explore the impact of Confucianism on Chinese democratization.

Defining Confucianism and Democracy

Confucianism contains many shades of meaning, and they are so intertwined with one another that people tend to shift from one meaning to another or lump all of them together. A careful analysis shows that three distinctive and separable conceptions of Confucianism have taken shape in a long historical process. The first conception refers to Confucian doctrine as mainly represented by *The Analects*, a book that was complied long after the death of Confucius (551–479 B.C.E.).[5] Like any other school of thought, Confucianism is a product of its time. Confucius lived in the period of the Warring States, characterized by immorality, anarchy, and war. H. G. Creel describes the political situations in Confucius's time by noting, "The process by which the power of the emperor was usurped by the rulers of states, and their power was usurped by their chief ministers, did not stop there. The officers of the ministers also encroached on the power of their superiors as much as they were able."[6] The chaotic situation called for explanations and solutions, which resulted in numerous schools of thought in China. Confucianism turned to morality for solutions; legalism emphasized the importance of the rule of law; Taoism advocated that the populace distance itself from societies; Mohism preached universal love as a panacea.[7]

In the course of history, Confucian doctrine has developed two major branches. One branch is associated with Mencius (372–289 B.C.E.), who distinguished himself by his view that human nature is good and that people are more important than rulers. Later, Mencian doctrine enjoyed such a high status that Confucianism denoted both Confucian and Mencian doctrines. The other branch is associated with Hsun Tzu (298–238 B.C.E.), whose doctrine rests upon the assumption that human nature is evil and that goodness results from conscious activity. Shunned by mainstream Confucianism, Hsun Tzu's assumption found favor with the legalists, the archenemies of Confucians.

The second conception of Confucianism refers to Confucianism as a state ideology that dominated China for more than two thousand years. Confucianism had its ups and downs after Confucius's death. Before 221 B.C.E., when Ch'in crushed all other states and unified China, Confucianism did not hold an upper hand over other schools in gaining official favor. In the short-lived Ch'in dynasty, Confucianism was ruthlessly suppressed by tyrannical rule amid a state ideology of legalism. Confucianism had its days when Emperor Wu, the sixth ruler of the Han dynasty, ascended the throne in 140 B.C.E. Confucian ministers had the 15-year-old emperor sign a decree respecting Confucianism, which did not prevent the emperor from taking a non-Confucian policy but did pave the way for the apotheosis of Confucianism.[8] As a state ideology, Confucianism had to fulfill its ideological function in the rulers' interests; it had to be associated with Confucian officials whose main interest was in making a living; and it had to accommodate itself to changing and complex realities. All this makes the second conception of Confucianism differ from the first.

The third conception of Confucianism, which has a more modern ring, uses Confucianism to denote the Chinese civilization itself.[9] Mistaken as it is, this conception does not merely come out of ignorance; it is also taken for the sake of convenience. To the extent that Confucianism prevailed in Chinese civilization for so long, it is understandable that non-Chinese and even contemporary Chinese tend to identify traditional China with Confucianism. Whatever the limitations, these three conceptions will continue to exist, because they reflect the different aspects of Confucianism and the different positions of its observers.

Like Confucianism, democracy has been subject to misunderstandings. Western democracy originated from ancient Greece more than 2,500 years ago, when Cleisthenes allowed all citizens of Attica to participate in public meetings and to criticize government in public. Etymologically, the term *democracy* means "rule by the people." For Aristotle, democracy embodies the spirit of liberty. While "the interchange of ruling and being ruled" forms political liberty, "living as you like" constitutes civil liberty.[10] Put another way, democracy comprises two conceptions: popular sovereignty and individual liberty.[11] Based on Aristotle's view of democracy, this article will define democracy in terms of freedom, which involves both positive and negative aspects.[12] Freedom in the positive sense means the situation in which people have the ability to intervene in government; freedom in the negative sense means the situation in which people have a right to live without arbitrary interference from government.

Whatever the differences between Greek and modern democracy,[13] the latter is still based on the same principles—popular sovereignty and individual liberty. Ideal as the principle of popular sovereignty may be, it is technically difficult, if not impossible, to let people in a nation-state decide everything.[14] In fact, modern democracies are not participatory, but representative. The principle of popular sovereignty in modern times hinges on two major mechanisms: the separation of powers advocated by Montesquieu and the competitive election highlighted by Joseph A. Schumpeter.[15] While the ruled choose their rulers during an election, rulers are mutually checked and balanced before and after the election. On balance, the competitive election is more important than the separation of powers in determining if and how a particular political system is democratic because the division of labor is employed in any government, especially a modern one. Robert A. Dahl goes on further to identify two dimensions of elections—public contestation and inclusiveness—and privileges the former over the latter.[16]

Individual liberty is another principle of democracy. Two modern British thinkers figure prominently in advocating individual liberty. While John Locke emphasizes that even a democratic government has no right to violate people's basic liberty, John Stuart Mill cautions that the tyranny of the majority poses threats to individual liberty, and stresses that society should be on its guard against the tyranny of both government and the majority.[17] It is important to point out that popular sovereignty takes precedence over individual liberty, because while the former refers to the source and purpose of government, the latter deals with the scope of government.

In modern times, democracy and totalitarianism are regarded as two ends of the political spectrum. To express it in terms of ideal types, a government respecting the principles of popular sovereignty and individual liberty is democratic; a government violating them is totalitarian. A hybrid system, which is neither democratic nor totalitarian in the strictest sense of the terms, contains two subtypes: one may respect popular sovereignty but violate individual liberty; the other may violate popular sovereignty but respect individual liberty. Throughout human history, few regimes have ever been totalitarian and most have been authoritarian. Compared with totalitarian regimes, authoritarian regimes are less willing and less able to damage people's rights and interests. In sum, in measuring whether a particular country is democratic or not, people should take into account the following questions: Are rulers elected or not? Does the separation of powers exist? To what extent do the people enjoy individual liberty?

Similarities and Differences

Defining Confucianism and Western democracy makes it possible to compare and contrast them. This section will examine ways in which Confucianism is similar to, and different from, Western democracy. Here Confucianism only means Confucian and Mencian doctrines, but for convenience, I will use the term *Confucianism* rather than *Confucian doctrine*.[18]

Confucianism and Western democracy have several things in common; in the first place, they find common ground in opposing despotism, a worse version of authoritarianism. Regarding what should be done for the people, Confucius's answer was to enrich and then to instruct them (Confucius, 13:9). Confucianism believes the interests of rulers and people to be closely related and mutually beneficial (Confucius, 12:9), so it is important for rulers to win the people's support. Among three prerequisites of the governments— sufficient food, sufficient weapons, and people's confidence in their ruler, Confucius gave priority to people's confidence (Confucius, 12:7). Confucius even specified four things rulers should avoid: cruelty, oppression, injury, and meanness (Confucius, 20:2).

In the second place, Confucianism not only opposes despotism, but defends people's rights and interests. The Confucian teachings mentioned above may strike people as utilitarian and commonsensical, because few political schools of thought in human history have regarded the relationship between the ruler and the ruled as antagonistic, encouraging rulers to milk the ruled.[19] But Mencius's defense of people's rights and interests surpassed that of Confucius and even partook of Kantian deontology.[20] In no uncertain words, Mencius put the interests of people before those of rulers. He maintains that "the people are the most important element in a nation; the spirits of the land and grain are the next; the sovereign is the lightest" (Mencius, 7b:14). Moreover, he defended the people's rights to rebellion. For him, killing a despot did not constitute regicide (Mencius, 1b:8). Although Mencius was not the first to justify the right to rebellion, which had been accepted by the Chinese since the twelfth century B.C.E. under the rubric of "mandate of heaven," he can be credited with popularizing this idea. Elbert Duncan Thomas attached such importance to this right as to declare it the basis of Chinese democracy.[21]

In the third place, like Western democracy, Confucianism advocates active participation in politics. Mencius identified three types of participation and withdrawal. The first type is represented by Pih-e, who participated in government when the situations were good and withdrew from it when they turned bad. The second type is represented by E Yin, who served the government in both good and bad times, because he thought his participation would not make the situation worse and might even make it better. The third type was represented by Hwuy, who dealt with all kinds of people, virtuous or vicious, intelligent or ignorant, without compromising his principles. Mencius did not make an invidious distinction among these types. Citing Confucius as an example, Mencius thought that the decision should depend on particular situations (Mencius, 5b:1). Despite this flexibility, a thread runs through Confucianism: gentlemen should deem it their responsibility to participate in government to make rulers benign and wise. This, however, should not be understood as a hunger for power. Confucianism often stresses the distinction between gentlemen, whose principle is righteousness, and mean-spirited people, whose principle is self-interest.

In the fourth place, both Confucianism and Western democracy place a premium on civic virtue. What distinguishes democracy from despotism is no less their purposes than their methods. Most rulers, democratic and despots alike, claim that their policies are to serve people's interests, but they employ different methods to pursue their objectives: despots are willful and unpredictable; democrats are careful and predictable. Confucianism sets store by two virtues: benevolence (*jen*) and propriety (*li*).[22] *Benevolence* is ill-defined, but Confucius did identify it once with loving people (Confucius, 12:22), and most Chinese use the word this way in modern times. *Propriety* denoted the rituals in sacrifice and ancestral worship, but later it came to mean the accepted standard. In social life, it represented self-discipline and mutual respect. If these virtues were hard to practice, Confucius advised people to follow the golden rule of means— that is, "whatever things you do not wish that others should do onto you, do not do unto them" (Confucius, 12:2). Democracy embodies the spirit of "live and let live," calling for civility, tolerance, and compromise. In this respect, Confucianism resembles Western democracy.

Finally, Confucianism has strong egalitarian tendencies, especially in socioeconomic terms. The Chinese know the Confucian ideal well that says, "I have been taught to believe that those who have kingdoms and possessions should not be concerned that they have not enough people or territories, but should be concerned that wealth is not equally distributed; they should not be concerned that they are poor, but should be concerned that the people are not contented. For with equal distribution, there will be no poverty; with mutual goodwill, there will be no want; and with contentment among the people, there can be no downfall and dissolution" (Confucius, 16:1).

No doubt, Western democracy places an emphasis on political and civil equality, but enhancing economic and social equality has received more and more attention. This emphasis on socioeconomic equality constitutes another similarity between Confucianism and Western democracy.

Whereas Confucianism resembles Western democracy in many ways, their differences are great and numerous. First, they differ in their views of human nature. No one expresses the basis of Western democracy better than Reinhold Niebuhr, who holds that "men's capacity for justice makes democracy possible; but men's inclination to injustice makes democracy necessary."[23] Confucianism concurs with Western democracy that human beings are rational and educable, but disagrees on whether human nature is good or bad. Generally speaking, Western democracy is predicated on the pessimistic assumption that human beings are neither omniscient nor omnipotent, and that their selfishness makes conflicts unavoidable. In contrast, Confucianism plays down the negative side of human nature. Confucius said that human beings were born upright (Confucius, 6:17); Mencius presented a systematic view of human nature, maintaining that human nature is good (Mencius, 2a:6). Although both assumptions contain partial truth, the Western assumption is superior to the Confucian one, for the assumption that "human beings are egoistic" is more valid than its null assumption that "human beings are not egoistic." What matters more is not the validity of the different assumptions, but the possible implications they carry. The Thomas theorem, named after American sociologist William J. Thomas (1863–1924), shows that if something is regarded as true, it will have an impact as such, no matter if it is true or not. A pessimistic assumption of human nature is more conducive to the emergence of democracy than an optimistic one: while the former necessitates external constraints to check rulers' power, the latter misleads people into pinning their hopes on enlightened rulers.

The second difference is that unlike Western democracy, which is associated with individualism, Confucianism places a premium on families. To emphasize family values does not necessarily conflict with Western democracy, since family has always been the basic social unit in human society. What makes Confucianism distinctive is that it regards filial piety as the uttermost virtue in society, thereby sacrificing individualism and patriotism at the altar of family. Two cases illustrate the Confucian emphasis on family values. In one case, Confucius thought that if a father had stolen a sheep, his child should conceal the misconduct instead of bearing witness against him (Confucius, 13:8). Mencius said that if Emperor Shun's father committed a murder, the emperor might abandon his empire and run away with his father (Mencius, 7a:35). Confucian emphasis on filial piety has had a great impact on Chinese society in general and China's political culture in particular.[24]

The third difference between Confucianism and Western democracy lies in their attitudes toward the dichotomy of hierarchy and equality. Neither Confucianism nor Western democracy denies the different endowments of human beings, but while Western democracy preaches equality as a goal worth pursuing, Confucianism accepts and beautifies hierarchy. Confucius wished to "let the prince be a prince, the minister a minister, the father a father, and the son a son" (Confucius, 12:11). Mencius claims that in society, "some labor with their minds, and some labor with their strength. Those who labor with their minds govern others; those who labor with their strength are governed by others." (Mencius, 3a:4). Besides this, Confucianism has made distinctions between the old and the young, and between men and women. In each case, the latter is supposed to obey the former. In fairness to Confucianism, this kind of attitude permeates all traditional societies and still exist in modern democracies. Yet without the tension between social realities and human ideals, society will barely make progress.

The fourth difference between Confucianism and Western democracy is that unlike Western democracy, which is characterized by the rule of law, Confucianism prefers ethics to law to such an extent that it obviates the need of law in society. Confucius argues, "Under a virtuous rule the orders of the government will be effective even though they are not followed by law and punishment; and that under a corrupt rule the people will not obey the orders of the government even though they are liable to severe punishment" (Confucius, 13:6). Highlighting the importance of morality in society is beyond reproach; without morality no society can survive. But Confucius mistook a necessary condition for government as a sufficient one. His argument begs the question: How can one be sure that rulers and people are as moral as he wished? In spite of or because of the immorality pervading Confucius's times, Confucianism is unrealistic in solely relying on morality.

The last and most important difference between Confucianism and Western democracy manifests itself in their attitudes toward rulers. As mentioned above, the essence of democracy is to select and control rulers. Without elections and the separation of powers, there is no democracy. Confucius did say that a commoner might become a prime minister overnight (Confucius, 12:22) and that one of his disciples might properly ascend a throne. But how to select rulers is not the concern of Confucianism. No doubt, traditions, customs, and rites constrained emperors just as modern laws constrain democratic leaders, but rulers could and did circumvent these constraints. In short, Confucianism does not provide an effective mechanism to check despotism, as does Western democracy.

What conclusions can be drawn from the comparison between Confucianism and Western democracy? In its opposition to despotism, defense of the people's rights and interests, support of participation, emphasis on civic virtue, and egalitarian tendency, Confucianism resembles Western democracy. But their similarities, especially in the humanistic spirit, do not provide legitimate reasons to believe that Confucianism is democratic. While Confucianism may advocate a government for the people, it does not call for a government of the people and by the people. The fact that Confucianism does not advocate popular sovereignty and individual liberty excludes the possibility that Confucianism is democratic. Likewise, in its view of human nature, emphasis on family, deference to authority, the rule of men, and a lack of mechanism against despotism, Confucianism differs from Western democracy. But these differences evince no evidence that Confucianism is antidemocratic. To advocate democracy is one thing; to oppose democracy is another. On the political spectrum, there exist numerous possibilities. E. R. Emmet says, "'Either it is or it isn't' may be a very misleading thing to say and the danger of the Contradictory of Formal Logic is that it may make us think in terms of clear-cut distinctions where none are, in terms of black and white when in fact there are many intervening shades of grey."[25] This passage clearly applies to the relationship between Confucianism and Western democracy. Confucianism is neither democratic nor antidemocratic; it is appropriate to call it "a-democratic."

Confucianism and Authoritarianism

Having compared Confucian doctrine with Western democracy, this chapter will now examine how Confucianism is related to China's political traditions. After all, the importance of Confucianism results less from its intellectual messages than from its practical implications. A well-known scholar, Lucian W. Pye, contends that "the gap between words and actions, between doctrinal theories and practice, in Chinese political culture is wider than in almost any other culture."[26] Even if one may challenge the validity of the statement, it is necessary to examine the gap between Confucian doctrine and China's political traditions.

There are several misperceptions among many scholars that China's political traditions were quite democratic. First, disobedience, ranging from protest to rebellion, indicates that China did not lack a democratic movement. No doubt, Chinese history witnessed a myriad of rebellions, which sometimes forced rulers to be more benign, and sometimes even succeeded in replacing one dynasty with another. To the extent that these rebellions represented the people's will, they were democratic. Yet what makes a political system democratic is not that it contains some democratic ideas or witnesses some democratic movements, but that the two democratic principles—popular sovereignty and individual liberty—are institutionalized. After all, democratic ideas and movements can be found in any society.

Second, Chinese rulers were subject to many constraints. Franklin W. Houn points out that Chinese rulers not only faced competition from many other social forces, but encountered numerous restrictions on their powers even within their regimes. Among them are local officials, imperial relatives and eunuchs, imperial officials, the decision-making process, remonstrances, ancestral precepts, precedents, public opinion, and divine visitations and prodigies.[27] Anyone with a knowledge of Chinese history will agree that Chinese emperors could not do whatever they wanted and were constrained by the natural environment, social interactions, and physical limitations. Indeed, some officials were courageous enough to remonstrate with the rulers at their own risk, and many rulers were wise enough to listen to different opinions. Yet democracy requires institutional constraints on rulers, and it is these constraints that were few and far between in traditional China.

Third, the Chinese people enjoy a great deal of socioeconomic freedom and equality. Bertrand Russell argues that "China has developed personal liberty to an extraordinary degree, and is the country of all others where the doctrines of anarchism seem to find successful practical application."[28] Equally important, the Chinese civil service system had an egalitarian and meritocratic cast; almost all people had opportunity to participate in civil service examinations; and most positions in China were not hereditary. All this made China a striking contrast to Europe, Japan, and India. In addition, China's lack of primogeniture represented and boosted Chinese socioeconomic equality. Given the fact that the Chinese preferred a large family and that the rich could afford to raise more children, the equal division of inheritance among all male descendants would make sons poorer than their fathers, hence narrowing the gap between the rich and the poor in the long run. A Chinese saying has it right: "Wealth cannot last more than three generations"(*fu bu guo san dai*). However free and equal the Chinese were, the phenomena mentioned above did not make China democratic. Freedom enjoyed by the Chinese depended on one thing—that the rulers' interests might not be damaged. Such freedom resulted from rulers' indifference, but did not represent a sphere of immunities.[29] Moreover, democracy demands equality in political and legal terms and gives preference to formal equality rather than substantial equality.

Finally, the local autonomy is regarded as one of the democratic elements in traditional China. The central government attempted to keep effective control over the local governments, but the imperial bureaucracy was so small that it merely reached the county level.[30] The limited capability of the central government allowed the local gentry to play an important role in local affairs. Local autonomy may indicate the limitation of China's political system, but it by no means makes that system democratic.

What then is the nature of China's political tradition, especially its political system? Making a sweeping generalization about the Chinese political system is risky, because the rule of men implied the possibility of enlightened rule and the Chinese political system did undergo changes.[31] Yet based on the definition of democracy elucidated before, it is not difficult to see that the Chinese political system as a whole is undemocratic. In terms of popular sovereignty, Chinese rulers might respect the people's interest, but sovereignty rested with emperors. The constraints they faced were neither institutional nor compulsory. Election of rulers by the people and the separation of powers in modern sense never took place. In terms of individual liberty, the fact that Chinese enjoyed much freedom does not hide another fact that their freedom was not political and might be rescinded if the rulers wanted.

An undemocratic regime does not amount to a totalitarian one. Exercising totalitarian rule in traditional China was neither necessary nor possible: unnecessary because traditional authorities faced less contestation than their modern counterparts do; impossible because the vast territory and backward technology in traditional China made it difficult for rulers to exercise effective control over society, let alone totalitarian rule. To idealize a traditional political system is naive; to demonize it is unfair. Based on our analysis, it is safe to say that China's traditional political system was neither totalitarian nor democratic, but was authoritarian at best and despotic at worst.

An important question naturally arises: How is Confucianism related to Chinese authoritarianism? The answer is that they are closely related. A comparison between Confucianism and Christianity in terms of their respective relationship with the state is enlightening. In theory, while Christianity at least makes a distinction between the emperor's affairs and God's affairs,[32] Confucianism deems it an ideal to serve emperors. In practice, both Christianity and Confucianism became involved with state affairs. In medieval times, Christianity imposed its will on secular rulers; in modern times, it is forced to keep a distance from the state.[33] By contrast, Confucianism served as an ideological underpinning of the authoritarian rule for twenty-odd centuries. It *intended* to get involved with the state, and succeeded in this respect.

Before elaborating Confucianism's role in traditional China, two caveats are necessary. First, it is unfair to say that Confucianism as a state idealogy merely serves as an obedient handmaid to despotism. Confucianism at least fulfilled two positive functions. On the one hand, it inculcated the basic sense of right and wrong among the Chinese, ruler and ruled alike. The sense of right and wrong does not necessarily make emperors benevolent and enlightened, but it certainly reduces wrongdoings. On the other hand, when wrongdoings occurred, Confucianism might attempt to censure them.[34]

Second, it is wrong to lay blame for China's authoritarianism solely at the doorstep of Confucianism. Throughout human history, the vast majority of political systems have been authoritarian rather than democratic, and all major doctrines—including Christianity, Islam and Hinduism—have been made to lend support to authoritarianism. Confucianism did not create, but was created by, authoritarianism. It is naive to believe that Chinese rulers merely followed Confucianism in ruling China. In fact, legalism played a very important role in Chinese politics. Furthermore, other factors, such as China's subsistence agricultural economy, its vast territory, and its Machiavellian tradition are also to blame for Chinese authoritarianism.[35]

Despite these caveats, Confucianism as a state ideology contributed to authoritarian rule in many ways. First, the Confucian homily on benevolence on the part of rulers paled before the Confucian sermon on loyalty and obedience on the part of the ruled. Rulers might be persuaded to be benevolent, but the ruled were forced to be loyal. In a conflict between rulers and the ruled, Confucianism as a state ideology would more often than not side with rulers. In Chinese history, few rebellions took their inspiration from Confucianism;

many turned to other doctrines, such as Taoism and even Christianity for inspiration. This conservative nature of Confucianism manifests itself even in modern times. Kam Louie found a pattern in modern China: "The demand for radical change, especially in the ideological sphere, has been thus linked with anti-Confucianism while a desire for stability has been linked with pro-Confucianism."[36]

Second, the Chinese bureaucracy, which is closely related to Confucianism, lent support to authoritarianism. In a negative sense, the Chinese bureaucratic system provided a safety valve for authoritarianism. By co-opting the talented people, this system defused their discontents with the existing order, which fulfilled the function of Vilfredo Pareto's so-called "circulation of elites."[37] In the positive sense, although Confucian scholars were not necessarily the brightest, they were certainly better than average. The Chinese bureaucracy as a whole did not constitute a force of opposition, but rather represented an important ruling tool. It deserves mentioning that these bureaucrats sometimes acted like despots themselves, their unscrupulous behaviors awaiting emperors' discipline and penalty. It is no wonder that many Chinese rebellions were aimed at overthrowing corrupt officials rather than emperors.

Third, Confucianism as an orthodoxy created a conservative mentality, which fit authoritarianism. Confucianism revealed no inclination to discover the natural rules that govern the world, and showed little interest in *philosophical issues* in the strict sense of the term. Max Weber points out, "Confucianism was in large measure bereft of metaphysical interest."[38] Confucian interests in imposing morality on human relations narrowed the Chinese horizon and created a conservative mentality. What is worse, Confucian ideology suppressed other schools of thought. Rather than encouraging pluralism or freedom of thought, it emphasized conformity and hierarchy. While the intellectual stagnation following the apotheosis of Confucianism constituted one of the biggest tragedies in Chinese history, it certainly helped preserve authoritarian rule in China.

Not the least of all, Confucian emphasis on family values was utilized to support authoritarianism. Compared with Europe, China lacked a civil society. In modern Europe, states fought with one another; the church competed with the states; cities enjoyed autonomy; and different classes held their own positions. On the contrary, China was a united empire for a long time; no religious order challenged the secular authority; cities were citadels of rulers; and the four-tier class structure (official, peasant, craftsman, and merchant) paled before the distinction between ruler and ruled.[39] The only powerful unit that competed with the state for loyalty was family. Yet the Confucian family system did not serve as a check against authoritarianism; rather, it was used to support authoritarianism. As Confucius well realized, the virtue of filial piety was a good preparation for loyalty to high authority. Furthermore, Chinese rulers invented collective responsibility to preserve social order. In a word, if Confucianism as a doctrine is of an anti-despotic nature, Confucianism as a state ideology is a handmaid of authoritarian rule.

Confucianism and Democratization

There are two tendencies in evaluating the impact of Confucianism on democratization, the effort to move toward democracy. One tendency is to dismiss Confucianism as useless or even harmful, as represented by the new cultural movement early in this century. The movement chanted the slogan "Down with Confucius and Sons" and turned to "Mr. Democracy" and "Mr. Science" for help. The other tendency is to exaggerate the positive influence of Confucianism, as Lee Kuan Yew does. For Lee, Confucianism can redress deficiencies or excesses of Western democracy, such as the preponderance of rights over duties and governments' assumption of family roles.[40] Among democratized and democratizing parts of East Asia, Lee is not a voice in the wilderness. It seems that the more developed East Asia is, the more assertive Confucianism grows. Interesting enough, Kim Dae Jung's criticism against Lee is to dismiss East Asia's antidemocratic values as myth.[41]

Taking diametrically opposed views is understandable because the object of the study and the position of the observers both affect people's judgment. From the previous analysis, we realize that Confucianism contains different messages, and that its relationship with authoritarianism is more complex than it seems. Equally important—no matter how objective observers may be—is that there is no denying that their different positions affect their conclusions. For example, it is well-known that nineteenth-century Europe held a negative view of the Chinese political system; less known is the fact that a quite optimistic view prevailed in Europe in the previous two centuries.[42] H. G. Creel even found that Confucianism had an impact on the thinkers of the Enlightenment, who, in turn, promoted Western democracy.[43] The reason why Europeans saw China in a different light is not that China's political system underwent great change during these three centuries, but that the changing nature of European societies enabled Europeans to reach a different conclusion.

This chapter argues that the question of whether Confucianism facilitates or obstructs Chinese democratization is simplistic precisely because it is too general. Therefore, it is more fruitful to study some specific questions, such as *in which ways* and *to what extent* Confucianism facilitates or obstructs democratization. In doing so, it is necessary for researchers to make sure which Confucianism they are talking about.

As mentioned above, Confucian doctrine is less political theory than it is ethical teaching. As an idealistic doctrine preaching morality, Confucianism fails to ask what should be done if morality fails, hence providing few realistic mechanisms to prevent rulers from abusing power. Furthermore, Confucian ethics are more applicable to traditional society than to modern society: the latter is larger in scope and more complex in nature than the former.[44] For all this, we should not expect Confucianism, which is mostly concerned about social relations in traditional society, to help democratization, which attempts to set right the relations between state and society in modern society.

In this century, Confucianism lost its status as a state ideology and ceased to be treated as a sacred doctrine, but the demise of "political Confucianism" does not imply that the "Confucian personal ethic" had lost its influence.[45] As an essential part of Chinese culture, Confucianism has shaped, and will continue to shape, Chinese attitudes and behaviors.[46] Specifically speaking, three factors in Confucian tradition stand in the way of democratization. The first is a Confucian conception of harmony and conflict.[47] Confucian tradition emphasizes stability and harmony, but ignores a basic fact that no society, especially a modern one, is stable or harmonious. Instead of resolving conflicts in a piecemeal and institutionalized way, Confucian tradition suppresses conflicts, only to find that they go out of control. Here it is important to make a distinction between two kinds of conflict. One is continuous but small-scale conflict, as exists in democratic societies; the other is occasional but large-scale conflict, as witnessed in nondemocratic society. Conflict inherent in democracy may be annoying, but conflicts associated with despotism are more violent and destructive. Between these two evils, the lesser evil should be chosen. Without a realistic understanding of social conflict, the Chinese will be reluctant to introduce democracy.

The second factor is Confucian opposition to the rule of law. This involves attitudes toward both authority and law. Confucians tradition is famous for its deference to authority. In this tradition, rulers are supposed to be benign and wise. The problem is that the benign and wise do not necessarily have as much chance to become rulers as do the malignant and shrewd. Western democracy is right in believing that power corrupts, and absolute power corrupts absolutely. Likewise, Confucian tradition is characterized by its aversion to law, which results both from the punitive nature of traditional laws and from Chinese preference of substantial justice to formal justice. Both attitudes bode ill for democracy. Without a suspicion of authority and an appreciation of the rule of law, democracy will be hard to establish; even if it is established, it is not easy to maintain.

The last factor is that Confucian ethics itself has weakness. Within society, the conflict of family and social interests is not resolved in a way suitable for modern society. Influenced by Confucian tradition, the Chinese are collectivist within their families, but tend to be uncooperative in society. Sun Yat-sen's dictum that "China is a dish of loose sand" is still echoed by contemporary scholars.[48] Familism arrests the development of the public spirits, hence rendering it difficult for China to establish democracy.

Within officialdom, Confucian tradition encourages ambitious people to participate in politics, but fails to elaborate on professional ethics. As a result, Confucian officials are characterized by their inefficiency and corruption. Since their primary objectives are to keep their positions, they do their best to shirk responsibilities. Moreover, the Chinese bureaucracy lacks functional specificity, an important characteristic of modern bureaucracy in Weber's view.[49] Confucian officials are not only inefficient, but also corrupt. Etienne Balazs's remarkable analysis of corruption deserves full quotation:

The required attitude of obedience to superiors made it impossible for officials to demand higher salaries, and in the absence of any control over their activities from below it was inevitable that they should purloin from society what the state failed to provide. According to the usual pattern, a Chinese official entered upon his duties only after spending long years in study and passing many examinations; he then established relations with protectors, incurred debt to get him appointed, and then proceeded to extract the amount he had spent on preparing himself for his career from the people he administered—and extracted both principal and interest. The degree of his rapacity would be dictated not only by the length of time he had had to wait for his appointment and the number of relations he had to support and of kin to satisfy or repay, but also by the precariousness of his position.[50]

Though Confucianism does not encourage inefficiency and corruption, it fails to set a high standard for public officials. Without efficient and honest public officials, democracy will not win full support of the people, but will instead foster cynicism in the society.

Although Confucian tradition affects Chinese democratization, contemporary studies on democratization and modern history in East Asia suggest that it is unjustifiable to exaggerate the negative influence of Confucian tradition. There are two major perspectives in studying the preconditions for democracy; one perspective emphasizes the importance of cultural factors, the other highlights the significance of economic factors.[51] Regardless of different theoretical orientations, the vast majority of scholars concur with Huntington that no single factor is a necessary or sufficient precondition for democracy.[52] This provides us with enough reasons to believe that the extent to which Confucian tradition affects Chinese democratization should not be exaggerated.

More important, twentieth-century history in East Asia demonstrates that Confucian tradition did little in arresting the democratic movement. It is Confucian China that established Asia's first democratic republic in 1911, when democracy had not even set foot in many advanced Western countries. Moreover, when the dynastic system was consigned to the dustbin of history and Confucianism receded into the background, the twentieth century saw a totalitarian regime emerge in China. The success of democracy in Taiwan provides the most convincing case: Confucianism has received much better treatment in Taiwan than it has in mainland China, but it is Taiwan that has succeeded in establishing a democratic system. In broader terms, Japan and South Korea, which were heavily influenced by Confucianism, have also been transformed into democracies since World War II. The origin of modern democracy in the advanced West, the adoption of democracy by some newly industrialized countries in East Asia, and the lack of democracy on mainland China indicate an important sequence: democracy will more easily settle in a modern society than in a traditional society.[53] For all these, it stands to reason that while Confucianism offers little help and even creates some problems in the democratization process, its negative impact on the process is not overwhelming, especially in our times.

Conclusion

To contribute to the enduring debate on the compatibility of Confucianism and Western democracy, this study argues that the previous debates suffered methodological problems and turned a complex issue into a simple one. Keeping these problems in mind, this study makes three distinctions: the first is between Confucianism as a doctrine and Confucianism as a state ideology; the second is between the democratic mechanism and the humanistic spirit; and the third is among democratic, "a-democratic," and antidemocratic notions.

This study reaches several conclusions. The first of these is that Confucian doctrine is neither democratic nor anti-democratic, but merely "a-democratic." Although Confucianism resembles Western democracy in many ways, these similarities do not qualify Confucianism as democratic, because it fails to meet the two requirements of democracy: popular sovereignty and individual liberty. Likewise, there are many differences between Confucianism and Western democracy, but these differences do not make Confucianism antidemocratic. It is therefore better to call Confucianism "a-democratic." Second, as a doctrine Confucianism is antidespotic, but as a state ideology it served the Chinese political system, which was authoritarian at best and despotic at worst. It is wrong to blame Chinese authoritarianism solely on Confucianism, but this study reveals that Confucianism did play a very important role in maintaining authoritarianism. Finally, although the abolition of the dynastic system decreases the influence of Confucianism, Confucianism as an essential part of Chinese culture does obstruct Chinese democratization in some ways. Nevertheless, contemporary studies on democratization and modern history in East Asia show that Confucianism does not present a huge obstacle to Chinese democratization.

Notes

1. For example, see Andrew J. Nathan, "Chinese Democracy: The Lessons of Failure," *Journal of Contemporary China* 4 (1993), 3–13; Martin King Whyte, "Prospects for Democratization in China," *Problems of Communism* 41, no. 3 (1992), 58–70.
2. The debate can be traced back to Western views on the nature of Chinese society. While Aristotle, Montesquieu, G. W. F. Hegel, and Karl Marx dismissed the oriental countries—including China—as despotic, G. W. Leibniz, Voltaire, and François Quesnay regarded the Chinese political system as admirable. For Western views of traditional China, see Andrew L. March, *The Idea of China: Myth and Theory in Geographic Thought* (New York: Praeger, 1974).
3. Take Samuel P. Huntington, for example. He asserts that "'Confucian democracy' is clearly a contradiction in terms." See his *Third Wave: Democratization in the Late Twentieth Century* (Norman: University of Oklahoma Press, 1993), 307.
4. For example, Franklin W. Houn, *Chinese Political Traditions* (Washington, D.C.: Public Affairs Press, 1965); Roger V. Des Forges, "Democracy in Chinese History," in Roger V. Des Forges, Luo Ning, and Wu Yen-bo, eds., *Chinese Democracy and the Crisis of 1989: Chinese and American Reflections* (Albany: State University of New York

Press, 1993), 21–52; Kim Dae Jung, "Is Culture Destiny? The Myth of Asia's Anti-Democratic Values," *Foreign Affairs* 73, no. 6 (1994), 189–94; Francis Fukuyama, "Confucianism and Democracy," *Journal of Democracy* 6, no. 2 (1995), 20–33.

5. According to Arthur Waley, between 100 B.C.E. and 100 C.E., two versions of *The Analects* were used, but not until the second century C.E. did it take the form similar to what we read today. *The Analects of Confucius*, translated, annotated, and introduced by Arthur Waley (New York: Vintage Books, 1938), 24.

6. H. G. Creel, introduction to his *Confucius: The Man and the Myth* (London: Routledge and Kegan Paul, 1951), 21.

7. For a review of these schools, see Yu-lan Feng, *A Short History of Chinese Philosophy* (New York: Macmillan, 1948); Benjamin Isadore Schwartz, *The World of Thought in Ancient China* (Cambridge, Mass.: Harvard University Press, 1985).

8. For the transformation of Confucianism from a doctrine to a state ideology, see John Knight Shryock, *The Origin and Development of the State Cult of Confucius* (New York: Paragon Book Reprint, 1966).

9. For criticism of this tendency, see David S. Nivinson and Arthur F. Wright, eds., *Confucianism in Action* (Stanford, Calif.: Stanford University Press, 1959); Arthur F. Wright ed., *The Confucian Persuasion* (Stanford: Stanford University Press, 1960).

10. Aristotle, *The Politics of Aristotle,* trans. and intro. by Ernest Barker (Oxford: Oxford University Press, 1961), 258.

11. Ibid., 234.

12. Isaiah Berlin makes a distinction between "positive freedom" and "negative freedom." See his "Two Concepts of Liberty," in *Four Essays on Liberty* (Oxford: Oxford University Press, 1969), 121–34.

13. Greek democracy differed form modern democracy in several ways. First, along with tyranny and oligarchy, democracy was regarded by the Greek as a corrupt form of government. Second, Greek democracy took the form of direct democracy, where citizens directly participated in making laws, although women, slaves and resident aliens were excluded. Finally, regardless of their properties and talents, rulers were selected by lots.

14. Theorists of different stripes deemed ideal democracy, namely direct rule by the people, to be impossible. For example, Robert Michels, an elitist theorist, claims that "The mass will never rule except *in abstracto.*" See his *Political Parties: A Sociological Study of Oligarchical Tendencies of Modern Democracy,* trans. E. Paul and C. Paul; intro. S. M. Lipset (New York: Free Press, 1962), 366. Even Jean-Jacques Rousseau, a staunch advocate of popular sovereignty, acknowledges, "Taking the term in its strictest sense, no genuine democracy has ever existed, and none ever will exist." See his *The Social Contract* in *The Essential Rousseau,* trans. Lowell Bair, intro. Matthew Josephson (New York: New American Library, 1975), 57.

15. Montesquieu, *The Spirit of the Laws,* trans. and ed. Anne M. Cohler, Basia C. Miller, and Harold S. Stone (Cambridge: Cambridge University Press, 1989), 157–66; Joseph A. Schumpeter has a point in reducing democracy to opportunities for the people to choose those who are to rule them. See his *Capitalism, Socialism and Democracy* (New York: Harper and Row, 1950), 269.

16. Robert A. Dahl, *Polyarchy: Participation and Opposition* (New Haven: Yale University Press, 1971), 4.

17. John Locke, *Second Treatise of Government,* ed. Richard Cox (Arlington Heights, Ill.: Harlan Davidson, 1982), 82–87; John Stuart Mill, *On Liberty* (Buffalo, N.Y.: Prometheus Books, 1986), 10–11.

18. In the remaining part of the article, Confucian and Mencian doctrines are based on Confucius's *The Analects* and Mencius's *The Book of Mencius.* The latter book can be found in *The Four Books: Confucian Analects, The Great Learning, The Doctrine of the Mean, and The Works of Mencius,* trans. and notes James Legge (Shanghai: The Chinese Book Company, 1930).

19. Vitaly A. Rubin thinks that legalism is an exception. See his *Individual and State in*

Ancient China: Essays on Four Chinese Philosophers, trans. Steven I. Levine (New York: Columbia University Press, 1976), 62.

20. Durkheim asserts that Kantian deontology and Benthemite utilitarianism are two main forms of ethical theory. See Anthony Giddens, *Capitalism and Modern Social Theory: An Analysis of the Writings of Marx, Durkheim and Max Weber* (Cambridge: Cambridge University Press, 1971), 68.

21. Elbert Duncan Thomas, *Chinese Political Thought: A Study Based upon the Theories of the Principal Thinkers of the Chou Period* (New York: Prentice-Hall, 1927), 216.

22. For the relationship between these two virtues, see Tu Wei-ming, "The Creative Tension between *Jen* and *Li*," *Philosophy East and West* 18 (1968), 29–39.

23. Reinhold Niebuhr, quoted in Samuel P. Huntington, "Young Democracies Face Big Challenges," *The Free China Journal*, September 8, 1995, 7.

24. Commenting on Chinese familism, Lin Yutang points out, "Graft or 'squeeze' may be a public vice, but is always a family value." See his *My Country and People* (New York: John Day, 1935), 180. John Leighton Stuart selected mutual jealousies and suspicions as more characteristically Chinese weakness and attributed the weakness to "the highly personalized element in their social structure." See his *Fifty Years in China: The Memoirs of John Leighton Stuart, Missionary and Ambassador* (New York: Random House, 1954), 290.

25. E. R. Emmet, *Handbook of Logic* (Totowa, N.J.: Rowman and Allanheld, 1984), 44.

26. Lucian W. Pye, *Asian Power and Politics: The Cultural Dimensions of Authority* (Cambridge, Mass.: Harvard University Press, 1985), 204–205.

27. Houn, *Chinese Political Traditions*, 45–98.

28. Bertrand Russell, *The Problem of China* (London: Allen and Unwin, 1966), 76.

29. Tang Tsou, *The Cultural Revolution and Post-Mao Reform: A Historical Perspective* (Chicago: The University of Chicago Press, 1986), xxiv.

30. In 1958 communist China employed almost eight million state functionaries; in 1948 nationalist China around two million; in the nineteenth century the Ch'ing dynasty only about forty thousand. Barrington Moore Jr., *Authority and Inequality under Capitalism and Socialism* (Oxford: Clarendon Press, 1987), 78–79.

31. For the variations of the Chinese political system, see Jack L. Dull, "The Evolution of Government in China," in Paul S. Ropp ed., *Heritage of China: Contemporary Perspective on Chinese Civilization* (Berkeley and Los Angeles: University of California Press, 1990), 55–85.

32. Matthew, 22:21; Mark, 12:17; and Luke, 20:25.

33. For the relationship between Christianity and democracy, see Alexander Dunlop Lindsay, *The Churches and Democracy* (London: Epworth Press, 1934).

34. The changing attitude of T'ai Tsu toward Mencius serves as a good example. T'ai Tsu, one of China's most despotic rulers, decided to rid Confucius's temples of Mencius's images for his disrespect of rulers and declared any remonstrator to be guilty of "contempt of majesty." President of the Ministry of Justice Ch'ien Tang, however, risked his life to remonstrate against the order and did change the emperor's mind.

35. For the Machiavellian side of the Chinese society, see Dennis Bloodworth and Ching Ping Bloodworth, *The Chinese Machiavelli: 3,000 Years of Chinese Statecraft* (New York: Farrar, Straus and Giroux, 1976).

36. Kam Louie, *Critiques of Confucius in Contemporary China* (New York: St. Martin's Press, 1980), 147.

37. For Vilfredo Pareto, "Society is harmed not only by the accumulation of inferior elements in upper strata but also by the accumulation in lower strata of superior elements which are prevented from rising." See his *Sociological Writings*, selected and introduced by S. E. Finer, trans. by Derick Mirfin (New York: Praeger, 1966), 159.

38. Max Weber, *The Religion of China: Confucianism and Taoism*, trans. and ed. by Hans H. Gerth, intro. by C. K. Yang (New York: Free Press, 1964), 154.

39. Karl A. Wittfogel holds that division into ruling class and ruled class is one of the

distinctive characteristics of Oriental despotism. See his *Oriental Despotism: A Comparative Study of Total Power* (New Haven: Yale University Press, 1957), 321.

40. Fareed Zakaria, "Culture is Destiny: A Conversation with Lee Kuan Yew," *Foreign Affairs* 73, no. 2 (1994), 109–26.

41. Political and economic modernization in East Asia rekindled people's interests in studying the impact of Confucianism on democratization. See, for example, Joseph P. J. Jiang, ed., *Confucianism and Modernization: A Symposium* (Taipei: Freedom Council, 1987); Robert Bartley et al., *Democracy and Capitalism: Asian and American Perspectives* (Singapore: Institute of Southeast Asian Studies, 1993). In addition, the International Conference on Consolidating the Third Wave Democracies was convened in Taipei in 1995.

42. William Theodore de Bary, *The Liberal Tradition in China* (Hong Kong: The Chinese University Press, and New York: Columbia University Press, 1983), 93.

43. For the impact of Confucianism on Western democracy, see H. G. Creel, "Confucianism and Western Democracy," in his *Confucius*, 276–301.

44. For an analysis of the differences between traditional and modern societies, see Ferdinand Tonnies, *Community and Society (Gemeinschaft und Gesellschaft)*, trans. and ed. by Charles P. Loomis (East Lansing: Michigan State University Press, 1957).

45. Tu Wei-ming makes a distinction between "political Confucianism," which supports a hierarchical political system, and "Confucian personal ethic," which influences everyday life. See his *Confucian Ethics Today: The Singapore Challenge* (Singapore: Curriculum Development Institute of Singapore, 1984), 90.

46. For analyses of Chinese political culture, see Lloyd E. Eastman, "Social Traits and Political Behavior in Kuomintang China," in his *The Abortive Revolution: China Under Nationalist Rule, 1927–1937* (Cambridge, Mass.: Harvard University Press, 1974), 283–313; Pye, *Asian Power and Politics*; Arthur H. Smith, *Chinese Characteristics* (Shanghai: North-China Herald Office, 1890); and Richard H. Solomon, *Mao's Revolution and the Chinese Political Culture* (Berkeley and Los Angeles: University of California Press, 1971). For Confucian influence on modern Chinese political thought, see Brantly Womack, "In Search of Democracy: Public Authority and Popular Power in China," in Womack, ed., *Contemporary Chinese Politics in Historical Perspective* (Cambridge: Cambridge University Press, 1991), 59–60.

47. See Derk Bodde, "Harmony and Conflict in Chinese Philosophy," in Arthur F. Wright ed., *Studies in Chinese Thought* (Chicago: University of Chicago Press, 1953).

48. For example, Fukuyama compares the Japanese to a "block of granite" and describes the Chinese as "a tray of sand, with each grain representing a single family." See his *Confucianism and Democracy*, 27.

49. J. R. Levenson regards antiprofessionalism as "one of the outstanding all-pervasive values of Confucian culture." See his "Confucianism and Monarchy at the Last," In Nivinson and Wright eds., *Confucianism in Action*, 262.

50. Etienne Balazs, *Chinese Civilization and Bureaucracy: Variations on a Theme*, trans. H. M. Wright (New Haven: Yale University Press, 1964), 10.

51. Samuel P. Huntington says, "In terms of explaining different patterns of political and economic development, however, a central independent variable is culture." See his "The Goals of Development," in Myron Weiner and Samuel P. Huntington eds., *Understanding Political Development: An Analytic Study* (Boston: Little, Brown, 1987), 22; Barrington Moore Jr., who emphasizes the importance of socioeconomic factors, dismisses the importance of traditional cultures. For him, "To explain behavior in terms of cultural values is to engage in circular reasoning." See his *Social Origins of Dictatorship and Democracy: Lord and Peasant in the Making of the Modern World* (Boston: Beacon Press, 1966), 486.

52. Samuel P. Huntington, "Will More Countries Become Democratic?" *Political Science Quarterly* 99, no. 2 (1984), 214.

53. Edward Friedman finds that democratization in East Asia fits general rules. See the introduction to *The Politics of Democratization: Generalizing East Asian Experiences* (Boulder, Colo.: Westview Press, 1994), 6.

4

Democracy in China

The Theory and Practice of Minben

ENBAO WANG AND REGINA F. TITUNIK

Did the concept of democracy arise in ancient China? A number of scholars and observers of China's political culture have identified a theory of democracy, akin to the Western democratic idea, in ancient Chinese thought. The view that a democratic tradition can be discerned in ancient China is expressed in Chin Yao-chi and colleagues' *San min Zhuyi yu Rujia Sixiang* (The Theory of "Three Principles of People" and Confucian Thought). The common theme of the essays in this volume is that Sun Yat-sen's theory of three principles of the people derives from a concept of democracy that existed in ancient Chinese thought.[1] The apparently successful transition to democracy that has occurred in Taiwan and South Korea lends credibility to the notion that some Asian cultural resources are compatible with democracy. Kim Dae Jung, former political dissident and current president of South Korea, has suggested that a democratic political culture existed in ancient China.[2]

As China struggles to define its political culture in the face of the collapse of communist ideology, the pronounced tendency is to mine China's cultural heritage for ideological resources on which to build a new foundation for political legitimacy. In the 1990s, Chinese scholars argued that the recovery of the traditional concept of *minben* and a reassertion of the importance and value of the people should attend their country's political liberalization.[3] More recently, Liu Ji, an advisor to President Jiang Zemin, draws on traditional notions of revolution and legitimacy in order to explain China's current policies and the manner in which the government will pursue democratic reforms.[4]

The concept that is the source of this most recent political thought in China is *minben*, which expresses the idea that the people are of primary importance in the political order. The centrality of the idea of "the people" and their constitutive significance in the state, conveyed by the concept of minben, invites comparisons with modern democratic ideas and explains the assertion of Kim Dae

Jung and others that ancient Chinese political values can be identified with modern democracy.[5] Both theories give priority to the well-being of the people and put forward the idea that the people should not be abused by those in power. Both outlooks also conceive of the people as having it within their power to bring down despotic government.

This chapter examines the concept of minben and considers the question of the affinity between this ancient Chinese concept and modern democracy. We will first attempt to explicate the meaning of minben. This concept appears early in Chinese history and has been variously interpreted by Chinese scholars. We will piece together the interpretations and reinterpretations of minben that have been put forward by classical and contemporary scholars. In addition, we will trace the use of the term as it has appeared at various stages of China's history and consider the ways that the concept influenced or failed to influence political practice in Chinese history. While the concept of minben has been influential in China, little attention has been given to sifting its meaning from the various literary and historical sources and constructing a general account of this term. It is our aim to develop such a comprehensive account of the term *minben*. In order to further illuminate the concept of minben and determine the extent of its resemblance to the western idea of democracy, we compare Chinese minben and the ideas central to western democracy.

The Original Concept of Minben

The word *minben* consists of two Chinese characters: *min* and *ben—min* means people and *ben* means root, source, or origin. Together these two characters signify the idea that the people are the original source of the political authority of a state.[6]

The term *minben* first appeared in a slightly different form in the *Shangshu,* one of the earliest pieces of Chinese literature. In the *Shangshu* the expression *min wei bang ben* is used and conveys the idea that the people are the root or essence of the state.[7] This expression was later contracted to *minben*. The concept of minben appeared in many ancient classics and was interpreted in a variety of ways. We will look at these diverse interpretations and attempt to develop a full picture of the concept drawing from ancient and modern sources.

In his research on the concept of minben, Liang Qichao, a famous Chinese scholar of the early twentieth century, found that, based on classic writings such as *Shujin, Shijin, Ya,* and *Song,* the concept of minben was well developed before the birth of Confucius.[8] Other scholars have argued, however, that the concept of minben was still in an embryonic stage before the time of Confucius (551–479 B.C.E.). It was formally established in the Spring and Autumn (770–476 B.C.E.) and the Warring States (475–221 B.C.E.) periods and continued its development until the twentieth century.[9] In the latter view, Confucius and Mencius were the major contributors to the concept. There is, then, some disagreement about minben's origins and historical manifestations. Liang Qichao's careful research on this issue and his argument that the concept is of ancient progeny is convincing in our view. According to Liang, the concept of minben was very influential prior to the Shang dynasty (1600–1100 B.C.E.). During the Western Zhou period (1027–770 B.C.E.), the concept of minben was still influential. During the Spring and Autumn periods, however, the idea of minben declined and was replaced by the concept and practice of tyranny.[10]

During the Spring and Autumn and Warring States periods, wars among kingdoms caused the people tremendous suffering. It was these conditions of disorder, strife, and hardship that formed the backdrop to the emergence of Confucian thought, with its emphasis on harmony and good government. Confucius and Mencius did not originate the doctrine of minben; rather, Mencius in particular "brought into prominence a doctrine that had dropped out of sight" and did so "in the late Chou era of dictatorial rulers and tyrannical governments."[11] In these circumstances, Confucius and Mencius retrieved the ancient concept of minben and evolved the theory of *ren* (loving the people) and benevolent government.

At a very broad level, interpreters agree that the concept of minben conveys the idea that the will of heaven is equal to the will of the people and that the people are the source of final authority. The concepts of *tian* (heaven), *di* (God), and *tianzi* (the son of heaven) appear in most of the ancient classics. Heaven, or *tian,* was understood in classical Chinese thought in terms of "a crude mixture of personal and impersonal aspects . . . heaven was sometimes described as an awesome and unfathomable force of limited space, pouring forth floods. At other times heaven was regarded as the source of righteous authority . . . [or] the highest ruler governing the people of the four corners to foster their well being."[12] The classical texts further identify the ruler of the people as *tianzi,* or "son of heaven." In other words, heaven, which is authoritative, appoints its son to rule the world. The duly appointed tianzi "is the parent of the people and also the king of the earth." This notion, which appears in several classics, is, according to Liang, the most important for understanding the concept of minben and includes the full meaning of the concept of tianzi.[13]

Heaven is, according to the classics, father of all human beings, including tianzi himself. Any human being, in principle, can be appointed as tianzi by heaven and, in this respect, all human beings are equal. Since every man is conceived to be eligible to be chosen as the "son of heaven," the position of tianzi does not belong to one person or one family indefinitely. Some scholars have drawn an expansive and perhaps exaggerated view of equality from this basic idea. Liang, for example, suggests that "[e]xcept the emperor alone, everyone in the state is equal in the sight of law, with equal personal and public rights. Even the authority of the Emperor is not a right divine, but is conditioned by the wish and consent of the people . . . the Chinese people have been taught to believe in the equality of men for so long that even the strongest of rulers has not been able to ignore it."[14] It is not clear that this more broad interpretation of the idea of equality is really implicit in the notion of minben. The idea of equality, as it is conveyed by the concept of minben in the ancient texts, appears to mean only that heaven can select from among equal human beings the one that is to rule.

That is, legitimacy is not conferred by family but is bestowed on the leader whom heaven deems as qualified to rule. We are not entitled to infer an equal status *between* citizens in respect to their relationships with each other from the way the term *minben* is used in the classics. The most we can conclude is that heaven may identify the competence for rule in an individual who may not be privileged by wealth, status, or family connection.

On what basis, then, does heaven choose a particular person to become the ruler of the people and how can the will of heaven be known? The classics equate the will of heaven with the will of the people: "What the people desire heaven will surely carry out."[15] In effect, the political authority of the tianzi rests on the will of the people. The tianzi will be respected as long as he is responsible to the people and promotes the interests of the people rather than his own private interest.[16] As Chin Yao-chi expresses it, the purpose of government is "to serve the people, not the king."[17] The people may invoke the name of heaven, overthrow the current ruler and choose another tianzi if the ruler fails to be responsible to the people. For instance, the *Shujin* (Book of History) relates the story of Jie, the last king of the Xia dynasty, who was a corrupt and cruel ruler. His regime was overthrown by the people of Shang. The *Shujin* author expresses his fears about such a revolt but remarks that overthrowing the king is the will of heaven, saying, "The sovereign of Hsia [Xia] has many crimes and heaven [*tian*] has commended me to destroy him.... Fearing the supreme God [*shangdi*], I dare not but punish him ... and carry out the punishment appointed by heaven [*tian*]."[18]

In accordance with the concept of minben, the people's rebellion against the government is justified in the name of carrying out the decree of the heaven. Logically, since the will and actions of the people can be interpreted as those of heaven, the people are, in fact, the source of highest authority. It is necessary to stress that the connection of divine will and the will of the people is key to understanding the concept of minben.

Mencius's Notion of Democracy

Mencius (372–289 B.C.E.) was the leading influential thinker of Confucianism after the death of Confucius (551–478 B.C.E.). At the time Confucius and Mencius theorized about government, China was divided into many small kingdoms and the kings of these entities sought to expand their power and their territories by dominating other states. As we have indicated, the continuous military conflicts among these kingdoms caused the people considerable adversity. Thus, the question of how to unify China and to end wars became a critical issue. Confucius proposed the theory of *ren* ("benevolence" or "loving the people"). In fact, ren is the cornerstone of Confucianism. For Confucius, "politics is that which sets things right"[19]; loving the people and making the world peaceful were the right things for rulers to do. Confucius argued that rulers should love the people and adopt a policy of benevolent government rather than the current policy of rule by force. He maintained that the virtuous ruler would be supported by the people. In other words, he attempted to convince rulers that real power or the source of genuine support derived from the people who respond to virtue rather than force. For Confucius, the main political goal was to find a virtuous and benevolent king, under whose rule stability, prosperity, and peace would prevail.[20] However, such an ideal state could not be realized in a day. Confucius said, "If a virtuous ruler rises to power it would take him a century to achieve ren. If a virtuous man rules for one hundred years he may eliminate killing and other forms of cruelty."[21] Confucius set a high standard of virtuous leadership but seemed to indicate that such an ideal was almost impossible to achieve in practice. Still, the point is that Confucius saw good government as connected with the rise of virtuous leadership.

Mencius was a disciple of Confucius and perpetuated Confucius's ideas of benevolence and benevolent government. For Mencius, however, the notion of *the people* was far more pronounced than for Confucius. Confucius gave primary attention to the quality of leadership, while Mencius stressed the importance of the people's perception of the their leaders. Therefore, contemporary scholars have linked Mencius's thought with the concept of minben. Some scholars suggest that Mencius originated the idea of minben. For instance, Gung-Hsing Wang argues that Mencius was "the first scholar in China who instilled the democratic spirit into our humanistic thought."[22] Yet as we have indicated, the concept of minben already appeared prior to Mencius. Mencius's ideas about government and the people represented a continuation and refinement of the concept of minben that had emerged in ancient times. Still, Mencius is a particularly significant figure for our purposes since he most fully develops the main ideas connected with this concept. Therefore, attention to Mencius's thought is crucial for further extending our understanding of the concept of minben.

Mencius traveled in several kingdoms, particularly Wei and Qi, and tried to advise the leaders of these kingdoms to accept his political ideas. He argued that a benevolent government would advance the unification of China and would be supported by the people who were then suffering under the cruel rulers. He reasoned that the peoples of all kingdoms, who hated wars and cruel rulers, would choose to immigrate to the state that has a benevolent government. As a result, the most populous state, whose government was supported by the people, would be the strongest state.

In advocating benevolent government to the kings, Mencius emphasized the importance of the people implicit in the traditional ideas associated with the concept of minben. Mencius argued that among the three main elements of a kingdom—the people, state, and the sovereign—the people are most consequential, saying, "The people are the most important element in a nation; the spirits of the land and grain [an expression often used to indicate the state] are the next; the sovereign is the slightest."[23] Mencius insisted that the function of government is to "give and multiply what the people want and to suppress what they dislike."[24] He also said, "To gain the peasants is the way to become sovereign; to gain the sovereign is the way to become a prince of a state; to gain the prince of a state is the way to become a great officer."[25] Consistent with the classical idea, Mencius suggests that the king's legitimacy originates from heaven, which is the source of invisible authority. Yet the authority of kings is dependent, finally, upon the consent of the people. In other words, the will of the people is equal to the will of heaven and the will of the people is the tangible expression on earth of the will of heaven. Therefore, when any political regime betrays the heavenly trust by causing the people suffering and hardship, it was the latter's right and obligation to destroy that regime on behalf of heaven.

In the following conversation with his student Wan-chang, Mencius explained the relationship among the people, the king, and heaven as follows:

> Wan-chang opened the conversation: "Is it true that King Yao gave his throne to Shun?"
>
> Mencius: "No, a king has no right to give away his throne to anybody."
>
> Wan-chang: "But Shun ascended to the throne, didn't he? Who else could have given it to him?"
>
> Mencius: "Heaven."
>
> Wan-chang: "Did heaven so decree?"
>
> Mencius: "No, heaven can't talk. One must listen by observing the trend of events and human deeds."
>
> Wan-chang: "How?"
>
> Mencius: "Yao recommended Shun to heaven as his successor. Heaven approved it because the people accepted Shun as their ruler."
>
> Wan-chang: "Please clarify the procedure once more."
>
> Mencius: "When Yao died, he wanted Shun to succeed him. Shun refused and fled to the country in favor of Yao's son. But the officials of the realm continued to seek counsel from Shun. The people continued to praise Shun. These are signs of heavenly decree as revealed through deeds and events among men. Let me quote a passage from the ancient classic: 'Heaven sees what the people see and hear.' This is what I have in mind."[26]

Mencius developed the traditional concept of minben by sharpening the identification of the will of heaven with the will of the people. He suggested that the people were more important than the state and king and that kings would lose their legitimacy if they failed to gain the support of the people. In a conversation with the King of Qi, to whom he was an advisor, Mencius intrepidly defended the idea of the people dethroning kings by force. The King of Qi asked Mencius: "Do you consider it justifiable to revolt against a king?" Mencius immediately answered: "When a king treads on virtue and throws away his moral obligation, he is no longer king but an ordinary individual. While no one has the right to harm his king, anyone can kill an undesirable individual."[27] For Mencius, a king by definition is a "sage-king," or is a king insofar as he embodies the Confucian virtue of loving the people. If kings do not continue to possess these virtues, their authority and qualification as kings are automatically lost, in Mencius's view. As a result, the people would rise up to dethrone the unqualified king and support a new king.

Mencius evidently failed to persuade the King of Qi to accept his idea that China could be unified by a benevolent government. On the contrary, the King of Qi chose to attack his neighboring kingdoms with military force. Mencius finally recognized that these rulers would not accept his idea of benevolent government and he gave up his position as an adviser to the King of Qi. Indeed, in Mencius's time, no kings attempted to adopt Mencius's idea of benevolent government as the policy for unification. China was finally unified by the first emperor of Qin by means of powerful military force.

Minben and Its Influence in Chinese History

It is difficult to make a judgment, based on the existing historical materials, regarding how minben as a political ideal had been actually put into practice in the early period of Chinese history. Liang Qichao only suggests that the concept was very influential prior to the Shang dynasty. Before the Xia and Shang dynasties, Chinese civilization could be said to have been at the stage of primitive society in the Marxist sense: private property was unknown and the tribes were classless. Most probably, Yao and Shun, the legendary sage-kings, were chiefs of primitive tribes. It is possible that in Yao's and Shun's time important decisions were made by the participation of all members of the tribes. For these tribes, the most important business was to choose their chiefs. Therefore, Yao gave his position as the chief of the tribe to Shun with the support of the community, and in a similar process Shun gave his position to Yu. However, when those primitive tribes grew into formal states like Xia, Shang, and Zhou, the kings of these new states did not give their throne to the individual preferred by the people, but to their sons. The legendary stories of passing power from one sage to another thus ended.

Since Qin Shihuang, the first emperor of China, unified the country in 221 B.C.E. and established a strongly centralized government in which the emperor maintained absolute power, the commitment to the practical realization of minben gradually declined. However, as an ideal, minben was deeply embedded in the heart of the nation and the people. Notwithstanding the fact that no leader actively adopted the idea of "benevolent government"—and indeed, as Confucius observed, virtuous government is almost impossible to realize in practice—the concept of minben was still discernible in the process of governance in Chinese history. The concept particularly influenced those rulers who themselves had participated in destroying the old dynasty through peasant uprisings. These new rulers, such as emperors, kings, and top governmental officials, personally experienced the power of the peasant uprisings. Consequently, in the beginning period of each new dynasty, the feudal governments always adopted a policy of concessions to the peasants by lowering taxes and rents and by demanding less corvée. These policies led to prosperity because the peasants had more time to work on their land. In the beginning of the Han and Tang dynasties, the feudal rulers deliberately adopted this "concession policy" to consolidate their rules. [28]

In the early period of the Han dynasty, the government adopted a tax policy of "one of fifteen" of the peasants' income and later further reduced the tax to "one of thirty." Tang Taizong, the second emperor of the Tang dynasty, discussed the relationship between the people and the end of the feudal government with his ministers. They concluded that the people are like water, the government is like a boat, and the water can carry the boat but can also submerge the boat.[29]

In effect, though the rulers of China were not sage-kings and did not establish a benevolent government, they recognized the power and importance of the people. While they exercised extensive power, they made concessions to the people over tax and corvée matters, fearing the people might overthrow their rule if their governments excessively violated the people's interests.

After a long period of stagnation, the idea of minben revived in the seventeenth century. Huang Zongxi, a scholar at the later period of the Ming dynasty, criticized the feudal dictatorship and argued that the government was *yi ren feng tianxia* (one person working for the people of the nation) not *tianxia feng yi ren* (the people of the nation working for one person). He proposed the theory of *jun ke min zhu* (the emperor is a guest, but the people are host). Huang's idea was a continuation of that of Mencius, and had a great impact on the further development of minben in the modern era.[30] Wang Fuzi, another later Ming scholar, argued that it was time for a revolutionary change in China's political system. A "society that will work for the public should be created based on the opinions of the people; consequently, the land under heaven will not belong to one family."[31]

The significance and persistence of the concept of minben is evidenced by the fact that appeals to legitimacy were made based on this concept up until the twentieth century. Sun Yat-sen, father of modern China, borrowed ideas from the ancient classics and advocated the famous slogan *"tianxia wei gong"* (land under heaven belongs to the public) during his campaign to overthrow the last feudal dynasty and establish the first republic in 1912. Sun's political philosophy—*san min zhuyi* (the three principles of the people, nationalism, democracy, and people's livelihood)—may be seen as a continuation and development of the traditional political philosophy of minben.[32]

The above survey of the uses of the concept of minben in Chinese thought ranging from the ancient classics to contemporary times allows us to put together the following main characteristics of the concept of minben. The concept of minben may be understood in several interrelated respects: the centrality of the people in the politics, the equality of people as regards their potential to be chosen by heaven to rule, the importance of the popular legitimation of leaders and the validity of withdrawing that approval through rebellion.

The Concept of Minben and the Western Notion of Democracy

The basic elements of the idea of minben that we have gleaned from Chinese history and thought indeed appear to suggest some similarities to the Western idea of democracy as has been noted by Kim Dae Jung and others, especially insofar as this theory also expresses an aspiration to ensure that people are not abused by those in power. We will examine this idea more closely by considering the notion of *democracy* as it developed in the West and comparing it with minben.

Politics refers to the activity of making authoritative decisions for a community and to the manner in which those decisions are made. *Democracy* means that the people make decisions or participate in some meaningful way in determining the authoritative decisions of the community. Democracy, as a type of a political system, first emerged in ancient Greece. In the direct democracy of Athens, all of the citizens of the state participated in the decision-making process and decisions were made based on the will of the majority of the citizens. Large-scale modern liberal democracies make use of the practice of "representative democracy," which signifies the participation of citizens through the choice of representatives to make authoritative decisions for the community.[33]

Other changes are also notable in the transition from ancient, direct democracy to modern representative democracy. The latter theory and practice of politics–more precisely designated as *liberal* democracy–prioritizes the individual in a way that was alien to ancient Greek democracy. The right of the individual to pursue her happiness as she sees fit is the fulcrum on which modern liberal democracy turns. The emphasis on the individual's capacity for autonomy is particularly pronounced in the thought of Thomas Hobbes,[34] with whom modern liberal democratic thought originated. Hobbes takes as his starting point the idea of free and equal individuals in a "state of nature" or a condition of complete freedom. This original state of nature is an insecure condition because these free and equal individuals continually harm one another in pursuit of their desires. Ultimately these individuals come together to form a "social contract" or a government to protect themselves from each other and better secure their interests. Modern political thought builds up from the supposition of the autonomous individual who enters into an agreement to create a government. This act of consent becomes the basis of legitimate politics.[35]

The arrangements of modern liberal democracy are intended to maximize each individual's natural right to live under his or her own control while also ensuring that one individual's exercise of freedom does not infringe on another's. The most extensive possible opportunity for people to participate in making laws, or "universal suffrage," is one means of guaranteeing the right of the individual to control his own life to the greatest possible extent. Democratic arrangements also require the unhindered diffusion of knowledge through a free press and education, the freedom of association that gives rise to more than one political party, and a division of powers among political institutions that prevents the concentration of power in the hands of one individual or group.

The general philosophical view of minben we have explicated above surely gives central attention to the well-being of the people. But in contrast to the democratic view described above, the exponents of minben never abandon the idea of an authoritative decision maker who, in some decisive sense, stands above the people. To be sure, the legitimacy of this ruler depends on the continued support of the people. Yet insofar as the ruler enjoys that support, his decisions are accepted as issuing from superior wisdom and enlightenment. Mencius suggested that only a sage-king had the legitimacy to rule the people and warned that a cruel king would be abandoned by the people. However, Mencius's political philosophy and the theory of minben itself failed to indicate a proper channel for the people to express their opinions to political authorities. The only mode of participation indicated by the concept of minben, as it was developed by Mencius, is overthrowing the leader and replacing him with a new one. In other words, the will of the people and the importance of the people can only be seen when dynasties or kings are changed through revolution and violence. It seems as if the discontent of the people is more akin to an act of nature rather than political participation in the Western sense. Wise rulers must, then, be cognizant of this possible "natural eruption" or "storm" in wisely guiding the ship of state. The persistence of the analogy of the will of the people and water supports this view. The people are seen collectively as a force to check abusive power. It seems that the will of the people is upheld as an ultimate sanction in order to induce rulers to be enlightened. In the same way that wise rulers would make adjustments to the natural ebb and flow of nature, rulers must be aware of the forces that move the people.

There seems to be some basis for comparing the legendary Yao-Shun China and democratic city-states in Greece, but we only know Yao and Shun were popular leaders of their communities. It is not clear how decision making actually proceeded in Yao and Shun's time. At least this much is clear: even if a sort of primitive democracy existed at this time, it was soon eclipsed by subsequent developments that emphasized the moral qualifications of the leaders rather than the participation of the people. Two Taiwanese scholars, commenting on democratization in Taiwan and the Chinese minben philosophy, observe that "[d]emocratic politics in Taiwan is not and can never be a derivative of Western liberal democracy. Given that Chinese political culture requires the nation's top leader to serve as a moral icon, elections matter only when they serve as occasional mechanisms for demonstrating public trust or to revive, periodically, the leader's moral conscience.... Thus a Confucian democracy could still be authoritarian in political action (e.g., mass mobilizations) even while liberal in institutional structure."[36] For these two scholars, the citizens in Taiwan as well as mainland China who support democracy only see it as "the most popular (and internationally accepted) means of installing virtuous, benevolent elite rule."[37]

The apparent similarities between minben and the theory of democracy, we contend, are misleading. To be sure, both concepts give primary importance to the well-being of the people; democracy, however, does not simply imply consideration of the good of the people or the public good. A consideration of the good of the people, or the "common good," is characteristic of all "good" government, and does not necessarily denote democratic government. Aristotle defines good governments, or "right constitutions," as those in which "the one, the few or the many rule with a view to the common interest." [38] He identifies three types of "right constitutions"—kingship, aristocracy, and polity—each of which aim at securing the common welfare. The bad regimes or the perversions of these three right constitutions, which aim to secure the private interest of the ruler rather than the good of the whole, are identified as tyranny, oligarchy and (extreme) democracy.[39] The question provoked by Greek political philosophy is, Which form of rule or combinations of rule—of the one, the few, or the many—is most conducive to achieving rule for the common good?

The answer to this question emerging from the Confucian tradition is that the rule of a wise or enlightened leader is the type of rule most conducive to public welfare and safety. Both the concept of minben and Mencius's ideal government are silent about people's participation in decision making. The implication is that the people have to passively rely on the benevolent king to rule them. Insofar as a king is wise, the people cede their power to their leaders. One American political scientist distinguishes Chinese political philosophy and the Western idea of democracy as follows: "China's political culture has deep obstacles to democratic reform. Since the time of Confucius over two thousand years ago, Chinese people have assumed and almost hoped that government would be authoritarian. An authoritarian government was needed to prevent chaos."[40]

The theory of democracy is based upon the presupposition that ordinary human beings are competent to participate in the guidance of their collectivities through participating in policy making. That is, the basic assumption of democracy is that people are capable of self-rule and that the aim of achieving "good government" is best realized when the people participate in decision making. The idea that people are the best judges of their own interests and, correlatively, that the rule of the people is most conducive to good government or justice may be erroneous. It is not clear that the people are in fact the best judges of their interests. Yet irrespective of which system better achieves the public good or "justice," the answer to what type of system is best is qualitatively different in the ancient Chinese and Western democratic views. Illuminating in this regard are the reported comments of president Jiang Zemin's advisor, Liu Ji, who observes that "[l]egitimacy is not produced by universal election, as westerners argue.... Hitler's government was elected but did not serve the interest of the people. The Chinese Communist regime, which was created in 1949, was legitimate because it was supported by the Chinese people. When it ceases to work for the people, it would be overthrown by the people."[41] The view developing in China's political tradition puts forward the ideal of a selfless, moral leader who makes wise decisions for the good of the whole. The role of the people is to give ultimate sanction to the legitimacy of the king. In the same way that the king could be delegitimized by natural catastrophes such as droughts, he is delegitimized by the uprisings of the people. The people, in their totality, are viewed as a significant force, but their value as individual beings capable of self-governance is not contained in the role of the people as envisaged in the Chinese tradition. The idea that people are equally eligible to be chosen by heaven to rule does not entail a conception of autonomous individuals. Rather, this idea represents another means of checking the improper use of power but does not break down class divisions and assert the inherent right of each individual to live her life as she sees fit.

In conclusion, though minben is a theory that emphasizes the importance of the people in a state, this does not entirely equate with a theory of governance that champions participation and governmental decision making by the people. Moreover, the idea of minben does not give central importance to the individual human being who is able to direct his actions to desired ends, an idea that forms the basis of modern liberal democracy. Thus the view, according to which minben anticipates modern democracy, is erroneous in certain respects. Yet though these two theories of government diverge, there are some points of convergence of which we also take note. Both ideas have spawned a revolutionary tradition. The concept of minben and its influence may explain why so many dynasties were replaced, one after another, in feudal China.

Minben and the Western Concept of Revolution

The most interesting comparison to be made between the Chinese concept of minben and theories of modern Western philosophers regards the notion of *revolution*. The notion of revolution in the West was classically formulated by John Locke in his *Two Treatises of Government*. Drawing from Hobbes's idea of a state of nature, Locke formulated the modern theory of liberal democracy. Locke argued that the people are born with certain natural rights to preserve life, liberty, and estate. [42] The government is created, based on a social contract, to protect these rights of the people. In the absence of government, in a state of nature, there is no common authority to adjudicate fairly if there is a conflict between human beings or if one individual infringes the liberty and property of another. Given that each individual is the only judge of the justness of his cause in the state of nature, everyone is compelled to defend his own interests and his life as he sees fit.[43] Consequently, the relationship of human beings in the state of nature is unstable and easily slides into a condition of mutual violence because in the absence of an impartial judge, conflicts are ultimately resolved by force.[44] Human beings, in Locke's view, establish a common authority or a government to more effectively protect each individual's rights and freedoms from the infringements of others. Yet if the government itself infringes the freedom of the people, it ceases to be a government properly speaking.[45] In this case, a "state of war" subsists between the people and government and the people have a right to "defend" themselves or, in effect, to overthrow the government.[46]

The classical notion of minben also puts forward this idea that "bad" government ceases to be government properly speaking. When any political regime betrays the heavenly trust by causing the people suffering and hardship, it is the latter's right and obligation to destroy that regime on behalf of heaven. Both Mencius and Locke argue that the government (kings) should be overthrown if the interests of the people are violated, and—at least in an ultimate sense—the people are the final judge of their interests. As discussed above, Mencius believed that if a king lost his virtue by ruling the people cruelly, he would lose his legitimacy as a king and become an undesirable person; he would therefore be driven away from the throne by the people.

The concept of violent overthrow in the Chinese tradition differs somewhat from that in the Western tradition insofar as the eruption of the people bears more resemblance to an act of nature than a people rightly reclaiming their rights in Locke's sense. Moreover, Locke's theory of revolution justifies such an action when the people only perceive that there is a "design" to deprive them of their liberties.[47] Yet the two theories are similar in as much as they evoke the threat of this ultimate sanction to coerce rulers and prevail against a spirit of resignation on the part of the people toward the injustices inflicted by government.

The revolutionary power of the idea of minben has had a significant impact in Chinese history. Feudal rulers, as we noted above, recognized the power and importance of the people. Under the influence of minben, the Chinese people frequently rebelled against cruel emperors and tried to find a more benevolent government.

Conclusion

We have noted the similarities and differences between the ancient Chinese concept of minben, and the idea of democracy as it evolved in the West. We have concluded that, despite apparent similarities, the two political philosophic traditions differ in significant respects. While the concept of minben promotes accountable government, it does not necessarily point to a democratic system as the solution to achieving accountability and the public welfare. Indeed the idea of the *good of the people,* predominant in classical Chinese thought, is serviceable for supporting authoritarian governments and presents few obstacles to the model of "soft authoritarianism" congenial to the current Chinese regime.[48] The concept of minben, insofar as it focuses on the "good of the people," may reinforce the juxtaposition between the common good, on the one hand, and the threat of "chaos" (*luan*) on the other, a juxtaposition that sustains authoritarianism.

Our analysis does not, however, point to the conclusion that some form of democracy will not emerge in China's future. Rather, our aim is to point out that any charting of China's political evolution requires clarity about its traditions and about the concept of democracy. Democracy requires not simply a political system that maximizes the public good, but a system that balances individual freedom and the collective good. James Madison's famous reflections on the new American government in his "Federalist No. 10" give classic expression to this idea that democracy requires a reconciliation of private freedom and public interest. Madison considers the question of how a political system can both preserve freedom and prevent the exercise of freedom from undermining the collective good. He suggests that a system that balances interest against interest achieves the optimal combination of private freedom and public welfare. It is conceivable that the current Chinese regime is in fact moving toward such a balance. China may be undergoing what Juntao Wang refers to as "gray" democratization or a piecemeal institutionalization of democratic practices. As Wang sees it, "both the people and the elites are self-interested, eager to maximize their own power and serve their own interests. As they jostle and complete with one another, it will become apparent that none can control the others completely. Thus they may be driven to agree upon rules to regulate the political process. The separation of powers, open competition among diverse factions, a more responsible administration and elections may all emerge in this way."[49] The successful achievement of this "gray" democracy requires clarification of what democracy is and an understanding of the uses and limitations of the traditional concept minben in fostering democracy in China.

Notes

1. Chin Yao-chi et al., *San min Zhuyi yu Rujia Sixiang* (*The Theory of "Three Principles of People" and Confucian Thought*) (Taipei: Zhongyang Wenwu Chubanshe, 1978), 26–28, 34–35, 44–45, 56–58, 65–66; see also Lin Zhenguo, *Mengzi* (*Mencius*) (Taipei: Shibao Wenhua Chubanshe, 1987), 75.

2. Kim Dae Jung, "Is Culture Destiny? The Myth of Asia's Anti-Democratic Values" *Foreign Affairs* 73, no 6 (1994), 191.

3. See "Sixiang Jiefang huigui Yiminweiben" (Liberation of the Mind Requires the Recovery of Minben Politics) in *Yazhou Zhoukan* no. 13 (1998).

4. Zhou Ruipeng, "How Will China Develop toward Democracy: an Interview with Liu Ji," *United Zaobao*, March 23, 1999, electronic edition (www.zaobao.com.sg).

5. For instance, Liang Qichao's use of the term *minben* was translated into "democratic ideas" in *History of Chinese Political Thought During the Early Tsin Period*, trans. L. T. Chen (New York: AMS Press, 1930 and reprinted in 1969), 150–52. Liang Qichao was an influential Chinese scholar of the early twentieth century. This book is translated from the translator's notes of Liang Qichao's lectures. Occasionally, this English version is different from the published Chinese version. We cite from both the Chinese and English versions of Liang's work.

6. Some scholars translate *minben zhengzhi* (politics) as "people-based governance" or "people as essence." See L. H. M. Ling and Chih-Yu Shih, "Confucianism with a Liberal Face: The Meaning of Democratic Politics in Postcolonial Taiwan," *Review of Politics* 60, no. 1 (1998), 61.

7. Chin Yao-chi, *Zhongguo Minben Sixiang zhi Shi de Fazhan* (The History of the Chinese Thought about *Minben*) (Taiwan: Jiaxin Shuisi Gongsi Wenhua Jijinhui, 1964), 1. This book is the thesis for Chin's master's degree and is the only special research on this topic.

8. See Liang Qichao, *Xian Qin Zhengzhi Sixiang Shi* (*The History of Political Theory of Pre-Qin China*) (Beijing: Dongfang Chubanshe, 1996) (hereafter, Chinese version), 44.

9. Chin, *Zhongguo Minben Sixiang zhi Shi de Fazhan*, 12–16. Chin divided the development of the political philosophy of minben into six periods. During the first period—from Xia to Shang to Western Zhou—the concept is in a period of embryo. During the second period—the Spring and Autumn and the Warring States periods—minben as a political philosophy was formally established. The concept of minben enters a period of stagnation (*tingzhi*) during the third period—the Qin (221–206 B.C.E.) and Western Han (206 B.C.E.–8 C.E.) dynasties. During the fourth period, which includes the Eastern Jin, Sui,

Tang, Song, and Ming dynasties, the idea of minben is dormant (*xiaochen*). The fifth period begins at the end of the Ming dynasty and it is the time of revival for minben. The sixth and last period includes the late nineteenth and twentieth centuries, during which time minben as a political philosophy was fully completed by Sun Yat-sen with his theory of *san min zhuyi*, a combination of minben and Western democracy.

10. Liang, Chinese version, 35–44.
11. Kung-chuan Hsiao, *A History of Chinese Political Thought*, trans. F. W. Mote (Princeton, N.J.: Princeton University Press, 1979), p.160.
12. Gung-Hsing Wang, *The Chinese Mind* (Westport, Conn.: Greenwood Press, 1968), 6–7. Regarding the early concepts of heaven, king and people, see also, Benjamin I. Schwartz, *The World of Thought in Ancient China* (Cambridge, Mass., Harvard University Press, 1985), 16–55; and Alfred Forke, *The World-Conception of the Chinese* (New York: Arno Press, 1975), 147–55.
13. Liang, Chinese version, 35.
14. Liang, English version, 8–9.
15. Ibid., 151.
16. Chin, *Zhongguo Minben Sixiang zhi Shi de Fazhan*, 8–12.
17. Ibid., 8–12. Chin Yao-chi suggests that *minben zhengzhi* (politics) includes six principles: (1) the importance of the people as the main body of the polity; (2) the importance of the consent of the people for the monarchical power of the king, who will work for the people; (3) the importance of the duty of the king to protect the people and ensure their livelihood; (4) the interest of the people as higher than the private interest of the king; (5) the importance of promoting benevolent governance (*wangdao*) and opposing the rule of force (*badao*); and (6) the purpose of government being to serve the people not for the king. Obviously, Chin's six points of minben also included the development of minben by Confucius, Mencius, and other philosophers. Chin's view is different from Liang Qichao, who argued that minben had already declined and even disappeared in Confucius' time. Yet both Confucius and Mencius actually developed their ideas by borrowing ancient philosophies.
18. Fung Yu-lan, *A History of Chinese Philosophy*, trans. Derk Bodde (Princeton, N.J.: Princeton University Press, 1952), 30.
19. See Liang, English version, 41.
20. Song Shuping, *Lunyu: Zhongguoren de Shen Shu* (*The Teachings of Confucius: The Sacred Book of the Chinese*) (Taipei: Shibao Wenhua Chubanshe, 1987), 107–30, 155–78.
21. Liang, English version, 52. Confucius had a famous saying about politics: "*zheng zhe zheng ye*" ("to govern is to set aright," or "to make upright"). He explained, "Once a man has contrived to put himself aright [*zheng*], he will find no difficulty at all in filling any government post. But if he cannot put himself aright, how can he hope to succeed in putting others right?" He also said, "If a superior love propriety, the people will not dare not to be reverent. If he love righteousness, the people will not dare not to submit to his example. If he love good faith, the people will not dare not to be sincere." See Hsiao, *A History of Chinese Political Thought*, 111, 113.
22. Wang, *The Chinese Mind*, 29. Also see Lin, *Mengzi* (Mencius), 78.
23. Francis C. M. Wei, *The Political Principles of Mencius* (Shanghai: Presbyterian Mission Press, 1916, reprinted in 1977), 52. This sentence has also been translated as "The people are of the first importance, the state next, and the Emperor is least important of all." Liang, English version, 61.
24. Liang, English version, 61.
25. Wei, *The Political Principles of Mencius*, 52-53.
26. Wang, *The Chinese Mind*, 31–32. Yao and Shun were legendary "sage-kings" in Chinese history. They lived in the time prior to the formation of states. Most probably, Yao and Shun were benevolent and successful chiefs of tribes and were beloved by the members of their tribes.
27. Ibid., 32.

28. The theory of "concession policy" was first proposed by an influential contemporary Chinese historian, Jian Bozan, who tried to explain the phenomenon that prosperity occurred at the beginning of each feudal dynasty in Chinese history. However, Mao Zedong, the Chinese communist leader, criticized Jian's theory of concession policy, and Jian was purged during the Cultural Revolution.

29. Jian Bozan, *Zhongguo Shi Gangyao* (*The Outline of Chinese History*) (Beijing: Renmin Chubanshe, 1983), vol. 1, 112–15, 424–25.

30. Chin, *Zhongguo Minben Sixiang zhi Shi de Fazhan*, 132; and Lu, *Zhongguo Zhenzhi Xixiang Shi*, vol. 2, 583–90.

31. Lu zhenyu, *Zhongguo zhengzhi sixiang shi* (The Political and Ideological History of China) (Beijing: Renmin Chubanshe, 1962) vol. 2, 596.

32. Chin, *Zhongguo Minben Sixiang zhi Shi de Fazhan*, 152–61; Chin argues that Sun's idea of *minquan* is the final and complete development of the ancient idea of minben. Regarding the relationship between Sun Yat-sen's san min zhuyi and ancient minben, see also Chin Yao-chi et al., *San Min Zhuyi yu Rujia Sixiang*. Sun Yat-sen himself said that one of the sources of his political idea of his san min zhuyi was ancient minben.

33. James Madison argued that the practice of representation and the large size of modern states prevailed against the tendency of democracies to destroy themselves through conflict among factions while preserving the principle of liberty. See James Madison, "Federalist No. 10," *The Federalist Papers* (New York: New American Library, 1961), 77–84.

34. Thomas Hobbes, *Leviathan* (Harmondsworth, U.K.: Penguin Books, 1968).

35. "China did not have political theorists comparable to Hobbes, Locke, or Rousseau, who suggested that the people themselves created government, and therefore the government should be responsible to the people." See Benedict Stavis, *China's Political Reforms: An Interim Report* (New York: Praeger, 1988), 69.

36. Ling and Shih, "Confucianism with a Liberal Face," 81–82.

37. Ibid., 78.

38. Aristotle, *The Politics of Aristotle*, trans. Ernest Barker (Oxford: Clarendon Press, 1949), 1279a.

39. Ibid.

40. Stavis, China's Political Reforms, 67.

41. Zhou Ruipeng, "China Does Not Need a Multi-Party System: An Interview with Liu Ji," *United Zaobao*, March 19, 1999, electronic edition.

42. John Locke, *Second Treatise of Government* (Indianapolis: Hackett, 1980), 9, 46; see also 31, 66.

43. Ibid., 9–14.

44. Ibid., 16.

45. Ibid., 114.

46. Ibid., 111.

47. Ibid., 113. This idea that the people's perception of a design to reduce them under despotism is sufficient to justify a revolution forms the basis of Thomas Jefferson's Declaration of Independence. The bulk of the Declaration is a long list of charges against the British king, the purpose of which is to show that such or "design" or "conspiracy," as we would say nowadays, is evident.

48. For a discussion of this model, see Francis Fukuyama, "Asia's Soft-Authoritarian Alternative," *New Perspectives Quarterly* 9, no. 2 (1992), 60–61.

49. Juntao Wang, "A 'Gray' Transformation," *Journal of Democracy* 9, no. 1 (1998), 48–53.

5

New Moral Foundations of Chinese Democratic Institutional Design

BAOGANG HE

Just as the West separated politics from religion in the period of secularization and set in motion a process leading to the death of ideology, China needs to separate politics from the official ideology and its morality; this separation is a hallmark of political modernity. With this attempt to free politics from the official ideology, initially there needs to be a radical desacralization of official morality, followed by the search for a new relationship between morality and politics. With this purpose in mind, this chapter will explore a potential alternative moral foundation for Chinese democratic institutional design.

To examine the moral foundation of a liberal theory of democracy in China, this chapter will discuss the idea that Chinese Marxist, goal-based morality and the traditional sage's conception of morality should be taken out of Chinese politics while rights-based morality should be infused into political institutions in China. Specifically, it explores the project of infusing rights-based morality into political institutions in China—that is, political institutional arrangements should be based on a morality that is characterized by urgent recognition of the following: equal liberties, institutional protection of rights, and fair procedures for democratic institutions. It will analyze that project by showing how a rights-based theory provides a moral critique of established political power in China as well as a constructive guidance for political institutional design. This paper is not so much a historical account of the decline of Chinese Marxist, goal-based morality and the rise of rights-based morality as a sociological and philosophical analysis of them.

I should say right at the beginning that the project of infusion of morality into politics in my present work is not one that concerns the moralization of individuals; rather, it is a question of seeking moral principles that are to guide institutional design for a particular form of government. The institution of politics is, first of all, the democratic institution of a civil state—the use of passions against passions, power against power, and threat against threat.

This chapter adopts Ronald Dworkin's classification of goal-based, rights-based, and duty-based theories,[1] and makes a conceptual distinction between three kinds of political morality. A *goal-based* morality would take some goal as fundamental. The official Chinese morality, for example, is goal-based in the sense that the establishment of a communist society is taken as the primary goal.[2] A *duty-based* morality takes as fundamental some duty, such as the duty to obey God's will as set forth in the Ten Commandments. Clearly, Confucian moral theory can be regarded as a duty-based theory. A *rights-based* morality takes as fundamental the right of all humans to the greatest possible overall liberty. The moral theories of John Stuart Mill and John Rawls are rights-based, and the new morality advocated by Chinese liberals is also a rights-based morality. This conceptual distinction is crucial to thinking about the moral foundation of Chinese democratic institutional design.

The Removal of Confucian Sage Morality from Democratic Institutional Design

In Chinese culture, the notion of duty traverses different spheres: loyalty in politics and filial piety in family. Chinese culture lacked a specific term for rights. A well-ordered Confucian society is completely duty-based; the management of the state relies on the management of family, and the management of family relies on a set of duties: the son's duty to respect and serve his father, the wife's duty to respect and serve her husband, and the father's duty to look after the whole family. At the level of the state, subjects have the duty to pay taxes and obey the law, and administrators have the duty to do whatever is necessary to provide service to the emperors. In return, any emperor has a moral obligation to look after the well-being of his subjects. To do so, all emperors are required by Confucianism to develop the humanist potential of *ren.*

Confucian *ren* (compassion) again is a duty-based theory that stresses love for others. From duty one looks to others, and serves families, local communities, and states. Ren implies a paternalistic government whose duty is to look after the poor. Moreover, within the Confucian theoretical framework, the state and paternal authority assume and oversee the common good.

In ancient and contemporary China, power was and is used to set an example of moral rectitude so that the conduct of all individuals should be exemplary. In this way, virtue is to be upheld and the consequence will be a peaceful, harmonious society rather than a society mobilized for mundane problem solving.

Politics, then, is solely a matter of ethics, not the use of power to maximize values.[3] According to Confucianism, politics is about how to select able persons for government, and should thus be managed by moral persons. Politics is one way to achieve morality, or to satisfy a moral principle. In other words, politics is an instrument for moral improvement, rather than a function for the articulation of individual interests. Politics is seen as a place where an individual can overcome self-interest and transcend oneself.

There is a long history of the admixture of Chinese morality and government; means and ends have become indistinguishable, and not only was and is ethical conduct the guide for government, but government was and is there to improve the ethical conduct of all.[4] Confucianism emphasizes the state's education to promote moral life. The state is obliged to provide a moral example—for example, to help the poor (*fuping*). In Zhejiang Province in China a law is made to punish someone who do not save the life of someone in danger. Does the state have the right to impose this morality? From the perspective of liberalism, such practice may be regarded as illegitimate. However, it is justifiable for the state to impose moral education on people. Political institutions are able to force people to have a "better" moral life defined by the state.

What is involved in this mix of politics and morality is the Chinese sage's conception of morality; this demands that human beings be altruists and sages who are the first to be concerned with the world's troubles and the last to rejoice in their own happiness. This kind of morality maximizes seeking for the highest ideal of the moral state.

This sage's conception of morality is related to the Confucian idea of liberty. The Confucian sage is an ideal self who has the highest liberty, or an inner freedom, which combines moral autonomy with spiritual happiness and peace. The essence of the moral autonomy of man is the subordination of individual desires to moral law. Such a Confucian notion of liberty is perfect liberty or positive liberty, which is not decided by material conditions.

Democratic institutional design rejects the Confucian duty-based theory, for it has led to suppression, conformity and the imposition of restriction; and Confucian moral elitism is a kind of morally arbitrary assertion. Democratic institutional design does not require the sage's concept of the maximization of virtue. There are at least three reasons for this.

First, *the very essence of rule by moral example is antipolitics;* that is, it precludes the kinds of activities associated with using power competitively in support of different values. The Confucian ideal of politics denies the trade or bargaining of politics, and attempts to remedy the extreme excess of individualism and the rightists, thus repressing negative liberty. Rule by moral example favors the ideal of a static, conformist social order. Everyone is expected to know what the moral standards are that have to be shared by the entire community in order to achieve the passive state essential for such a style of governance. Those who are safely included in the elite could engage in debates about alternative definitions of virtue, but for society as a whole there should be conformity and consensus. Yet precisely because the norm of stylized rule allows no concessions to the realities of contention, the counternorms of officialdom have to allow scope for devious tactics, intrigue, subtle ploys, and ingenious dissimulation among those certified as the most virtuous. Thus, the life of officialdom was and is built upon the foundation of hypocrisy.[5] Furthermore, the Chinese cultural belief that rule should be by virtuous persons and not by impersonal laws makes it difficult for the Chinese to institutionalize authority since they are reluctant to invest power in impersonal arrangements.[6]

Second, *institutional arrangements are less likely to be implementable* the more they demand of people. Liberals, in adopting the assumption that humans should be assumed potentially evil or knavish, take a pessimistic view of the effectiveness of the sage-moral appeal. Conceivably, one who is seriously committed to the democratic enterprise would be willing to sacrifice his time, salary, and even life. But we cannot really expect that moral rules of this kind will be followed, and cannot expect too much of the average person. Although the sage-moral approach may also admit of the assumption that most persons will not be sages, it assumes that all people are, by nature, potentially moral sages, and thus encourages people to make self-sacrifices.

Third, *one of the purposes of democratic institutional design is to avoid personal morality*, which is the great flaw of the operation of totalitarianism or authoritarianism. Democratic institutional design aims to make democratic arrangements function independent of the manners of humans and the goodness or badness of rulers, making it in the interests of even a bad person to act for the public good. The science of politics, therefore, is not concerned with manners and morals, but with the balancing of separate interests and the skillful division of power in order to best secure public interests.[7] Institutional design should economize on virtue in the following two senses: (1) the social contract from which it derives assumes an impersonal model unconcerned with the best virtues, and (2) fair procedures on which liberal institutional design is based should aim to regulate how institutions (and rules of law) operate, rather than to regulate how individuals behave virtuously.[8] Thus, the sage's moral appeal constitutes neither a starting point nor a guiding principle for democratic institutional design. Consequently, the institutions should not be seen as tools to produce ideal human beings as defined by one doctrine or one organization, but rather as an instrument of rational control in the management of evil.

Individual Rights as Moral Foundation

Democratic institutional design looks for a new moral foundation for democratic polity. This new moral foundation should be seen as a result of a long process of moral evolution, or an ideological transformation that is still unfolding in China: from the supposition of good to evil in human nature; from local loyalty to the loyalty to democracy; from duty-centered theory to rights-centered theory; from passion to interests; and from collectivity to individuality. Among these transformations, the most important thing is the rise of individualism and its notions of individual interests and rights.

Despite controversially alleged Chinese traditions of individualist ideas and practices in Taoism, Buddhism, and Confucianism,[9] both Chinese traditional and modern societies are essentially collectivist; the life purpose of individuals is to do good *for society*, the very existence of individuals is believed to rely *on society*, and the way of thinking and behavior of individuals is said to be defined *by society*. Society, its hierarchy and custom, is a great source of individuals' values and beliefs; it is a safe haven in which individuals secure their belonging. Society constitutes an authority or vindication, and society has the right to impose its authority on individuals. Chinese people seem to live for their society (in the forms of family, kinship, local community, work unit, and nation-state), rather than on their own. It is uncommon for Chinese people to hold the idea that society is made *of individuals*, that society is only an association *of individuals*, or that society ought to provide service *for individuals*. Chinese people seem to have difficulty in developing the view that society has no right to impose its authority on individual life—in particular, the intellectual inquiry of individuals.

In Western political culture, it is often acknowledged that the political process can legitimately be used by individuals and groups to try to force the state to serve their interests. By comparison, in Chinese political culture, individual interests are never taken as a fundamental principle in politics; even the interests of individual leaders have no legitimacy in Chinese political culture. In Confucian thinking, the interests of the collective must not be challenged by individuals. Terms such as *patriot* and *public,* representing the Confucian ideal of disinterested public service, are often used to combat the individualist attempt to advance personal ambitions or sectional interests.

When conflicts occur between the collective interests and individual interests, Chinese Confucian culture affirms the collectivism principle—the supremacy of public interests over individual interests, and individual interests must be subordinated to collective interests. In the era of Mao Zedong, this principle was enforced in such a way that the legitimacy of individual interests and rights in public discussion was denied. As a result, people acted one way in public and another in private, so that China became a nation of hypocrites. And Chinese society is "mass society" without individuality and individual creation. In the era of Deng Xiaoping, extreme collectivism has been modified to take into account individual, local, and immediate interests. The interest of individuals is legitimized in social and political thinking.

Chinese collectivist thinking and practice have influenced the process of Chinese learning from Western democracy. The starting point, purpose, and premise for the demand for Chinese democracy are collectively (rather than individually) oriented, and the underlying attitude to democracy is functional (rather than idealistic). The Chinese often sees democracy as a means for establishing China as a great power; such a view is likely to overlook individual interests, freedom and rights, and the development of individual potentialities. Chinese elites and intellectuals have modified the ideas of individualistic democracy within their own collectivist framework and paternalistic culture. For example, when Liang Qichao referred to the concept of individual freedom, he did not emphasize individual liberty but the freedom of participation by the citizenry as a whole, and "national freedom." Another example is Deng Xiaoping's stress on the strict distinction between collective and socialist democracy on the one hand and individualist and bourgeois democracy on the other.

Great changes have taken place since the 1980s. The Chinese people have now become more individualistic. More important, the idea of individuals has gained a primary *ontological* position in Chinese liberals' social and political thinking. Individuals are now regarded as equal without being affected by their social status and class. Chinese liberals believe that in evaluating social and political arrangements, the well-being of the individual must be a central criterion. In this regard, the Chinese totalitarian or authoritarian system is seen as a form of enslavement because it regards suppression of individuality as the basic condition of its survival. In contrast, liberal democracy is believed to allow the full development of each individual's abilities and the protection of each individual's interests. It is deemed as a form of social cooperation because it articulates the interests of individuals through a set of institutional representation and compromise, and encourages the development of individuality as the basic condition of its existence.[10]

Chinese liberal thinking regarding the individual has developed the idea of how a political society should be constituted and formed. Individuals and their individuality should be given the highest value; the aspiration of individuality should impose itself on the idea and practice of government. To meet the demands of individuality the government should be capable of transforming the interests of individuals into rights and duties. Individuals have the inviolable right to dignity and security; and any restriction by the state on individuals' pursuit of happiness should be denied. Governments must be powerful enough to preserve the social and political order for individuals to realize their aspirations, but not so powerful as to constitute a threat to individuality. And a government must respect the autonomy of philosophy as an intellectual activity and it must desist from relying on the power of the state to control opinion and thought.[11] This should be the moral foundation for any Chinese government. At the level of practice, the rise of the coastal regions' power, the legitimate status of individual and local interests, and the emergence of the political bargaining between center and localities in China suggest that legitimacy cannot come from the center, and that the establishing the legitimacy of a political society should be based on the protection of individual rights and interests, and on the interplay of political forces among competing interests.

At the level of international politics, a substantive moral theory of human rights can mandate minimal standards and protections that governments must provide for their citizens—as formulated, for example, in the United Nations Universal Declaration on Human Rights. For example, rights of personal security (freedom from arbitrary arrest, torture, or death) should be respected by all cultures. This minimal international morality is seen in Rawls's universal character of justice as fairness in at least two ways. First, it extends to the international society and binds all its members, the nation-states. Second, insofar as certain of a society's domestic institutions and policies are likely to lead to war or to expansionist aims, or to render a people unreliable and untrustworthy as partners in a confederation of states or in a cooperative arrangement, those institutions and policies are open to censure and sanctions of varying degrees of severity by the principles of international justice.[12]

One Confucian scholar might reject the rights-based theory on the grounds that rights-based morality does not allow for the moral significance of supererogation. Acts are supererogatory if their performance is praiseworthy and yet it is not morally wrong to omit them. There is no obligation to act in a supererogatory way in the framework of rights-based morality. Consequently, rights-based moralities cannot include the intrinsic moral value of virtue and the pursuit of excellence.

A contemporary revised version of Confucianism will also challenge rights-based morality on the grounds that it logically contains the idea of a right to do wrong. As an example, to consume drugs in a private home is seen as a private right and it is morally wrong to interfere with this kind of action.[13] Confucian criticism of a right to do wrong is based on its concept of the priority of goodness over rights. In the eyes of Confucianism, we have rights only insofar as we use them to promote the ethical life, or *ren*. In other words, one is free to choose the good. As Yu-wei Hsieh argues, "On condition that we choose within the limits of goodness, we can choose freely. Outside the limits of goodness, one should not be free. . . . Whatever freedom you want, you should not violate this ethical principle of freedom to choose the good."[14] There is, thus, a priority of goodness over rights and liberties; Confucianism allows no priority of rights over goodness.

In contrast, Chinese democratic institutional design ought to choose rights-based morality: rights should take priority over truth, goals, and duties. Why should we take the priority of rights seriously? First, *they reflect the conditions* under which it becomes possible for an agent to recognize and act on considerations such as these.[15] Second, rights have *special importance*, an importance that warrants overriding other values and ideas whenever they conflict with the protection of rights. A right is nothing but a particular interest: it is assigned a greater weight than ordinary interests and therefore counts for more in utilitarian or other welfarist calculations.[16] Third, as J. L. Mackie argues, "rights have obvious advantages over duties as the basis and ground of morality. Rights are something that we may well want to have; duties are irksome. . . . Duty for duty's sake is absurd, but rights for their own sake are not."[17]

Take as an example the paternalist benevolence of the government in Singapore, which provides people with state houses. By 1994, more than 85 percent of the 2.7 million population lived in public housing, of whom more than 70 percent were owner-occupiers. The government has adopted a quota system that mingles multiethnic groups in these state houses, a policy intended to prevent the development of racial enclaves, promote cross-cutting communities, and reduce the polarization of ethnic groups. Some evidence shows that the level of interracial neighborliness has increased over the years,[18] and this policy is praised as promoting interethnic harmony.

However, no questioning of this benevolent policy can be raised within the Confucian theoretical framework. In contrast, within the liberal theory of minority rights, people could criticize the repressiveness of the quota rules and charge that minorities are unable to defend racial enclaves. Individuals can defend their interests and criticize government only if they are empowered by the correct discourse; they are less likely to defend their interests if they have only duty-based theory available to them. In this regard, liberalism is more effective than Confucianism, because liberalism recognizes that conflict is a basic human condition while in Confucianianism there is a denial of conflict. The Confucian emphasis on harmony often leads to suppression, and its success in achieving harmony often lies in paternalistic authority, of which liberalism is very skeptical.

In short, the principle of the priority of equal rights serves us best as a guide to democratic institutional design. There are three points that must be clarified if rights are to be a starting point for political morality.

First, the idea of equal natural rights constitutes the source of all rights; a multiplicity of rights derive from fundamental natural rights. Civil and political rights are inviolable, universal, and superior to economic and social rights, which are historically determined and contingent upon concrete circumstances. When conflicts between rights occur, the principle of the priority of fundamental rights over economic and social rights should take effect.

Second, it is possible theoretically to derive both *duties* and *rights* from basic goals, as is done in consequentialist arguments; it is also possible to derive both *goals* and *rights* from duties as is done in Immanuel Kant's categorical imperative. However, a rights-based morality begins with basic rights from which both goals and duties can be derived. It does not reject moral goals, but constitutes a premise from which we set up as a political goal that institutional arrangements should respect and protect human rights and liberty and recognize the proper autonomy of citizens. Thus, if a rights-based political morality is infused into politics, it logically requires that democratic institutions should grant rights to good people as well as to potentially evil people so as to ensure a counterbalance mechanism that can effectively control and manage the problem of evil. To protect equal human rights thus becomes the first and most important goal of democratic political institutions. At the same time, one of the goals of the democratic state should be to dismiss utopian goals such as the realization of a communist society.

Third, a rights-based political morality also does not ignore moral obligation, but constitutes a premise from which human beings have the duty to respect the rights of others. If A has the moral right to do X, then A has a duty to take responsibility for doing X. If A is also protected in doing X, it follows that others are morally required not to interfere or prevent A from doing X. One who enjoys rights has a duty to respect the rights of others, and, more important, has a duty to follow "the rules of the game." The complete fulfillment of the different kinds of rights involves the performance of multiple kinds of duties; for example, the right to physical security implies a duty not to eliminate a person's security, a duty to protect people against deprivation of security by other people, and a duty to provide for the security of those unable to provide for their own. Also, as seen below, the procedural conception of morality requires that the procedure itself should be fair, and that people have a duty to obey the rules.

Not only do rights presuppose duty, but also a kind of spiritual support that highly respects procedure, rules, and norms. This spiritual source comes from our sympathy for fellow countryman and our concern with all lives and whole nature. This perhaps is the deepest and biggest source of morality.

Procedural Morality

The above idea, that the well-being of individuals must be a central criterion in evaluating social and political arrangements, raises a number of questions. When the interests of individuals are conflicting, how does the well-being of individuals constitute a concrete benchmark in the evaluation of political institutions? Do we look for the improvement in the average income of individuals? Do we take the interests of the least-advantaged group seriously? Evaluation and redesign of political institutions will face more difficulties when different individuals hold diverse views of what is moral or immoral. One way out of these kinds of difficult questions is the development of the idea of procedural morality. Democratic institutional arrangements need to build on a procedural conception of morality as a way to deal with the conflicting interests of individuals.

The procedural conception of morality emphasizes rule-following and fair procedures. The virtue of justice is nothing but a disposition to obey the rules of law. The procedural conception of the good person is not seen as the Confucian good person, but, as Montesquieu argues, the politically good person who loves the laws and procedure and who acts from love of the law and procedure.[19] Thus, the procedural conception of morality and the good person is less demanding than the sage's conception in the sense that it only requires a *minimal* criteria: people have to follow the rules of the game.

This minimal demand facilitates the feasibility of institutional design, because institutional arrangements are more likely to be implementable the less they demand of people. The possibility and operation of democratic institutions also depend on the procedural view of morality; otherwise democratic institutions cannot work. Democratic institutional design, therefore, presupposes the procedural conception of virtue, or institutionalized morality, in the sense that it does not stress that people should behave virtuously but requires people to follow rules through institutional devices such as the mechanisms of reward and punishment. For example, Mill's morality is composed of "coercive rules," rules that indicate when coercion may be used to compel or punish.[20]

Now it is time to examine a possible tension in Chinese liberals' thought. Although Chinese democrats have advocated procedural morality, they have unconsciously retained vestiges of traditional moral idealism.[21] They share two implicit assumptions about goodness: (1) the democratic enterprise should be guided by those who are concerned only with the interests of the people and less with personal interests—leaders of democratic movements, therefore, should be, and can be, moral sages; and (2) it is the critical and creative intellectual, and not the political ruler, who represents, advocates, and holds truth and social justice. The power of Chinese intellectuals is based on or comes from morality and "cultural capital" rather than from class, property, or political position. The role of intellectuals is to point out the right path of politics, and this role has more status than that of political leaders.

If these assumptions are taken as an intellectual basis for institutional design, then they undermine the claim in their argument for democratic institutions that human beings are self-interested, further undermine the principle of equal liberty at the institutional design level, and possibly deny the civil and political rights of peasants in the process of democratization in terms of the superiority of intellectuals. This possible theoretical tension in the Chinese liberal theory of democracy comes from the absence of a distinction between morality as virtues (sages) and as rules (procedures). If this distinction is made, the sage's conception of morality is taken out of democratic institutional design, and the procedural conception of morality is adopted at the institutional design level. The contradiction is then resolved, because the procedural conception of morality recognizes the legitimacy of self-interests and social conflicts that are seen as a permanent feature of human life. The theoretical tension also stems from an absence of a distinction between institutional design and practical moral advocacy. The former does not require the sage's view of morality, but rather the procedural conception of morality. Moral advocacy calls for the moral sentiment to deal with practical problems, such as factional fights among democrats. And it may be useful in reducing tensions among democrats and speeding up the process of democratization *if* all the Chinese democrats are "sages." While the good intentions of Chinese democrats are highly laudable, the political results are likely to be dubious; thus, when all is said and done, this moral advocacy has to be rejected at the institutional design level in order to avoid or dissolve the inbuilt tension at the theoretical level.

Procedural Principle That Should Be Fair

The problem of the abuse of procedure challenges the procedural idea of morality. A purely procedural principle would legitimate the adoption of a policy imposing any deprivation, such as deprivation of property, or of equal opportunity in politics, in employment or in education, provided only that it is supported by procedure specified by the decision rule. This is a theoretical defect of formalistic proceduralism.[22]

In order to protect everyone from such deprivations and to overcome the theoretical defect of proceduralism, a principle that is not merely procedural would be required. In this context, Rawls's deontological theory of the priority of rights and his idea of pure procedural justice is suitable. To put it very simply, a principle should take rights as "trumps"; and procedure should be fair in terms of equal political opportunities or the principle of equal liberty.[23] This procedural fairness can help us to decide on adjudicative procedures when we have exhausted the arguments showing procedures to be more or less apt to yield reasonable determinations. If a fair procedure is set up, the outcome is likely to be fair, whatever it is, provided that the procedure has been properly followed. [24] Thus, pure procedural justice constitutes a normative basis for democratic institutions.

Human beings need procedural fairness to regulate their actions. When procedural politics is not fair, then political force justified by so-called procedure becomes a mere brutal solution; thus, procedure becomes a tool in the interests of a minority of politicians. It is important to stress that the considerations of procedural fairness result from the tragedy of the Cultural Revolution, and from the historical lesson that theoretical justifications of the violation of human rights always depend on the denial of the principle of equal liberty. The fact that procedures have been abused through "autocratic rules of law" or certifies that it is necessary to implement both the principle of pure procedural justice and a real rule of law to protect and maintain liberty. To do so, the crucial thing is that procedure and law must themselves be just. That a constitution should be just, therefore, is the foundation of the rule of law. It is here that Rawls's liberalism appeals as a fundamental solution to procedural and legal problems in China; that is, by securing basic rights and liberties, and assigning them a due priority, the most divisive questions are taken off the political agenda.[25] Without this fundamental reconsideration and solution, China will repeat its old mode of rule by law.

Here Rawls's political morality indeed apprehends the fundamental problems pertaining to a moral foundation for sound politics and better political arrangements for society. Political liberalism wisely identifies the most urgent value, equal liberties: a fair procedure is set up, and any principles agreed to will be just; if the institutions of the basic structure are framed according to the value of equal liberties, intractable conflicts are unlikely to arise.[26]

Against the Argument of the Independence of Politics from Morality

Those Chinese who hold a nihilistic attitude to morality, as revealed in the call for "the death of Lei Feng" which could be equated with the death of God in the West, might argue that there is no need to discuss morality in Chinese political life at all. The argument is about *the independence of politics from morality*. Drawing on Carl Schmitt, they might argue that the crucial political distinction is that between friend and foe. The political foe need not be morally evil or aesthetically ugly. The friend-foe antithesis is seen as independent of other antitheses, such as good and evil in morality. Politics is further seen as autonomous only in the sense that the validity of political categories is independent of morality. Politics is then a battle to conquer and retain political power, regardless of all normative bonds.[27] Thus, proponents of this line of argument dismiss our moral effort as naive and idealist. Moral idealism is perceived as failing to understand the essence of politics: moral principles do not guide and regulate political life; rather, they are always manipulated by politicians in their own interests.

No doubt the nature of politics is the conflict between foe and friend and the struggle over competing values within or outside a political community. However, friend-foe politics does not exclude the moralistic and normative aspect of politics. Friend-foe politics can be incorporated in or subordinated to a constitutional-democratic framework, because those who understand politics in friend-foe terms might well choose to respect rules and encourage others to respect rules in the hopes of minimizing their potential losses.

Furthermore, a democratic constitution itself is devised to address and resolve the enduring problem of conflict of interest. The key issue is how to deal with such conflict. For a liberal, this conflict can be resolved or controlled by commonly held norms and compromise within *just* institutional devices. Regardless of who is friend or foe, one must comply with an appropriate procedure in dealing with basic conflicts in political life.

Against One Practical Argument

One might argue that the project of infusing politics with moral principles has led to catastrophic consequences in China: Mao Zedong's appeals to a moral movement, so as to change the old face of China, did result in tragedies during the Cultural Revolution. Such moralistic appeals actually comforted and caused people to back Mao's dictatorship. If moral appeals could serve the mere task of providing solace to Mao's supporters, that is more than enough to give us pause in our project of trying to infuse morality into politics.

One easy reply would be to distinguish, at this point, between the "true morality" that we hope to infuse into politics and the "pseudo-morality" on which Mao's rule relied. The counterexamples of Mao's pseudo-morality and the like should not necessarily give us pause, the argument would follow, because Mao and his supporters were not really acting on moral principles— on *true* moral principles—at all. The objection, therefore, is not to the infusion of moral principles into politics, but rather *against* the infusion of *false* moral principles.

However, this strategy of distinction between true and false moralities is intellectually unsatisfactory. It poses, in Robert Goodin's view, genuine problems on two levels. First, the distinction between true and false moralities appeals to practices so as to identify true morality and reject false morality. Since those employing this device will never be prepared to say what is a true moral principle until they see how it turns out in practice, they are never in a position to say in advance what morally we *should* do. The second relating to the first is an institutional design problem posed by such an approach. If we do not know what the right principles are until we see how they turn out, we can never set things up in such a way as to guarantee that the right principles are put into practice in the first place. People trying to design the system so that the right principles are put into effect will simply be chasing their own tails, if this line were adopted. On that account, the whole project of infusing morality into politics would become a logical impossibility.[28]

Given this lack of success in distinguishing true and false moralities, a distinction among the rights-based, duty-based, and goal-based moralities is employed to avoid the question of true or false and to focus on the question of the most urgent value. This alternative strategy, I suggest, is useful in defending the project of infusing morality into political institutions.

The practical argument against the project of infusing morality into politics fails because it rejects and condemns *all* morality and ideology as providing a potential weapon for totalitarianism, and fails to recognize the fundamental fact that the liberal ideas of rights are totally different from those expressed in Chinese Marxist morality. Goal-based Chinese Marxist morality shows concern for what is taken to be the interest of society as a whole, such as national glory; however, it overlooks rights, and has even become a tool used to deprive people of their rights. The official goal-based morality demands that individuals should be sacrificed for the well-being of collective interests. What is more, this kind of morality even denies the right to complain about making such a sacrifice. Conversely, rights discourse defends natural rights and rejects any idea that denies civil and political rights.

Now let me make a comment on fears regarding the project of infusing politics with morality. As Goodin suggests, one might fear the general effects of "moralizing" politics, and the sorts of attitudes people may, as a result, take toward their political opinions. The fear is that people will come to regard most of their political opinions as if they were matters of high moral principle, whether or not they really are. The further fear is that people will, in consequence, become increasingly adamant, inflexible, and intolerant even in the smallest matters of politics. Most particularly, the fear is that people's treating political opinions as if they were sacred values in this way will, from time to time, lead them to support the egregious excesses of an Adolf Hitler, Joseph Stalin, Mao Zedong, or Pol Pot. And even if matters stop well short of that, regarding political opinions as sacred values generates nonnegotiable demands of a sort that normally prove utterly intractable to ordinary political processes; what cannot be settled by bargaining is left to be resolved by other, more bloody means. Such are the fears of those who resist the proposal to infuse morality into politics.[29]

These fears are reasonable if goal-based morality is infused into politics, which might produce the above negative effects that people fear. However, those who have these fears have no objection to the rights-based morality and democratic mechanisms that Chinese liberals have been advocating. Their objection is instead to the tendency toward inflexibility and intolerance that comes from introducing the unifying official Chinese goal-based moral principles into politics. By comparison, the rights-based theory, like Rawls's theory of two just principles, has a definite advantage: rational persons run no chance of having to acquiesce to a loss of freedom over the course of their lives for the sake of a greater good enjoyed by others.[30]

Here I do not adhere to the view that political institutional design based on the rights-based moral principle is *always* for the better. Following Goodin, I support a weaker claim: political institutional design based on the rights-based moral principle in political life usually works out for the better.[31] It usually does not lead to a holocaust, or to the killing fields, or any such horror. This is an empirical claim, not an analytic one. Being a mere empirical claim, it can only be contingently (rather than necessarily) true, and that, in turn, means that it may well prove to be false—certainly in particular instances, and perhaps in general. Just like Goodin, though, I hope and believe that this is not the case. There seem to be many good grounds for supposing that the rights-based moral principles and democratic mechanisms will help to prevent such tragedies as the Cultural Revolution, rather than causing them. Also, a rights-based political morality is capable of withstanding abuse because it contains an internal mechanism of self-corrective procedure and principle, and because rights, in Ronald Dworkin's view, are "political trumps" held by individuals.[32] In short, although the matter of use of theories depends on the user rather than the theories themselves, Rawlsian rights-based morality and fair procedures can help to reduce the number of cases of abuse, while the official Chinese goal-based morality lacks an internal mechanism against abuse by a despot.

Against a Cultural Relativist Argument

A Chinese cultural relativist would not accept the project of infusing morality into politics because of her rejection of a universal doctrine of right-based political morality. Julia Tao claims that the Chinese way of thinking about the self and about moral agency is in stark contrast to the image of the self as a bearer of rights in the deontological conception. She further suggests the inadequacy of the moral individualism of a rights-based morality and argues for an alternative view of morality that places importance on the intrinsic value of collective goods and on membership in a society.[33] Thus, a Chinese culturalist would like to infuse Confucian duty-based morality into politics.

Drawing on Julia Tao's argument, a Chinese cultural relativist might argue that rights-based political morality is too alien to be applicable in China. Morality, in a cultural relativist's view, is something rooted in the particular practices of actual communities. So the idea of seeking to uncover abstract principles of morality by which to evaluate or redesign existing societies is, it is argued, an implausible one. There are, in a cultural relativist's view, no universal principles of morality or justice discoverable by reason. For a cultural relativist, to seek to apply rights-based political morality in China is to look for the wrong thing, for universal principles to serve as solutions to universal (or at least generalizable) problems—the problem of the nature of the best form of political association. The truth of the matter, it is argued, however, is that there is no such rights-based political morality except in the minds of liberal philosophers.

I disagree with the above idea, but I would like first to acknowledge the following: (1) cultural relativism is true as an empirical description of the moral practices of diverse cultures around the world; indeed there is a great deal of moral diversity in different cultures; (2) cultural integrity and national identity, as cultural relativists always claim, should be maintained within a community; and (3) cultural relativism is also useful in stressing differences, in encouraging creativity and in challenging dominant Western thought.

On a theoretical level, the cultural differences between China and the West are not the problem that Julia Tao has suggested. As Chandran Kukathas argues well, cultural diversity does not preclude the possibility of moral criticism or of developing universal moral standards; nor does it make it impossible to compare moral values, or to acquire moral knowledge.[34] The fact of moral diversity across cultures by no means entails the sceptical conclusion that there are no rational grounds for overlapping consensus on the idea of human rights as a universal principle.

Indeed, Chinese scholars have been arguing that the Confucian notion of *ren* can provide a moral foundation for rights[35] and that the Confucian notion of duty entails the idea of rights. For example, Mencius's idea of the right to rebel is similar to Locke's notion of the right to revolution. Joseph Chan presents a Confucian notion of human rights as supplementary or auxiliary: when virtues do not obtain, or human relationships clearly break down, rights are a fallback auxiliary apparatus.[36]

At a practical level, the problem associated with cultural relativism, in the context of Chinese practice, is that such relativism has always been used as an excuse to abuse rights or to confuse the issues at hand.[37] There are the following four types of evidence against the cultural relativist argument.

First, most Chinese liberal intellectuals, like liberals in Eastern Europe following the global trend, regard liberalism as a universal doctrine. The Chinese, among other peoples, are culturally universalistic in their belief in human rights and democracy. There are common points between Western and Chinese conceptions of rights, such as the belief in the social usefulness of free speech. Liberals in both the West and in China share a certain level of recognition of rights, a level of institutional guarantee of rights and a level of the substructure of philosophical assumption that a concept of social justice must take persons as the ultimate units of moral concern. For example, Yan Jiaqi has argued that humanism, democracy, human rights, freedom, and the like, belong to an essentially universal culture;[38] Fang Lizhi also argues that the idea of human rights is a common treasure shared by the global community, just as science is.[39] This fundamental agreement constitutes a basis for us to agree on a minimal international morality.

Second, the rights-based morality is also rooted in China in the sense that it is demanded by Chinese democratic practice. The Chinese demand for just principles lies not only in philosophy but also in Chinese politics. Chinese liberals' search for a better form of political association arises from within the Chinese political community, particularly after the tragedies of the Cultural Revolution.

The Chinese liberal philosophers would follow Rawls in asking the same questions about possible abstract principles of morality by which to evaluate or design democratic institutions and a sound governmental structure. Chinese liberals' acceptance of the universal truth of rights-based political morality is of relevance and of great significance to the Chinese political community. Also, the idea of infusing rights-based morality into political institutions also mirrors the emergent economic civil society in China, as fairness is required by the development of market economics. Under Mao's planned economics, the state often took what it wanted from enterprises without a return gain, through the so-called *yiping erdiao* (gratis transfer of materials). With the development of market economics in Deng Xiaoping's time, a rudimentary norm of fairness—which each of us must be prepared to give as well as to take—has gradually taken root in economic life and become guaranteed by legal regulations. For example, Article 5 of the Development of Contract Law was set up especially to guard against the practices of absolute egalitarianism and gratis transfer of materials. Also, the development of contract economics together with the legal regulation of contract in China requires a further ethical norm of fairness: people must be morally obliged to keep their agreements, even when all their gains are in the past and all their costs in the future.

Third, there is an emerging international law of human rights that sets standards for all states, and the Chinese are moving toward acceptance of this international law. Furthermore, the Chinese government has recognized the importance of human rights and appraised highly the Universal Declaration of Human Rights.[40]

Fourth, the idea of infusing the rights-based morality into politics is not arbitrary at all; nor is it purely speculative. It in fact mirrors the development of the moral and ideological lives in China—that is, the crisis of the official morality and the growing demands, in the past decades, for the protection of human rights in China. In other words, the rights-based morality seems to be an attractive and promising alternative to other forms of morality—the official goal-based morality and traditional Chinese underground morality. The crisis of Chinese Marxism and its morality is well known. The old control mechanisms of the official goal morality have lost their former effect. There was a revival of virtuocratic control mechanisms in the late 1980s, when the Chinese Communist Party stressed moral education as one of the top priority issues before and after 1989, and stated that improving morality among youth was a decisive factor in creating China's future. However, the conflict between traditional socialization methods and the emerging democratic demands concerning socialization that we find in modern society, as well as the danger of technocracy and even a form of industrialization of morality, have made official Chinese morality ineffective.[41] Moreover, the vacuum of faith among the Chinese which followed the death of Maoism was filled by traditional values such as *hao han* (the good man), *gemenr* (mateship), and *yiqi* (the honor of the *hao han* tradition) in the language of the Chinese underworld. However, these values, as W. J. F. Jenner points out, have always been too destructive to build something new.

They glorify gangsterism and help to cement bonds among criminal or rebel gangs.[42] Given the problems associated with the above two kinds of morality, Chinese liberals think that it is worthwhile for China to implement a rights-based morality in political life.

Conclusion

Democratic institutional design does not require a sage's conception of morality, or a Chinese Marxist, goal-based morality. Yet it would be wrong to take this further and argue that no form of morality constitutes a normative basis for democratic politics. Contrarily, I have argued for a rights-based morality as being a solid moral foundation for Chinese liberal institutional design, and a procedural conception of morality as an actual basis for well-founded democratic institutions.

I have examined and rejected a number of arguments against the project of infusing politics with morality. The argument of the independence of politics from morality fails because the problem of the abuse of procedure intrinsically requires the moral remedy that procedure should be fair. The practical argument concerning the catastrophic consequences of infusing politics with moral principles fails because it fails to distinguish between goal-based and rights-based moralities. The cultural relativist argument fails again because empirical moral diversity does not exclude a normatively minimal international morality and because a *universal* doctrine of rights-based morality is rooted in today's Chinese politics.

Notes

1. Ronald Dworkin, *Taking Rights Seriously* (London: Duckworth, 1977), 171–72.
2. T. H. Rigby and Ference Feher have discussed goal rational legitimation in communist regimes. They argue that legitimacy in Soviet society reflects the goal-rational character of its social order. The validity of orders issued by the rulers is derived from the validity of the principal social goals that the authorities claim to represent and promote. See Rigby and Feher, *Political Legitimation in Communist States* (London: Macmillan, 1982).
3. Lucian W. Pye, *Asian Power and Politics: The Cultural Dimensions of Authority.* (Cambridge, Mass.: Harvard University Press, 1985), 56.
4. Ibid., 63–64.
5. Ibid., 42.
6. Ibid., 200.
7. David Hume, *The Philosophical Works*, vol. 3, ed. Thomas Hill Green, and Thomas Hodge Grose (London: Scientia Verlag Aalen, 1964), 99; Duncan Forbes, *Hume's Philosophical Politics* (Cambridge: Cambridge University Press, 1975), 227.
8. Geoffrey Brennan and James M. Buchanan, *The Reason of Rules: Constitutional Political Economy* (London: Cambridge University Press, 1985).
9. See Lucian W. Pye, "The State and the Individual: An Overview Interpretation," *China Quarterly* 127 (1991), 443–66; and Donald Munro, ed., *Individualism and Holism: Studies in Confucian and Taoist Values* (Ann Arbor: the University of Michigan, 1985).
10. For detailed discussion of this, see chapters 3 and 4 of Baogang He, *The Democratization of China* (London: Routledge, 1996).

11. Baogang He, "Separation Ideology and Politics," *Zhengming* 124, (1988), 41–42; a different version appeared in *The Quest* 1 (1989), 49–52.
12. John Rawls, "The Domain of the Political and Overlapping Consensus," *New York University Law Review* 64, no. 2 (1989), 252.
13. Jeremy Waldron, "A Right to Do Wrong," *Ethics* 92 (1981), 21–39.
14. Yu-wei Hsieh, "The Status of the Individual in Chinese Ethics," in Charles A. Moore, ed., *The Chinese Mind* (Honolulu: University of Hawaii Press, 1967), 313.
15. Gregory Vlastos, "Justice and Equality," in Jeremy Waldron, ed., *Theories of Rights* (London: Oxford University Press, 1984), 41–77.
16. Jeremy Waldron, introduction to his *Theories of Rights*, 14–15.
17. J. L. Mackie, "Can There Be a Right-Based Moral Theory?" in Waldron, *Theories of Rights*, 171.
18. Beng-Huat Chua, *Communitarian Ideology and Democracy in Singapore* (London: Routledge, 1995), 140–41.
19. Montesquieu, *The Spirit of the Laws*, trans. and ed. Anne Cohler, Basia Miller, and Harold Stone (Cambridge: Cambridge University Press, 1989), xli.
20. Gerald F. Gaus, "Mill's Theory of Moral Rules," *Australian Journal of Philosophy* 58, no. 3 (1980), 266.
21. See Yan's conversation with Zhu Gaozheng, *Zhongyang Ribao*, May 15, 1990, 7; Hu's conversation with Zhu Gaozheng, in Hu Ping, *Gei Woyige zhidian* (Give Me a Fulcrum), in *Book Title* (Taipei: Lianjing Chuban Gong Shi, 1988), 238–66.
22. James Fishkin, "Tyranny and Democratic Theory," in Peter Laslett and James Fishkin, eds., *Philosophy, Politics and Society*, 5th ser. (Oxford: Basil Blackwell, 1979), 214.
23. I acknowledge different understandings of fairness in the Western political theories, and tensions between fairness as mutual benefit and fairness as impartiality. For a utilitarian concept of fairness, see Robert Goodin, *The Politics of Rational Man* (London: John Wiley and Sons, 1976), chapter 6. For a discussion of tension between theories of justice, see Brian Barry, *Theory of Justice: A Treatise on Social Justice*, vol. 1 (London: Harvester-Wheatsheaf, 1989). I adopt Rawls's conception of justice as fairness in my present study.
24. I acknowledge that institutional arrangements such as markets, legal regulations, and decision rules of unanimity cannot guarantee fair outcomes.
25. Rawls, "The Domain of the Political," 253.
26. John Rawls, *A Theory of Justice* (Oxford: Clarendon, 1971), 136; John Rawls, "The Idea of an Overlapping Consensus," *Oxford Journal of Legal Studies* 7, no. 1 (1987), 16.
27. Carl Schmitt, *The Concept of the Political,* trans. George Schwab (New Brunswick, N.J.: Rutgers University Press, 1976), 25–37.
28. Robert E. Goodin, *Motivating Political Morality* (Cambridge: Basil Blackwell Publishers, 1992), 163–64.
29. Goodin, *Motivating Political Morality*, 166–67.
30. Rawls, *A Theory of Justice*, 176, 180.
31. Goodin, *Motivating Political Morality*, 165.
32. Ronald Dworkin, "Rights as Trumps," in Jeremy Waldron, ed. *Theories of Rights*.
33. Julia Tao, "The Chinese Moral Ethos and the Concept of Individual Rights," *Journal of Applied Philosophy* 7, no. 2 (1990), 119–27.
34. Chandran Kukathas, "Explaining Moral Variety," *Social Philosophy and Policy* 11, no. 1 (1994), 1–21.
35. Lin Yu-sheng, "The Evolution of the Pre-Confucian Meaning of Jen and the Confucian Concept of Moral Autonomy," *Monumenta Serica* 31 (1974–75), 172–204; see also William Theodore de Bary and Tu Wei-ming, eds., *Confucianism and Human Rights* (New York: Columbia University Press, 1998).
36. Joseph Chan, "The Asian Challenge to Universal Human Rights: A Philosophical Appraisal," in James T. H. Tang, ed., *Human Rights and International Relations in the Asia-Pacific Region* (London: Pinter, 1995), 25–38.

37. For example, the Chinese government used the idea that human rights are circumscribed by historical, social, economic, and cultural conditions to argue against international condemnation of the Beijing Massacre in 1989.

38. Yan Jiaqi, *Wode Sixiang Zichuan (My intellectual Autobiography)* (Hong Kong: San Lian Shuju, 1988), 59–66.

39. Fang Lizhi, *Farewell to an Era: Writings of Fang Lizhi,* ed. J. Williams (New York: Knopf, 1991).

40. Guo Jisi, "China Promotes Human Rights," *Beijing Review,* January 28–February 23, 1991, 12–17.

41. Borge Bakken, "The Modernization of Morality in the People's Republic of China: Paradoxes of the Socialization Process," paper presented at the Contemporary China Centre, Research School of Pacific Studies, Australian National University, September 13, 1989.

42. W. J. F. Jenner, *The Tyranny of History: The Roots of China's Crisis*

Part III

Chinese State–Society Relations and Democracy

6

The Conceptual Evolution of Democracy in Intellectual Circles' Rethinking of State and Society

YIJIANG DING

Western discussions of the state-society relationship in China have mostly focused on social and economic change instead of formal intellectual change. Nevertheless, a few scholars in the West have noticed the Chinese rethinking issues relating to democracy and the state-society relationship. Among them are Merle Goldman's and Xue Liang Ding's discussions of Chinese intellectuals and their positions on democracy and the state-society relationship,[1] Shu-Yun Ma's and He Baogang's analyses of the Chinese discourses on civil society,[2] Ronald Keith's discussion of the Chinese debate on the rule of law and human rights in relation to the changing "structure of interests,"[3] Bill Brugger and David Kelly's analysis of the erosion of orthodox Leninism,[4] and Barry Sautman's discussion of the Chinese debate on "neo-authoritarianism."[5] The scale of the Chinese rethinking of democracy and the state-society relationship, however, requires a more comprehensive and focused analysis than was thus far offered. In attempting a detailed analysis highlighting more updated materials, this chapter deliberately encompasses a two-part discussion of the pre- and post-Tiananmen intellectual conceptualization of the state and society, and the relationship between them.

Pre-Tiananmen Discussions

In the late 1980s, the intellectual circles' discussion of democracy resulted in a redefinition of the concept of society and its relationship with the state. The growing importance given to *society* was directly connected with the shift of focus from *class struggle* to *contradictions among the people*; the change of *the people* from a social class concept to a largely all-inclusive concept almost identical to *society*; and the change of the state's functional focus from *dictatorship* to *the managing of public affairs*.[6] These changes provided the foundation for the emergence of new ideas about the state and society that explicitly or implicitly challenged orthodox Leninist democracy.

The Orthodox Position on Democracy

The regime's orthodox view of democracy effectively emphasizes the unity of interests both within the people and between the people and the Communist Party. In essence, then, democracy means rule by the party in the unified interest of the people. Theoretically, the party is regarded as having no special interest of its own and as acting solely on behalf of the most fundamental, unified, and long-term interests of the people.

Mao Zedong expounded on the structure of interests in socialist society as a structure of unity among three different kinds of interests—those of the state, the collective, and the individual—reflecting the ownership system prior to the economic reform, in which state ownership was regarded as the advanced form of public ownership, "collective ownership" as in transition toward state ownership, and private ownership as no more than a tolerated remnant of old society. "Contradictions among the people" were acknowledged but assumed a secondary position and were considered "questions involving the distinction between right and wrong among the people," originating in economic, cultural, or ideological underdevelopment. Such contradictions basically indicated negative aspects of life; the positive aspects were related to unity. The way to handle such contradictions was Mao's well-known formula: "unity—criticism—unity," which was "to start off with a desire for unity and resolve contradictions through criticism or struggle so as to achieve a new unity on a new basis."[7]

This orthodox emphasis on unity was reiterated by Deng Xiaoping in 1979, who said, "Under the socialist system, individual interests are subordinate to collective interests, the interests of the parts are subordinate to the interest of the whole.... This is because, in the final analysis, the interests of the individual and of the collective are in unity with each other under the socialist system, so are the interests of the parts and of the whole.[8]

Such emphasis on the unity of interests has obscured the conceptual distinction between the state and society and provided justification for the party's unchallengeable control of political power.

The orthodox idea of democracy based on the unity of interests, however, was challenged by many scholars in the late 1980s. Available evidence indicates that it was challenged in three ways: first, its validity was directly questioned; second, society was increasingly viewed as a separate entity from the state; and third, society itself came to be regarded as a plurality of equally legitimate social interests.

Unity as a Target of Criticism

The unity issue was raised in early 1986 at a conference on political reform organized by *Zhongguo Shehui Kexue*, an influential journal published by the Chinese Academy of Social Science (CASS). It was suggested at this conference that one of Stalin's mistakes was to conclude that after the elimination of enemy classes, a socialist state would be highly unified and devoid of conflicts of interest. It was also suggested that "the issue of 'interest pluralism' (*liyi duoyuan zhuyi*) is worthy of our study and investigation." [9] After the conference, a number of articles appeared in official newspapers and academic journals, attacking the orthodox idea of "the unity of interests." Several related arguments were presented in these articles, as well.

First, the orthodox idea was criticized for ignoring an important social reality: the existence of differing interests. Second, arguments were made against "imposing unity" upon people with different interests—a common practice in line with the Leninist orthodoxy. It was suggested that the principle of minority right should be included in the idea of democracy, assuming that different interests in society were equally legitimate and deserved equal protection.[10] Third, "overemphasis on the unity of interests" was accused of contributing to the supremacy of the state and obstructing social and economic development, because the modern economic system—the market economy—was characterized by the recognition of diverse interests and individual rights.[11] Fourth, the emphasis on the unity of interests was blamed for the lack of democracy in China. This last point deserves our special attention, since it is directly related to the understanding of democracy itself.

Several authors tried to establish a negative correlation between unity and democracy, but in different ways, revealing two related but different approaches to the issue of democracy. One argument focused on the state-society relationship and suggested that the difference in interests between the state and society provided a basic motivation for democracy: to allow society to protect itself from the state. In order to develop democracy, the difference in interests between the state and society must be recognized. Emphasis on the unity between the state and society, on the other hand, implies that the people's interests would be completely embodied in the state, thus making it unnecessary for people to have democratic rights.[12] The other argument focused on the diversity within society itself: pluralism was said to be a precondition for democratic politics because the purpose of democracy is to allow the articulation of various social interests by people of different social groups. In other words, the motive for democratic participation lay in the difference between social interests and the need to voice the difference. The past emphasis on the unity of interests created "a false sense of social unity," thus removing the need for interest articulation by different social groups.[13]

During the late 1980s, emphasis on the difference rather than the unity of interests as the foundation of democracy became well-established among scholars and gained some official acceptance, as was evidenced by the ensuing scholarly discussions on the state and society. Even *Hongqi*—a conservative voice within the regime—published an article that somewhat reluctantly acknowledged "a certain lack of complete unity of interests in the relationship between different regions, ethnic groups, social groups, and even between the state, groups and the individual."[14] Interestingly, the author replaced "the collective" (*jiti*) with the more trendy "groups" (*qunti*) in the orthodox formula of interests. While the collective is viewed as transcending the individual, a group is more regarded as a simple aggregation of individuals.

The Differentiation of Society from State

The conceptual differentiation of society from state appeared to be a natural extension of the earlier arguments for decentralization and the division of power. Theoretically, when decentralization exceeds the boundary of the state system, power is transferred from the state to society. In the late 1980s, more people began to argue that a truly effective decentralization would have to involve transferring some power to an increasingly autonomous society.

In early 1986, an article in *Zhengzhixue Yanjiu* suggested that the past measures of decentralization were ineffective because they "focused only on the allocation of power among different levels of government," while the problem of excessive centralization could be solved only by "the return of power to society"(*huan quan yu shehui*). The use of the word *return* indicates that the power of the state originated in society; to transfer power to society was thus to return it to where it had originated. The author argued that it was necessary to distinguish government and nongovernment affairs and to establish legally defined boundaries of government power, as well as legal protection for the autonomy of social and economic life.[15]

This new position on the state-society relationship was supported by several leading scholars. For example, Yan Jiaqi agreed that different levels of government should have legally defined powers and that the state should give up its total control of society, allowing individuals and social organizations autonomy from the state. He proposed a plan for a four-direction division of power that included not only the division and decentralization of power in the traditional sense but also the giving of some power to nongovernment organizations.[16] Su Shaozhi suggested that, contrary to what Karl Marx had assumed, the existing system in China was that of state socialism, under which the party "developed into an omnipotent structure in charge of everything." Consequently, social and political life became "a unified domain," a system that was said to have "suffocated democracy and freedom."[17] In other words, freedom and democracy required separation between social life and political life.

The most systematic theory for the separation of the state and society was proposed by Rong Jian, a prominent young scholar from Renda, who later became a main participant in the debate on "neo-authoritarianism." Rong published several articles in 1987 and 1988, in which he interpreted Marx's position on the relationship between civil society and the political state and proposed a theory of the state-society dualism (*eryuanhua*). This reform Marxist position was clearly the rationale behind the return of power to society advocated by many scholars.

Rong explained that, according to Marx, the state originated in society and came to control society when society lost its self-control in its internal conflicts. When society regained its "self-consciousness," a historical process would begin during which society could "take back the power of the state." This is the process of "returning power to society."[18] Historically, this process was to be accomplished in two steps: First, society would "regain the power of economic self-determination from the state." This would result in the state-society dualism. Second, society would regain political power and come to control the state through democratization. This would result in the "withering away" of the state. In this way, the state-society relationship was to go through three evolutionary stages in a Hegelian negation of the negation: (1) the unity of the two through the state domination, (2) the "dualism" (the separation of the two), and (3) final unity through the "withering away" of the state.[19]

According to Rong Jian, precapitalist society featured a high degree of integration of the state and society, and "a great achievement of capitalism was to have completed the process of separation of civil society from political life."[20] Here, *civil society* was defined as a separate sphere of social and economic freedom. The key to the development of civil society, therefore, was to separate social and economic life from the political life of the state. This second stage of development in the state-society relationship—the "dualism"—was what China was faced with: since China had never been through capitalism, the separation of the state and society would have to be achieved through economic and political reforms. Rong emphasized, "The purpose of the reform is to complete the dualism."[21] In other words, the reform would be aimed at creating a separate sphere of social and economic freedom: a civil society in China.

Rong Jian's theory of state-society dualism as a reform Marxist justification for the separation of the state and society and for economic freedom enjoyed much support among Chinese scholars and provided a theoretical foundation for a general consensus on the development of the state-society relationship in China. Two central issues emerged in the discussions on the state-society relationship, representing two interrelated perspectives: The society perspective emphasized the need for economic freedom. The state perspective focused on the need to change the role of the state. Both could be derived from the theory of dualism.

The issue of *economic freedom* was raised by many authors in the late 1980s. The chief justification for it was that it was a precondition for political freedom and democracy. For example, a *Gongren Ribao* article argued that "if economy is controlled by a centralized power and without freedom, political freedom is merely empty talk."[22] Lin Yunong, in *Zhongguo Shehui Kexue*, also held that the growth of democracy depended on the development of free market.[23] Sometimes, economic freedom was made a criterion for the distinction between "autocratic politics" and "democratic politics": the former was said to be "the politicization of social and economic powers," while the latter was "the separation of social and economic powers from the political power."[24]

Several authors attempted to establish a "natural" correlation between a free market economy and political democracy, in order to argue that the former would pave the way for the latter. The market economy was said to "naturally favor equality ... in economic relations" and require economic players to be independent, free, and equal. This in turn would foster demands for political freedom and democracy, since democracy as a kind of political relationship reflected the economic relationships of the free market.[25] It was therefore argued that any kind of democracy, whether socialist or capitalist, would require a highly developed market economy as a precondition.[26]

Some cited Marx's notion of communism as "communities of free people" as evidence that the kind of socialism he envisioned was built on the basis of a free contractual relationship, whereas in China, socialism was "grafted" onto a "society of ascribed status" (*shenfen shehui*). Reform, in this sense, was to replace a status relationship with a free contractual relationship.[27] Liao Xun, a well-known economist from the CASS, held that societal autonomy was the key meaning of the term *socialism,* and that economic organizations in socialist society ought to be "communities of free people."[28] These authors identified the free individuals in market economy with Marx's "communities of free people" and turned Marx's idea of communism into a justification of the free market.

Ironically, the argument for economic freedom as a condition for democracy often seemed to assume that the current priority was economic freedom rather than political democracy. Indeed, this underlying assumption was implied in Rong Jian's theory of dualism. It became explicit in the 1988 and 1989 debate on neo-authoritarianism. The two sides in this debate disagreed on the priority given to democratization, but not on the meaning of democracy as political expression of individual freedom and equality and the need for economic freedom as a foundation for democracy. Main advocates of neo-authoritarianism, including Wu Jiaxiang and Zhang Bingjiu, clearly shared Rong Jian's view on the three evolutionary stages of the state-society relationship. The distinction they made between traditional authoritarianism and neo-authoritarianism highlighted their emphasis on the need for economic freedom. In their view, economic freedom fostered by an authoritarian state—the East Asian model—was the only way to create social, economic, and cultural preconditions for the eventual democratization.[29]

The issue of *the role of the state* was raised in the early 1980s. The focus then was on changing the function of the state from dictatorship to social management in accordance with the change of focus from class struggle to "contradictions among the people." In the late 1980s, however, the emphasis was increasingly placed on the return of power to society. The main argument was that the role of the state should be weakened, limited, and "societalized" (*shehuihua*), meaning that the social management function of the state should be partially replaced by society's self-management through the return of power to society.[30] Proposals were made for transferring power from government to nongovernment organizations.[31]

For example, an article in *Tianjin Shehui Kexue* defined "societalization of government functions" as "the transfer of many affairs formerly controlled by the government to localities, enterprises, social organizations and mass organizations." This, according to the author, was a "general trend in the transformation of the state" in both socialist and capitalist countries, while in the former, it was more of a self-conscious effort, because "the basic task of the socialist state is to self-consciously create material and spiritual conditions for its own withering away," and "the societalization of government functions is the only way" to that end.[32]

One might argue that using mass organizations as means of social control was part of the traditional mass-line approach to the government-versus-masses relationship, which was a kind of state corporatism that underlined the fundamental unity between the state and society and reserved the decision-making power to the state. However, the rationale behind the "societalization of government functions" differed fundamentally from the mass-line tradition in that it emphasized the separation between the state and society and the need for societal autonomy. While mass-line aimed at strengthening the power of the state, "societalization" attempted to weaken it.[33]

During this period of time, a well-publicized formulation for changing the government functions was "small government, big society" (*xiao zhengfu, da shehui*), which was said to be first proposed by Liao Xun.[34] Liao himself cited both liberalism and Marxism to justify his proposal. The liberal principles of personal freedom and limited government laid the foundation for the model of "small government, big society." Marx, on the other hand, accepted utopian socialist ideas of small government, societal autonomy, and communism as made up of "communities of free people." In sharp contrast to Marx's idea of socialism, Liao suggested, was the Soviet model of statism, in which there was only the state, no society.[35]

A much discussed model of small government, big society was the Hainan model. While there is evidence that a liberal perspective existed among some scholars, viewing Hainan as an experiment of limited government and legally protected individual rights and freedoms,[36] the Marxist theory of the state-society relationship as expounded by Rong Jian appeared to be a more accepted justification of small government, big society. For example, an article in *Shehui Kexue* suggested that "small government, big society" was an inevitable result of the "dualist differentiation of society from the state"—a necessary stage in the return of power to society. It was, therefore, completely in accordance with the Marxist idea of the "withering away" of the state.[37]

To sum up, in the late 1980s, the idea of an autonomous society free from control by the state was suggested by many scholars in China. A Marxist theory of the civil society and its relationship with the political state was proposed to justify a degree of separation of society from the state. According to this theory, the state should abandon part of its power over society in order to allow members of society to enjoy a degree of freedom in social and economic life.

Civil society in China became a hot issue among Western scholars after the Tiananmen incident in 1989. According to Shu-Yun Ma, Western scholars generally believed that Chinese intellectuals were then almost totally unaware of this issue. The available evidence not only supports Ma's claim that the Chinese discussion on civil society appeared as early as 1986, well before "most Western scholars may have assumed," but also indicates that the Chinese discussions went well beyond the debate on how the term had been used by Marx, how it should be translated into Chinese, and what its implicit meanings were.[38] In the late 1980s, some Chinese scholars were already using the Marxist concept of civil society to justify the development of an autonomous society in China.

However, the meaning of *civil society* as explained by Chinese scholars during this period was a rather weak and passive one. Instead of a well-organized political society confronting the state, as was thought by some Western scholars, it was no more than a depoliticized sphere of social and economic life, while the state was given the power to dominate the political life of society. The focus then was not on the right of society to participate in the political process, but on limiting the state power to the political sphere. The emphasis was on separation rather than participation. In this sense, the autonomy of society as it was argued for was still quite limited.

The relationship between such a civil society and political democracy was ambiguous at best. Indeed, this concept of civil society was employed to justify neo-authoritarianism. Nevertheless, the meaning of democracy based on societal autonomy differed fundamentally from the orthodox idea of democracy based on the unity of interests between the state and society, in that the state control of society was now rejected as "autocratic politics," and societal autonomy itself was regarded as democracy at its early stage of development. The current economic and political reforms were subsequently viewed in essence as efforts to create an autonomous society and pave the way for an advanced form of democracy: political freedom and mass participation.

Social Interest Differentiation and Pluralism

While the conceptual differentiation of society from the state challenged the unity of interests between the party and the people, interest differentiation (*liyi fenhua*) and social pluralism (*shehui duoyuanhua*) broke away from the idea of fundamental unity among the people. This breaking away was connected with the earlier shift of emphasis from *class struggle* to the *contradictions among the people*. The discussions on the *contradictions among the people* in the early 1980s already displayed the tendency to exceed the orthodox meaning of the term in that the negative connotation attached to such contradictions was replaced by an implicit recognition of the legitimacy of different social interests. In the late 1980s, this implicit recognition developed into a general acceptance of interest differentiation and social pluralism.

The issue of *interest pluralism* (*liyi duoyuan zhuyi*) was raised during the conference on political reform organized by *Zhongguo Shehui Kexue* in early 1986.[39] This conference marked the beginning of a series of attacks on the orthodox idea of unity, which I discussed earlier. Initially, arguments for social pluralism generally tried to establish as fact that every society was made up of different interest groups, since individual members formed social groups according to their shared interests.[40]

A few people suggested that the difference of interests had always existed in socialist society, and simply came into the open and multiplied as a result of economic reform.[41] Mainstream opinion began to assume that interest differentiation and pluralism were the inevitable outcome of economic reform and the process of modernization. Reform directly resulted in economic pluralism, which in turn contributed to the emergence of social groups with distinctly different interests. This position was held by well-known scholars such as Wang Huning of Fudan; Zheng Yongnian of Beida; Min Qi, a political scientist who coordinated the first national survey of political culture in China in 1987; and many others.[42]

Unlike the arguments for the separation of the state and society, which was made primarily on the basis of the Marxist theory of the state-society relationship, the idea of pluralism appeared to result more from the influence of the Western theory of modernization and political development, which assumed a causal relationship between economic development, differentiation of social structure and interests, increased demand for participation, and the development of a rational and efficient political system through structural-functional differentiation and democratization.

Assuming interest differentiation and pluralism as a fait accompli resulting from the economic development since the beginning of reform, some Chinese scholars suggested that the essence of economic reform was to reorganize, readjust, and coordinate the relationships among different social interests, so as to "create equal opportunity,"[43] "mobilize productive initiatives,"[44] and resolve conflicts of interest.[45] Their discussions seemed to indicate the uneven impact of economic reform, the acute feeling among many people that the reform benefited others far more than themselves, and the fear that the conflicts of interests between social groups might escalate into social crises. For example, Min Qi warned that interest differentiation and social pluralism would lead to increasing demands for political participation, which would result in a "participation crisis."[46]

The solution to the potential crises was said to be political modernization—a process of political development concurrent with economic, social, and cultural development and leading to the establishment of a "rationalized political authority" (lixinghua de zhengzhi quanwei), in order to keep pace with social and economic modernization.[47] It was suggested that this "rationalization" of political authority contained two different, and sometimes conflicting, dimensions: efficiency and democracy. The former required structural differentiation and functional specialization, as well as system integration and institutionalization. The latter required the political system to become open to mass participation, and responsive to societal demands. There was general agreement on the meaning of political modernization, but clear disagreement on the priority given to its two different dimensions.[48]

Those who held that the current priority should be efficiency rather than democracy believed that democracy required certain social, economic, and cultural conditions that were underdeveloped in China. Under these circumstances, pushing for democratization would intensify rather than alleviate existing social conflicts, and jeopardize economic development.[49] Those who preferred democracy, on the other hand, believed that the only way to avoid social crises was to open up the system to mass participation and develop "political pluralism"(*zhengzhi duoyuanhua*) to allow different social groups to press for their demands within the political system.

With a degree of approval by the Zhao Ziyang regime, the notion of "social consultation and dialogue"(*shehui xieshang duihua*) was proposed as a limited measure for opening up the political system. Recognizing diversity of interests, social *consultation and dialogue* was explained as a system of interest articulation by different social groups.[50] It was suggested that its purpose was to facilitate input and output between the political system and the social environment.[51]

In addition to social consultation and dialogue, "political pluralism"—a much more radical idea—was proposed by some scholars. Min Qi, for example, suggested the need to modify the current one-party system in order to accept the new social forces into the political process and avoid the "participation crisis."[52] An article in *Tansuo: Zhesheban* also argued that social interest pluralism required differentiation of political institutions and the separation of powers, a process "usually accompanied by the emergence of multi-partyism."[53] An article in *Shulin* went so far as to praise the "bourgeois democratic system" as the "best achievement of political civilization that has been made by mankind so far," and to suggest that China's political reform should aim at the establishment of a "pluralist democratic political system with social interest groups as its main participants and checks and balances as its core content."[54]

The notion of political pluralism as an integral part of democracy corresponding to economic and social pluralism indicated another important change in the Chinese understanding. Democracy came to mean a process of interests accommodation, coordination, and compromise, in contrast to the politics of class struggle, which suppressed the expression of different interests.[55] In the same way, democratization came to be understood as "a process of admitting different interests into the political process." Therefore, a balance of different interests was preferred over domination by one interest because the former would create favorable conditions for democratization.[56] In line with this understanding of democracy was the proposal that various social organizations should become autonomous representatives of different social interests,[57] and that people's congresses should be modeled after Western parliaments and act as "coordinators of social interests."[58]

This understanding also implied that democracy was the politics of peace and stability, in contrast to class struggle, which was the politics of violence and instability. Political coordination (*zhengzhi xietiao*) was explained as a system of "consultation and compromise" on the principles of "peace and moderation" and of "seeking common ground while maintaining differences."[59] Democracy was said to be able to ensure political stability because it "was capable of comprehensive coordination of various interests and demands of the modern society."[60]

There was clear agreement that democracy was in essence a process of peaceful accommodation, coordination, and compromise of diversified social interests. This understanding is similar to the meaning of democracy suggested by a number of contemporary Western political scientists, such as Arend Lijphart,[61] Giuseppe Di Palma,[62] Samuel P. Huntington,[63] and Georg Sorensen.[64] The influence of Western political science theories was indicated by the vocabulary and overall rationale of these Chinese scholars.

To sum up, the acceptance of the plurality of social interests, together with the conceptual differentiation of society from the state, profoundly influenced Chinese intellectual circles' understanding of the meaning of economic reform and political democracy in the late 1980s. Economic reform came to be understood both as a process of separation of society from the state and as readjustment of relationships among different social interests. These can be viewed as two dimensions of the same reform process, during which large sections of society are being freed from direct state control, new social interests have emerged, and their relationships with one another and with the state are being readjusted.

In the same way that economic reform was understood as a readjustment of economic and social relationships, political reform was viewed as a readjustment of political relationships. Those who focused on the state-society relationship viewed democracy as society's freedom from the state at its early stage, and society's control of the state in its advanced form. Those who emphasized social interest differentiation and pluralism viewed democracy as a process of interest accommodation, coordination, and compromise. These were two related aspects of change different from the orthodox Leninist democracy.

This new understanding of democracy was well illustrated by "the first nationwide conference on the building of democratic politics" held in Changsha in 1988. The participants expressed the view that democracy was "in essence society's control of the state," and that democratization was required by the development of social pluralism. Since "each group has its own interest and has right to press for its interest" in the political system, it was necessary to seek common ground among the majority through negotiations and democratic procedures. This was said to be "the negation of the political system in which a power standing above society exercises unified control of all aspects of social life."[65]

The Post-Tiananmen Discussions

The 1989 Tiananmen incident was a crucial test of the vitality of the new ideas about state and society that developed in the late 1980s. Immediately after the incident, almost all of the new ideas about state and society were attacked in both the official media and academic journals. People who had advocated them were completely silenced.

Many of those who had pioneered them belonged to either what Merle Goldman termed the "democratic elite"—Hu Yaobang's intellectual network and their associates, or Zhao Ziyang's "think tanks." Both groups were purged after the incident. Their members either were jailed, fled overseas, or simply ceased publication in academic journals. In her book *Sowing the Seeds of Democracy in China*, Goldman described the fate of some of these scholars after the incident, which partially explained why most of these people became silent.[66] However, the new ideas about state and society not only reappeared soon after they were criticized, but gained greater acceptance among the intellectuals. Even the most sensitive issue of "political pluralism" was raised again. The revival of these ideas also coincided with the appearance of a large number of new names in Chinese academic journals, indicating the emergence of a new,

Table 6.1 Post-Tiananmen Chinese Scholars

Name	Academic Degree, Position, and/or Institutional Affiliation
Bao Xinjian	Shangdong Provincial Social Science Association
Cai Tuo	
Chen Binhui	Xiamen University
Chen Shi	
Chen Zhen	Professor of Law, Shandong University
Cui Peiting	Professor, CCP Central Party School
Deng Zhenglai	Chief editor, *Zhongguo Shehui Kexue Jikan*
Fan Yongfu	
Gong Zhihui	Nanjing Institute of Politics
Gu Benhua	
Guo Daohui	Chief editor, *Zhongguo Faxue*
Guo Dingping	Professor of political science, Fudan University
He Zengke	Ph.D. in political science; associate researcher, Institute of Modernity, CCP Central Bureau of Compilation and Translation
Jia Dongqiao	Department of Political Science, Northwestern Normal University
Jing Yuejing	Associate professor of political science, the People's University (Renda)
Li Jing	CCP Sichuan Provincial Party School
Li Jingpeng	Professor of political science, Beijing University (Beida)
Liu Wujun	Department of Law, Beijing University (Beida)
Liu Zuoxiang	Associate professor, Northwestern Institute of Politics and Law
Lu Pinyue	Professor, Southeastern University
Ma Changshan	Heilongjiang Provincial Bureau of Civil Affairs
Shi Xianmin	Ph.D. in sociology from Beida; Shenzhen Institute of Administration
Shi Xuehua	Ph.D. in political science from Fudan University; associate professor, Hangzhou University

post-Tiananmen generation of Chinese scholars. Most of the authors listed in table 6.1 appeared in Chinese journals after the Tiananmen incident; quite a few of them are home-trained Ph.D.s and in their thirties.

From Hibernation to Revival

The Tiananmen crackdown was followed by a campaign of criticism, which targeted key concepts such as the state-society dualism, marketization, the return of power to society, economic freedom, individual freedom, social pluralism,

---

Table 6.1 (cont.)

Name	Academic Degree, Position, and/or Institutional Affiliation
Sun Guohua	Professor of law, the People's University (Renda)
Sun Li	
Sun Liping	Professor of sociology, Beijing University (Beida)
Sun Xiaoxia	Department of law, Hangzhou University
Wang Huning	Professor of political science, Fudan University
Wang Jiangang	China Youth Institute of Politics
Wang Jianqin	Assistant professor, Central Cadre Institute of Politics, Law, and Management
Wang Puli	
Wang Song	Professor, East China Normal University
Xie Hui	
Xie Pengcheng	Graduate School of the CASS
Xie Qingkui	Professor, Beijing University (Beida)
Xu Guodong	Professor, Central South Institute of Politics and Law
Yan Qin	
Yin Guanghua	General Office of the Central Commission for the Size of State Institutions
Yu Keping	Ph.D in political science from Beida; associate researcher, Institute of Modernity, CCP Central Bureau of Compilation and Translation
Zhang Chengfu	
Zhang Jingli	
Zhou Yezhong	Ph.D in law; professor of law, Wuhan University
Zhu Changping	

Sources: Chinese journals that published articles by these authors; blanks indicate lack of information.

political pluralism, checks and balances, and so on. In the second half of 1989 and throughout 1990, the criticism campaign more or less dominated the official and academic publications. However, a year after the Tiananmen incident, dissenting voices began to appear in academic journals. For example, in mid-1990, *Zhongguo Faxue* carried several articles discussing democracy and the rule of law. One author claimed that during the "preliminary stage of socialism," it was still necessary to fight for freedom, democracy, and civil rights.[67] Another author emphasized the similarities between "socialist democracy" and "bourgeois democracy" and declared that "democracy is a spiritual wealth that belongs to the whole of mankind."[68] An article in *Ningxia Shehui Kexue* suggested that the lack of institutionalized participation was responsible for the 1989 social unrest. The author cited Huntington's theory of the relationship between institutionalization and participation to argue for the necessity to institutionalize democratic participation so as to avoid participation crisis and political alienation caused by participation failure.[69]

In 1991, the criticism campaign clearly began to flag. Unorthodox ideas reappeared in terms that were acceptable to the regime leadership. For example, an article in *Fujian Xuekan* repeated the old argument that the function of the state was not simply "class suppression," but primarily the management of public affairs for all of society.[70] An article in *Shehui Kexue* pointed out that democracy needed to recognize individual rights: there could be no sovereignty of the people to speak of if people did not have human rights.[71] A *Guangming Ribao* article suggested that democracy was a process of social interest articulation, exchange, and coordination, and that the so-called people's fundamental interest was simply the "optimal point of combination" of different social interests.[72] An article in *Zhengzhi yu Falu* carefully distinguished between restriction of power and checks and balances in order to justify the former.[73][7]

If 1991 was a year of cautious testing of political water, then 1992 was a year of drastic change of political climate, caused primarily by Deng Xiaoping's *Nanxun* (southern China tour) speeches. Deng probably intended no more than to revive the sluggish economy and to gain some lost ground from the other elders. Nevertheless, his speeches triggered a wave of articles in the official Chinese media that criticized the left, meaning orthodox Leninism, and demanded the liberation of the mind. In June, *Renmin Ribao* carried an article by Rong Yiren, who reasserted that "practice" was "the sole criterion of truth."[74] In July, the "anti-Left" and "liberation of the mind" themes were further played up by a *Renmin Ribao* editorial.[75] One immediate effect of this sudden change of climate was the revival of all the key ideas about the state and society developed in intellectual circles in the 1980s—their hibernation had ended quite abruptly.

The discussions on the state-society relationship in the 1990s focused on a few familiar topics, namely, the role of the government, societal freedom and independence, social pluralism, and political pluralism. What was new was that the issue of civil society attracted much greater attention and some new ideas were proposed, apparently stimulated by the Western interest in civil society in China in the early 1990s.[76]

Changing the Role of the Government

Changing the role of the government was an old and "safe" topic: it had received the regime's approval and did not suffer from criticism in 1989 and 1990. The regime's focus was on downsizing government institutions to make them more efficient. Many in intellectual circles, on the other hand, used this topic to break up the post-Tiananmen silence on the state-society relationship and revive those ideas criticized in 1989 and 1990. Their chief interest was in limiting the government power and giving society more freedom and independence. Many articles on this topic had appeared in newspapers and journals since the late 1980s. The authors included both scholars and officials, including top regime leaders such as premier Li Peng. However, a careful reading of these articles reveals the difference between the regime and the scholars.

In May 1992, Chen Shi, who argued for economic freedom in 1986, suggested, again in *Gongren Ribao*, that direct government intervention in the economy contributed to the problem of "big government, small society." Government, he proposed, should be a servant rather than the leader of the reform; social management ought to be its sole function and most of its economic functions should be eliminated. Its role in the economy should change from that of player to that of rule maker and referee.[77]

In July, *Renmin Ribao* published an article by premier Li Peng on county-level government reform. Li proposed the formulation "small offices, big service" (*xiao jiguan, da fuwu*); his focus was on government, not on society. Nevertheless, he agreed that the government should reduce its direct intervention in economy, so as to allow "a greater proportion of adjustment by market." In Chinese terminology, "adjustment by market" (*shichang tiaojie*) differs from "market economy" (*shichang jingji*). It means using the market as a complementary measure in a planned economy. Li's position signaled only a reluctant acceptance of the market.[78]

A *Renmin Ribao* editorial in August, however, went a step further and suggested that there should be a clearly defined boundary limiting the power of the government in social and economic affairs.[79] A signed article in *Renmin Ribao* went even further than the editorial and demanded "the return of power to enterprises and to the market"(*huanquan qiye, huanquan shichang*)[80] These discussions were followed by a large number of articles on this subject by both scholars and government officials.

In these articles, changing the role of the government was discussed in relation to the broad topic of the state-society relationship. It was equated to "small government, big society," and was explained as a movement from political "monism"(*yiyuan*), meaning the politicization of economy and society through the state domination, to the "dualism of politics and economy, the state and society, and the government and citizenry," a process that formed part of the "political modernization" and contributed to the transition of society from tradition to modernity.[81]

It was suggested that a legally defined boundary of the state power was necessary in order to turn an "unlimited government" into a "limited government."[82] It was warned that "the cycle of decentralization and recentralization of power purely between government institutions" must not be repeated.[83] Not only the size of government, but the role of the government itself, had to be reduced to the point that government would "only be concerned with what has to be done by the government."[84] A correlation between changing the role of the government and the development of a civil society was also suggested: the former promoted the latter by contributing to the separation of the state and society. The latter promoted the former by creating a "social momentum" for it.[85]

Yin Guanghua, a member of the Central Commission for the Size of the State Institutions, acknowledged that though there would still be many difficulties in changing the role of the government, "on the issue of (the need for) the government to return power to enterprises, a general agreement has been reached throughout society."[86] An indication of this general agreement was the vocabulary of the officials participating in the discussion. They generally used the term *the return of power (huanquan)* to refer to the transfer of power to societal organizations, as if they were aware that power originated in society and not the state.

Developing Civil Society

Unlike *small government, big society*, *civil society* never received official recognition. Nevertheless, the term appeared in scholarly discussions in the 1980s and became a hot issue in the early 1990s. Many scholars offered their opinions on it. In their discussions, the reform Marxist theory of the state-society dualism proposed by Rong Jian in 1987 was clearly revived.[87] The issue of changing the role of the government was also connected with the need to develop civil society in China.

In late 1992, Deng Zhenglai and Jing Yuejing published an article on civil society in *Zhongguo Shehui Kexue Jikan*,[88] in which they defined *civil society* as "a private sphere of autonomous economic and social activities based on the principle of voluntary contract, and a public sphere of unofficial participation in politics."[89] The inclusion of "a public sphere of unofficial participation" marked their difference from Rong Jian's notion of civil society, which was economically free but politically passive. Based on this more active definition, they proposed a relationship of "positive interaction" between the state and society. In this relationship, civil society would play an active role protecting societal freedom, opposing state domination, developing social pluralism, and promoting democracy.[90]

In their opinion, the previous focus on the transformation from one type of political authority to another (*quanwei zhuanxing*)—highlighted by the democratization–versus–neo-authoritarianism debate—failed to recognize the fact

Table 6.2.   The Two-Stage Process: Deng and Jing compared with Rong

	Stage One	Stage Two
Rong Jian	Transfer of economic power to society; state-society dualism; civil society based on economic freedom.	Transfer of political power to society; democratization; the "withering away" of the state.
Deng and Jing	The same as Rong's stage one: civil society within the private sphere.	"Positive interaction" based on state-society dualism; civil society's expansion into the public sphere; democratization.

that the main difficulty with China's political modernization was the lack of a "dualist structure" in the state-society relationship. In other words, state-society dualism must be accomplished before it is possible to democratize. Therefore it was necessary to shift the focus from the transformation of the authority type to the development of societal autonomy and civil society.[91]

Deng and Jing envisaged a two-stage development of civil society: the first stage aimed at setting up a "dualist structure" in the state-society relationship; the second was characterized by the "expansion of civil society from the private to the public sphere" and the development of "positive interaction" and democratic politics.[92] This seemed to resemble Rong Jian's two-stage process for the return of power to society. Indeed, Deng and Jing incorporated some of Rong's stage-two targets into their second stage. However, their stage two was in essence part of Rong's stage one: it was part of the development of civil society based on the state-society dualism, rather than the state-society reintegration through democratization and the "withering away" of the state (see table 6.2).

Deng and Jing's article marked the opening of heated discussions on civil society and the state-society relationship. In August 1993, more than forty scholars attended a conference on civil society in Shanghai.[93] The proposed shift of focus from the transformation of the authoritarian system to the development of civil society and the idea of positive interaction between the state and civil society appear to have received wide support.

For example, Guo Dingping agreed that the development of civil society had to precede the transformation of the authoritarian system, since the latter required certain economic, social, and cultural preconditions that could only be created through the development of civil society.[94] Lu Pinyue held that "if society itself [did] not have a system of self-management," efforts to transform the political system would only result in a vicious circle in which "decentralization leads to anarchy; recentralization leads to overcentralization" (*yifang jiu luan, yitong jiu si*).[95] In other words, transformation of the political authority depends on the ability of society to impose order on itself through self-management.

Meanwhile, there is indication of disagreement on the meaning of *positive interaction,* whether it signifies a cooperative or a competitive relationship with the state. Deng and Jing themselves proposed a combination of the two: civil society's "positive ability to participate" and its "negative ability to check and balance."[96] Others, however, tended to prefer one to the other. For example, He Zengke contended that *positive interaction* meant constructive engagement, not antagonism. Dualism required a contractual relationship based on mutual respect.[97] Lu Pinyue agreed that cooperation and mutual complement, rather than the people versus the government, was the appropriate model for civil society in China.[98] These arguments generally emphasized common interests between the state and society.

On the other hand, Liu Wujun held that the essence of positive interaction lay in the checks and balances between rights and power.[99] Similarly, an article in *Ningbo Daxue Xuebao—Renwen Kexue Ban* contended that the basic structure of modern society was a division of power, and checks and balances between the state and society.[100] This disagreement somewhat resembles the difference between two Western models on China's state-society relationship: civil society and corporatism. The former emphasizes societal independence and confrontation with the state, while the latter depicts a relationship of dependence and cooperation.

Rong Jian's influential theory of dualism remained the basis of broad agreement on the meaning of civil society and the evolution of the state-society relationship. Civil society was generally viewed as a sphere of social and economic life separated from the political life of the state. Within this "dualist" structure, civil society was seen as a dynamic process of development instead of a static model. It was believed that different elements of civil society could be achieved in stages.[101] Meanwhile, a few people, such as Sun Liping and Xu Guodong, emphasized property rights, a contract system, and degrees of social organization as crucial elements of civil society. The more rigid definition of civil society led to the conclusion that civil society was yet to be developed in China.[102]

In spite of these disagreements, everyone agreed that China needed a *civil society,* and the term came to represent a combination of economic, social, cultural, and political elements that were considered preconditions for democracy. These elements include economic freedom, autonomous social organizations, a political culture that values individual rights and freedoms, equality and independence, and the ability of society to manage its own affairs and to participate in the political process. In short, the development of civil society came to mean the establishment of the foundation for democracy.[103]

In the discussions, legal scholars joined political scientists and sociologists and became influential. Their theoretical justification for the rule of law was anchored in the *social origin of law*—a theory of the relationship between law, society, and the state that was pioneered in China by Guo Daohui in a series of articles published between 1993 and 1995.[104] Guo suggested that legal rights originated in "spontaneous social rights," which were transformed into the former through the lawmaking function of the state.[105] Therefore, *law (fa)* differed from *laws (falu)* in that law was the common will of society, while the state-made *laws* were in essence the expression of *law.*[106] Guo made two parallel distinctions: between the "rule *of* law" and the "rule *by* law," and between social-ism and statism. *Rule of law* was found in socialism and placed both society and law above the state. *Rule by law* and statism signified the state domination of society. Guo concluded that socialism demanded the return of power to society and state-society dualism.[107]

A similar idea was expressed by Ma Changshan, who distinguished "the *form* of law" from "the *essence* of law." The former reflected the will of the state, but was determined by the latter, which embodied the demands of civil society. The orthodox notion of law as originating in the will of the ruling class was wrong because it mistook the form of law for its essence and justified the state domination of society. The development of civil society presupposed the liberation of society from the state.[108] Xu Guodong expressed the view that civil law was the law of civil society, based on property rights and contract system. These were denied by public ownership and economic planning—the means of state domination. The true meaning of *small government, big society,* he held, was to replace the state domination with the separation of the state and society, implement market economy, and develop civil society in China.[109]

Xie Pengcheng suggested that, instead of embodying the will of one social class, law actually resulted from coordination, compromise, and common understanding among different social interests. Modern democracy was to re-place statism with socialism, and the supremacy of the state with the supremacy of law.[110] Liu Wujun also held that the development of dualism and the emer-gence of civil society in China would be a process of establishing the rule of law in China, since law expressed the interests of civil society.[111] These discussions provided a legal science perspective on the issue of the state-society relationship and democracy in China.

Social Pluralism and Political Pluralism

Social pluralism received some official approval at the Communist Party's thir-teenth congress in 1987, came under attack in 1989 and 1990, and reemerged in 1992; it is now largely assumed to be a given. Many people, such as Deng Zhenglai, Jing Yuejing, Guo Daohui, and Xie Pengcheng, mentioned it in their discussions of related issues. Focused treatment of this issue was also brought about by many scholars. People generally agreed that the market economy inevitably led to social pluralism. It was suggested that, in a pluralist society, the common interests of society resulted from compromise between particular interests, and that democracy as the political expression of such common inter-ests could only grow out of free and equal articulation of interests by different social groups.[112]

The possibility of a "participation crisis" was again raised. The need for proper, institutionalized channels of interest articulation in order to meet soci-etal demands was suggested, indicating the persistent influence of the Western modernization theory.[113] It was argued that the emergence of social pluralism demanded "political integration,"[114] and that a pluralist society needed to develop "common understanding" on basic political values and procedures.[115]

These arguments appeared to emphasize the integrating function of the political system in an effort to avoid possible social disintegration caused by the "participation crisis."

A few people discussed the recent social structural changes in China. It was suggested that social differentiation was not merely functional differentiation, but a reconstruction of society—a complete breaking away from a society of ascribed status dominated by the state,[116] and that the emergence of group interests based on the individualization of social interests promoted the "group interest consciousness," which in turn would foster democratization.[117]

Sun Xiaoxia proposed a new "structure of interests" made up of the individual, group, and social interests. *Individual interests* were primary, and *group interests* were aggregations of individual interests. *Social interests,* on the other hand, were the general interests transformed from individual and group interests and shared by most individuals and groups. The problem with Mao's orthodox structure of interests was that it replaced social interests alongside state interest, which was a particular interest that might not be transformed into a social interest. Therefore, the state could legitimately intervene in social affairs only in the name of social interests, not in the interest of the state.[118]

Political pluralism was one of the most sensitive issues in China's political discourse and had been the target of the most vicious attacks in the 1989 and 1990 criticism campaign; the issue was raised, however, in many post-1990 discussions on democracy. For example, Yan Qin's criticism of "political monism" contained an implicit argument for political pluralism, since monism (*yiyuan*) is the opposite of pluralism (*duoyuan*). Yan suggested that China should adopt a Western-style competitive campaigning in elections, and the checks and balances among the National People's Congress (NPC), the State Council, and the Supreme Court.[119] An article in *Hunan Shifan Daxue Shehui Kexue Xuebao* discussed the emergence of enterprise managers and intellectuals as increasingly independent social groups that demanded participation in the political process, and concluded that economic and social pluralism would result in pluralism in the structure of political power.[120]

Jia Dongqiao held that the "mechanism of free competition" in a pluralist society would inevitably be introduced into politics.[121] Wang Jiangang argued for the transformation of the current party system into a "one-party-dominant system," which was "pluralist in its composition," so as to create a "stabilizing mechanism" for a pluralist society.[122] Wang Song proposed the idea of "socialist political pluralism"—an attempt to legitimize political pluralism by adding the term *socialist* to it.[123] Zhou Yezhong held that pluralism was in the meaning of democracy, which was a process of interest coordination, concession, and compromise.[124] Even Wang Huning, who maintained close ties with the regime leadership, agreed that pluralism was a necessary principle of modern democracy.[125] We can see that political pluralism was generally accepted as an inevitable outcome of social pluralism and a necessary ingredient of democracy.

Conclusion

In the late 1980s, many Chinese intellectuals rejected the orthodox Leninist democracy, which was based on a monolithic view of "the people" and justified centralized control by the party-state. Two key concepts were developed: *state-society dualism* and *social pluralism*. Society was conceptually differentiated from the state and came to be understood as made up of a plurality of legitimate social interests. The role of the state was reduced to controlling political life and providing necessary services for society. This new understanding of state and society contributed to the conception of democracy as the control of the state by an autonomous society, and decision making undertaken by different social groups through peaceful coordination and compromise. However, the notion of *civil society* developed in this period was a passive one. It simply meant a depoliticized sphere of social and economic life that was not dominated by the state, while the state controlled the political process; in other words, it demanded only economic freedom under an authoritarian state. Economic freedom, viewed as a condition for economic development, was given priority over political freedom. Democracy remained an ideal for the future.

The progressive development of these new ideas was only briefly interrupted in the political backlash of 1989 and 1990. Beginning in 1991, these ideas not only revived, but continued to develop among Chinese intellectuals—now made up largely of a new generation of scholars. Stimulated by Western debates, *civil society* became the subject of heated discussions and replaced the *transformation of the authoritarian system* as the key issue in China's political modernization. A more active role for civil society was proposed and gained wide intellectual acceptance. It now included both a private sphere of economic freedom, as previously suggested, and an "unofficial public sphere" of political participation. This resulted in a closer connection between civil society and democracy. *Civil society* came to mean a combination of economic, social, cultural, and political conditions for democracy that were to be obtained in a dynamic process of development.

In view of the political reality in China, it is quite understandable that the focus of scholarly attention turned from the transformation of the authoritarian system in the 1980s to the development of civil society in the 1990s. Many now believe that it is the latter that holds the key to political modernization. Apart from recognizing the political reality, the scholarly focus on civil society also undoubtedly reflects changes in socioeconomic reality, such as the rapid development of the private-sector economy, associational activities, and village "self-government," that have begun to draw attention from the outside world only in recent years.

What is puzzling is that, while the regime appears to be more repressive toward political dissidents, the reemergence and development of the ideas discussed in this paper seem to indicate its greater tolerance. This raises questions concerning both the authors cited in this article and the overall relationship between intellectuals and the regime.

In table 6.1, about two-thirds of the scholars with some biographic information are from institutions of higher education—including universities, various institutes of politics, and the graduate school of the CASS. However, we cannot say that other groups are less important. The two chief editors clearly played crucial roles in developing cutting-edge ideas. Among the eleven whose biographic information is not available, five published in newspapers, which seldom provide such information. Ability to publish in nationwide newspapers such as *Guangming Ribao, Renmin Ribao, Jingji Ribao,* and *Gongren Ribao* usually indicates a degree of prestige. The remaining six published in university or provincial social science journals, indicating possible affiliations with the respective universities or provincial social science academies.

Taken as a whole, these authors and their ideas are quite influential in this particular area, and their influence can be viewed from several perspectives. Individually, it is demonstrated by their ability to publish in prestigious journals and newspapers, and to introduce new ideas that incite active responses from others such as Rong Jian, Deng Zhenglai and Jing Yuejing, Guo Daohui, and the like. Collectively, their influence can be seen in the intellectual focus of attention created by their discussions. In China, this focus sometimes may directly affect the political atmosphere, as demonstrated in the months prior to the 1989 Tiananmen incident. Their influence is also evidenced by the long-term impact on intellectual development. For example, the pre-Tiananmen discussions on the state-society relationship clearly influenced post-Tiananmen discussions.

There is strong evidence that the Chinese scholars participating in the discussions are highly aware of one another. Evidence of active interactions includes frequent discussions among them on specific ideas. A good tendency among Chinese scholars in the 1990s is that they pay more attention to giving credit to other authors whose ideas they have cited. This is reflected in the increased number of notes in their articles, which provide evidence of interactions among them, and of the presence of Western influence. Academic conferences have also played a role in building connections among scholars. Jing Yuejing's report on the first nationwide conference on civil society offered a vivid description of this type of interaction among Chinese scholars.[126] On the whole, interactions among intellectuals make them more influential as a group.

If the intellectuals involved in this discussion are influential, and their ideas are clearly unorthodox, then the question is: Why does the regime tolerate them? In my own opinion, the answer lies in the nature of the present regime and its relationship with these intellectuals.

As a result of the decline of the communist ideology and the weakening of the party-state, the present regime has lost much of its radicalism and become selectively repressive, targeting those who have directly challenged its rule, while leaving others alone so long as they do not present a direct threat. It now "has neither the will nor the capacity" to exercise comprehensive control over intellectuals.[127] Meanwhile, the post-Tiananmen political alienation, combined with unprecedented opportunities in the market economy, has increased the independence of the intellectuals and their distance from the regime. Consequently, the Chinese intellectuals today are "changing from their traditionally dependent and close relationship with government to one of increasing autonomy." They now seek to use their "independent channels to influence society directly rather than indirectly through political patrons."[128]

Seemingly paradoxically, while the intellectuals appear to become more alienated from the regime, there is also evidence of a closer partnership between them, in that the regime actively seeks advice from the intellectuals in important issue areas such as human rights and the legal system reform. In recent years, virtually all the important issues concerning the politics and economics of reform have become subjects of heated intellectual debate. This debate undoubtedly influences the policy-making process. In fact, the partnership between the intellectuals and the regime does not necessarily contradict the increasing independence of intellectuals.[129]

We should of course be aware that the Chinese scholars reviewed in this article belong among the relatively liberal part of the intellectual community. There is another part of that community that is relatively conservative, as represented by such journals as *Zhenli de Zhuiqiu*. On the whole, however, the conservative journals appear to be less influential among the younger generation of intellectuals when compared to the large number of journals published by academic institutions, which are considered to be more "academic"—meaning less orthodox.[130]

Given this changing relationship between the regime and the intellectuals, it will be interesting to observe how post-Deng Chinese leadership will respond to the further development of the new political ideas that have seriously challenged the Leninist orthodoxy.

Notes

1. Merle Goldman, *Sowing the Seeds of Democracy in China: Political Reform in the Deng Xiaoping Era* (Cambridge: Harvard University Press, 1994); Xue Liang Ding, *The Decline of Communism in China, Legitimacy Crisis 1977–1989* (Cambridge: Cambridge University Press, 1994).
2. Shu-Yun Ma, "The Chinese Discourse on Civil Society, " *China Quarterly* 137 (1994), 180–93; He Baogang, "The Ideas of Civil Society in Mainland China and Taiwan, " *Issues and Studies* 31, no. 6 (1995), 24–64.
3. Ronald C. Keith, *China's Struggle for the Rule of Law* (New York: St. Martin's Press, 1994); "The New Relevance of 'Rights and Interests': China's Changing Human Rights Theories, " *China Information* 10, no. 2 (1995), 38–61.
4. Bill Brugger and David Kelly, *Chinese Marxism in the Post-Mao Era* (Stanford, Calif.: Stanford University Press, 1990).
5. Barry Sautman, "Sirens of the Strongman: Neo-Authoritarianism in Recent Chinese Political Theory," *China Quarterly* 129 (1992), 72–102.
6. For some of the discussions on these related issues by Chinese scholars in the 1980s, see Gu Shicheng, "Zhubu jianshe gaodu minzhu de shehuizhuyi zhengzhi zhidu" (Gradually Establishing a Highly Democratic Socialist Political System), *Faxue Zazhi* (*Journal of*

Legal Science) 1 (1982), 7–10; Chen Zhonghua and Ma Runqing, "Lun guojiade guanli zhineng" (On the Management Function of the State), *Guizhou Shehui Kexue* (*Social Sciences in Guizhou*) 3 (1982), 1–7; Qiu Zhen and Yu Chi, "Shilun woguode guoti he zhengti" (A Tentative Theorizing on China's Form of State and Form of Government), *Xuexi yu Yanjiu* (*Learn and Study*) 7 (1982), 14–19; Zhou Yongchuang, "Guanyu bu shuyu jieji douzheng fanwei de shehui maodun" (On Social Contradictions That Do Not Belong to the Realm of Class Struggle), *Shehui Kexue* (*Social Science*) 8 (1982), 28–29; Lei Yun, "Lun tuidong woguo shehui fazhan de zhongyao maodun" (On Important Contradictions That Promote China's Social Development), *Shehui Kexue* (*Social Science*) 8 (1982), 41–42; the Writing Group of the Scientific Socialism Teaching and Research Office of the CCP Central Committee Party School, "Lun shehuizhuyi shehui de maodun" (Contradictions of Socialist Society), *Guangming Ribao* (*Guangming Daily*), October 31, 1983, 3; Li Detian and Yuan Minwu, "Dui guojia zhineng de zairenshi" (Rethinking the Function of the State), *Lilun Yuekan* (*Theory Monthly*) 4 (1986), 21–25; Situ Yan, "Zhongguo zhengzhi tizhi gaige de beijing yu qianjing" (Background and Prospect of China's Political System Reform), *Zhengzhixue Yanjiu* (*Political Science Research*) 1 (1987), 1–6; Zhu Qinjun, "Lun guojiade minzhu zhineng jiqi zai zhengzhi tizhi gaige zhongde xiaoying" (On Democracy as a Function of the State and Its Effect in Political System Reform), *Anhuisheng Dangxiao Xiaokan* (*Journal of the Anhui Provincial Party School*) 1 (1987), 75–78, 84; Xu Bin, "Zhengzhi tizhi gaige yu zhengti lilunde gengxin— guanyu guoti zhengti, minzhu jizhong guanxide zai renshi" (Political System Reform and the Renewal of the Theory of Political System—Rethinking the Form of State, the Form of Government, and the Relationship between Democracy and Centralism) *Zhejiang Xuekan* (*Zhejiang Journal of learning*) 5 (1987), 30–33; Ju Xingjiu and Li Guangzhi, "Minzhu zhengzhi lilun shi zhengzhi tizhi gaige de lilun yiju" (The Theory of Democratic Politics Is the Theoretical Basis for Political System Reform), *Lilun Tantao* (*Explore Theory*) 4 (1988), 25–28; Yu Haocheng, "Guanyu woguo zhengzhi tizhi gaige he fazhi jianshe de jige wenti" (A Few Questions in China's Political System Reform and Legal System Construction), *Wen Hui Bao* (*Wen Hui News*) January 14, 1989, 4; Lang Yihuai, "Zhongguo shinian zhengzhi gaige de jiben zouxiang" (Basic Directions in China's Ten Years of Political Reform), *Shehuizhuyi Yanjiu* (*Studies of Socialism*) 1 (1989), 20–24, 11.

7. Mao Tse-tung, *On the Correct Handling of Contradictions among the People*, (Beijing: Foreign Languages Press, 1957), 8–9.

8. Deng Xiaoping, "Shixian sige xiandaihua bixu jianchi sixiang jiben yuanze" (The Four Cardinal Principles Must Be Upheld in Order to Realize the Four Modernizations), *Zhongguo Zhengzhi* (*Chinese Politics*) 5 (1987), 23.

9. Li Ping, Shen Jian and Ding Wang, "1987 nian gaige shehui xingli diaocha baogao" (Report on the 1987 Survey on Social Psychology of Reform), *Jingji Ribao* (*Economic Daily*) October 24, 1987, 2, and October 27, 1987, 2. See also Lei Dongsheng, "Shehui xieshang duihua zhidu zhi wojian" (My Opinion on the System of Social Consultation and Dialogue), *Hubei Shehui Kexue* (*Social Science in Hubei*) 4 (1988), 51.

10. Su Shaozhi, "Zhengzhi tizhi gaige yu fandui fengjianzhuyi yingxiang" (Political System Reform and the Fight against Influence of Feudalism), *Renmin Ribao* (*People's Daily*) August 15, 1986, 8. See also "Shaoshu yao fucong duoshu, duoshu yao baohu shaoshu— minzhu jianshe zhongde yige wenti" (The Minority Should Be Subordinate to the Majority, and the Majority Should Protect the Minority—an Issue in the Development of Democracy), *Guangming Ribao* (*Guangming Daily*) October 7, 1986, 1. Qin Xiaoying, "Shehuizhuyi minzhu yeying baokuo 'shaoshu yuanze'" (Socialist Democracy Should Also Include the 'Minority Principle,'") *Qiushi* (*Seeking Truth*) 8 (1988).

11. Zheng Chengliang, "Shangpin jingji, minzhuzhengzhi de fazhan yu faxuede chonggou" (Development of Commodity Economy and Democratic Politics, and the Rebuilding of Jurisprudence), *Zhengzhi yu Falu* (*Politics and Law*) 1 (1989), 10–12. Yang Haikun, "Shehuizhuyi chujijieduan liyiqunti lun" (Interest Groups in the Preliminary Stage of Socialism), *Zhengzhi yu Falu* (*Politics and Law*) 2 (1989), 1–5.

12. Lin Yunong, "Lun shehuizhuyi minzhu fazhan yu jingji tizhi gaige de tongbu guanxi" (On the Parallel Development of Socialist Democracy and Economic System Reform), *Zhongguo Shehui Kexue* (*Chinese Social Science*) 5 (1986), 9–10.

13. Wu Zhilun, "Bixu jianli zhengzhijia yu putong qunzhong de youji lianxi" (An Organic Relationship Must Be Built Up between Politicians and Ordinary People), *Zhengzhixue Yanjiu* (*Political Science Research*) 1 (1988), 24–29. See also Zhang Qian, "Shehuizhuyi zhengzhi tizhi yu duoyuanhua" (Socialist Political Systems and Pluralization), *Lilun Xingxi Bao* (*Theoretical Information News*) September 26, 1988, 4.

14. Wang Jue, "Minzhu zhengzhi de xinfeng" (A New Style of Democratic Politics), *Hongqi* (*Red Flag*) 8 (1988), 29.

15. Zheng Shiping, "Lun Zhongguo zhengzhi tizhi jichu de gaige" (On Reforming the Foundation of China's Political System), *Zhengzhixue Yanjiu* (*Political Science Research*) 1 (1986), 29.

16. Yan Jiaqi's 1986 article titled "The Division of State Power in Four Directions" was republished in a collection of his works, *Toward a Democratic China* (Honolulu: University of Hawaii Press, 1992). In this article, he proposed dividing the state power in four directions: (1) horizontally, between legislative, executive and judicial, and between the party and the government; (2) vertically, between different levels of government; (3) between government institutions and social organizations; and (4) between government and the public, in the form of popular participation.

17. Su Shaozhi, *Democratization and Reform* (Nottingham, U.K.: Spokesman, 1988), 179. This is a collection of his works, including his 1986 article titled "Rethinking Socialism," which first appeared in *World Economic Herald*, November 24, 1986.

18. Rong Jian, "Lun Makeside minzhu sixiang" (On Marx's Democratic Ideas), *Zhengzhixue Yanjiu* (*Political Science Research*) 3 (1987), 6–7.

19. Rong Jian, "Makesizhuyi guojia xueshuo yu zhengzhi tizhi gaige" (Marxist Theory of State and Political System Reform), *Guangzhou Yanjiu* (*Guangzhou Research*) 2 (1987), 22, 27.

20. Rong Jian, "Cong zhengzhi he jingji de eryuanhua kan jingji gaige he zhengzhi gaige de guanxi" (The Relationship between Political Reform and Economic Reform from the Perspective of Dualism of Politics and Economy), *Zhengzhixue Yanjiu* (Political Science Research) 6 (1987), 13.

21. Ibid., 14.

22. Chen Shi, "Jingji gaige yu zhengzhi ziyou" (Economic Reform and Political Freedom), *Gongren Ribao* (*Worker's Daily*) August 15, 1986, 3.

23. See Lin Yunong, 38.

24. Liu Junning, "Shehui quanli, zhengzhi quanli, jingji quanli" (Social Power, Political Power, Economic Power) *Gaige* (*Reform*) 4 (1988), 161.

25. See Lin Yunong, 38. See also Xing Fensi, "Xianjieduan Zhongguo shehui gaige de ruogan lilun wenti" (A Few Theoretical Problems Concerning China's Social Reform at the Present Stage), *Shehui Kexue Zhanxian* (*Social Science Front*) 1 (1988), 14.

26. He Peiyu, "Lun minzhu zhengzhi de shehui jingji jichu" (On Social, Economic Foundations for Democracy), *Tansuo—Zhesheban* (*Exploration—Philosophy and Social Science Edition*) 1 (1988), 24.

27. Zhou Jianming, "Cong shenfen guanxi dao qiyue guanxi zhuanbian zhi wojian" (My Opinion on the Transition from Status Relationship to Contractual Relationship), *Zhengzhi yu Falu* (*Politics and Law*) 6 (1986), 9–11.

28. Liao Xun, "Lun 'da shehui, xiao zhengfu'" (On Big Society, Small Government), *Zhongguo Xingzheng Guanli* (*Chinese Administration*), 8 (1988), 4–6.

29. Wu Jiaxiang, "Xinquanweizhuyi shuping" (Explaining Neo-Authoritarianism), *Shijie Jingji Daobao* (*World Economic Herald*) January 16, 1989, 12. Wu Jiaxiang and Zhang Bingjiu, "Jijinde minzhu haishi wenjiande minzhu—Wu Jiaxiang and Zhang Bingjiu dui-hualu" (Radical Democracy or Stable Democracy—a Dialogue between Wu Jiaxiang and Zhang Bingjiu), *Guangming Ribao* (*Guangming Daily*) March 31, 1989, 3.

30. Tang Daiwang, "Shehuizhuyi chujijieduan de guojia zhineng" (The Function of the State

at the Preliminary Stage of Socialism), *Zhengzhixue Yanjiu* (*Political Science Research*) 6 (1988), 16–18.

31. Such proposals were made by many Chinese scholars, among them Zheng Shiping (see note 27, above), Yan Jiaqi (see note 16, above), Cai Tuo, "Zhengfu zhineng xintan" (A New Exploration of Government Functions), *Tianjin Shehui Kexue* (*Social Sciences in Tianjin*) 1 (1988), 25–27, and Wu Yue, "Shehui guanli zhineng yu zhengfu jigou gaige" (Social Management Function and the Reform of Government Institutions), *Qinghai Shehui Kexue* (*Social Sciences in Qinghai*) 4 (1988), 4–7.

32. See Cai Tuo and Wu Yue.

33. See Tang Daiwang.

34. Gao Changyun and Shi Yuan, "'Xiao zhengfu da shehui' de Hainan mushi—yizhong zhengzhixue de sikao" (The Hainan Model of 'Small Government, Big Society—A Political Science Reflection), *Hainan Kaifa Bao* (*Hainan Development News*) September 23, 1988, 3.

35. See Liao Xun, 4–6.

36. See Gao Changyun and Shi Yuan.

37. Han Zhulin, "Xiao zhengfu, da shehui—guanyu zhengfu jigou gaige mubiao mushi de tantao" (Small Government, Big Society—Explore the Model for the Reform of Government Institutions), *Shehui Kexue* (*Social Science*) 3 (1989), 31.

38. See Shu-Yun Ma, 182–84.

39. Li Kejing, "Woguode zhengzhi tizhi gaige yu zhengzhixuede fazhan—Zhongguo Shehui Kexue zazhishe zahaokai de 'zhengzhi tizhi gaige' xueshu zuotanhui zongshu" (China's Political System Reform and Development of Political Science—A Summary of the Conference on Political System Reform Organized by the Chinese Journal of Social Sciences), *Zhongguo Shehui Kexue* (*Chinese Social Sciences*) 4 (1986), 3–14.

40. See, for example, Shen Rendao and Yang Ming, "Liyi jituan de gainian he fenlei" (The Concept and Typology of Interest Groups), *Zhengzhixue Yanjiu* (*Political Science Research*) 3 (1986), 19–22.

41. Gu Jialing and Wu Zhilun, "Zhengzhi tizhi gaige de mubiao xuanze" (The Choice of Target for Political System Reform), *Zhengzhixue Yanjiu* (*Political Science Research*) 6 (1987), 10.

42. Wang Huning, "Zhongguo zhengzhi-xingzheng tizhi gaige de jingji fenxi" (An Economic Analysis of China's Political—Administrative System Reform), *Shehui Kexue Zhanxian* (*Social Science Front*) 2 (1988), 115. Zheng Yongnian, "Jingji fazhan yu minzhu zhengzhi" (Economic Development and Democratic Politics), *Guangming Ribao* (*Guangming Daily*) February 13, 1989, 3. Min Qi, "Guanyu zhuanxingqi de Zhongguo zhengzhi" (Chinese Politics in the Transition Period), *Xuexi yu Tansuo* (*Study and exploration*) 4 (1988), 78. See also Bai Wei, "Luelun jingji gaige yu zhengzhi xiandaihua" (On Economic Reform and Political Modernization), *Rencai yu Xiandaihua* (*Human Resources and Modernization*) 1 (1986), 20. Liu Junning, 164. Huang Shaohui, "Lun shehui xieshang duihua zhidu" (On the System of Social Consultation and Dialogue), *Guangming Ribao* (*Guangming Daily*) December 7, 1987, 3. Chi Dao and Ji Ning, "Shehui xieshang duihua 'xin' zai nali?" (What Is 'New' about Social Consultation and Dialogue?), *Liaowang* (*Outlook*) 16 (1988), 18. Zu Xuguang, "Xietiao maodun shi minzhu dangpai canzheng de yige zhongyao fangmian" (Coordinating Contradictions Is an Important Aspect in the Democratic Parties' Participation in Politics), *Renmin Zhengxie Bao* (*The People's Political Consultation News*) June 17, 1988, 3.

43. See Li Ping, Shen Jian, and Ding Wang, 42.

44. See Bai Wei, 30.

45. Jiang Nanyang, "Shehuizhuyi gaige zhongde 'hunluan' zhuangtai jiqi duice" (The State of 'Confusion' in Socialist Reform and the Way to Handle It), *Tansuo—Zhesheban* (*Exploration—Philosophy and Social Science Edition*) 4 (1987). See also Zu Xuguang, 3. Wang Junchang, "Shehui gaige lilun chutan" (An Initial Exploration of the Theory of Social Reform), *Zhejiang Xuekan* (*Zhejiang Journal of Learning*) 3 (1988), 10.

46. See Min Qi, 78.

47. See Bai Wei, 21. See also Wang Huning, "Jianli yizhong xinde zhengzhi fazhan guan" (Form a New Concept of Political Development), *Zhongguo Qingnian Bao* (*China Youth News*) August 19, 1988, 3.

48. See Situ Yan, 5–6. Bai Wei, 21, 23. Wang Huning, Ibid. Xu Yong, "Zhengzhi xiandaihua: shijie yu Zhongguo" (Political Modernization: The World and China), *Shehuizhuyi Yanjiu* (*Socialist Studies*) 4 (1988), 8–13.

49. See Situ Yan, 6; Gu Jialing and Wu Zhilun, 1–3; Zhou Zhongshu, "Zhengque renshi zhengzhi tizhi gaige de jinqi mubiao" (Correctly Understand the Short-Term Target of the Political System Reform), *Xuexi yu Jianshe* (*Learning and Construction*) 5 (1988), 27. Wang Yaohua, "Tan zhengzhi tizhi gaige de changqi mubiao he jinqi mubiao" (On the Long-Term and Short-Term Targets of Political System Reform), *Lilunjie* (*Theoretical Circles*) 5/6 (1988), 18–19. This position appeared to be supported by the regime. See Huang Hai, "Jinxing zhengzhi tizhi gaige de qiangda sixiang wuqi" (A Powerful Ideological Weapon for Political System Reform), *Renmin Ribao* (*People's Daily*) July 27, 1987, 5. Chi Fulin, "Zhengzhi tizhi gaige dadao shenme mudi, baokuo naxie neirong?" (What Are the Objectives and Substances of Political System Reform?), *Liaowang* (*Overlook*) 8 (1987), 9–11.

50. See Chi Dao and Ji Ning, 18.

51. See Huang Shaohui.

52. See Min Qi, 79.

53. Wang Renbo, "Guanyu fenquan mushi de jiazhi sikao" (Evaluative Reflections on the Model of Separation of Powers), *Tansuo—Zhesheban* (*Exploration—Philosophy and Social Science Edition*) 4 (1988), 34, 36.

54. Lu Zhen, "Shi nian fansi: gaige de si da wuqu" (Rethinking the Past Ten Years: Four Big Errors in Reform), *Shulin* (*Books*) 4 (1989), 4.

55. Chen Ziming, "Gaige zhongde zhengzhi yu jingji" (Politics and Economy in the Reform), *Zhengzhixue Yanjiu* (*Political Science Research*) 1 (1987 7–9.

56. See Zheng Yongnian.

57. See Chi Dao and Ji Ning, 18.

58. Xiao Rong, "Guanyu guojia minzhu zhidu de jianshe" (On the Building of the State's Democratic System), *Guangming Ribao* (*Guangming Daily*) January 26, 1989, 3.

59. Huang Shaohui, "Lun zhengzhi xietiao" (On Political Coordination), *Sichuan Shifan Daxue Xuebao: Sheke Ban* (*Journal of Sichuan Normal University: Social Science Edition*) 4 (1988), 5.

60. Li Mingyao, "'Liyi fenhua yu liyi xietiao,' 'zhengzhi minzhu yu zhengzhi wending' xueshu taolunhui zongshu" (A Summary of the Conference on "Interests Differentiation and Interests Coordination" and "Political Democracy and Political Stability"), *Zhengzhixue Yanjiu* (*Political science research*) 2 (1989), 35.

61. Arend Lijphart, *Democracy in Plural Societies* (New Haven: Yale University Press, 1977).

62. Giuseppe Di Palma, *To Craft Democracies* (Berkeley and Los Angeles: University of California Press, 1990).

63. Samuel P. Huntington, *The Third Wave* (Norman: University of Oklahoma Press, 1991).

64. Georg Sorensen, *Democracy and Democratization* (Boulder Colo.: Westview Press, 1993).

65. Zhao Chengxing, "Zhongguo minzhu zhengzhi lilun chutan—quanguo shouci minzhu zhengzhi jianshe yantaohui zongshu" (An Initial Theoretical Exploration on the Building of Democratic Politics in China—A Summary of the First Nationwide Conference on the Building of Democratic Politics), *Lilun Xingxi Bao* (*Theoretical Information News*) November 7, 1988, 1.

66. See Goldman, 332–37.

67. Sun Guohua, "Minzhu jianshe bixu naru fazhi guidao" (The Building of Democracy Must Be in Accordance with the Rule of Law), *Zhongguo Faxue* (*Chinese Legal Science*) 5 (1990), 9.

68. Chen Zhen, "Minzhu shi renlei jingbu he wenming de jiejing" (Democracy Is the Crystalization of Human Progress and Civilization), *Zhongguo Faxue* (*Chinese Legal*

Science) 5 (1990), 11–12.

69. Zhu Changping, "Lun gongmin zhengzhi canyu de zhiduhua" (On Institutionalization of Citizens' Political Participation), *Ningxia Shehui Kexue* (*Ningxia Social Science*) 4 (1990), 15–17.

70. Chen Binhui, "Guojiade guanli zhineng xintan" (New Exploration into the Management Function of the State), *Fujian Xuekan* (*Fujian Journal of Learning*) 3 (1991), 65, 69–71.

71. Li Jing, "Minzhu wenhua yu Zhongguode minzhu jianshe" (Democratic Culture and Democratic Construction in China), *Shehui Kexue* (*Social Science*) 9 (1991), 15–18.

72. Wang Puli, "Lun minzhujizhongzhi de shizhi" (On the Essence of Democratic Centralism), *Guangming Ribao* (*Guangming Daily*) October 7, 1991, 3.

73. Liu Zuoxiang, "Yanjiu quanli zhiyue wenti de lilun jiazhi he shijian yiyi" (The Theoretical Value and Practical Significance in Studying the Issue of Restriction of Power), *Zhengzhi yu Falu* (*Politics and Law*) 1 (1992), 7–10.

74. Rong Yiren, "Jianchi ba shijian zuowei jianyan zhenli de weiyi biaozhun" (Insist on Taking Practice as the Sole Criterion of Truth), *Renmin Ribao* (*People's Daily*) June 15, 1992, 5. Rong was then president of the All China Federation of Industry and Commerce. He later became vice-president of the PRC.

75. "Lun jiefang sixiang" (On the Liberation of the Mind), *Renmin Ribao* (*People's Daily*) editorial, July 4, 1992, 1.

76. Western authors were frequently cited, their views summarized, by Chinese scholars participating in the discussion.

77. Chen Shi, "Zhengfu zhineng bixu zhuanbian" (The Role of Government Must Be Changed), *Gongren Ribao* (*Worker's Daily*), May 15, 1992, 3. While no biographic information about the author is available, we may guess that he has some connection with *Gongren Ribao*, a newspaper controlled by the All China Federation of Trade Unions and known for frequently taking liberal, unorthodox positions. For example, when Wang Ruoshui was barred from publishing in *Renmin Ribao*, he began publishing in *Gongren Ribao* (Goldman, 159, 163, 171).

78. Li Peng, "Jiji tuijing xianji jigou gaige" (Actively Promoting Institutional Reform at the County Level), *Renmin Ribao* (*People's Daily*), July 7, 1992, 1.

79. "Yao qieshi zhuanbian zhengfu zhineng" (The Role of Government Should Be Truly Changed), *Renmin Ribao* (*People's Daily*) editorial, August 5, 1992, 1.

80. Zhang Jingli, "Jiefang hongguan" (Macro-Level Liberation), *Renmin Ribao* (*People's Daily*), August 8, 1992, 3.

81. Shi Xuehua, "Lun shehui zhuanxing yu zhengfu zhineng zhuanbian" (On Social Transition and Changing the Role of the Government), *Tianjin Shehui Kexue* (*Tianjin Social Science*) 2 (1995), 21–23. Yan Qin, "Guanyu zhengzhi tizhi gaige de ruogan sikao" (Reflections on Political System Reform), *Shehui—Shanghai* (*Society—Shanghai*) 9 (1992), 11–13. Cai Tuo, "Shichang jingji yu zhengzhi fazhan" (Market Economy and Political Development), *Tianjin Ribao* (*Tianjin Daily*), February 9, 1993, 6.

82. See Cai Tuo, ibid. See also Yu Keping, "Shehuizhuyi shimin shehui: yige xinde yanjiu keti" (Socialist Civil Society—a New Subject of Research), *Tianjin Shehui Kexue* (*Tianjin Social Science*) 4, 1993, 45–48. Xie Qingkui, "Zhengfu zhineng zhuanbian de hanyi" (The Meaning of Government Role Change), *Jingji Ribao* (*Economic Daily*), May 13, 1993, 7.

83. Fan Yongfu, "Xiang Gang de shehui zizhi he zixun xitong jiqi dui neidi jigou gaige de qishi" (Society's Self-Management and Consultation System in Hong Kong and Its Implications to Institutional Reform in the Mainland), *Hainan Tequ Bao* (*Hainan SEZ News*), October 26, 1993, 3.

84. Wang Jianqin, "Dangqian woguo zhengfu jigou gaige weishenme nanyi tuijing?" (Why Is It Difficult to Carry Out Government Institutional Reforms?), *Qiyejia Bao* (*Entrepreneurs News*), January 6, 1994, 3.

85. See Shi Xuehua, 24–26.

86. Yin Guanghua, "Zhengfu zhineng zhuanbian de san da nandian" (Three Big Difficulties in Changing the Role of Government), *Jingji Ribao* (*Economic Daily*), April 15, 1993, 7.

87. Rong's name was never mentioned in the discussions, perhaps to avoid political controversy.

88. This journal was published in Hong Kong, but many of its contributors were scholars in the mainland. Deng Zhenglai, the chief editor, was a mainland scholar and had been one of the authors of the well-known book series titled *Zouxiang Weilai (Toward the Future)*.

89. Deng Zhenglai and Jing Yuejing, "Jiangou Zhongguode shimin shehui" (Building Civil Society in China), *Zhongguo Shehui Kexue Jikan (Chinese Social Science Quarterly)* 1 (1992), 61.

90. Ibid., 64.

91. Ibid., 59.

92. Ibid., 66.

93. Jing Yuejing, "'Shimin shehui yu Zhongguo xiandaihua' xueshu taolunhui shuyao" (A Summary of the Conference on Civil Society and China's Modernization), *Zhongguo Shehui Kexue Jikan (Chinese Social Science Quarterly)* 5 (1993), 197–202.

94. Guo Dingping, "Woguo shimin shehui de fazhan yu zhengzhi zhuanxing" (Development of Civil Society and Political Transformation in China), *Shehui Kexue (Social Science)* 12 (1994), 52–55, 60.

95. Lu Pinyue, "Zhongguo lishi jingcheng yu shimin shehui zhi jiangou" (China's Historical Progress and the Development of Civil Society), *Zhongguo Shehui Kexue Jikan (Chinese Social Science Quarterly)* 8 (1994), 174.

96. Deng Zhenglai and Jing Yuejing, 66.

97. He Zengke, "Guanyu shimin shehui gainian de jidian sikao" (Some Reflections on the Concept of Civil Society), *Xiandai yu Chuantong (Modernity and Tradition)* 4 (1994), 44–45.

98. Lu Pinyue, 178.

99. Liu Wujun, "Shimin shehui yu xiandai fa de jingshen" (Civil Society and the Spirit of Modern Law), *Faxue (Legal Science)* 8 (1995), 30.

100. Xie Hui, "Quanli yu quanli de gongneng beifang" (The Opposite Functions of Rights and Power), *Ningbo Daxue Xuebao—Renwen Kexue Ban (The Journal of Ningbo University—Human Sciences Edition)* 2 (1995), 96–104.

101. For example, Lu Pinyue suggested that the economic, social, and politial elements of civil society could be attained in three stages. See Lu Pinyue, 178.

102. Sun Liping, "Guojia yu shehui de jiegou fenhua" (Structural Differentiation of State and Society), *Zhongguo Shehui Kexue Jikan (Chinese Social Science Quarterly)*, premier issue, November 1992, 69–76. Xu Guodong, "Shimin shehui yu shimin fa" (Civil Society and Civil Law), *Faxue Yanjiu (Studies in Law)* 4 (1994), 3–9.

103. Jing Yuejing, "Shimin shehui yanjiu jiqi yiyi" (The Study of Civil Society and Its Significance), *Xiandai yu Chuantong (Modernity and Tradition)* 4 (1994), 32. See also Guo Dingping, 54–55, 60; Yu Keping, 48; Zhang Chengfu, "Xingzheng minzhu lun" (On Administrative Democracy), *Zhongguo Xingzheng Guanli (Chinese Administration)* 6 (1993), 23–27.

104. Guo Daohui is a very influential legal scholar, and chief editor of *Zhongguo Faxue*.

105. Guo Daohui, "Renquan, shehui quanli yu fading quanli" (Human Rights, Social Rights, and Legal Rights), *Zhongguo Shehui Kexue Jikan (Chinese Social Science Quarterly)* 3 (1993), 37–49.

106. Guo Daohui, "Shehuizhuyi ziyou—dangdai shehuizhuyi fade jingshen" (Socialist Freedom—the Spirit of Law in Contemporary Socialism), *Faxue (Legal Science)* 10 (1994), 2–6.

107. Guo Daohui, " (Fazhi guojia yu fazhi shehui" (Rule of Law by the State and Rule of Law by the Society), *Politics and Law (Zhengzhi yu Falu)* 1 (1995), 17–20.

108. Ma Changshan, "Cong shimin shehui lilun chufa dui fa benzhi de zai renshi" (Rethinking the Essence of Law According to the Theory of Civil Society, " *Faxue Yanjiu (Studies in Law)* 1 (1995), 41–48.

109. See Xu Guodong, 3–9. Xu's article was named by the editorial board of *Faxue Yanjiu* as one of the best articles published in *Faxue Yanjiu* since 1978.

110. Xie Pengcheng, "Lun dangdai Zhongguo de falu quanwei" (On the Authority of Law in Contemporary China), *Zhongguo Faxue (Chinese Legal Science)* 6 (1995), 3–13.

111. See Liu Wujun, 28–30.

112. Cui Peiting, "Jianli shehuizhuyi shichang jingji tizhi yaoqiu shenhua zhengzhi tizhi gaige" (Building a Socialist Market Economy Requires Further Political System Reforms), *Lilun Yanjiu (Theoretical Studies)* 2 (1993), 2–4.

113. Gong Zhihui, "Zhengzhi tizhi gaige zhongde zhengzhi wending" (Political Stability in Political System Reform), *Shehuizhuyi Yanjiu (Socialist Studies)* 5 (1993), 15–19. See also Cai Tuo, "Shichang jingji," 6; Bao Xinjian, "Jiji tuijing shehuizhuyi zhengzhi xiandaihua" (Actively Promoting Socialist Political Modernization), *Guangming Ribao (Guangming Daily)* December 14, 1992, 3.

114. Wang Song and Sun Li, "Lun jingji liyi duoyuanhua yu zhengzhi yitihua" (On Pluralism of Economic Interests and Political Integration), *Zhongguo Xingzheng Guanli (Chinese Administration)* 7 (1993), 24–27.

115. Guo Dingping, "Cong duoyuan shehui tanji zhengzhi gongshi" (Political Common Understanding in Plural Society, " *Shehui Kexue (Social Science)* 8 (1993), 28–31.

116. Shi Xianmin, "Zhongguo shehui zhuanxingqi de jiegou fenhua yu shuang eryuan shehui jiegou" (Structural Differentiation in China's Transitional Stage and Double Dualist Social Structure), *Zhongguo Shehui Kexue Jikan (Chinese Social Science Quarterly)* 5 (1993), 55–65.

117. Li Jingpeng, "Dangdai Zhongguo shehui liyi jiegou de bianhua yu zhengzhi fazhan" (Changes in the Structure of Social Interests and Political Development in Contemporary China), *Tianjin Shehui Kexue (Tianjin Social Science)* 3 (1994), 31–37.

118. Sun Xiaoxia, "Lun falu yu shehui liyi" (On Law and Social Interests), *Zhongguo Faxue (Chinese Legal Science)* 4 (1995), 52–60.

119. See Yan Qin, 13–14.

120. Gu benhua, "Shichang jingji tiaojianxia quanli jiegou de zouxiang" (The Way the Structure of Power Changes under the Conditions of a Market Economy), *Hunan Shifan Daxue Shehui Kexue Xuebao (The Social Science Journal of the Hunan Normal University)* 2 (1994), 17–21. Recognition of entrepreneurs and intellectuals as influential social groups can also be found in Deng Zhenglai and Jing Yuejing, 61.

121. Jia Dongqiao, "Shichang jingji dui woguo zhengzhi de yingxiang qiantan" (A Brief Discussion of the Impact of a Market Economy on Chinese Politics), *Shehui Kexue (Social Science)* 10 (1993), 12, 25–28.

122. Wang Jiangang, "Duodang hezuo yu shehui zhengzhi wending" (Multiparty Cooperation and Social, Political Stability), *Zhongguo Qingnian Zhengzhi Xueyuan Xuebao (Journal of the China Youth Political Institute)* 6 (1993), 41–45, 49.

123. Wang Song, "Jingji liyi duoyuanhua yu dangdai Zhongguo zhengzhi fazhan" (Pluralism of Economic Interests and Political Development in Contemporary China), *Tansuo yu Zhengming (Exploration and Debate)* 10 (1994), 39–41.

124. Zhou Yezhong, "Lun minzhu yu liyi, liyi jituan" (On Democracy, Interests, and Interest Groups), *Xuexi yu Yanjiu (Learn and Study)* 2 (1995), 70–76.

125. Wang Huning, *Minzhu Zhengzhi (Democratic Politics)* (Hong Kong: Joint Publishing, 1993), 64–68.

126. See Jing Yuejing, "'Shimin shehui yu Zhongguo xiandaihua'," 197–202.

127. Merle Goldman, "Politically Engaged Intellectuals in the Deng-Jiang Era: A Changing Relationship with the Party-State," *China Quarterly* 145 (1996), 49.

128. Ibid., 51.

129. An interesting example of this paradoxical relationship is the one between Wang Huning and Jiang Zemin: Wang is said to have twice rejected Jiang's invitation to go to Beijing before finally accepting it. This may indicate Wang's reluctance to get too close with the regime leadership even though his advice has been actively sought by the latter.

130. This impression is based on my own conversations with a few young Chinese scholars.

7

Plural Institutionalism and the Emergence of Intellectual Public Spaces in China

A Case Study of Four Intellectual Groups

E D W A R D   X .   G U

In contemporary scholarship concerning China's state-society relationship in the 1980s, the conceptual schema of "civil society versus the state" has been widely employed to describe the reemergence of an autonomous social arena independent of the state. The existence of such an arena, much of which was opened up by intellectuals, is further utilized as an important factor for explaining the social upset that erupted in spring 1989. However, a debate over the strength and nature of the emergent arena of societal independent activity in China, and whether the concept of "civil society" is at all applicable to the Chinese case, is now under way.[1] A number of scholars avoid using the concept of *civil society*.[2] Some take a critical view of the simplistic usage of this concept in the present literature.[3] Xue Liang Ding argues that the concept of civil society has little relevance to China, and instead he proposes the model of "institutional parasitism" as an alternate scheme, highlighting that the boundary between state and society in China is vague and indeterminate, and that the nature of so-called independent or autonomous social organizations were actually quasi-autonomous, or "amphibious."[4]

One of the fundamental problems with the civil society approach is that it treats state-society relations as dichotomous, confrontational, and zero-sum. As Ding contends, "the binary conception of civil society versus the state, when bestowed on nonconformity and opposition movements in communist systems, is usually misleading, being applicable only in rare, extreme cases."[5] Therefore, the sceptics of the civil society approach are inclined to offer empirical proof for the interrelated nature of state and society. Yet the pros and cons of the approach are common in that state and society are unnecessarily (and perhaps inaccurately) portrayed as two monolithic blocs, and the relationship between them is singular. The point of difference is the rival characterizations of the two blocs: either confrontational or interrelated.

I do not want to get entangled in a debate on whether a civil society existed in China before the Tiananmen movement or to decribe how an emergent Chinese civil society was dependent upon the party-state. Instead, this chapter's primary attention is given to the following question: Under which institutional constraints could Chinese intellectuals create a number of different types of public spaces in which to pursue their own intellectual activities?[6] To answer this question, this article, first of all, develops another alternative model to the conceptual scheme of "civil society versus the state," what I would like to call "plural institutionalism."[7] Second, the case of four intellectual groups is utilized for an examination of the explanative power of the new model. And, finally, an analysis of how political choices and actions of intellectuals during the 1989 Tiananmen movement were structured by various institutional and historical factors will be provided in light of the new framework.

Plural Institutionalism and the Politics of Intellectuals

The departure point of plural institutionalism is that the holistic images of both state and society should be discarded. Within the communist state, as Jerry F. Hough's model of institutional pluralism has shown, there exists a multiplicity of interests and preferences. The political process revolves around conflicts among a complex set of crosscutting and shifting alliances of persons and groups with divergent interests and preferences.[8] Society is also in fragmentation. There are different social groups, which hold different interests, opinions, identities, orientations, and goals. Even in a social group such as that of intellectuals, there are different segments, which are inclined to establish different relations with the party-state. From the perspective of plural institutionalism, therefore, the institutional forms that shape state-society relations show a great diversity among different social groups and state organs. The diversity of organizational forms of social groupings also evolves in its concrete manifestation, depending upon different institutional and/or noninstitutional (e.g. historical) environments, as well as different patterns of interactions between them over time. In short, plural institutionalism suggests the plurality of the state, the plurality of social groupings, and the plurality of state-society relations.

To examine the numerous complexities of the state-society relationship, plural institutionalism draws insights from new institutionalism, which as a theoretical orientation has aroused an increasing interest among political scientists, economists, sociologists, and historians.[9] The core of new institutionalism as an analytical framework lies at its new definition of *institution*. The English term *institution* has a twofold meaning: "rule" or "regulation" on the one hand, and "organization" on the other. Using this term in its ordinary sense, the institutional and organizational analyses are not separated from each other in the existing literature on Chinese intellectuals. In contrast, a crucial conceptual distinction between "institution" and "organization" is made in the literature of the new institutionalism. According to Douglass North, institutions are the rules of the game in a society, and "organizations" are bodies created by certain groups of individuals bound by some common purpose to achieve certain objectives. The focus of new institutionalism is on institutions as the rules for social actions, and organizations (e.g. state organs, enterprises, institutes, universities, etc.) are treated as the agents of institutional maintainance and institutional change.[10]

The basic point of new institutionalism is that institutions as the rules for social actions should be taken seriously. On the one hand, how institutions sustain and change can become the object of study. On the other hand, institutions are treated as a kind of independent variable for explaining the formation of interests, political choices of social agents, and the outcomes of social actions. New institutionalism of course does not regard the institutional factors as the exclucively decisive variable. Rather it holds that, in explaining how institutions shape the political strategies and influence the outcomes of sociopolitical actions, the complicated interactions between institutional factors and other social, political, economic, and ideational factors should be brought to light by in-depth empirical studies. For one branch of the new institutionalism, so-called historical institutionalism, historical factors have attracted particular attention.[11]

There is no doubt that if the role of rules for social actions in shaping social life is neglected we cannot profoundly understand social life, just as we cannot understand a football match if we do not know its rules. Certainly the rules of social actions are much more complicated than those of sports. Apart from many explicitly written formal institutions (e.g. constitutions, laws, regulations, etc.), there are many informal institutions (such as conventions, customs, and codes of behavior) that to some extent play a more significant role than formal institutions do in shaping social life.[12]

As a kind of social game, the activities of intellectuals to create public spaces and thereby to restructure intellectual-state relations under communist rule must be constrainted by historically evolving institutional settings. The model of plural institutionalism examines a variety of institutional factors as independent variables, from the macrolevel operations of the party-state system to intermediate-level ones such as existing institutional arrangements in different social sectors, and the micro-level conventions, like the importance of personal connections (*guanxi*) for doing everything in China. The distinctiveness of different institutional settings over historical periods and across social realms can lead a variety of intellectuals to different political choices.

Plural institutionalism might also provide us with a theoretical means to probe into the relationship between the "men who make history" and the circumstances under which they are able to do so.[13] It thus avoids the possible structural determinism that often characterizes structural-functionalist, behavioralist, and system-theory approaches. Political choices made by social groups (in particular their core members) are structured, constrained, and refracted by institutions. Yet institutions are themselves also the outcomes (conscious or unintended) of deliberate political strategies, political conflicts, and political choices. Above all, the creation of intellectual public spaces means the change of existing institutional arrangments for the relationship between intellectuals and the state. Hence, while some institutional factors are taken as independent variables, others may be taken as dependent variables. The role of specific individuals contributing to construct various institutional and organizational forms to bridge society and the state—those whom I might call "institution-building entrepreneurs"—is highly emphasized in plural institutionalism. They play an important role in finding out the institutional leeways within the exisiting institutional configuration and establishing public spaces for themselves as well as their followers in as many ways as are legally possible.

For political scientists who wish to understand the politics of intellectuals, plural institutionalism has another advantage: it offers an image of intellectuals not only as social critics but also as rational interest-calculators. This approach, against which Jerome Karabel calls "the grand moralist tradition of discourse about intellectuals" and along with which he favors the "realist" tradition,[14] puts its primary focus on identifying the historically evolving institutional conditions and political processes that shape the actual political actions of different groups of intellectuals. In the meantime, although doubting the applicability of the civil society approach, plural institutionalism by no means rules out the existence of a confrontational relationship beween intellectuals and the state. Rather, its new institutionalist orientation contains a potentially powerful analysis of intellecual radicalism.

Approaching the Intellectual Public Spaces in Post-Mao China: Four Relational Patterns and Four Organizational Forms

There are few intellectuals who would not be willing to be able to freely express their views on public affairs, and to live in a public space with independence and autonomy. The fulfillment of these desires, however, is not always guaranteed. On the one hand, the legal guarantee for intellectual autonomy from the state may not be sufficient. On the other hand, the societal structure underlying independent public spaces may be underdeveloped. In communist China, the institutional basis of intellectual public spaces was always extremely weak before the time of reforms. As the most institutionalized forms of public spaces, newspapers and magazines were almost totally controlled by the party-state. In the late period of the Cultural Revolution, the control capacity of the party-state bureaucracy upon society declined under the lash of Maoist revolutionary waves, and the ultra-leftist official ideology was losing its persuasiveness. Thus, some small circles, networks, or "salons," as they were named—wherein young intellectuals were keen to discuss public affairs and engage in nonofficial (or even underground) literary and theoretical writings—became more and more active in several large cities, particularly in Beijing. During the 1978 and 1979 Democracy Wall Movement, big-character posters (dazibao) and nonofficial magazines (samizdat) were institutional forms by which young intellectuals expressed their arguments. However, these institutional forms basically disappeared in the wake of Deng Xiaoping's suppression of the movement in early 1979.[15]

In the 1980s, with the deepening of the reforms and the further loosening of ideological control brought about by the reforms, the Chinese party-state and society came to be more and more complicated and plural, and, as a consequence, a few institutional leeways for the development of public spaces were available. Chinese intellectuals quickly invented many organizational forms for establishing their public spaces. Nevertheless, Chinese intellectuals never formed an integrated societal group or class. Among them there were many groups, informal or formal, and there were also many individuals who were not affiliated with any group. They held various ideas, showed diverse preferences, and took a variety of actions. The confrontation of Chinese intellectuals with the party-state was neither a coherent nor a mainstream phenomenon. Chinese intellectual life was mainly characterized as the cautious and careful development of its members' own independence within the plurally channeled and frequently changing institutions and organizations. The institutionalization of intellectual public spaces was developed in a moderate manner.

Intellectual public spaces belong to what Philip C. C. Huang calls the "third realm" and defines as "a space intermediate between state and society in which both participated."[16] Along with such a conception, we further divide the third realm into different subspaces to analyze the influence of state, society, or both, on the formation and operation of public spaces. To do that, four ideal-typical patterns—in terms of the roles of either state or society, or both, in the formation of intellectual public spaces and in terms of the structuring of their relations with the state—can be presented here. The first of these is the *state-generated and establishment* pattern, in which the intellectual-power elite within the state establishes some official or semiofficial institutions, and attempts to operate them as a transmission belt, serving the party-state. The second is the *society-originated and establishment* pattern. With this model, nongovernmental intellectual activists form their own organizations in society, and later they enter into the establishment, making their own organizations as a part of the establishment. The third is the *autonomous from the state* pattern. In this type, nongovernmental intellectuals have their own organizations in society, but later they—intentionally or unintentionally—do not enter into the establishment and only maintain a lukewarm relationship with the party-state. Failing to be integrated within the establishment, the organizations they establish seem to be, to a considerable extent, independent of or autonomous from the party-state. The fourth is the *confrontational with the state* pattern. This pattern characterizes the public space for dissident intellectuals, who keep a position of confrontation with or opposition to the party-state.

In the first two of the above-listed relational patterns, while the organizations established by establishment intellectuals are within the party-state and in principle are official, they exist, as Tang Tsou says, "at the outer limit of the boundary of the state, touching on society in many ways."[17] In the last two, the intellectual public spaces are located within society and outside the state.

The last model shows the lowest degree of institutionalization, because all the institutionalized or organized activities run by those who are suspected by the party-state to be dissidents would suffer serious suppression. After the crackdown on the Democracy Wall Movement in 1979, there were actually no dissident organizations or groups, merely dissident individuals in China.

Among the intellectual organizations formed in the state-generated manner, the most important are those research institutes of the Chinese Academy of Social Sciences (CASS), various media and publishing houses, and a set of premier Zhao Ziyang–backed research centers under the State Council that was founded between 1980 and 1982.[18] The CASS mainly serves the ideological-theoretical constructions necessary for the party-state's rule; media and publishing houses serve to produce ideological propaganda and theoretical dissemination; and the research centers under the State Council serve (or served) as information collection and policy consultancies. Many influential academic associations are also formed in a state-generated way.

The members of the "democratic elite," as Merle Goldman calls them, wielded their power and influence in state-generated public spaces. Some of them (e.g. Yu Guangyuan, Su Shaozhi, Yan Jiaqi) were high-ranking officials in the reform-inclined institutes of the CASS, and some were senior editors of official newspapers and magazines, for example, the *People's Daily*'s Wang Ruoshui and Hu Jiwei and the *New Observer*'s Ge Yang.[19] Most of them actively participated in the so-called Emancipate the Mind movement, which was launched in 1978 by Hu Yaobang. The movement heavily attacked the legitimacy of Maoism and thereby created an ideological atmosphere conducive to the political victory of the reformists, represented by Deng Xiaoping, in an intense power struggle within the Communist Party.[20] Formal intellectual groups were as hardly found in the state-generated and establishment types of intellectual public spaces, however. While it was because of the party-state's serious crackdown that formal organizations scarcely emerged among disssident intellectuals, it was because of the intellectuals' own self-disciplinary behavior, resulting from long-term institutional restraint, that it was difficult for a formal group life to exist within the establishment. Under certain conventional norms of the party-state, formal group activities not run by party leaders could not avoid the political charge of factionalism. Thus, the democratic elite never formed an independent political group, still less an organization; it was just an informal network, which Goldman calls "Hu Yaobang's intellectual network" since its main members had various personal and organizational connections to Hu.[21] Of course, there were a few members of the democratic elite, such as astrophysicist Fang Lizhi and historian Bao Zunxin, who had nothing to do with the network.

Intellectual group life existed mainly in the two intermediate types of public spaces. Here I will focus on four intellectual groups, which were not only among the most influential groups in 1980s Chinese intellectual life, but also typical of the four organizational forms of intellectual groupings; they are: (1) research groups, (2) editorial committees engaging in editing series of books, (3) nonofficial institutions, and (4) nonofficial academies. All four groups were society-originated, but only one of them was incorporated into the establishment.

The four groups were all based in Beijing. Ideologically, they encouraged intellectuals to cast off the yoke of the party-state's cultural hegemony. Organizationally, they vacillated between the party-state and society. The first group, the Research Group on Problems of China's Rural Development (hereafter abbreviated as the Development Group), stepped from society to the establishment after successfully helping the reformers within the Communist Party (represented by Zhao Ziyang and Wan Li) defeat their political rivals during the policy dispute over the implemetation of the household responsibility system (HRS) in rural areas. The second group, the editorial committee of the Toward the Future book series (hereafter abbreviated as the "Future Group"), experienced an arduous process of institutionalization, although it might be seen as the "cultural wing" of the first group. The third group consisted of young intellectuals who were concerned with the problem of China's political development, Chen Ziming and Wang Juntao being its core. They established an autonomous, nongovernmental organization, the Beijing Social and Economic Sciences Institute (hereafter abbreviated as BSESI). The fourth group was the International Academy of Chinese Culture (*Zhongguo Wenhua Shuyuan* in Chinese, hereafter abbreviated as the "Culture Academy"), which, as a nongovernmental organization, pursued independent academic research in cultural studies and undertook culturally related education.

None of the four relational patterns of the intellectual-state relationship and the four organizational forms of intellectual groupings was dominant in the 1980s. The different relationship between intellectuals and the state depended upon varying choices by the different intellectuals, and their different choices, in turn, were structured in a host of ways by various institutional and historical conditions. Among these restraining conditions, some were universal, some particular; some were macro-level, some intermediate level, some microlevel, and some very personal. Focusing on those particular intermediate-level and personal elements, as well as their interactions with those universal and macrolevel in nature, we may provide answers to the prior question of why the political choices and outcomes (that is, the institutionalized relationship between intellectual groups and the party-state) differed from one intellectual group to another.

Group Formation in the Chinese Intellectual Life: Institutional Constraints and Personal Choices

This section describes in detail the formation of the four intellectual groups, analyzes the different processes of their institutionalization, and discusses the parts they played in changing the state-society relationship in 1980s China.

The Development Group: From a Research Group to Two Think Tanks

In the mid to late 1970s, as a new development of the power struggle inside the Communist Party, the reformist faction that argued for the abandonment of the

Maoist political and economic policies got the upper hand within the establishment. In society, young intellectuals intensively concerned about their country and their people were increasingly active. Small personal networks of such people multiplied, their scope extended, and the content of mutual exchange became richer. By 1978 there were many "seminars" or "salons" in Beijing, where young intellectuals exchanged plenty of political information and rumors, as well as theoretical arguments, with each other.[22] All the salons were informal, with no established hosts, no regular locations, and no fixed participants. Nevertheless, in each salon, there were some core members whose personal characters, family backgrounds, and political preferences were among the important factors in attracting and selecting participants.

A few research groups were born from these salons and, among them, the Development Group later became the most well known.[23] The founder and the later organizational leader of the Development Group was Chen Yizi. As an activist of youth work, Chen in the 1950s got to know Hu Yaobang, then secretary general of the Central Committee of the Communist Youth League (CYL). During the Cultural Revolution, Chen fell at the hands of the political purge and was sent down to a commune in Henan province.[24]

In 1978, Chen returned to Beijing. With the direct help of Hu Yaobang (then director of the Department of Organization of the Chinese Community Party [CCP], in charge of the party-state's personnel affairs), Chen obtained a research job at the Institute of Agricultural Economics of the CASS. In many salons, mainly in biweekly meetings, Chen got to know more active-minded young intellectuals. Among them, Wang Xiaoqiang and Wang Xiaolu, both editors of the CASS-based journal *Drafts* (*Weidinggao*), kept in touch with many small intellectual circles at that time.[25] Because of their encouragement, a number of youngsters published their virgin writings in *Drafts*, giving novel, courageous evaluations of the Communist Party's ideology and practice. Among intellectual circles, Chen Yizi was conspicious due to his association with anti-Maoist rural reform, the introduction of the HRS.

From 1978 to 1980, the HRS policy, which had been viewed by Maoists for a long time as a kind of "capitalist means," was secretely carried out by peasants in some provinces, in particular in Anhui and Sichuan, where Wan Li and Zhao Ziyang, both the top leaders of the two provinces before 1979, backed the institutional change pushed voluntarily by peasants. In Beijing, however, an intense political struggle was conducted within party leadership on whether or not the HRS should be implemented. Large numbers of high-ranking leaders deeply influenced by Maoism, including then party chairman Hua Guofeng, were firmly against the HRS policy and regarded it as a sign of the so-called capitalist restoration.[26]

During the spring-summer of 1980, Chen Yizi went to Anhui to conduct a comprehensive investigation. In his report, he presented a clear-cut stand on supporting the Anhui reformist practice, commending the HRS as the "great creation of the Chinese peasantry."[27] This report at once attracted Hu Yaobang's and Deng Liqun's attention. In order to attract more official attention, Chen formed the Development Group, with twenty or so core members, then mostly students of economics at the Chinese People's University, the Beijing College of Economics, and Beijing University (hereafter "Beida"). At the beginning the group was informal, amateur, and with little difference from other university students' academic associations.[28] In January, 1981, the Development Group's formal inaugural meeting was held at Beida. Deng Liqun (then secretary of the Secretariat of the CCP Central Committee) and Du Runsheng (then director of the Rural Policy Study Office of the CCP Central Committee) attended the meeting and gave speeches, expressing their support to the group.[29]

In late 1980 and early 1981, the university and college election campaigns for the representatives of local People's Congresses, the only free and democratic election campaigns in China, had just ended,[30] and authorities were highly sensitive to any voluntarily organized students' group activity, normally taking measures to bar such activities. Only the Development Group was quickly given official recognition and support. According to Zhu Jiaming, a leading establishment economist and adviser to Zhao Ziyang who had intimate ties with Chen Yizi, Wang Xiaoqiang, and others, the Development Group obtained powerful support from Deng Liqun, Du Runsheng, and Zhao Ziyang succesively in the process of its development. They worked like a three-stage rocket, pushing the members of the group up to the top status of the establishment policy advisorship.[31] Yet why did the Development Group enjoy such a privilege?

First, the membership structure of the Development Group is of significance. Some members of the group were the sons and daughters of high-ranking cadres, and the main leaders of the group were party members. In addition, none of the group had been involved in nonestablishment political activities like the Democracy Wall Movement and university and college election campaigns. Thus, all the members of the group were politically reliable in the eyes of the old cadres. Second, being personally connected to high-ranking officialdom has always served as a key factor for the Development Group's political rise. Among the group membership, Deng Yingtao and Du Ying are the son and the son-in-law of Deng Liqun, and Bai Ruobing is the son of Bai Jiefu, then vice governor of Beijing, who had been a close comrade-in-arms with Du Runsheng since the Yan'an period. Through these personal connections, some core members of the group were often the honored guests of Deng's and Du's family.[32] Third, and most fundamentally, on the policy debate over the implementation of the HRS, Deng Liqun, Du Runsheng, and Zhao Ziyang all stood on the side of reform. Yet, since this reform had not been endorsed by the party-state, the bottom-to-top information flow within the existing bureaucratic hierarchy was highly selective, generally pandering to the political preference of the more orthodox side. Most of the information beneficial to the reformers was blocked at a variety of low and intermediate levels within bureaucracy. Therefore, to the reformers within the party-state, there was a need for the emergence of outside experts who had not yet been influenced by bureaucrats and who were capable of providing reformers with accurate information on the basis of actual investigations.

In the summer of 1981, the Development Group conducted a large-scale on-the-spot investigation into the actual effects of the HRS in Chu County of Anhui Province. The investigation fund was from the CASS Research Project on Rural Development in China, and this project, according to a contract signed between the group and the Institute of Agricultural Economics of the CASS, was solely undertaken by the Development Group.[33] It is believed that the financial arrangement for the project was made under the guidance of Deng Liqun, who then was also the vice president of the CASS. As Yang Guansan recalls, the fund amounted to more than one million yuan, a huge amount in China.[34] In addition, the Development Group also had letters of introduction from the Study Office of the CCP Central Secretariat under Deng's rule. Without these letters, the local authorities would not have allowed the group to conduct its investigation.[35]

The results of the investigation, often called "Chu County Reports" (*Chuxian baogao*), provided the reformers with the theoretical weapon to defeat the conservatives within the party-state. Premier Zhao Ziyang wrote comments on the reports, praising them for clarifying the rural situation since the implementation of the HRS. The reports, with Zhao's commendation and endorsement, were transmitted throughout the bureaucratic organizations at all levels, and caused wide repercussions.[36]

After this, under the political sponsorship of Zhao Ziyang and Deng Liqun, the status of the Development Group shifted from an informal, amateur students' research group to a formal but privileged section in the Institute of Agricultural Economics of the CASS, directly under the leadership of Du Runsheng. In October 1981, the legitimation of the HRS was endorsed by the CCP Central Working Conference on Rural Affairs. The summary of the Conference as CCP Central Committee Document No. 1 of 1982 was transmitted throughout the party. Since then, the HRS has quickly spread over the whole country, and China's rural reform has achieved a breakthrough.[37] Some core members of the Development Group participated in drafting Document No.1.

The formal institutionalization of the Development Group within the establishment signaled the growing influence of the middle-aged and young economists on China's economic policy making. Besides the Development Group, there were a few other small middle-aged and young economist circles in the CASS, which came to show their talents in the policy studies on China's urban economic reforms in the mid-1980s. From 1985 onward, with Zhao Ziyang's promotion, certain research organizations, mainly consisting of middle-aged and young intellectuals, were set up one after another. The most well-known among them were the Chinese Institute for the Study of Reforms in the Economic System (*Zhongguo jingji tizhi gaige yanjiusuo*, hereafter abbreviated as the CISRES), the Chinese Institute for the Study of the Rural Development (*Zhongguo nongcun fazhan yanjiushuo*, CISRD), and the Beijing Association of Young Economists (*Beijing qingnian jingji xuehui*, BAYE). Some of the leading members of the Development Group split off to be the main leaders and key researchers of the first two institutes. The BAYE converged almost all of the elite of the middle-aged and young establishment economists, and Zhao Ziyang's political secretary, Bao Tong, was taken up as its first chairman.[38] These organizations have been widely called "Zhao Ziyang's think tanks."

The Future Group: The Emergence of the Chinese Encyclopedia School

From an ideological standpoint, the 1980s were characteristic of the influx of Western ideas in social sciences and humanities. With the alteration of the structure of ideological alternatives, the legitimacy of the Communist Party's orthodox ideology, Marxism-Leninism and Maoist thought, collapsed. All China specialists agree that the legitimacy crisis was one of the most important historically contextual factors in the events leading to the 1989 Tiananmen movement. The large-scale influx of Western learning was promoted by the so-called series fever (*congshu re*), which was initiated by the enormous success of the Toward the Future book series edited by the Future group.

The intellectual and organizational leader of the Future group, Jin Guantao, a researcher affialiated with the Chinese Academy of Sciences, was one of the most influential figures in 1980s Chinese intellectual life. In the late 1970s and early 1980s, Jin and his wife Liu Qingfeng became famous among various circles (or salons) of young intellectuals for their historical theory on the superstable structure of China's premodern society, which echoed the criticism of the Chinese ancient authoritarian tradition in the Emancipate the Mind movement.[39] Nevertheless, Jin was not satisfied with this limited-scope influence and intended to spread it to the young generation of university students. What was in his mind was to form a Chinese "encyclopedia school," launching a mighty enlightenment movement in China.[40] In 1982, Jin organized an editorial committee (EC), the Future Group, purporting to edit an all-embracing series entitled "Towards the Future," introducing the newest intellectual tides home and abroad, in particular the works of Jin himself. His ambitious enterprise would take off.

In the early 1980s, however, there were many institutional barriers in getting this series published. The press system was seriously under the party's control. On the one hand, most of the translated books, in particular the translations of Western works, could only be published and distributed "internally," which meant that these books were only accessible to those who held a certain high-status post within the establishment hierarchy. On the other hand, according to the related regulations, the ultimate power for going over manuscripts was held by the party's committee for the press. To impose their own influence upon the publishing decision, the Future Group strove from the very beginning to seize the ultimate power over manuscripts for their own hands. Three conditions needed to be met. First, they needed to get the EC attached to a formal institute within the establishment, and to ideologically receive the leadership of the party organization of this institute; second, with respect to the problem of who holds the ultimate power for going over manuscripts, they needed to reach a tacit agreement with the press, letting its party committee grasp the power in principle while the EC would hold it in reality; and, finally, it was significant for them to obtain recognition or even support from high-ranking party officials.

Virtually all of these institutional obstacles were overcome, one by one, by Jin and his comrades. First, they gained support from the party committee of the CASS Institute for Youth Studies. Its head, Zhong Peizhang, a reformist middle-level party official and intellectual, admired and encouraged Jin's proposal for a Chinese enlightenment movement. Zhong's subordinate, Tang Ruoxin, an admirer and student of Jin's historical theory, became the co-vice-director of the EC. Second, the Sichuan People's Press decided to publish the series through the recommendation of Liu Maocai, Liu Qingfeng's brother, who then was a leader of the Sichun Province Academy of Social Sciences and thereby had a certain influence upon local publishing circles. A tacit agreement on the ultimate power over manuscripts was settled between the two sides. Finally, Jin's plan received "spiritual support" (*guanhuai*) from Deng Liqun; personal connection was of absolute importance in their obtaining Deng's support. Liu Qingfeng's father was once a close comrade-in-arms to Deng Liqun in Yan'an. Deng's daughter was a good friend of Jin and Liu. And *The Economic Cybernetics*, the first work by Deng's son Deng Yingtao, had been accepted by the EC to be published in its series.[41]

In the spring and summer of 1984, the first parts of the Toward the Future series were published and quickly became best-sellers. Historical timing was crucial to the series' success; at that time, rural reform had achieved preliminary gains, and urban reform had been put on the policy agenda of the party-state. The media was virtually dominated by a plethora of pro-reform propaganda. Under such an ideological atmosphere, the craving of young intellectuals (in particular, university students) for knowledge was awakened. Yet what the present press system had offered were still books full of platitudes. There was a small number of the so-called internally distributed books in translation at the time, but it was difficult for university students to have access to them. As well, these internally distributed books were mostly the translations of Western academic books, which were too abstruse for university students.

The Toward the Future series, with its completely novel design format, writing style, and intellectual content, filled a vacancy in the book market. It combined Western, mass-market format with modernist cover designs. In the style of writing, the series is characterized as popular and easy to understand. Its content highlights the interdisplinary character, in particular stressing the combination of natural and social sciences. Among the twelve books of the first batch are Jin Guantao's book, popularizing his historical theory, and Liu Qingfeng's book, discussing the reasons why modern science did not emerge in China (a question put forward by Joseph Needham). Both incorporate theories from the natural sciences, such as system theory, information theory, and cybernetics, into historical studies.

Within one year, the Toward the Future series was reprinted twice, with more than 200,000 copies of each book produced. By 1988, there were seventy-four books in the series, including translations of Max Weber, Robert Merton, Kenneth Arrow, János Kornai, and Joseph Levenson, to name a few. Jin's six important books on history and philosophy were also published in the series.

The series' success in the market brought a twofold benefit to both the publisher and the EC: increased visibility and an improved financial state. As luck would have it, in mid-1984, the conservative "Eliminating Spiritual Pollution" campaign was beaten in an election against a more large-scale ideological countercampaign, backed by Hu Yaobang and Zhao Ziyang. This latter campaign propagated the "Third Wave" and the "Western new technological revolution" in name,[42] and the reform-and-openness policies in reality.[43] Because of the interaction of the microlevel benefit in cultural and economic interests and the macrolevel change of an increasingly looser ideological atmosphere, the arrangement that editorial committees organized by intellectuals would edit a number of book series and presses would publish them became a model followed by others. A "series fever" took place.

The significance of this series fever was embodied not only in the alternation of the structure of the ideological alternatives through the massive introduction of Western ideas, but also in institution building in the realm of the state-society relationship. The EC became an organizational form for intellectual group life and the public space, within which intellectuals with similar orientations met regularly to discuss a wide range of subjects and carry out research, writing and publishing their favorite books. The EC also provided a source of solidarity within each intellectual group. Rarely did any intellectual groups exist without their ECs and book series, which provided the institutional means for different groups to form their own collective identities. Administratively, all the ECs registered themselves as organizations affiliated with working units with the party-state establishment, accepting their leadership in name but possessing a considerable autonomy in reality. This institutional arrangment later evolved into a so-called affiliation (*guakao moshi*), which was applicable to the administrative registration of all the nongovernmental organizations (NGOs). From 1986 onward, with the deepening of the economic reform, presses were mostly ordered by the state to assume sole resposibility for their profits or losses. Under the financial pressure, then, many presses directly sold their rights of publishing[44] to ECs run by intellectuals or even private book-publishing businessmen, and did not fundamentally care about the concrete content of books as long as they were not "politically incorrect." It thus came to be increasingly difficult for the party-state to impose ideological control on the publishing of books. Although there would periodically be trouble for publishing directly anti-Marxist books, it was increasingly possible for non-Marxist or indirectly anti-Marxist books to get published, even become best-sellers.

The members of the Future Group around the EC of the Toward the Future series consisted of several well-known middle-aged and young establishment economic policy intellectuals. Chen Yizi was among the advisorship for the EC; Wang Xiaoqiang and He Weiling, both former vice-directors of the Development Group, were core members. Some books written by members of the Development Group were published in the Future Group's series. In 1986, after the CASS Institute for Youth Studies (the EC's pendant-and-dependent unit) was eliminated in the administrative reform, the EC reestablished its pendant-and-dependent relationship with the CISRES.[45]

After the first batch of the series was published, Jin Guantao made a great effort to get the activities of the Future Group institutionalized. For this purpose, Jin first sent an application to Deng Liqun, attempting to establish the Toward the Future Press and to let Jin himself be its manager-in-chief. However, this plan failed to gain Deng's support, and eventually ended up with nothing settled.[46] As a second step, Jin adopted a suboptimal strategy, sending a letter to Deng Liqun to seek his support in the publishing of a journal, *Toward the Future*.[47] In August 1986, the publishing of the quarterly began with Jin Guantao as its editor-in-chief and Wang Xiaoqiang one of the vice editors-in-chief.

By the second half of 1988, the success of the BSESI, mastered by Chen Ziming, and the Cultural Academy, led by Tang Yijie, set up for intellectuals good examples for imitation. There emerged a wave of establishing *minban* (literally meaning "run by people," equivalent to "nongovernmental" or "nonofficial") institutes among intellectuals. With the highest degree of institutionalization, the minban institute became the intellectuals' most favorite organizational form for the public space, in which they could not only freely discuss, freely express, and freely engage in research, but also make more money. In other words, by establishing their own minban institute, intellectuals could shake off control by the party-state, both intellectually and economically.

As the wave continued, the earnest wish that Jin Guantao kept in mind was to set up his own formal organization, run by the members of the Future Group, named the Twenty-First Century Institute. According to his plan, this institute should make a reference to the institutional model of the Cultural Academy, but the focal point of the educational and academical activities in the institute should be geared toward his own historical, philosophical, and cultural theories. Jin was aware that a new cultural hegemony of his thoughts would not be formed until they could be learned, studied, and finally accepted by the younger generation of intellectuals.[48] The Twenty-First Century Institute was established at the end of 1988, but, largely because of its poor financial situation, it was not successful. It seemed that the only public activity it involved was the cosponsorship with the Cultural Academy of an international conference on the May Fourth Movement, convened on May 28–30, 1989.

The BSESI: The Establishment of a Nongovernmental Institute

The emergence of the group around Chen Ziming and Wang Juntao and their organizational base, the BSESI, has been widely seen as the mark of the emergence of a civil society in China.[49] This supposition looks by no means groundless. The BSESI was a minban institute, independent of the state. In particular, it achieved completely finicial autonomy. Of course, to say the BSESI was independent of the state does not mean that it was totally separated from the state. During the process of its institutionalization, the Chen-Wang group once obtained a number of small grants from the establishment for their research on the civil servant system and personnel management.[50] And, as a necessary condition for the registration, every minban institute must be affiliated with (*guakao*) an organization within the establishment, politically under the leadership of the Party committee in these establishment organs (*guakao danwei*). Normally, however, the political supervision of the etablishment organs upon the minban institutes is just an empty principle, and the former scarcely intervene in the everyday activities of the latter.[51]

The formation of the independent intellectual public space was not necessarily the one Chen Ziming (or his comrades) would have deliberately chosen for themselves; it was forced upon them by interactions between the institutional environment in which they acted and their own personal experiences. In the mid-1980s, Chen, Wang, and their comrades had been widely regarded as veteran democratic activists. They were active participants in all previous democratic movements: the 1976 Tiananmen demonstration (later known as the April Fifth Movement), the 1978 and 1979 Democracy Wall Movement, and the 1980 University and College Election Campaign.[52] Their deep involvement in these pre-1981 democractic movements imposed a double influence upon their activities throughout the 1980s: both the psychological basis of their group identity and the historical burden for their group institutionalization. Not only political strategies but also political preferences they held and goals they pursued were shaped by both institutional and historical contexts.

After the election campaigns at the end of 1980, a few campaigners organized a Research Group on Problems of National Conditions and Youth (hereafter abbeviated as the Youth Group), and Chen was a core figure. For a while this group enjoyed equal popularity with the Development Group among young intellectuals; the former was called the "Youth Party," the latter the "Peasantry Party."[53] At the beginning the members of the Youth Group wished to model themselves on what the Development Group had done, entering into the establishment to be policy advisers to high-ranking reformist leaders. Hu Yoabang once showed his personal concern about the Youth Group, dispatching some staff members of the Communist Youth League (CYL) to interview its core figures. The Youth Group was affiliated with the Institute for the Study of Youth Studies of the CYL, and undertook some contract research projects with grants from the CYL, the State Science and Technology Commission (SSTC), and the State Economic Reform Commission (SERC).[54]

However, the Youth Group did not possess the political advantages that the Development Group did: more high-ranking cadres' children, more party members, and fewer former democratic activists. Therefore it was very hard for the Youth Group to earn political support from high-ranking officials, whereas it was very easy to be confronted with political suspicions. Not surprisingly, the Youth Group quickly experienced growing political pressure. At the that time, the majority of the 1980 election campaign activists, except for those who were high-ranking cadres' children, suffered varying degrees of political discrimination after they graduated from universities or colleges. Chen and Wang were also burdened by their involvement in the April Fifth Movement. Although taking a political stand to support Deng's reform line, they were seen as troublemakers and blacklisted by the police. Their whereabouts and activities were closely monitored. Many party-state institutes, which originally had no idea about these people and would have liked to entrust them with research projects, later broke their promises one after another because of the fear of possible political troubles. Thus, the sources of research funds were almost exhausted. By 1984, the Youth Group was disbanded.[55]

From 1984 onward, in the wake of economic reforms in urban China, waves of "business fever" began. Without funds from official channels, the only option to Chen and his comrades was to make money on their own. Chen Ziming, Wang Zhihong (Chen's wife), and Li Shengping (who was a participant in the 1980 election campaign at Beida's First Branch College and elected as the people's representative[56]) set up a highly profitable business, the North Books and Magazines Distributing Corporation. Later, Chen and his wife established two correspondence colleges, at which the tuition income was very sizable.[57] When they had enough funds, the discussion on politics became active again; a set of informal or formal seminars on political problems were hosted by Chen and his comrades. On July 27, 1986, they organized the Preparatory Group for the Young Political Scientists Association, in order to establish their own organization imitating the BAYE. The members of this group also founded the Chinese Institute for Politics and Administration (CIPA).[58]

Not only did Chen's successful reconstruction of the institutional sphere for his own and his comrades' research activities result from the direct loosening of political control, but it also benefitted from the diversification of the party-state institutions. In the mid-1980s, under the party-state's reform program on its science and technology management system, the establishment of minban research or consultancy institutes was encouraged by policies.[59] There were two main institutional conditions for setting up such an institute: not applying for the state's financial appropriations, and finding an establishment organ with which an affiliation relationship could be established. The institutional changes that took place in other social realms, but not the direct change in the institutional arrangement for the party-state's control over intellectuals, gave the institutional leeway to Chen Ziming to establish their own organizations. The financial resources of the CIPA were mainly the incomes of the two correspondence colleges mastered by Chen, plus fragmentary funds collected from other minban companies. Institutionally, it was pendant and dependent upon the Talents Exchange Center of the SSTC.[60] Here again, personal connections were indispensable to the establishment of the pendant-and-dependent relationship: Chen had the personal friendship of the director of the Talents Exchange Center.

Even at this stage, Chen and his colleagues had not abandoned the hope of entering into the establishment. What they did both intellectually and organizationally was to imitate what the middle-aged and young establishment economic policy intellectuals had done. At that moment, the CCP's Thirteenth Congress was about to be held, and the reform of the political system would be on its agenda. Under the leadership of Bao Tong, the Research Office on the Reform of Political System (RORPS) was formed in charge of the proposal discussions and policy advice on political reform; it was controlled by some members of Zhao Ziyang's think tanks.[61] Some members of the CIPA were recruited into the RORPS, but Chen Ziming, Li Shengping, Wang Juntao, and Min Qi, the backbone of the CIPA, were pushed aside because of their personal backgrounds and the intense competition between them and the establishment's economic policy intellectuals. Once again, they lost a chance to enter into the establishment.[62]

In December 1986, the members of the CIPA faced another political setback when student demonstrations demanding democracy broke out in Shanghai and Beijing.[63] Because of the gratuitous suspicion and neurotic vigilance over the activities of the former democratic campaigners, the CIPA was seen as a "black hand" of the student campaigns by some organs of the party-state system and was for a while subject to political harassment. Meanwhile, an internal conflict on management affairs occurred between the two leaders of the CIPA, Chen Ziming and Li Shengping. Beset with both internal and external difficulties, the CIPA was compelled to disband. A couple of months later, some of the leading members of the CIPA split off to form two new minban institutes, Chen Ziming's BSESI and Li Shengping's Beijing Scientific and Social Development Institute (SSDI).[64]

In envisaging the political reality with which they were faced, Chen began a serious discussion of the development strategy of the BSESI with its backbone members, Wang Juntao, Min Qi, and others. They decided to cast off the illusion of being establishment advisers and took an independent and autonomous road, deciding to run the BSESI as a nongovernmental think tank.[65] During the two-year period from 1987 to 1989, the BSESI established two branch organs, the Beijing Talents Evaluation and Examination Center and the Chinese Poll Center. With the growing interest shown in theories on political modernization and political culture, Chen and his friends engaged in a number of ambitious translation and research projects.

In 1988, after nearly one year of effort, the everyday operation of the BSESI was proceeding normally. Still, one defect was that the BSESI did not yet issue its own regular publications. Hence, Chen acted very quickly when found out that the newspaper *Economics Weekly*—run by the Chinese Union of Societies for Economic Studies (CUSES), the largest state-generated academic association, set up by the veteran reform-oriented establishment theoretican Yu Guangyuan—was urgently seeking investment due to budget constraints. Under the party-state's regulations on publishing affairs, running a newspaper requires the specific permission of both the party's propaganda department and the state institutes in charge of managing media and publications. Conventionally, it was (and still is) impossible for a minban institute to get this sort of permission. For Chen, to take over the editorship of the *Economics Weekly* by investing in it was a good way to bypass all the institutional barriers for running a newspaper. On Febuary 29, 1988, an agreement concerning the takeover of the editorship was mutually signed by the office of *Economics Weekly* and the BSESI. The posts of editor-in-chief and vice editor-in-chief were taken up, respectively, by He Jiadong, the former editor-in-chief of the Workers Publishing House and now an advisor to the BSESI, and Wang Juntao. The post-takeover *Economics Weekly* published from March 20 onward, and, among intellectual circles, quickly won a reputation similar to that of the Shanghai-based *World Economic Herald*.[66]

The Culture Academy: The Revival of the Chinese Tradition of Private Education

The independent stance of the Chen-Wang group was not one they had originally chosen for themselves. On the contrary, the founders of the Culture Academy intended from the outset to break away from party-state control and open up an independent, autonomous space for academic freedom. Unexpectedly, their efforts easily made considerable headway. Among the four intellectual groups discussed here, the Culture Academy was founded last, but institutionalized first. The Culture Academy is virtually the only nongovernment intellectual organization that has survived since the June Fourth incident in 1989.

The founding of the Culture Academy was a result of "culture fever," the popular name for the ongoing debate over the nature of China's traditional culture and its influence upon China's modernization. In mid-1984, inspired by culture fever, a few middle-aged and young Beida teachers, who taught mostly Chinese philosophy, expressed a desire to open up an educational and academic space outside the existing university and college system. The Chinese traditional academy was regarded as an institutional form of this space by this young generation of cultural intellectuals. Their ideas received warm encouragement from their senior colleagues. Professor Tang Yijie was chosen to be the leader of the Culture Academy.[67]

The academy (*shuyuan*) as an organizational form for the nonofficial education has premodern roots. The educational system in premodern China can be roughly divided into two parts: *guanxue* (official education) and *sixue* (private education). The purpose of the guanxue system was mainly to foster state bureaucrats. The objectives of the sixue system, in contrast, were diverse. To educate the literati, the reserve force of the state bureaucrats, was merely one task; more important was the fact that only in the sixue system did Confucian intellectuals emerge. Functionally, the sixue system consisted of *sishu* (private schools) and *shuyuan* (academies), the former analogous to present-day primary and secondary schools, and the latter to the universities and graduate schools. It is widely recognized that Confucius was the founder of the Chinese sixue educational system, having established the first private school in China, wherein Confucianism generated. The academy as an educational institution began to take shape in the Tang dynasty, and in its mature form was a legacy of the Song period. Imitating the institutional model of Buddhist temples, Confucian intellectuals repeatedly founded academies in places with scenic beauty, engaging in the collection, publication, and research of Confucian classics and giving lectures to propagate their views on social morality and order. A few academies also conducted rites venerating Confucius. Ideologically, Confucianism dominated in both guanxue and sixue systems. Nevertheless, because of its bureaucratic nature, the guanxue system was always dominated by one or another Confucian orthodoxy during different periods, whereas both orthodoxies and heterodoxies might be in communication or development in the nonofficial system of academies. Neo-Confucianism as a heterodoxy was born in the academies of the Song period, but it later became the orthodoxy. In general, the sixue academies were much more liberally colored than the schools of the guanxue system. One of the traditions of these academies was that of plurality and tolerance. A well-known story demonstrates this. Zhu Xi, a famous Song neo-Confucian, invited his theoretical rival Lu Xiangshan, another famous Song neo-Confucian, to lecture at the Zhu-mastered Bai-Lu-Dong (White Deer Grotto) Academy.[68] It was from the outset that the founders of the Culture Academy consciously regarded inheriting the traditions of Chinese academies as their duty. In their opinions, the sixue tradition made a greater contribution to the development of Chinese traditional culture, while the guanxue made less contribution, if any, because genuine scholars could not be fostered within the guanxue system.[69]

Throughout the whole of the 1980s, China's economic reform had been advancing alone, while the reform of the educational system had basically been marking time. The particulars of education in, and the administration of, universities and colleges were seriously under the control of a centralized educational planning system. The Education Ministry (which later altered its name to the State Education Committee) was the main maker and implementer of educational plans, and universities and/or colleges were just agents of the state.

The founders of the Culture Academy intended to open up an independent intellectual public space outside the existing educational system, enabling them to freely research, discuss, and spread their own views on Chinese traditional culture.[70] Yet they were also very much aware that this independent space could not be opened up without support from the party-state. Thus they attempted to influence the party-state by utilizing the reputation of veteran professors and taking the way of *shangshu* (which literally means "submitting a written statement to the highest authority")—a frequently seen practice within both Chinese traditional and communist institutions. In October 1984, several Beida-based professors, led by Feng Youlan and including Tang Yijie, Ji Xianlin, and Zhang Dainian, among others, wrote a letter to the present general secretary, Hu Yaobang, winning support from the state for their proposal.[71]

Since the aims of the Culture Academy ("to expand and propagate the Chinese cultural tradition" and "to promote modernization of Chinese traditional culture"[72]) were to a considerable degree compatible with the policy of cultural nationalism implemented by the party-state in the post-Mao period, since the veteran scholars were consistently a kind of social force with which the Communist Party had been working to unite, and since he himself had respected veteran intellectuals all along, Hu Yaobang quickly gave a written instruction to the officials who were in charge of educational affairs, consenting to the proposal for establishing the Culture Academy and asking them to offer support. Peng Peiyun, then vice-minister of the Education Ministry, immediately gave calls to Tang and the party leaders of the Beida, hoping the Culture Academy would be established as an internal institution of Beida. This plan to integrate the emergent Culture Academy into the establishment, however, eventually fell through because the firm demands by the founders of the Culture Academy that they possess independent powers of personnel management, finance, and teaching were flatly refused by the party leaders of Beida.[73]

In December, based on personal connections, the Culture Academy, pendant and dependent upon the Beijing Universities and Colleges' Marxism-Leninism Study Society, and registered at the Beijing Bureau of Adult Education, formally proclaimed its founding.[74] From 1987 to 1989, the Culture Academy initiated four symposia, on Chinese traditional culture, comparisons between Chinese and foreign cultures, culture and sciences, and culture and the future. The first symposium on Chinese traditional culture, begun in March 1987, created a furor and did much to upgrade the Culture Academy's reputation and popularity. The Culture Academy also provided a two-year correspondence course on comparative cultural studies. Under the intellectual climate of "culture fever," large numbers of students, including a few from Singapore, enrolled in these educational activities, thereby bringing a considerable amount of tuition income to the Culture Academy. As Wang Shouchang (vice-president of the Culture Academy) recalls, in 1987 and 1988, the tuition income alone amounted to more than one million yuan.[75] The Culture Academy also made money from selling textbooks as well as other publications. In addition, it received donations and sponsorship from a variety of sources, both domestic and international. Now in a strong financial state, the Culture Academy organized many international academic conferences on cultural studies and formulated several ambitious publishing programs, some of which are still in press today.[76] In the sphere of cultural discourse, the notion of plurality took shape, and the official orthodox Marxist views on China's history and culture were pushed from center to periphery.

In addition to keeping the nonofficial tradition, the Culture Academy inherited the tradition of academic pluralism from Chinese traditional academies. This point was well embodied in the constituency of its teachers, consisting of almost one hundred well-known Chinese and foreign scholars speecializing in China's history, philosophy, and culture. Among them were Liang Shuming and Feng Youlan who, as early as the 1920s and 1930s, were well-known as leading Chinese cultural conservatives; Marxist cultural theoreticians such as Li Zehou, Pang Pu, and Zhang Dainian; cultural radical Bao Zunxin; and other philosophers, historians, and literary critics who were to varying degrees liberally inclined. The age distribution of its teachers ranged from over thirty to over ninety. Harvard professor Tu Wei-ming was on the first list of its teachers; later, Chung-ying Cheng from the University of Hawaii, Yü-sheng Lin from the

University of Wisconsin-Madison, and Frederic Wakeman Jr. from the University of California-Berkeley joined it. There were (or are) other teachers from Hong Kong, Taiwan, Australia, Canada, and Japan. The lecturers of the Culture Academy symposia were also diverse, both geographically and ideologically. Among them were Jin Guantao, and Tang Tsou of the University of Chicago.[77]

The return of Liang Shuming, then over ninety, to the rostrum was of twofold symbolic significance to contemporary Chinese cultural discourse and caused a stir for the public in the mid-1980s. I use the word *symbolic* because Liang was one of the intellectuals who had adhered to his own thoughts after Communist rule began, and, in particular, was the only Chinese intellectual who once had a public run-in with Mao Zedong.[78] To the new generation of intellectuals who were pursuing intellectual autonomy in the 1980s, Liang no doubt represented the backbone of the Chinese intelligentsia. Second, Liang's return symbolized the revival of Chinese modern cultural conservatism in the 1980s "culture debate."[79] In the history of Chinese modern ideas, Liang Shuming is widely treated as a representative figure in cultural conservative movements in general, and one of the initiating figures of New Confucianism in particular.[80]

However, Liang's return was only of symbolic importance to the Culture Academy because his thoughts did not occupy the mainstream position in contemporary Chinese cultural discourses. Both his ideas and his social practice (the Rural Reconstruction Project) had become the objects of study for a few historians, but to the majority of the younger generation of intellectuals, they were only remote historical memories; the contemporary spokesman of New Confucianism in 1980s mainland China was Tu Wei-ming. As a result of his introduction, New Confucianism became a subtopic arousing debates in the culture fever.

Despite its plurality, the important, mainstream representatives of the Culture Academy's discourse were a few senior Chinese Marxist cultural theoreticians and historians, such as Tang Yijie, Pang Pu, and Li Zehou. Trained in the 1950s in Marxist philosophy under the dominance of communist ideology, in the 1980s they abandoned a variety of then ruling doctrines of the official Marxist-Leninist ideology; drew a great deal of intellectual nourishment from Chinese traditional thoughts, Western Marxism, or both; and developed their own Chinese neo-Marxist cultural theories. To a great extent, their theories represented the main body of the mainland intellectuals' reponses to overseas New Confucianism.[81]

A Chinese Civil Society as a Phantom in the Air: Fragmented Intellectual Life and Tiananmen

All the above-mentioned attempts to restructure the party-state, to rebuild society, and to establish a viable state-society relationship were made after the destruction of the Maoist regime and during the transition from a revolutionary totalitarianism to a "fragmented authoritarianism," to quote Kenneth G.

Lieberthal's term.[82] The newly emergent situations of state-society relationship very much impressed the scholars in Chinese politics and society. Most of them found in the Chinese intellectual life on the eve of the Tiananmen people's movements "an emerging civil society struggling to surface,"[83] or "the beginning of organized opposition."[84] It seemed to them that some fundamental changes would be under way in Chinese society—perhaps the rise of a cohesive civil society.

Such a conclusion would be, however, very misleading. It results from incomplete observations on Chinese intellectual life. Chinese intellectuals' identical yearning for liberty and democracy, their common enthusiasm for China's modernization and reforms, and their similar hatred of conservative forces have concealed other similarly fundamental and real facts: they worked in different organizations, were bound by different institutions, and thereby held different political preferences. Their different political actions were structured by the interaction between different institutional constraints and different political preferences. Like the Chinese party-state characteristic of fragmented authoritarianism in its operation, the reformist intellectual elite acting in society was divided into various factions, intellectually and organizationally. Every faction had its own identity, its own way of consensus mobilization, and its own manner of membership selection and determination.[85]

More important, no consensus on China's reforms was formed among different intellectual factions, except for some abstract goals—for instance, liberty, democracy, and the rule of law. The enormous divergence of views on reform came to be exposed in 1988 and early 1989, the time of the most lax ideological atmosphere. The overt neo-authoritarianism versus democracy controversy brought to the surface the conflict between those literary intellectuals who took radical views on China's political reform and those social scientists who took politically realistic positions. [86] The members of the "democratic elite" and many literary intellectuals like Li Zehou belonged to the former camp, and the establishment economic policy intellectuals of Zhao Ziyang's think tanks and the nonestablishment intellectuals at the BSESI to the latter.

The split within the intellectual elite was embodied not only in their arguments, but also in their political actions. From January to March 1989, several intellectuals advanced three petitions by publishing open letters appealing to the government to release Wei Jingsheng as well as other political prisoners, and calling for the comprehensive guarantee of the political rights of citizens. The organizers of and participants in these petitions were several writers, artists, natural and social scientists, and scholars in humanities, including some members of the "democratic elite," some teachers from the Culture Academy, and the core members of the Future Group. These three petitions have been taken as important evidence of "the beginning of organized opposition." It is worthwhile to note, however, that neither the establishment economic policy intellectuals (i.e., the members of Zhao Ziyang's think tanks) nor the nonestablishment political scientists (i.e., the members of the Chen-Wang group) participated in these petitions.

Many students of China's politics ignore or underestimate the political implications of the split within the intellectual elite. This fact is relevant to our perception of the 1989 Tiananmen tragedy, which left a series of spectacular, contradictory, and puzzling phenomena that no one had expected, and which now social scientists must seek to put into proper perspective. On a list of these phenomena given by Tang Tsou, the spectacular relationship between intellectuals and students is at the top, as he explains that "not since the May Fourth period had the intellectuals qua intellectuals exercised such profound influence over the ideological orientation of the students and general public, and yet they were unable to provide the latter with guidance in political actions."[87]

The intellectual-student relationship at that time, in fact, was remarkably characterized by the lack of institutionalized communication channels between moderate intellectuals and students and the dominance of the influence of radical intellectuals upon students. The party ideology was in a deep legitimacy crisis among students.[88] The intellectual vacuum that existed among students, however, was not filled by analytical, realistic, or constructive arguments. What students had seen, understood, admired, and eventually accepted were no more than serious criticisms of reality and ideal goals woven by a few "beautiful" slogans. This phenomenon can be best illustrated by mentioning briefly the informative case of the development of the "democratic salon" at Beida, organized by Wang Dan, who later became a prominent student leader in the Tiananmen movement. The influence of intellectuals upon this students' group was exclusively imposed by radical intellectuals, among them Fang Lizhi, Xu Liangxing, Zhang Xianyang, Bao Zunxin, Yan Jiaqi and Ren Wanding.[89]

There was no way for establishment economic policy intellectuals to impose substantive influence upon the political attitudes and orientation of students. On the one hand, their duty was to provide policy makers with information and advice, but not to influence students. On the other hand, the establishment economic policy intellectuals would violate the rules and norms of the political game under a structure of the party-state if they directly communicated with students through nonofficial channels. Moderate nonestablishment intellectuals like Chen Ziming and Wang Juntao also failed to make effective efforts to influence students. In order to avoid arousing suspicions from the party-state, they had kept a distance from any student activities since December 1986.

The sudden eruption of the students' demonstration, which was sparked by Hu Yaobang's death on April 15, 1989, left all intellectuals at a loss. During the initial period of the movement, many intellectuals, as if by prior agreement, adopted noninvolvement as their first choice. The leaders of the establishment CISRES and the nonestablishment BSESI both warned their junior members. Obviously, intellectuals knew very well the rule and convention that the party-state dealt with students' strikes. The victims of every political purge after every students' strike ("settling the account after the autumn harvest") were frequently intellectuals, but not students. The main concern of intellectuals was to conserve and further build on their limited but hard-won spaces for academic freedom and intellectual autonomy. With such a strategic consideration, noninvolvement seemed a rational choice at that time.

The hunger strike that began on May 13 was a turning point that marked the beginning of the growing radicalization of the student movement. This sudden action was apparently planned by a few radical intellectuals behind the scenes, but it again left most intellectuals at a loss. As an inevitable result of the developing circumstances, Chen and Wang decided to get involved in the movement.[90] The decisive factor that led them to get involved, however, was that Yan Mingfu, head of the United Front Department (UFD) of the CCP and a leading reformer, invited the members of the BSESI to be mediators between the government and the students, persuading the hunger strikers to withdraw from Tiananmen Square before the Sino-Soviet summit scheduled for May 16.[91] Yan's manner of tackling political problems was similar to that of Hu Yaobang—that is, he had a liberal attitude toward intellectual criticisms. His invitation provided Chen and Wang with a chance to fulfill their willingness to participate politically. Under the current political situation, the possibility that the government would make some concessions and, as a result, the students' hunger strike would end peacefully could not be ruled out. If Chen and Wang refused to take notice of Yan's invitation, they would let a golden and historic opportunity slip once the party reformers had succeeded in finding a peaceful solution to the student movement.[92]

Yet, partly because the moderate intellectuals had no influence upon the students, and partly because the students from radical factions ruled out any compromise, no settlement was made. After the Sino-Soviet summit, the polarization of Chinese intellectuals accompanied the radicalization of the student movement. At the frontier of the radicalization of intellectuals were some members of the "democratic elite" as well as poets, writers, and artists who scarcely manifested rational judgment on political situations and deliberation over political issues. The climax of the radicalization was the so-called May Seventeenth Declaration, drafted by Yan Jiaqi and Bao Zunxin and signed by a group of thirty-five leading intellectuals, which condemned Deng Xiaoping in the strongest possible terms.[93] Wang Juntao and Chen Ziming refused to sign this declaration and *Economics Weekly,* which they edited, refused to publish it.

In contrast to the deep involvement by the members of the "democratic elite" and nonestablishment middle-aged and young intellectuals like Chen and Wang, the core members of Zhao Ziyang's think tanks did almost nothing during the one-month political storm from mid-April to mid-May. However, on May 19, several hours before the proclamation of martial law, a joint declaration suddenly issued by the CISRES, the CISRD, the BAYE, and the Institute for the Study of International Problems (*Zhongxin guoji wenti yanjiushuo,* hereafter abbreviated as the ISIP),[94] praised the "patriotic democratic movement" of the students and the masses and denounced the government for their errors and delays that had created the crisis.[95] That step was the first and the last collective political action by the three institutes and one association, Zhao Ziyang's most trusted clique of advisorship.

Tang Tsou is inclined to interpret this action as a sign that the establishment economic policy intellectuals "had shaken off their official links and sought to become the voice for an emergent civil society. In other words, the student movement magnified the split within the party, which in turn led some actors on the border areas between the state and society to break with the party and assert their separate identities as spokesmen for society."[96] As Zhu Jiaming (then the vice director of the ISIP) analyzed five years later, however, the publishing of the joint declaration was of no more than symbolic significance, a mere demonstration of their political position *after* their political patron was forced to step down.[97] Chen Yizi reminisced later that, according to their analysis then, the hard-liners within the party backing Li Peng had from the outset adopted a strategy of constantly stimulating the students and, eventually, by utilizing the intensifying contradiction between state and society, staged a coup d'état forcing Zhao to step down. ("When the nest is overturned no egg stays unbroken.") As Zhao's advisors, they anticipated that they would not live on even in degradation under the rule of the Li Peng regime. In order to vindicate their honor of reformist intellectuals, the only choice for them was to break their silence and to expose their noncooperative position with Li Peng to the public.[98] The cost of the pursuit of independence by establishment economic policy intellectuals under the communist regime was a political crackdown. The three institutes disbanded after the June Fourth suppression; some of their core members were arrested, and some forced into exile.

Conclusions

By proposing a new theoretical model, "plural institutionalism," for approaching the relationship between intellectuals and the state in the 1980s, this chapter has attempted to go beyond such methodologically problematic and empirically misleading conceptions as that of the "civil society against the state." In light of this new model, Chinese intellectuals as a whole should be seen as a highly segmented entity with differentiated links to the state. The institutional base for intellectuals' opposition to the party-state was weak, and the actions characteristic of the intellectuals against the party-state were not mainstream. What was mainstream was that intellectuals utilized the institutional leeway made by the changes in different institutional sectors and policy fields to develop their group life and to get intellectual groupings institutionalized.

One means of institutionalization took place in that the nongovernmental groups spontaneously formed in society received recognition and support from the party-state and further established their own organizations within the establishment. Another means was the formation of nongovernmental organizations outside the establishment. The outcome of group institutionalization was determined by complicated interactions between actors' preferences, institutional conditions, and historical factors.

Of the four intellectual groups this article has discussed, one was finally institutionalized within the establishment, the other three evolved in one way or another into nongovernmental organizations. Yet the core members of two of the latter three groups, who are treated as "institution-building entrepreneurs," originally intended to imitate the first group, which entered into the establishment. This preference was shaped by institutional and historical elements. A majority of intellectuals preferred to "be establishment" because an overwhelming majority of resources were grasped and wielded by the party-state. In particular, to enjoy the advice of high-ranking officials seemed to be the optimum choice for economists and political scientists.

The path of the Development Group from an amateur research group to the think tanks of Zhao Ziyang was extremely smooth, mainly because of an institutional demand created by the rapid and ongoing economic reform whereby the leading reformers within the party-state needed research organizations outside the existing bureaucratic hierarchy in charge of economic affairs to supply nonbureaucratic information conducive to policy making related to the reform. The difficulties in institutionalizing the Chen Ziming–Wang Juntao group within the establishment arose mainly because the party-state had not undertaken deep reforms in political and ideological realms, and the institutional demand for advice in these two realms was not as strong as in the economic field; the Future Group faced a similar problem.

Concerning the significance of noninstitutional elements, the active involvement in the pre-1981 democratic movements by members of the Chen-Wang group constituted another reason why it had so few opportunities to receive official recognition and support. However, thanks to the changes that took place in other institutional sectors, such as the regulation of adult education and the management of the scientific-technological research system, Chen and his comrades overcame the resource crisis through nongovernmental channels, established the extra-establishment organizational base of their group activities, and even ran a newspaper of their own. It is worth noting that having personal connections with leading (but not necessarily very high-ranking) figures within the establishment was always key for organizational leaders of groups in institutionalizing their group life, whether within the establishment or outside the establishment.[99]

Because of the different historically bounded foundations of group identity, because of the divergence of political preferences, and because of the differentiated links to the party-state, the Chinese intellectual community was in the de facto split, as the party-state was characterized as fragmented. This split was embodied not only in the intellectual clashes they had with each other, but also in the lack of consistent political action. In hard and bitter struggles for the institutionalization of their group life, intellectuals had almost no time to be concerned with the establishment of institutionalized channels for influencing students. The lack of a more institutionalized relationship between intellectuals and students was also strongly affected by a variety of intermediate-level institutions working in the university and college educational system, a social sector relatively less reshaped by the reforms and remolded by intellectuals. A consequence of such an intellectual-student relationship was that the nearly innate student radicalism was enhanced by the radical side among intellectuals.

The fragmentation of the Chinese intellectual community and the noninstitutionalization of the intellectual-student relationship was branded on the failed People's Movement of 1989. When the student protest erupted, intellectuals found that not only was there little consensus on the current situation enabling them to carry out any constructive joint action, but there were also few channels enabling them to constructively exercise their influence upon the students. Simultaneously, bound by their great knowledge of the conventions and rules the party-state had employed in past political campaigns to deal with conflicts between state and society, intellectuals were reluctant to be involved in the movement in any organized manner. Similarly restrained by party-state institutions, the establishment failed to play the role of bridge in the interaction between state and society. The radicalization of the student and mass movement proved that the fragmented involvement of intellectuals in the movement was fruitless.

To conclude, the institutional analyses demonstrate that Chinese civil society being a phantom in the air was not simply a matter of the balance of strength between the party-state on the one side and society on the other. For better or worse, as Tang Tsou points out, the party-state still shaped society even as society labored to reemerge from its control.[100] The political choices and actions of intellectuals in the newly emergent public spaces were often structured and refracted by the party-state–centered institutions, which at first glance appeared to be negligible, insignificant, conventional, or outdated, some of them being exactly what intellectuals strove to break away from, and some of them not attracting the attention they deserved from intellectuals.

Notes

1. For a comprehensive review of this debate, see Gu Xin, "A Civil Society and Public Sphere in Post-Mao China? An Overview of Western Publications," *China Information* 8, no. 3 (1993–94), 38–52.

2. See, for example, Andrew G. Walder, "The Political Sociology of the Beijing Upheaval of 1989," *Problems of Communism* 38, no. 5 (1989), 30–40; and Dorothy J. Solinger, "Urban Entrepreneurs and the State: The Merger of State and Society," in Arthur Lewis Rosenbaum, ed., *State and Society in China: The Consequences of Reform* (Boulder, Colo.: Westview Press, 1992), 121–41.

3. For example, see Philip C. C. Huang, "'Public Sphere' and 'Civil Society' in China," *Modern China* 19, no. 2 (1993), 216–17; and Heath B. Chamberlain, "On the Search for Civil Society in China," *Modern China* 19, no. 2 (1993), 199–215.

4. See Xue Liang Ding, *The Decline of Communism in China: Legitimacy Crisis, 1977–1989* (Cambridge: Cambridge University Press, 1994).

5. Ibid., 26.

6. The reason that I use the term *public spaces* rather than *public sphere* is similar to the reason for my reluctance to talk about "civil society in China." Jürgen Habermas's model of the public sphere is too value-laden to be used as a paradigm for empirical studies. It is better used as a normative category for political and social critique. For the elaborations of the limitations of Habermas's model, see Michael Schudson, "Was There Ever a Public

Sphere? If So, When? Reflections on the American Case," in Craig Calhoun, ed., *Habermas and the Public Sphere* (Cambridge, Mass.: M.I.T. Press, 1992), 141–63.

7. I am indebted to T. W. Ngo for suggesting the term *plural institutionalism.*

8. See Jerry F. Hough, *The Soviet Union and Social Science Theory* (Cambridge, Mass.: Harvard University Press, 1977), 22–24.

9. Two useful articles are Vivien Lowndes, "Varieties of New Institutionalism: A Critical Appraisal," *Public Administration* 74, no. 2 (1996), 181–97; and Junko Kato, "Institutions and Rationality in Politics: Three Varieties of Neo-Institutionalists," *British Journal of Political Science* 26, no. 4 (1996), 553–82.

10. See Douglass North, *Institutions, Institutional Change and Economic Performance* (Cambridge: Cambridge University Press, 1990), 3–5.

11. See Sven Steinmo, Kathleen Thelen, and Frank Longstrech, eds., *Structuring Politics: Historical Institutionalism in Comparative Analysis* (Cambridge: Cambridge University Press, 1992).

12. See North, *Institutions*, 36–53. See also Peter A. Hall, *Governing the Economy* (New York: Oxford University Press, 1986), 19; here *institutions* are defined as "the formal rules, compliance procedures, and standard operating practices."

13. Bo Rothstein, "Labor-Market Institutions and Working-Class Strength," in Steinmo, Thelen, and Longstreet, eds., *Structuring Politics*, 35.

14. See Jerome Karabel, "Towards a Theory of Intellectuals and Politics," *Theory and Society* 25, no. 2 (1996), 205–33. In this seminal article, Karabel tries to establish an empirical theory on intellectuals and politics in light of neofunctionalism. In my view, however, his theory can be greatly strengthened by incorporating the insights of new institutionalism into the analysis.

15. For an analysis of the Democracy Wall Movement, see Andrew J. Nathan, *Chinese Democracy* (New York: Alfred A. Knopf, 1985); for a discussion of the *samizdat* as well as its Chinese version, see H. Gordon Skilling, *Samizdat and an Independent Society in Central and Eastern Europe* (London: Macmillan, 1989), chapter 1.

16. Huang, "'Public Sphere' and 'Civil Society' in China," 224.

17. Tang Tsou, "The Tiananmen Tragedy: The State-Society Relationship, Choices, and Mechanisms in Historical Perspective," in Brantly Womack, ed., *Contemporary Chinese Politics in Historical Perspective* (Cambridge: Cambridge University Press, 1991), 281.

18. For a description of these research centers and a discussion of their functions, see Nina P. Halpern, "Information Flows and Policy Coordination in the Chinese Bureaucracy," in Kenneth G. Lieberthal and David M. Lampton, eds., *Bureaucracy, Politics, and Decision Making in Post-Mao China* (Berkeley and Los Angeles: University of California Press, 1992), 125–48.

19. See Merle Goldman, *Sowing the Seeds of Democracy in China: Political Reform in the Deng Xiaoping Era* (Cambridge, Mass.: Harvard University Press, 1994).

20. For a detailed description of the Emancipate the Mind movement, see X. L. Ding, *The Decline of Communism in China: Legitimacy Crisis, 1977–1989* (Cambridge: Cambridge University Press, 1994), 83–113.

21. See Goldman, *Sowing the Seeds*, 25–61.

22. Tang Tsou, "The Tiananmen Tragedy," 279. See also Chen Yizi, *Zhongguo: Shinian Gaige Yu Bajiu Minyun* (*China: The Ten-Year Reforms and the 1989 Democratic Movement*) (Taipei: Lianjing chuban shiye gongsi, 1990), 5.

23. See John P. Burns, "China's Governance: Political Reform in a Turbulent Environment," *China Quarterly* 119 (1989), 504–505. Here Burns presents a brief introduction of the group and takes its relations to some political leaders as an example of the client-patron relationship.

24. See Chen Yizi, *China*, 4–5.

25. Author's interview with Wang Xiaolu on July 10, 1994, in Canberra, Australia. Wang now is a doctoral candidate at the Australian National University.

26. For a vivid description of the Chinese peasants' carrying out the rural reform and the intraparty political struggle between the Maoists (led by Chairman Hua Guofeng) and the supporters of the reform (represented by Wan Li and Deng Xiaoping), see Yang Minqing and Tian Xuexiang, "Cong Xiaogang Heihui dao Wan Li Bianfa" (From the Underground Xiaogang Meeting to the Wan Li Reform), *Hainan Jishi* (*Hainan Magazine of On-the-Spot Reports*) 2 (1989), 2–11.

27. See Zhongguo Nongcun Fazhan Wenti Yanjiuzu (The Research Group on Problems of China's Rural Development, abbreviated as the Development Group), ed., *Nongcun, Jingji, Shehui* (*The Countryside, Economy, and Society*), vol. 1 (Beijing: Zhishi chuban-she, 1985), 33–53.

28. Author's interview with Yang Guansan, one of the core members of the Development Group, on December 20, 1994, in Beijing.

29. See Zhou Qiren, editorial preface to Zhou Qiren, ed., *Nongcun Biange yu Zhongguo Fazhan: 1979–1989* (*Rural Change and Development in China: 1979–1989*) (Hong Kong: Oxford University Press, 1994), xi. For the texts of Deng's and Du's speeches, see *The Countryside, Economy and Society*, vol. 1, 1–11.

30. For the best disccusion of the 1980 election campaigns, see Nathan, *Chinese Democracy*, 205–22.

31. Author's interview with Zhu Jiaming, in Beijing.

32. Based on the information provided in author's interview with Yang Guansan.

33. This contract is described in *The Countryside, Economy, and Society* 1, 23–24.

34. Author's interview with Yang Guansan.

35. Author's interview with Bai Nansheng, a core member of the Development Group and a participant in the Chu County investigation, December 8, 1994, in Beijing.

36. See Zhou Qiren, editorial preface, xi; Chen Yizi, *China*, 37; and John P. Burns, "China's Governance," 504–505.

37. See the Compiling Group of Contemporary China, *Dangdai Zhongguo de Nongye* (*Agriculture in Contemporary China*) (Beijing: Zhongguo shehui kexue chubanshe, 1992), 314–15.

38. Author's interview with Zhu Jiaming in Beijing.

39. See Daniel Kane, "Jin Guantao, Liu Qingfeng and their Historical Systems Evolution Theory: A New Theory of Chinese History," *Papers on Far Eastern History* 39 (1989), 46–73.

40. Author's interview with Zhu Jiaming and Bao Zunxin, who were both important members of the Future Group.

41 From author's interviews with Jia Xinmin and Chen Xiaoya, who were members of the Future Group; in Beijing.

42. Alvin Toffler's *The Third Wave* was read and discussed by almost everybody, at Zhao Ziyang's recommendation.

43. For a discussion of the ideological struggle then taking place among the leadership, see Carol Hamrin, *China and the Challenge of the Future* (Boulder, Colo.: Westview Press, 1990), 75–78.

44. Apart from the ISBN number, every formal Chinese publication has to have another publishing code (*shuhao*), which is printed on its copyright page. The ISBN and the Chinese publishing code are not freely available to everybody; they are given only to those presses endorsed by the party-state.

45. Author's interview with Zhang Gang, November 1992, in New York. Zhang Gang was a core member of the EC and on the staff of the CISRES.

46. Author's interview with Chen Xiaoya.

47. The text of the letter is available in Zhong Weiguang, "Jiquan zhuyi de wanquan yishix-ingtaihua he kexue sixiang taolun" (The Complete Ideologization and the Discussion on Scientific Thoughts), *Dangdai* (*The Contemporary*) 86 (1993), 8–35.

48. Author's interview with Chen Xiaoya. While Antonio Gramsci was scarcely read by

Chinese intellectuals in the 1980s, many of them derived similar views to Gramsci's of "cultural hegemony" from their own experiences from communist ideological life, and put it into their political practice.

49. See David Kelly and He Baogang, "Emergent Civil Society and the Intellectuals in China," 30; He Baogang, "Dual Roles of Semi-Civil Society in Chinese Democratization," *Australian Journal of Political Science* 29, no. 1 (1994), 154–71; and Merle Goldman, *Sowing the Seeds of Democracy*, 358–60.

50. Author's interview with Chen Ziming on December 18, 1994. Chen was released from jail in May 1994. In June 1995, Chen was arrested again, and remains in prison as of this writing.

51. In his interesting book dealing with the legitimacy crisis of the official ideology in China, X. L. Ding proposes the concept of "institutional parasitism" as an alternate scheme to the concept of "civil society versus the state," describing the symbiotic relationship between "independent" or "autonomous" organizations within the society and the party-state establishment (see his *The Decline of Communism*, 22–35). However, the concept of "institutional parasitism" is as similarly oversimplistic as the scheme of "civil society versus the state" at least on the point that it is hard to probe into the difference between minban, or nonofficial, institutes and corporatist organizations, which is not in degree, but in nature.

52. The sources for much of the biographical information on Chen Ziming and Wang Juntao are Chen Ziming, "Shui Shi Lishi de Zuiren?—Wo de Bianhushu" (Who is the Guilty Person Condemned by History?—My Defense), in his *Chen Ziming Fansi Shinian Gaige* (*Chen Ziming's Reflections on the Ten-year Reform*) (Hong Kong: Gangdai yuekan, 1992), 361–441; and Hou Xiaotian, "Wang Juntao de Xinlu Licheng" (Wang Juntao's Career and Ideas), in Wang Juntao and Hou Xiaotian, *Wang Juntao Qiren Qiyan Qi"zui"* (*Wang Juntao: His Career, His Speeches and His "Guilt"*) (Hong Kong: Dangdai yuekan, 1992), 21–33. The former has been partly translated into English; see "China: Defense Statement of Chen Ziming," *Asia Watch* 4, no. 18 (1992), 1–17.

53. Author's interview with Min Qi, July 18, 1994, in Beijing. Min Qi was consistently a core member of the Chen-Wang group. The information provided by Min Qi was also confirmed by the author's interview with Yang Guansan.

54. Author's interview with Min Qi. See also Chen Ziming, *Reflections*, 377–78.

55. See Chen Ziming, "My Defense," 376–78.

56. Hu Ping, et al., *Kaituo—Beida Xueyun Wenxian* (*Exploration—Peking University Student Movement Materials*) (Hong Kong: Tianyuan shuwu, 1990), 368–71.

57. See Min Qi, "Cong Zhinangtuan dao Sixiangku" ("From the [Establishment] Brain Trust to the [Nonestablishment] Think Tank"), *Ming-Pao* (Hong Kong), July 26, 1993. This essay was writen for the fourth anniversary of the BSESI. When it was published, Chen and Wang were still in jail.

58. Information here is mainly provided from the author's interview with Min Qi. All information is based on the archives of the Chen-Wang group; the task of putting them in order is underway.

59. "Collectives and individuals," according to the decision of the Central Committee of the CCP Concerning Reform of the Science and Technology Management System, "should be permitted to set up scientific research or technological service organizations." See Tony Saich, *China's Science Policy in the 80s* (Manchester: Manchester University Press, 1989), 167.

60. The emergence of talents exchange centers at various levels was a new phenomenon in the personnel system of the mid-1980s, and came about to satisfy the growing demand and mobility of talented people. For a detailed description of the reform in this institutional realm, see Saich, *China's Science Policy*, 104–44; on talents exchange centers, see particularly 133–35.

61. Chen Yizi was the executive director of the Research Office. See Chen Yizi, *China*, 106–10.

62. See Min Qi, "From the Brain Trust to the Think Tank."

63. A vivid description of the 1986 student demonstrations can be found in Orvill Schell, *Discos and Democracy: China in the Throes of Reform* (New York: Doubleday, 1989), 211–44. Among the aftermath of the demonstrations was Hu Yaobang's forced resignation from his post as the party's general secretary.

64. Author's interview with Min Qi.

65. See Min Qi, "From the Brain Trust to the Think Tank."

66. Author's interview with He Jiadong, July 20, 1994, and Feng Lanrui on December 14, 1994, in Beijing. Feng was the general secretary of CUSES and the former director of *Economics Weekly*. For a study of *Economics Weekly*, see Edward X. Gu, "The *Economic Weekly*, the Public Space and the Voices of Chinese Independent Intellectuals," *China Quarterly* 147 (1996), 860–88.

67. See Chang Hua, "Zhongguo wenhua shuyuan dashi xinian" (A Chronology of the Academy of Chinese Culture), in Li Zhonghua and Wang Shouchang, eds., *Wenhua de Huigu yu Zhanwang* (*The Retrospections and Prospects of Culture: The Commemorative Collection for the Tenth Anniversary of the Academy of Chinese Culture*) (Beijing: Beijing daxue chubanshe, 1994), 53.

68. For a discussion of traditional academies, see Linda Walton, "The Institutional Context of Neo-Confucianism: Scholars, Schools, and *Shu-yüan* in Sung-Yüan China," in W. Theodore de Bary and John W. Chaffee, eds., *Neo-Confucian Education: The Formative Stage* (Berkeley and Los Angeles: University of California Press, 1989); for studies of Zhu Xi (Chu Hsi)'s activities in academies, see Wing-tsit Chan, "Chu Hsi and the Academies" in the same volume. See also John W. Chaffee, "Chu Hsi and the Revival of the White Deer Grotto Academy, 1179–1181 A.D.," *T'ong Pao* 71 (1985), 40–62.

69. Author's interview with Tang Yijie, the president of the Culture Academy from its inception to the present, December, 20, 1994, in Beijing.

70. Author's interview with Tang Yijie.

71. Ibid. See also Chang Hua, "Chronology," 54–55.

72. See the Culture Academy's own introductory pamphlet (1988 version), 4.

73. Author's interview with Tang Yijie.

74. See Chang Hua, "Chronology," 54.

75. Author's interview with Wang Shouchang, in Beijing.

76. See the Culture Academy's own introductory pamphlet (1993 version), 2–3.

77. The lists of the Culture Academy's teachers over different periods are available in its introductory pamphlets (1988 and 1993 versions).

78. For a brief description of the conflict between Liang and Mao, see Guy S. Alitto, *The Last Confucian: Liang Shu-ming and the Chinese Dilemma of Modernity* (Berkeley and Los Angeles: University of California Press, 1979), 324–33.

79. The best studies of Chinese modern conservative ideas are collected in Charlott Furth, ed., *The Limits of Change: Essays on Conservative Alternatives in Republican China* (Cambridge, Mass.: Harvard University Press, 1976).

80. For a study of the Hong Kong–based New Confucianism, see Hao Chang, "New Confucianism and the Intellectual Crisis of Contemporary China," in Furth, ed., *The Limits of Change*. For a study of Xiong Shili's ideas, see Tu Wei-ming, "Hsiung Shih-li's Quest for Authentic Existence," in the same volume.

81. See Chen Lai, "Sixiang Chulu San Dongxiang" (Three Directions for the [Chinese] Intellectual Outlet), in Gan Yang, ed., *Zhongguo Dangdai Wenhua Yishi* (*The Cultural Consciousness in Contemporary China*) (Hong Kong: Sanlian shudian, 1989), 584–85.

82. Kenneth G. Lieberthal, "Introduction: The 'Fragmented Authoritarianism' Model and Its Limitations," in Lieberthal and Lampton, eds., *Bureaucracy, Politics, and Decision Making*, 1–30.

83. Quoted in Tang Tsou, "The Tiananmen Tragedy," 295.

84. This idea comes from Goldman, *Sowing the Seeds*; it is the title of her chapter 10.

85. For a vivid description of factionalism in Chinese intellectual group life, see Su Wei,

"Quanzi, Shalong yu Gonggong Kongjian" (Circles, Salons and the Public Sphere), in Yü Ying-shih et al., *Cong Wusi Dao Heshang* (*From the May Fourth [Movement] to the River Elegy*) (Taipei: Fengyun shidai chuban youxian gongsi, 1992), 171–88.

86. This controversy has been described by many authors. Among them, see Barry Sautman, "Sirens of the Strongman: Neo-Authoritarianism in Recent Chinese Political Theory," *China Quarterly* 129 (1992), 72–102; and Ma Shu Yun, "The Rise and Fall of Neo-Authoritarianism in China," *China Information 5*, no. 3 (1990–1991), 1–18.

87. Tang Tsou, "The Tiananmen Tragedy," 274.

88. See Stanley Rosen, "Students and the State in China: The Crisis in Ideology and Organization," in Rosenbaum, ed., *State and Society*, 167–92.

89. See Goldman, *Sowing the Seeds*, 293–94.

90. Hu Ping's interview with Wang Juntao, 26.

91. See Wang Juntao and Hou Ziaotian, *Wang Juntao: His Career, His Speeches and His "Guilt,"* 31.

92. For a detailed analysis of Chen and Wang's involvement in the movement, see Edward X. Gu, "Elitist Democracy and China's Democratization: A Graduate Approach toward Democratic Transition by a Group of Chinese Dissidents," *Democratization* (forthcoming).

93. Tang Tsou, "The Tiananmen Tragedy," 311.

94. This institute, as a branch organization of the CITIC, China's largest corporation for international investment, was formed by Li Xianglu, a former secretary of Zhao Ziyang, and Zhu Jiaming, a leading economic advisor to Zhao Ziyang.

95. The text of the declaration is collected in the Students' Association of the Hong Kong Chinese University, ed., *Bajiu Zhongguo Minyun Ziliaoce* (*The Collected Materials of the 1989 Chinese Democratic Movement*) (Hong Kong: The Students' Association of the Hong Kong Chinese University, 1991), 198–99.

96. Tang Tsou, "The Tiananmen Tragedy," 281.

97. Author's interview with Zhu Jiaming.

98. See Mei Zi's interview with Chen Yizi, published in *Open Magazine*, June 1991, 69–71.

99. That personal connections serve as an important institutional element (although being conventional in nature) in sociopolitical games in China, whether in revolutionary or in postrevolutionary phases, has been illustrated by some Western scholars of China's politics and society. See David Apter and Tony Saich, *Revolutionary Discourse in Mao's Republic* (Cambridge, Mass.: Harvard University Press, 1994), 322; and Mayfair Mei-hui Yang, *Gifts, Favors and Banquets: The Art of Social Relationships in China* (Ithaca, N.Y.: Cornell University Press, 1994).

100. Tang Tsou, "The Tiananmen Tragedy," 302.

8

The Limits of the Chinese State

*Public Morality and
the Xu Honggang Campaign*

DAWN EINWALTER

For nearly two decades, the Chinese state has been actively dismantling the mechanisms of collective production in favor of a more market-oriented approach, known as the "socialist market economic system." In brief, politics are to remain socialist, while economics are to become increasingly market-oriented.

Socialist morality, with its emphasis on the primacy of the group over individual interests, has been an important basis for the Chinese Communist Party's political legitimacy. The state, under party direction, claims to embody socialist morality and retains the right to propagate this morality throughout society. However, market reforms have introduced concepts of competition, profit, and the satisfaction of self-interest. By introducing market reforms without reformulating moral prerogatives that suit the new system, the state has diluted the relevance of socialist morality and made it appear antithetical to the new demands of the market. Consequently, though the state has tried to restrict self-interest to the economic realm and has continued to provide such models of selfless behavior as soldier-hero Lei Feng to guide noneconomic behavior, the leakage of self-interested action into areas of life outside the economic realm has proven unavoidable, and socialist moral imperatives have continued to fray. This essay looks at one attempt to shore up socialist morality with the Xu Honggang campaign of 1994.

The campaign drew inspiration from Maoist principles that deny the moral validity of particularistic relations such as those based on *guanxi* (personal connections).[1] Such universalist principles demand that one be willing to render assistance to anyone in need, whether a stranger or familiar. Nowhere is the need to render selfless assistance more pertinent than at moments of crisis—the scenes of accidents, crimes, or arguments—and the state has chosen to pinpoint such moments of crisis as a means to contrast selfless behavior in keeping with socialist morality with what it views as the continuing degeneration of morality caused by the extension of self-interest outside the realm of market economics. Self-interest, the state argues, is running amok, and citizens have become apathetic to the misfortunes of others. If such public apathy is not checked, it may have the potential to threaten the ultimate success of current reforms with social breakdown, and ultimately to lead to the corrosion of the state itself.[2] As Wu Qinying has noted, "These days some say heroism is not good for much. Stocks, deposits, and automobiles are the current reality.... When people see a place with lots of money and little love, when people fall in the river and nobody pulls them out, when they see a place where good people disband and bad people become a group, and when the masses fear the thief while at home and catastrophe while on the street, how can people not call out from the bottom their heart: Heroes! Where have you all gone?"[3]

The media are replete with stories of callous indifference: a child falls in a river and a man standing on the bank insists on negotiating a price for pulling him out.[4] Thirty people stand by and watch while a woman is raped, while "[a]mong those thirty, there were even those who climbed up onto the windows to see more clearly."[5] A child is hit by a bus and a passenger tries in vain to get cars to stop and take her to the hospital.[6] Public officials are also targeted, and when considered remiss in their duties are pointed out as moral delinquents. A Shanghai tax official, for instance, was dismissed from his job for failing to help a boy who had been injured in a traffic accident.

Stories of indifference reached a peak in the spring and summer of 1994, when the government launched an anticrime, pro-morality campaign that highlighted the exploits of Xu Honggang, a handsome People's Liberation Army soldier. Xu had rescued a young woman from being robbed and injured by thugs on a long-distance bus traveling from Yunnan to Sichuan, and in the process was severely wounded.

Standing Up for Righteousness

Xu Honggang's story was first presented to a national audience via the *People's Daily* (*Renmin Ribao*), as follows:

> At around 10:00 in the morning, a battle of righteousness and evil occurred. Ren, a thug, suddenly demanded money from Wu, a young woman leaning against the window in one of the bus seats. Wu resolutely replied that she didn't have any money.
>
> "If you don't have any money, then give me your watch." Ren grabbed at Wu's watch in order to pull it off her. Wu removed her watch and stuffed it in her pocket.
>
> "If you don't give me the watch, then I'll take your clothes!" Ren grabbed Wu's shirt and ripped it.
>
> Ren then shouted, "If she doesn't have any money, then I'll toss her from the bus!" And so saying, Ren grabbed Wu by the neck and, along with several of his cohorts, moved to toss her out the window of the moving bus....
>
> During this moment of crisis, which seemed like 10,000 minutes, the shouting

awakened a young soldier who had been napping in the back of the bus. Xu Honggang was returning from a visit home to Jinan where he was the signal company squad leader. Observing the situation, Xu's blood began to boil. He stood up with a cry and with eyes as wide as a tiger's, shouted, "Put your hands down! Don't do this!" Hearing Xu's thunderous voice, Ren was so frightened that he let go of the window and Wu was saved.

"Punk [*xiaozi*]! Is this any of your business?" Ren and his three cohorts rushed Xu like mad dogs and surrounded him.

Unarmed, Xu was still without the slightest caution in opposing these four knife-wielding thugs. He bravely strode forward and struggled with them. If he lifted a foot, a thug kicked him to the floor. If he raised a fist, another thug beat him. Thus hopelessly outnumbered, he was stabbed many times. Fresh blood flowed onto his clothes and his intestines protruded from his body.

By this time, the driver heard the ruckus and immediately stopped the bus and hurried over. . . . "Catch the murdering thugs!" the passengers yelled as the four leaped from the bus. Using his hand to hold his intestines in, Xu also leaped from the bus to give chase . . . but soon fell to the ground leaving a trail of blood more than fifty meters long.

At this point, several officials drove by in a car, saw the situation and slammed on the brakes. When they asked Xu how he was, he answered, "I'm a People's Liberation Army soldier. Quickly go after those thugs!"[7]

The story then relates that the officials followed Xu's instructions and chased after the thugs, with Xu in the passenger seat. When they realized how deathly ill he was, however, the officials took him to the hospital, where elaborate care was taken to save his life. (His injuries and the medical care required to treat them are then described in all their gory detail.) The total cost of this medical care amounted to over fifty thousand yuan (around U.S. $6,000), but "no price was too great to save this type of hero."[8]

Approximately six months after the initial incident, Xu was brought to Beijing, where he received a personal commendation from President Jiang Zemin for his bravery. He was then sent on a strenuous nationwide speaking tour. The story of his bravery and ensuing tour were widely publicized, and in the weeks that followed the initial media coverage, his story was used as a template for numerous other morality tales of selflessness and bravery.

The Xu Honggang template is based on a type of model socialist hero that predates the campaign—a *jian yi yong wei zhe*, or "someone who sees his duty and bravely takes action"—a "morality hero." Xu Honggang–like morality heroes are descended from the line of soldier-heroes characterized by Wang Jie, Ouyang Hai, and Zhang Hua, who like the more familiar hero, Lei Feng, became general character models known for their penchant for doing small, considerate acts, for their patriotism, and for their willingness to struggle with everyday hardships. Unlike Lei Feng, however, such soldier-heroes also became famous for their willingness to commit the ultimate self-sacrifice for the public good. Wang Jie sacrificed himself in 1963 to save a train by pushing a horse loaded with ammunition out of its path, while Ouyang Hai was killed in 1965 when he threw his body over a defective land mine during a training drill.[9] In the early 1980s Zhang Hua won official accolades for dying while rescuing an elderly peasant from a manure pit.[10]

Like soldier-hero campaigns of the past, the Xu Honggang campaign maintains a tension between the grand deed and the soldier's humility, and demands that acts of self-sacrifice be carried out in the Lei Feng tradition of the "rustless screw." Such a hero is shown offering his selfless act to society in a "spirit of a reverential offering" (*fengxian jingshen*) as one would humbly offer a gift to a superior. Heroes are often quoted as saying, "I simply did what I was supposed to do. Anyone would do the same."[11]

Injury or violent death is a prerequisite for achieving jian yi yong wei stature. This motif of blood is common in many of these heroes. Through their self-sacrificial shedding of blood, the mundane acts of Zhang Hua and Wang Jie are transformed into the heroic. The Xu Honggang campaign differs from this tradition in context rather than technique, as the crimes depicted can hardly be considered ordinary. The lurid scenarios of morality heroes like Xu Honggang raise the specter of national instability, and hearken back to the revolution, when the state's control over the country was still in some question and danger was a fact of daily life. They capitalize on the actual increase in crime in China to invoke the fear that socialism is being eaten away by a powerful and cunning criminal element, and they mobilize a popular response to this organized threat. The lone morality hero is often shown confronting an audacious knife-wielding criminal who is invariably backed by a gang of cronies.

As law enforcement officials are popularly perceived as brutal and corrupt, particularly in the wake of Tiananmen, the motif of the unarmed hero is particularly designed to show officials exercising restraint in their dealings with citizens. Even armed police (*wu jing*), who generally carry nightsticks, cattle prods, and handguns, are represented as too benign to use their weapons even in self-defense. As one story put it, "[F]or an armed policeman to subdue a ruffian is a very easy matter, [but] our soldiers put down their weapons and used their hands."[12] In another example, Luoyang traffic police officer Yao Cihui, who for a time received nearly as much attention as Xu himself, was killed when he fought a group of thugs bare-handed. Yao was also lauded for his loyalty (he never refused an assignment) and his poverty (the implication being that he did not succumb to bribes).[13]

Citizens can also be campaign heroes, as a common slogan, "heroes are by our sides," suggests that anyone is capable of countervening crime. The campaign decries the average citizen who is increasingly apathetic and willing to "see death without saving the victim" (*jian si bu jiu*), as the following story exemplifies:

> When faced with a thug and his blood-dripping dagger, female train employees Zhang Shaolan and Wang Hongxia fearlessly took concrete action to compose a *jian yi yong wei* song of praise.[14]
>
> On the evening of April 6, around 11:30, the #375 had just left Xiping station [bound for Hankou]. At this time, four Guangxi passengers on the #13 car allowed a tall youth to sit next to them on their short bench. After declining the

seat, the tall youth motioned five or six other male youths over to these four guys from Guangxi and started a fistfight. The tall youth pulled out a knife and stabbed passenger Zhou Xiong in the left side of his chest. Zhou fell onto the floor with blood streaming out. Frightened, the other three Guangxi men pleaded for mercy. The tall youth yelled to the other passengers around Zhou, "Look! It's a fistfight!" After saying this, he proceeded to hit and kick the other three Guangxi passengers.

At this time, the #13 car worker, Zhang Shaolan, and the #12 car worker, Wang Hongxia, heard the commotion and came running. One grabbed the tall youth's arm. The other thugs saw that the situation was beginning to look bad for them and took off. The tall youth said to the two women: "Let me go or I will certainly get you for this [baoda]!" But the two paid absolutely no heed to him, and Yang Yunzhang, the #9 car worker, wrapped his arms around the tall youth and hustled him toward the dining car. Arriving at the dining car, the tall youth suddenly pulled out the knife and plunged it into Zhang Shaolan's neck, and viciously said, "If anyone dares to go ahead, she will be stabbed [again]!" Zhang Shaolan simultaneously struggled and called out, "Quick, go get the train police!" When the youth saw that Zhang Shaolan was completely without fear, he turned and hit her, then abruptly ran off. At this time, the assistant train director, Chen Wenwu, arrived with two male train employees and ran after the thug. He yelled at the other passengers to catch the man, but the passengers in the car invariably got out of his way and not a single person tried to stop him. In this way, he was able to get to the #8 car and leap from the train.

The regret of people today is that when the train director, He Xinyi, asked passengers in the #13 car to help point out the other thugs, not a single one of the nearly two hundred passengers stepped forward to give evidence. Some passengers even made irresponsible and sarcastic remarks like, "Paid nothing, we still have to be sentinels. Be on duty!"

Zhang Shaolan indignantly responded, "While the entire country is studying Xu Honggang's heroism, where has these passengers' sense of social responsibility gone?"[15]

While many campaign stories, particularly those in national newspapers such as the *Renmin Ribao* and *Guangming Ribao*, followed the template of Xu Honggang's initial exploit nearly to the letter, local newspapers often adapted the formula extensively. As Lynn White notes, local papers are allowed relative leeway that gives editors "options, a language for debate" that may end up maintaining the contradictions between propaganda and local news, rather than airbrushing them.[16]

The remainder of this essay shows how these local adaptations reveal a disjuncture between the campaign's avowed concern to encourage selfless altruism and its methods, which often discourage such behavior. It first looks at how the campaign can advocate improved official/citizen cooperation, but fail to acknowledge that this relationship is being redefined to minimize the role of the citizen activist. The way in which self-sacrifice is being diluted by the state's provision of generous monetary rewards will then be considered. Finally, it is noted that the campaign fails to address the issue of reasonable personal safety and the limits of self-sacrifice.

The Role of Citizen Intervention in Transition

In the story of train conductors Wang Hongxia and Zhang Shaolan related above, the passengers are reproached for not cooperating with train personnel in the capture of the criminals. This is a common theme in morality hero stories; it suggests that if a partnership between citizens and officials could be reforged, then crime could be brought under control, a message in keeping with mass-line techniques of policing.

Under mass-line techniques, citizen intervention played a crucial role in maintaining social order. Neighborhood residents, work unit employees, and even strangers on the street were encouraged to be vigilant for signs of deviance and ideally intervened themselves or reported the behavior to volunteers filling administrative positions in such organizations as the neighborhood committee (*jumin weiyuanhui*) or the local police subunit (*paichusuo*). Effective social control in this form necessitated a mutually dependent relationship between citizens and officials.[17]

The Xu Honggang campaign's call for a return to citizen/official cooperation overlooks a number of factors that actually repress mass-line policing, some of which are being propagated by the state itself. In the neighborhood, the partnership between neighborhood administration and residents has become more tenuous as the authority and influence of the neighborhood committee has declined and the attention of local police has been diverted away from monitoring signs of political deviance toward investigating more serious crimes such as theft and assault.[18] So too, the easing of the state's emphasis on political reliability means that less stress is currently placed on citizens to engage in mutual surveillance. Residents now have considerably greater latitude to retreat from the affairs of their neighbors if they so choose.[19]

In addition, the state has significantly strengthened the role of law enforcement professionals, who are charged with enforcing a host of new regulations. The overall number of police has increased, and a new form of police, "patrol police" (*xunluo jingcha*), has been instituted to provide urban areas with more flexible law enforcement jurisdictions.[20] Police units are becoming more specialized and professionalized and in some areas are replacing citizen activism entirely.

In fact, the police have begun to consider citizen intervention at moments of crisis to itself be a source of public disorder. It has been typical for a crowd to gather at the scene of an argument, crime, or accident, and to become an active part in the resolution.[21] However, police regularly disperse such crowds in keeping with instructions found in law enforcement manuals.[22]

The following campaign news report describes an instance in which police found crowd intervention in a crime to be a potential threat to themselves. According to the story, when a Commerce Department inspector and police officer were patrolling a Shanghai neighborhood, they noticed several members of the Golden Oxen gang extorting money from a migrant (*waidiren*). The two officers attempted to intervene, but were attacked by several Golden Oxen and forced to run. They then enlisted help from several passing patrol police, but a gang member cleverly turned the tables, as he shouted to the patrol officers,

> "Come quickly! Come catch the culprit!" [The three patrol officers follow the gang member.] They find a black-jacketed "Golden Oxen" lying on the ground.
>
> "Armed police are hitting someone! Quick, come look!" several "Golden Ox" shouted unfounded charges. In order to prevent the situation from escalating and to keep a crowd from blocking traffic, [a patrol officer] decided to catch the illegal elements and deal with the situation in nearby Tianjin St. #182 alley.
>
> "Armed police are beating someone!" the tan-jacketed ruffian continued to yell, brandishing his fist. . . . [23]

The Golden Oxen gang member attempted to draw a crowd by appealing to their sympathies with the accusation that the police were beating someone. The police perceived the crowd not as a cooperative partner, but as a potential competitor that might be as likely to support the gang members as themselves, or even offer some physical threat to the police.

If, as the slogan goes, heroes are indeed among us, then such stories might be used to provide examples of citizen/official cooperation. Instead they serve to deny the feasibility of such cooperation, and reveal that actual police practice does not coincide with that encouraged by the campaign.

The Commoditization of Selflessness

In addition to its lack of clarity on the nature of official/citizen cooperation in public, the Xu Honggang campaign problematized the motivational basis for citizen activism. It displayed a commitment to conservative socialist morality by insisting that citizens must put aside their personal interests and be willing to sacrifice their safety, health, or life on behalf of another without thought for reward or celebrity. However, the overt commoditization currently found in many realms of Chinese life leaked into the Xu Honggang campaign, and its moral injunctions were diluted by the provision of significant material rewards to those designated as heroes.

The state has been providing benefits to designated heroes for years in the form of symbolic rewards such as laudatory songs and titles, which in China's "virtuocratic" system could possess instrumental value when parlayed into career advancement.[24] The provision of symbolic rewards continued in the Xu Honggang campaign in the form of official designations (Jian Yi Yong Wei Gongmin), songs extolling the virtues of the hero (alluded to in the first paragraph of the train conductors' story), and merit citations.[25]

What is different about the Xu Honggang campaign's approach to rewards, however, is the recent addition of generous benefits in the form of cash, housing, and expensive medical care being provided to officially designated *jian yi yong wei* heroes under the auspices of the Jian Yi Yong Wei fund, established in June 1993.[26] By 1994, the fund drew on a pool of ten million yuan, which it claimed to have accumulated primarily from private donations.[27] This money was used to provide awards to "five hundred national morality heroes by comforting and compensating them with more than 2.8 million yuan."[28] Hospitals were instructed to provide free medical care on the understanding that they would be reimbursed from the fund.[29]

When a school teacher lost her legs after leaping from a train to save a child, she was awarded 12,500 yuan for disabled care and artificial limbs, and allocated a three-room apartment suite.[30] On another occasion, when a thirty-four-year-old male worker threatened an eight-year-old boy with a knife, a female neighbor saved the boy's life by intervening but lost the use of her left hand, and was awarded ten thousand yuan and a lifetime pension over and above what was to be provided by her work unit.[31] A Liaoning fire brigade hero, Xu Shaoqiang, was awarded ten thousand yuan for saving a woman from a mugger.[32]

The state appears to have initiated large material rewards for two primary reasons. First, rewards have been an attempt to respond to criticism that persons who were injured while acting on behalf of others had no real financial safety net, while a few activists found themselves impoverished as a result of their injuries. A Nanjing man whom I interviewed, for instance, described a man from Changzhou (a city in southern Jiangsu Province) who had been severely burned while helping put out a fire. As a consequence, the man was no longer able to work and was reduced to begging in the streets with his child. The city of Beijing, for example, created a local fund to rectify such oversights, stating that there were some citizens who "due to having received injury and become disabled as a result of their heroism have suffered many difficulties with their work, livelihood, and medical care."[33] The Beijing fund was established on the basis of "bodily mishap and injury insurance" and is managed by the city's insurance company, which sets a cap of 20,000 yuan (U.S. $2300) for individuals who have been injured helping others and subsequently designated "capital Jian Yi Yong Wei Good Citizens." In 1994, twenty Beijing residents were so designated.

In addition, the creation of jian yi yong wei funds and the provision of material rewards were implicit attempts to provide extra incentive to would-be activists during a period of waning volunteerism. The result of this effort was to commoditize selfless intervention and foreground its motivation. Ideally, if the purpose of selfless action is to sublimate one's personal interests in favor of that of the collective—to offer it as "tribute" to the larger society— then selflessness should logically be its own reward. The Xu Honggang campaign encouraged such selfless intervention, yet it simultaneously introduced rewards that brought this selflessness into question. This mixed message fueled a public debate over whether or not citizen activists were intervening in crisis situations simply to obtain a reward. While from a practical standpoint it is difficult to believe that someone might court injury or death in order to obtain the benefits of being named a jian yi yong wei hero, some heroes were accused of receiving undeserved material rewards because they were seen as acting in their own benefit.

In one story, a major, Pi Yongxin, was awarded Merit Citation Third Class, designated a Jian Yi Yong Wei Advanced Hero, and received three hundred yuan from his unit's Jian Yi Yong Wei fund for receiving serious injury while defending his apartment from a burglar. Fellow soldiers complained that the award was excessive, especially since Pi was simply defending his own property, and insinuated that Pi acted as he did simply in order to obtain reward money. The complaints became so vociferous that a nine-member party committee was convened to hear the problem. The committee registered a certificate of approval stating that "[the designation of] jian yi yong wei does not distinguish between outside [the home] and inside," and Pi "had a strong feeling of social responsibility that is typical of [heroic] behavior," and had not acted intentionally to obtain any award money.[34]

The grousing over Pi's award can also be attributed to the resentment often felt toward activists. Resentment arises from the popular perception that activists are often mercenary, engaging in a form of "self-serving others" in order to obtain "honour and privileges."[35] Would-be activists now complain that they hesitate to undertake socially concerned actions because they are often subject to taunts, criticism, and even bullying.[36]

By 1995, the Xu Honggang campaign was effectively over and the party appeared to be engaged in damage control by downplaying material rewards. A story in the July 1995 issue of the Shanghai paper *Xinmin Wanbao* displays a hero motivated entirely by his selfless desire to assist others. This young man successfully rescued three children (and attempted but failed to rescue a fourth) while they were playing at a local lake.[37] For a week, the four household heads attempted to find the man in order to give him reward money in gratitude, but were unsuccessful as he had chosen to remain anonymous. When they finally did locate the young man and visited his home, their attempts to give him the reward money were ritually rebuffed on three occasions. "I'm just doing an act that builds spiritual culture. What can money represent?" the man is quoted as saying. The article applauds the household heads for their attempts to reward the man, stating, "Society should certainly reward those who struggle for others without concern for themselves (*dou bu gu shen*) as an act of social tribute (*fengxian*). But the greatest desire of these ... heroes is clearly not to obtain money and other material reward."[38]

Heroes or Fools?

Not only has the state's provision of material awards brought the meaning of selflessness for its own sake into question, but the high level of violence represented in the stories undermines the reasonableness of intervention. The heinous acts of criminals may be resisted in morality stories, but the criminals themselves are seldom caught and the hero is often severely injured. From a practical standpoint, the long-term outcome seems to be that the criminal will be able to continue unencumbered while the hero will suffer physical pain and disability. Are morality heroes in fact heroes or fools?

In interviews, the most frequent reaction, not surprisingly, was one of cynicism. One man in his thirties, for instance, exclaimed, "Everybody gets killed!" in the campaign's stories. He then mentioned that he had a friend who was learning martial arts in order to be ready to handle a crime situation. His friend was convinced, he said, that if he had to defend himself like Xu Honggang, then he had better have the weaponry to do so.

Another man questioned whether the injuries sustained by morality heroes were worth the item protected. He scoffed at stories that showed heroes sustaining injuries for small amounts of money or property. He related a news story in which a female bank worker in a small town had been stabbed by a robber. At the time, the bank only had about five to six thousand yuan on the premises (approximately $590–$700). "Why," he asked, "should she risk her life for such a small amount of money? The cost of the medical care to save her was probably more than the value of the money that she protected." He believed the campaign assumed that the protection of public property is "more important than people. I think that this is a major problem with party ideology, that property is more important than life. Life should be sacred."

One campaign story echoes the popular sentiment that personal safety should outweigh the protection of property. The story employs a full front-page spread to describe the exploits of three men who manage a popular private restaurant established in Beijing during the early 1980s.[39] When a thief came into their restaurant and began stealing from the customers, these "dumbhat" managers chased him out into the street. Once outside, the thief was reinforced by several knife-wielding cronies who attacked and injured the managers, still escaping with the stolen money.

"Was it worth it," the story asks, "for three 'big moneys' to shed blood over two hundred yuan? When all of us encounter this type of situation, what should we do?" The story provides a mixed answer. It condemns the passive bystanders outside the restaurant, noting that even though the managers yelled at them to catch the thief, "not a few people coldly 'allowed the net to open' and the thief escaped." Yet the reporter's solicitation of the man-on-the-street response to the story reveals generally negative reactions to the managers' heroism. Several people derided the three for being "Xu Honggang's little brothers." When the reporter suggests to one interviewee that he would probably respond like the managers if he were in the same situation, the man retorts, "If it were me, I wouldn't go after them." Even the attending doctor of the three says that it is highly unusual for *getihu* (private business) managers to behave in this fashion, especially given the seriousness of their injuries.

The three restaurant managers' heroism is further diminished when the reporter speaks to them directly. Normally, they admit, even they would not be likely to go after a thief. They claim to have chased him only because they wanted to maintain their restaurant's good reputation. "If we were somewhere else and saw someone steal something," one of them said, "we probably wouldn't care or do anything about it," observing that people nowadays have cultivated a certain blindness for the troubles of others.

The Xu Honggang campaign can claim a certain level of victory in perpetuating the state's claim that the problem of crime is severe and that it is being fed by a corresponding decay in the level of public morality. Despite the campaign's avowed intent to encourage greater citizen participation, however, nurturing the fear of crime and moral decay through presentations of violent self-sacrifice, however, is not likely to lead to greater participation on the part of the public, but to ward them off further from public intervention in the interests of self-protection. Instead of promoting selflessness, the campaign may have the unintended effect of encouraging self-interest, as individuals act to avoid risk and protect themselves from the sort of violent outcome experienced by Xu Honggang and similar heroes.

This is in keeping with the earlier assertion that police frequently discourage citizens from participating in crisis intervention. Michael Dutton notes that campaigns such as the Xu Honggang campaign that tout a return to mass-line techniques are little more than a "formal shell" designed primarily to frighten the public rather than transform them into more moral citizens.[40]

Conclusion

In many ways, the Xu Honggang campaign seems like a rehash of the morality that has been trotted out since the Yan'an period (1936–47), when the Maoist mythology of sacrificial bravery was first formulated.[41] The Xu Honggang campaign attempts to revive self-sacrifice in a recognizably Maoist guise, with motifs of revolutionary struggle utilized in order to create a sense of urgency at the threat of a new enemy—violent criminals and morally apathetic citizens. Maoist morality rejected all self-interest as "bourgeois" in favor of a dedication to the public interest.[42] Originally, the call for selflessness and sacrifice was inextricably bound with class struggle, which would ultimately give way to an egalitarian society based on universal values in which the interest of the individual was identical to the interest of the group. However, with the elimination of class markers after 1979, and the acceptance that China was only in the early stages of socialism and thus should tolerate differential remuneration, the moral justification for the radical denial of self-interest disintegrated. The new call for self-sacrifice found in the Xu Honggang campaign not only finds few concrete referents in Maoist ideology, but it barely conceals the callous determination of the state to ensure its own perpetuation by using a crisis of public order to justify intensified regulation of urban spaces.

The Xu Honggang campaign's pedigree is further weakened by the inclusion of language reminiscent of humanism that would have been anathema only a few years ago.[43] In addition to its conventional invocation of self-sacrifice reminiscent of the revolutionary period, the campaign adds the language of universal love, good samaritanism, and concern for others. As Jiang De and Zhang Huijin explain, "Without economic exchange, society will not progress, but if it were not for economics and money, would people be unable to interact? Of course not. In addition to money, people still need spirituality, which is everyone for me, myself for everyone. . . . Selfless tribute (*fengxian*) is a synonym for love and is love's highest realm."[44]

Yet even with its humanist bent, and having discarded the elements that gave it political legitimacy, the Xu Honggang campaign cannot quite embrace the moral possibilities of the new market-oriented social order, which would require a humanistic concern for others tempered by a *reasonable and practical* level of self-sacrifice. Without this rapprochement, the net effect of the Xu Honggang campaign is that it has served primarily to further delegitimize the state's hold on public morality.

Notes

1. See Mayfair Mei-hui Yang, *Gifts, Favors, and Banquets: The Art of Social Relations in China* (New York: Cornell University Press, 1994); Andrew Kipnis, "'Face': An Adaptable Discourse of Social Surfaces," *Positions* 3, no. 1 (1995), 119–48; Yan Yunxiang, "The Culture of *Guanxi* in a North China Village," *China Journal* 35 (1996), 1–25.
2. Huang Wei, "Call to Promote Socialist Culture and Ethics," *Beijing Review* 37, no. 17 (1992), 9–13.
3. Wu Qinying, "Yingxiong Zhuyi: Shiluo Yu Changdao" (Heroism: Lose and Advocate), *Guangming Ribao* (*Guangming Daily*), January 5, 1994, 1.
4. Sun Fengzhi, "Ni de Liangzhi Na Qu Le?!" (Where Has Your Intuition Gone?!), *Fazhi Shibao* (Current Legal News) 65 (1993), 1.
5. "Funu Dang Jie Bei Gan; Guanzhe Wu Dongyu Zhong" (A Woman Is Raped on the Street; Onlookers Are Unmoved), *Jiangsu Fazhibao* (*Jiangsu Legal News*) 45 (1993), 3.
6. Sun Fengzhi, 1.
7. Jiang Yongwu, "Yi Qu Shidai Zhengqi Ge" (A Song of Modern Times), *Renmin Ribao* (*People's Daily*), February 18, 1994, 1.
8. Jiang Yongwu, 1.
9. For more on Wang Jie and Ouyang Hai, see Mary Sheridan, "The Emulation of Heroes" *China Quarterly* 33 (1968), 47–72.
10. For a description of Zhang Hua, see Beate Geist, "Lei Feng and the 'Lei Fengs of the Eighties'—Models and Modeling in China," *Papers of Far Eastern History* 42 (1990), 72–124.
11. Yu Ji, Wei Xin, and Guo An, "Miandui Daitu Shibao Shi" (While Facing Violent Thugs . . .), *Shanghai Fazhibao* (*Shanghai Legal News*) March 11, 1994, 1.
12. Yu Ji, Wei Xin, and Guo An, 1.
13. Zhang Huijin and Jiang De, "Guangda Fengxian Jingshen" (Brighten the Spirit of Tribute), *Fazhi Ribao* (*Legal Daily*), April 7, 1994, 1.
14. Honorary songs are often written to praise heroes, but in this instance, the reference is probably metaphorical.
15. Chen Binglin and Liu Xinli, "Lieche Nu Yongshi Re Xue Dou Daitu" (A Female Train Warrior Hot-Bloodedly Struggles with a Thug), *Fazhi Ribao* (Legal Daily), May 18, 1994, 2.
16. Lynn T. White III, "All The News: Structure and Politics in Shanghai's Reform Media," in Chin-chuan Lee, ed., *Voices of China* (New York: Guilford Press, 1990) 104.
17. For a good explanation of this relationship, see Victor H. Li, *Law without Lawyers* (Boulder, Colo.: Westview Press, 1978); Elmer H. Johnson, "Politics, Power and Prevention: The People's Republic of China Case," *Journal of Criminal Justice* 14 (1986), 449–57; Amy Auerbacher Wilson et al., *Deviance and Social Control in Chinese Society* (New York: Praeger, 1977).

18. For more on police reform, see Hualing Fu, "Police Reform and Its Implication for Chinese Social Control," *International Journal of Comparative Criminal Justice* 14, no. 1 (1990), 41–48.

19. For a good description of these changes in urban areas, see Deborah S. Davis et al., *Urban Spaces in Contemporary China* (New York: Cambridge University Press, 1995).

20. China's enthusiasm for Singapore's methods of enforcing public civility has led it to adopt many of the city-state's procedures. See Denny Roy, "Singapore, China and the 'Soft Authoritarian' Challenge," *Asian Survey* 34, no. 3 (1994), 231–42.

21. See William R. Jankowiak's chapter on public mediation in his *Sex, Death and Hierarchy in Inner Mongolia* (New York: Columbia University Press, 1993); Charlotte Ikels, *The Return of the God of Wealth* (Stanford, Calif.: Stanford University Press, 1995) 30–33; Dawn Einwalter, "Soft-Authoritarianism and the Decline of Mediation in Chinese Public Space" (unpublished paper, 1997).

22. See Nie Shiji, *Gongan Baowei Renyuan Shiyong Zhishi Shouce* (Public Security Protection Worker's Handbook) (Chengdu: Sichuan People's Publishing, 1989); Song Zhansheng, *Zhongguo Gongan Baike Quanshu* (China Public Security Encyclopedia) (Guilin: Guilin People's Publishing, 1989).

23. Yu Ji, Wei Xin, and Guo An, 1.

24. See Borge Bakken, "On Models, Modeling and the Exemplary," Report Series 9, (University of Oslo, 1994) 22.

25. Tian Lingbi, "Tang Jinlong Chishou Kongquan Dou Daitu" (Tang Jinlong Struggles Bare-Handed with a Ruffian), *Wen Huibao* (*Cultural Report*), March 18, 1994, 1; Yu Ji, Wei Xin, and Guo An, 1.

26. Wu Yongli, 2.

27. Wu Qinying, 1.

28. Wu Qinying, 1.

29. Wu Jianzhong, "Mianfei Wei Jian Yi Yong Wei Zhe Liao Shang Zheng Rong" (Free Medical Treatment of Injuries and Plastic Surgery is Provided on Behalf of Jian Yi Yong Wei Heroes), *Fazhi Ribao* (*Legal Daily*), May 11, 1994, 3.

30. Zhang Nengxiang, "Beijing Wei Jian Yi Yong Wei Zhe Pai You Jie Nan" (Beijing Takes Care of Anxieties and Puts Difficulties in Order on Behalf of Jian Yi Yong Wei Heroes), *Fazhi Ribao* (*Legal Daily*), March 13, 1994, 1.

31. Wang Zhongduo, "Bei Qiu Shaonian Li Dengren 'Mu' Ganji Bai Leijie Qiuming Zhi En" (The Youth, Li Dengren, Saved by "Mother" Bai Leijie Feels Grateful for Her Kindness), *Zhoumo* (*Weekend*), June 4, 1994, 1.

32. Chi Hongjiang, "Xueran de Fengcai" (The Charisma of Bloodstains), *Zhongguo Qingnian Bao* (*China Youth News*), March 30, 1994, 2.

33. Zhang Nengxiang, 1.

34. Yu Wenlong, "Shi Zhengchang Ziwei Haishi Jianyiyongwei" (Is It Normal Self-Defense or Heroism?), *Shenghuo Zhoukan* (*Living Weekly*), October 31, 1993, 3.

35. Beate Geist, 112.

36. Only the truly naive would engage in activism, according to Luo Weiyang; "*Toujizhe yu Laoshiren*" (Opportunists and the Simple-Minded), *Shehui* (*Society*), January 20, 1990, 29–30.

37. Chen Xiangyang, "Qian Neng Daibiao Shenme?" (What Can Money Represent?) *Xinmin Wanbao* (*New People's Evening News*), July 16, 1995, 1.

38. Chen Xiangyang, 1.

39. Hu Yinhong, "Geti Laoban Jianyiyongwei Yin Chu de Huati" (A Conversation with the Private Manager Heroes), *Beijing Fazhibao* (*Beijing Legal News*), April 24, 1994, 1.

40. See Michael Dutton, "Dreaming of Better Times: 'Repetition with a Difference' and Community Policing in China," *Positions* 3, no. 2 (1995), 415–47.

41. David Apter, "Discourse as Power: Yan'an and the Chinese Revolution," in Tony Saich and Hans van de Ven, eds., *New Perspectives on the Chinese Communist Revolution* (Armonk, N.Y.: M. E. Sharpe, 1995), 200.

42. Lowell Dittmer, "The Radical Critique of Political Interest, 1966–1978," *Modern China* 6, no. 4 (1980), 363–96; Richard Madsen, "The Maoist Ethic and the Moral Basis of Political Activism in Rural China," in Richard W. Wilson, Sidney L. Greenblatt, and Amy Auerbacher Wilson, eds., *Moral Behavior in Chinese Society* (New York: Praeger, 1981), 170.

43. Wendy Larson, "Realism, Modernism, and the Anti-'Spiritual Pollution' Campaign in China," *Modern China* 15, no. 1 (1989), 37–71.

44. Jiang De and Zhang Huijun, "Guangda Fengxian Jingshen" (Brighten the Spirit of Tribute), *Fazhi Ribao* (*Legal Daily*), April 7, 1994, 2.

Part IV

The Prospects for Democracy in China at the Dawn of the Twenty-First Century

The Prospects for Democratization in China

Evidence from the 1995 Beijing Area Study

DANIEL V. DOWD, ALLEN CARLSON, AND MINGMING SHEN

The process of democratization in the People's Republic of China—or equally important, the lack thereof—will likely be one of the most important developments in the world in the early twenty-first century. While the normative aspects of democratization in China are both important and interesting, this paper focuses on survey-based public-opinion evidence to assess the prospects for democratization. In particular, we consider the long-term implications of the distribution of public opinion on a specific question asked of respondents in Beijing: to select their "most important value" relating to politics.

The findings of this chapter suggest that there is little apparent public opinion pressure for democracy, especially in comparison to other values. At the same time, we find that the future is likely to bring pressure for a more liberal society, with more "private space" for the individual. In addition, we find that income has no effect on the respondents' preferences for political democracy or individual freedom. These results call into question to what extent citizens in post–June Fourth Beijing possess political values supportive of democracy and what the likely future trends will be in public opinion related to democracy.

Previous Research

In the literature on democratization in China there is universal agreement that the economic reforms have created at least limited political liberalization or opening in China.[1] Yet concurrently there is widespread disagreement over the speed, scope, and most salient features of this change.[2] One way of categorizing these debates is by noting where authors locate the impetus for change. In looking at change in communist systems from a broad comparative perspective, Giuseppe Di Palma suggests that we can identify two main approaches: an application of the modernization thesis that draws on the importance of changes in the structural relationship between political and economic actors, and the more process-oriented approach that is derived from Janos's devolutionism (a focus on the shift from charismatic to legal-rational regime legitimacy)[3]

The second approach is based on Max Weber's understanding of regime legitimacy, and leads authors in the direction of analyzing elite politics. In China studies, this has meant a focus on the competition between the so-called liberal and conservative factions within high levels of the party as the key variable in pushing forward the reform process. Authors such as Harry Harding, Kenneth Lieberthal, and Michel Oksenberg employ this approach in tracing the path or reforms during the 1980s.[4]

In this chapter, we are not primarily concerned with the accuracy of this elite-centered approach. Indeed, we feel that such work offers a great deal of insight into the intricacies of the decision-making process in Beijing. However, such work also has its limitations, because it emphasizes the importance of elites over that of structural changes in society. We believe that this approach is limited, because while elites may have been self-motivated by power struggles or concerns with inner party legitimacy at the start of the reform crisis, over time the dominant role of central decision makers in the reform process declines, and other factors begin to play a more important role in forcing change. Therefore, a wider concern for structural factors is needed—if not to replace the work of those looking at shifts from charismatic to legal-bureaucratic government, then to complement and augment their approach.

A survey of the literature reveals that many scholars have taken up precisely this task—identifying structural changes in the Chinese polity. Examples of work influenced by the structure-oriented approach include that of Edward Friedman, Stephen Young, and Minxin Pei.[5]. However, an obvious limitation of the work of these authors is a failure to specify the manner in which public opinion and political values are changing in China. While this is not a major problem for authors studying elite politics, for those attempting to explain structural change and the formation of certain cultural prerequisites or preconditions of a more open polity it is a major oversight. Public opinion and political values are crucial variables in the reform process in that they are indicators of the extent to which societal pressures exist for a more open political system. Such variables would seem to merit close attention and analysis. Instead, it is more common in the literature to find generalized statements and prognoses that in reality tell us very little about how public opinion and political values are changing. For example, while discussing the emergence of civil society in China, Edward Friedman observes that "the late-twentieth-century unwillingness among Chinese to accept any political line should be understood as more than cynicism or a crisis of faith; it is also a part of a healthy skepticism that makes possible an open and free polity."[6] Stephen Young notes that in China, "the evidence clearly indicates that the rudiments of civil society are already emerging, albeit without much formal organizational structure."[7] Barrett McCormick and David Kelly add, "Increasing numbers of Chinese are explicitly pondering liberal ideals, and as a practical means of organizing a complex modern society, liberalism has still wider appeal."[8]

None of these articles offer replicable evidence that supports such observations. Rather, they are filled with references to informal interviews held with taxicab drivers, discussions with academics, and the rehashing of simplistic understandings of early versions of the modernization thesis. Nowhere do we find empirical evidence that either supports or contradicts the stated positions. While this may have been acceptable five years ago, we believe that a higher standard of evidence is now appropriate. In particular, we must begin more carefully examining the accumulating evidence about public opinion in Beijing and elsewhere, and whether or not political values are emerging in China that are supportive of a more open political system.

As mentioned above, some authors have begun to investigate this question. First, a number of recent articles and books have attempted to more accurately identify the relationship between state and society in China.[9] These works have contributed a great deal to our understanding of the formation of a civil society, and the manner in which different segments of the population relate to local-level party and government; they attempt to identify whether or not, and in what form, the space of civil society is developing. However, their works do not go far in explaining and quantifying the nature of political values in China today; in order to do this, it is essential to analyze reliable public opinion data.

This chapter is not the first to consider the importance of public opinion and changing political values in China. Indeed, Andrew Nathan and Tianjian Shi's *Daedelus* article deals directly with this question. More recently, Alfred Chan and Paul Nesbitt-Larking, Yongnian Zheng, and Jie Chen and colleagues have also written about this issue.[10] Interestingly, these authors do not report the same findings. Nathan and Shi optimistically report, "In general, as theory predicts, the more urban and educated sectors showed more democratic attitudes, supporting expectation as derived from modernization theory that China's culture will move closer to the patterns characteristic of democratic countries as the economy grows" (116). Zheng, and Chan and Nesbitt-Larking, while not as explicitly endorsing the modernization thesis, echo Nathan and Shi. Zheng observes that although his data does not necessarily show strong support for democracy, there are indications of an emerging liberalism. Chan and Nesbitt-Larking's emphasis on "critical citizenship" in China is consistent with Zheng's observations. Chen and colleagues find that popular support for the regime runs high, but do not extensively analyze the nature of the political values they report on, nor do they consider the extent to which their survey indicates the degree to which residents of Beijing are interested in democracy and a more open political system.

Overall, these articles are disappointing for the student of current structural changes in the Chinese polity. The work of Nathan and Shi, while promising, is already dated, as it is based on a 1990 survey conducted in Beijing. Chan and Nesbitt-Larking, and Zheng depend on data from the late 1980s, which was of questionable validity even then. While Chen and colleagues use contemporary data, their analysis is not particularly insightful, as it is restricted to gauging the level of support for the current regime, and fails to explore the more interesting question of how political values may be changing in Beijing.

Our chapter addresses these weaknesses, as we are using some of the newest, most reliable data available. In addition, we employ these cross-sectional data in a manner that allows us to assess the likelihood of future trends. In particular, we address the changes in the distribution of public opinion with respect to support for democratization and liberalization that are likely to be caused in the foreseeable future by generational replacement as well as caused by probable trends in the Chinese economy and educational systems.

Theory

As is clear from the above review, there is ample room in the existing literature for an analysis that focuses on public opinion in China regarding the issues surrounding democratization. In fact, we believe it is worth noting that public opinion climate favorable to a transition toward democracy is a necessary condition for the emergence of a democratic polity. That is to say, if all of the circumstances that lead to democracy were present but the public was opposed to democracy, it is difficult to imagine that a democratic polity could emerge.

As such, we believe it is time to focus explicitly on attitudes about democracy and liberalization. This paper does just that by examining data from a survey of the residents of Beijing that asks a very specific question: "The following are various qualities; which do you feel is the most important?"[11] The choice set offered to the respondents consists of *individual freedom, public order, fair administration of justice, social equality, political democracy, national peace and prosperity,* and *"don't know."* Only one choice was allowed. We have chosen in this article to focus on two of those choices, *political democracy* and *individual freedom.*[12]

If the prospects for democratization in China are good, there are some obvious patterns that we would expect to observe among the residents of Beijing.[13] First and foremost, if younger people are more favorably disposed toward democracy than older people, then it seems reasonable to expect that the future public opinion climate would be more amenable to a democratic transition than it is now because of generational replacement. This, of course, makes the assumption that individual attitudes are stable over an individual's life cycle. While this is certainly not true all of the time, there is a great deal of evidence in other contexts to suggest that this is a reasonable assumption.[14] In addition, this assumption can be relaxed to suggest merely than any microlevel attitude change across the life cycle is random. This implies that at the macro level, the changes balance out, leaving the distributions within and across age cohorts roughly the same. We expect to find that younger people are more supportive of democracy than older people.

If wealthier respondents are more likely to support democracy, assuming that China continues to progress economically, that would seem to suggest that more people in the future would likely favor democracy. China's economic growth over the last fifteen years has been nothing short of spectacular. This growth, however, has led to a significant increase in economic inequality. While increasing wealth in absolute terms may lead to changes in attitudes about democratization, it is also conceivable that the preference for democracy may be a function of increases in relative wealth. Fortunately, with respect to our data, the conclusions drawn about the prospects for democratization are the same in either case. Barring an economic disaster, China's future is both wealthier and less egalitarian. We remain somewhat agnostic about our expectations for wealthier people. On the one hand, wealthier people may be those most benefitting from the current system and may, therefore, be loath to see any changes. On the other hand, wealthier people may have more time to concern themselves with issues other than the necessities of life, and so prefer to see a more open polity.

In addition, it is reasonable to expect that China will continue to raise the average level of education of its citizens if the economic growth continues. If we find that people with more education are more likely to support democracy, then that would also bode well for the prospects for democratization. We suspect that education is strongly positively related to democratic values. Given the state of China's education system and the limited exposure to Western ideas of governance prior to higher education, it seems unlikely that those with a limited education would be very supportive of democracy.

We also suspect that the respondents who are dependent on the state for their income may be much less likely to support democratic values because they are more beholden to the current government than those employed in the private sector. We defined this dummy variable as those who are retired or who are employed in state-owned industries. The precariousness of many of the state owned industries may lead these respondents to be especially concerned about near-term employment prospects as opposed to other issues that are more remote. In the context of a question about the most important value, those who think they may be unemployed in the foreseeable future are probably more likely to select options such as "national peace and prosperity."

Finally, we will consider the effect of gender on support for democratic values. A priori, it is not clear what effect the gender of a respondent would have on political issues. Because there are important gender differences in other countries, however, we will analyze this variable as well.

Bivariate Analysis

We begin with a series of univariate or bivariate analyses of these data to see if the expectations noted above, in their simplest form, are borne out. We follow this up with a series of multivariate analyses that will answer questions about the effect of the variables of interest on the dependent variables, independent of the effect of the other variables.

Perhaps not surprisingly, a majority of Beijing residents, 56 percent (see table 9.1) report that national peace and prosperity is their most important value. [15] The next most popular response was *fair administration of justice,* which was selected by 13 percent of the respondents. *Social equality* was selected by 10 percent of the respondents, while only 4.7 percent selected *public order.* The two responses that directly address the preference for democracy are, of course, the *political democracy* option selected by 5.8 percent of the respondents, and *individual freedom,* which was selected by 6.3 percent. We believe that those who value *individual freedom* would support greater liberalization of the polity (as well as, perhaps, limitations on societal pressure and other forces) but that this is not necessarily a democratic value. At the same time, we suspect that most democratic revolutions (or transitions) are not the result of a burning theoretical desire for a multimember district, nontransferable vote system (or some other variant of an electoral system), but rather a desire to be left alone by the government. Given the extraordinary restrictions still placed upon ordinary Chinese with respect to, for example, where one can live, when one can marry, the number of children one can have, and so on, it seems entirely plausible that these kinds of issues, if not addressed by the government, could lead citizens to press for a change.

At first glance the prospects for democratization based on the responses to this question seem bleak. It is worth noting, however, that the appropriate comparison is not 100 percent support for democratic values, but rather, a level of support that is similar to other countries in the years leading up to a transition. Second, recall that the question reads, "Which is the *most* important value . . . ?" These data say nothing about secondary and tertiary values. In addition, there is nothing inherently undemocratic about valuing a fair judicial system or wanting your country to be peaceful and prosperous. [16]

Table 9.1.   Which of the Following Values Is Most Important?

Category	Percentage of Respondents
Individual Freedom	6.3%
Public Order	4.7%
Fair Administration of Justice	13.0%
Social Equality	10.0%
Political Democracy	5.8%
National Peace and Prosperity	56.0%
Don't Know	4.2%

Table 9.2.   Cross-Tabulation of Most Important Value by Age Cohort

Age	Individual Freedom	Public Order	Fair Justice	Social Equality	Political Democracy	National Peace and Prosperity	Don't Know	Total
18–25	13.3%	5.0%	16.7%	10.0%	5.0%	48.3%	1.7%	6.6%
26–34	8.5%	2.8%	18.6%	10.7%	0.6%	58.8%	0.0%	19.4%
35–44	5.8%	3.9%	11.0%	13.3%	5.2%	59.5%	1.3%	33.9%
45–54	4.4%	7.4%	14.8%	6.7%	10.4%	55.6%	0.7%	14.8%
55–64	4.2%	6.3%	9.9%	5.6%	7.7%	55.6%	10.6%	15.6%
65–74	4.5%	4.5%	9.0%	9.0%	9.0%	44.9%	19.1%	9.8%

The cross-tabulation of age cohort by the responses to the most important value question (see table 9.2) is the first indicator of trends due to generational replacement. It appears from here that the preference for *individual freedom* decreases with advancing age. While 13.3 percent of those between the ages of eighteen and twenty-five rated individual freedom as the most important value, 8.5 percent between the ages of twenty-six and thirty-four did the same. Those between the ages of fifty-five and sixty-four selected the *individual freedom* option only 4.2 percent of the time, while those between sixty-five and seventy-four selected *individual freedom* 4.5 percent of the time.

While the data on individual freedom support our a priori theoretical expectations, the apparent pattern among those who selected political democracy is surprising. It appears that older respondents were more likely to select political democracy as the most important value. While only 5 percent of the eighteen-to-twenty-five age group selected *political democracy,* and only 5.2 percent of those between thirty-five and forty-four, 10.4 percent of those between forty-five and fifty-four and 9.0 percent of those between sixty-five and seventy-four selected this option. It also looks as if there is a trend for younger people to be more concerned about the fair administration of justice. The other responses show no clear age trends. It is also worth noting that the two age cohorts over the age of fifty-five have dramatically higher incidences of choosing "*don't know*" than the younger respondents.

The cross-tabulation of education level with the responses to the most important value question is displayed in table 9.3. Before analyzing this table, there are several important points to be noted. One is that it is not possible to draw reliable inferences about the respondents who hold master's degrees, Ph.D.s, or went to a university but did not complete a degree, because the sample sizes within those categories are too small. Second, note the very high

Table 9.3.   Cross-Tabulation of Most Important Value by Level of Education

Education Level	Individual Freedom	Public Order	Fair Justice	Social Equality	Political Democracy	National Peace and Prosperity	Don't Know	Total
None	6.4%	2.1%	6.4%	12.8%	4.3%	31.9%	36.2%	5.2%
Primary School	6.5%	9.7%	12.9%	3.2%	0.0%	48.4%	19.4%	3.4%
Elementary School	4.9%	4.9%	3.3%	13.1%	13.1%	52.5%	8.2%	6.7%
Junior High	8.4%	3.5%	11.9%	14.1%	6.6%	53.3%	2.2%	25.1%
High School	7.6%	4.2%	13.8%	10.4%	3.5%	59.2%	1.4%	31.9%
Technical College	2.0%	6.1%	14.9%	6.1%	7.4%	63.5%	0.0%	16.3%
University (Incomplete)	0.0%	0.0%	33.3%	0.0%	16.7%	33.3%	16.7%	0.7%
University (Complete)	3.4%	6.8%	20.5%	5.7%	4.5%	59.1%	0.0%	9.7%
Master's Degree	14.3%	0.0%	0.0%	0.0%	14.3%	71.4%	0.0%	0.8%
Ph.D.	0.0%	0.0%	50.0%	0.0%	0.0%	50.0%	0.0%	.2%

incidence of those with no education or with just a primary school education who selected the "*don't know*" option. Third, these data starkly point out one of the ways in which Beijing is not representative of China as a whole. Almost 10 percent of the respondents report that they have a college degree, far higher than the Chinese population as a whole. It seems that there is an unusually high proportion of those with an elementary school education who prefer political democracy as the most important value. In addition, respondents with a higher education seem more concerned about the fair administration of justice than those with less education. Other than that, there are no clear trends evident from this table.

Table 9.4 presents a cross-tabulation of monthly family income grouping with respect to the most important value question. Again, note that based on income, Beijing is clearly not representative of China nationally. While 29.6 percent of the respondents report a family income of between 1000 and 1499 renminbi[17] per month, while another 22.2 percent have family incomes between 1500 and 1999 renminbi per month. [18] Note also that reliable inferences about those respondents who reported monthly incomes in excess of 3500 renminbi are not possible because of the small-within-category sample size.

The implications of these data are nothing short of stunning. It appears that family income is utterly unrelated to the respondents' answers to the most important value question. The only exception to this is the *"don't know"* category: those with low incomes are much more likely to report that they don't know than those with higher incomes. It seems reasonable to expect that this is a result of the fact that income is correlated with education. That is, we believe that mostly what causes people not to express an opinion is that they are relatively uneducated, or undereducated, not the fact that they are relatively poor.

Table 9.4.   *Cross-Tabulation of Most Important Value by Monthly Income Grouping*

Monthly Income (in RMB)	Individual Freedom	Public Order	Fair Justice	Social Equality	Political Democracy	National Peace and Prosperity	Don't Know	Total
None	6.4%	2.1%	6.4%	12.8%	4.3%	31.9%	36.2%	5.2%
< 300	6.3%	6.3%	18.8%	0.0%	0.0%	37.5%	31.3%	1.8%
300–499	5.9%	2.9%	11.8%	5.9%	8.8%	50.0%	14.7%	3.7%
500–999	8.8%	7.5%	8.8%	13.8%	7.5%	47.5%	6.3%	17.6%
1000–1499	5.9%	4.1%	13.4%	13.4%	5.6%	55.4%	2.2%	29.6%
1500–1999	3.5%	5.0%	13.4%	5.9%	6.4%	62.9%	3.0%	22.2%
2000–2499	8.3%	4.6%	11.0%	11.9%	2.8%	58.7%	2.8%	12.0%
2500–2999	0.0%	0.0%	17.1%	8.6%	0.0%	71.4%	2.9%	3.9%
3000–3499	10.5%	2.6%	28.9%	0.0%	5.3%	52.6%	0.0%	4.2%
3500–3999	0.0%	7.1%	14.3%	14.3%	0.0%	64.3%	0.0%	1.5%
4000–4999	15.8%	5.3%	10.5%	0.0%	5.3%	63.2%	0.0%	2.1%
5000–5999	20.0%	0.0%	0.0%	0.0%	40.0%	40.0%	0.0%	0.6%
>6000	0.0%	0.0%	14.3%	0.0%	28.6%	57.1%	0.0%	0.8%

Table 9.5.   Cross-Tabulation of Most Important Value by Type
              of Employment

Employment	Individual Freedom	Public Order	Fair Justice	Social Equality	Political Democracy	National Peace and Prosperity	Don't Know	Total
State-Dependent	5.5%	4.8%	12.8%	9.5%	6.0%	57.7%	3.8%	90.2%
Other	13.5%	4.5%	15.7%	14.6%	4.5%	39.3%	7.9%	9.8%

Table 9.6.   Cross-Tabulation of Most Important Value by Gender

Gender	Individual Freedom	Public Order	Fair Justice	Social Equality	Political Democracy	National Peace and Prosperity	Don't Know	Total
Male	6.1%	5.0%	16.5%	8.8%	7.7%	52.7%	3.2%	48.6%
Female	6.2%	4.5%	9.8%	11.1%	4.1%	59.2%	5.1%	51.4%

Table 9.5 presents a cross-tabulation of the most important value question according to whether or not the respondent is economically dependent on the government.[19] Two trends are clear from this table: first, those who are dependent on the state are more likely to select *national peace and prosperity* as the most important value; second, those who are not employed by the state are more likely to select *"don't know."* While respondents who were not dependent on the state were more likely to select *political democracy* or *individual freedom* as the most important value compared with those who were dependent on the state, it is not clear from the table if the differences are large enough to merit any inferences. We will come back to this point in more detail when we consider the more sophisticated analyses later in this article.

Table 9.6 is a cross-tabulation of gender of respondent as regards the most important value variable. Interestingly, women appear more concerned about *national peace and prosperity* than men do. While 59.2 percent of women selected *national peace and prosperity* as the most important value, only 52.7 percent of men made this selection. Men and women appear virtually identical on the *individual freedom* variable while men seem a bit more likely to have selected *political democracy* as the most important value. As a result, we will include gender as a control variable in each of the multivariate analyses later in this article.

Tables 9.7 and 9.8 report the results of a series of five separate *bivariate* logistic regressions of each of the two dependent variables with which we will concern ourselves for most of the remainder of this paper on each of the indicated independent variables. The dependent variable in table 9.7 is dichotomous, and is scored 1 if the respondent selected *individual freedom* as the most important value, and 0 otherwise. The dependent variable in table 9.8 is also a dichotomous variable, and is scored 1 if the respondent selected *political democracy* as the most important value and 0 otherwise. Both of these variables treat "*don't know*" responses as "missing."

The independent variables employed in this analysis are the same substantively as those presented in the cross-tabulations above, but some differ somewhat in their definition. Instead of regressing the dependent variables on the age cohort, they are regressed simply on the age of the respondent. This was calculated by subtracting the year of birth of the respondent from 1995, the year of the survey.[20] The age of the respondents varies from eighteen to seventy. The education variable has the same categories as indicated in table 9.3, with those with no education scored 0 to those with a Ph.D. scored 9. The income variable is also the same as the categories presented in table 9.4. It is scored 1 for those making less than 300 renminbi per month, to 12 for those making more than 6000 renminbi per month. The state employment variable is scored 1 for those who are employees of the state, and 0 otherwise. The gender variable is scored 1 for men and 0 for women.

The results of the bivariate logistic regressions confirm the intuitions from the cross-tabulations in tables 9.2 through 9.6, above. Unfortunately, logistic regression coefficients do not reflect simply the change in the dependent variable for a one-unit change in the independent variable.[21] Rather, a logistic regression coefficient reflects the change in the log odds of the dependent variable that a one-unit change in the independent variable would cause. It is, however, the appropriate technique with which to analyze a dichotomous dependent variable. For the remainder of this paper we will adopt the convention of providing the unstandardized logistic regression coefficients in the tables and indicating the substantive interpretations of these coefficients in the text.

Table 9.7.   *Bivariate Logistic Regression of "Political Democracy" Dummy Variable on the Indicated Independent Variables*

Variable	Intercept (constant)	Coefficient	Standard Error	Significance	−2 Log Likelihood
Age	−4.6042	.0400	.0105	.0001	378.901
Education Level	−2.5747	−.0462	.0889	.6037	393.305
Income	−2.8109	.0152	.0744	.8386	399.523
State-Dependent	−2.9704	.2542	.5335	.6337	399.322
Gender	−3.1076	.6577	.2948	.0257	394.380

Table 9.8. *Bivariate Logistic Regression of "Individual Freedom" Dummy Variable on the Indicated Independent Variables*

Variable	Intercept (constant)	Coefficient	Standard Error	Significance	−2 Log Likelihood
Age	−1.7627	−.0216	.0113	.0553	417.547
Education Level	−2.0487	−.1676	.0869	.0539	411.523
Income	−2.6472	−.0026	.0732	.9712	421.151
State-Dependent	−1.7636	−1.0431	.3481	.0027	413.545
Gender	−2.6610	−.0371	.2764	.8931	415.795

Table 9.7 demonstrates that the age and gender of the respondent are statistically significant predictors at the .05 level or higher of the probability that the respondent selected *political democracy* as the most important value. At the same time, neither the level of education of the respondent nor the monthly family income of the respondent nor whether the respondent is dependent on the state has effects that are statistically distinguishable from 0. The coefficient for the age variable is positively signed, indicating that the increases in the age of the respondent lead to increases in the probability that a respondent selected *political democracy* as the most important value. The negative sign on the coefficient of the dependent-on-the-state variable implies that those who are retired or state employees are less likely to select *political democracy* as the most important variable. The positive sign of the coefficient of the gender variable implies that men are more likely to have selected *political democracy* than women.

Table 9.8 indicates that age and level of education are statistically significant predictors at the .1 level of the probability that a respondent selected *individual freedom* as the most important value. The dependent-on-the-state dummy variable is a significant predictor at the .05 level. This time, however, supporting our a priori expectations, the increasing age of the respondent leads to a decrease in the probability that the respondent selected *individual freedom* as the most important value. Surprisingly, increasing levels of education appear to lead to decreasing probability that the respondent selected *individual freedom* as the most important value. Again, being dependent on the state leads to a decrease in the probability that the respondent selected *individual freedom*.

Multivariate Analysis

The foregoing analysis, however, does not enable us to assess the effect of each of the independent variables on the dependent variable, conditional on the effects of the other independent variables. Tables 9.9 and 9.10 overcome this

Table 9.9. Multivariate Logistic Regression of "Political Democracy"
Dummy Variable on the Indicated Independent Variables

Variable	Coefficient	Standard Error	Significance
Constant	−5.6006	.9051	.0000
Age	.0447	.0115	.0001
Education	.0667	.0892	.4549
Income	.0566	.0786	.4713
State-Dependent	−.1420	.5508	.7966
Gender	.6795	.3032	.0250

−2 Log Likelihood = 371.310

Table 9.10. Multivariate Logistic Regression of "Individual Freedom"
Dummy Variable on the Indicated Independent Variables

Variable	Coefficient	Standard Error	Significance
Constant	.8137	.9622	.3977
Age	−.0382	.0142	.0070
Education	−.3257	.1281	.0110
Income	−.0137	.0809	.8654
State-Dependent	−.7340	.3671	.0456
Gender	−.0157	.2832	.9558

−2 Log Likelihood = 390.565

limitation by reporting multiple logistic regression analyses of each of the dependent variables defined above on all of the independent variables simultaneously. This analysis allows a more complete understanding of the prospects for democratization in China because we will be able to disaggregate the effect of each of the independent variables controlling for the effect of the other independent variables.

Table 9.9 reports the logistic regression of the *political democracy* dummy variable on the five independent variables of interest. We find that the age variable is still, contrary to our expectations, a significant predictor and the sign continues to indicate that increasing age leads to increases in the probability of selecting *political democracy* as the most important value. Being dependent on the state is not statistically distinguishable from 0. Gender remains a statistically significant predictor and the sign implies that men are more likely than women to value *political democracy.*

Table 9.10 reports the multivariate logistic regression of the *individual free-dom* dummy variable on each of the relevant independent variables. This analysis suggests, similar to our expectations, that age is a significant predictor of *individual freedom* as a value. Younger respondents are more likely to have selected *individual freedom* as the most important value. Education level and the dependent-on-the-state dummy variable are also significant predictors. Again, increasing levels of education lead to decreasing importance of *individual freedom*. Being dependent on the state also dramatically decreases the probability of having selected *individual freedom* as the most important value.

Discussion

The multivariate model presented in table 9.9 provides no evidence to suggest that there will be increasing pressure for democratization based on generational replacement effects. The fact that increasing age leads to a decreasing probability that the respondent selected *political democracy* as the most important value would seem to suggest that there will not be any long-term, generational-replacement-driven pressure for democratization. In fact, these particular data would seem to suggest that there will be a decrease in public opinion pressure for democratization. In addition, these data suggest that despite the fact that the Beijing and China of the future will be better educated, have a higher income, and have fewer people who are state dependent, these changes will not have any apparent effect on pressure for democratization because none of these variables are statistically distinguishable from 0.

The sign of the age variable in the *political democracy* model is puzzling. We have to admit that younger people are less interested in democracy as a primary value than older people. At the same time, it is possible in the context of a question that asks respondents to select their *most* important value that younger people are systematically drawn into other categories. In fact, we observe that younger people are systematically more interested in *individual freedom* as well as the *fair administration of justice* as the most important value (see table 9.2). One explanation for this phenomena might be that those who have come of age shortly before or after the events of 1989 may have concluded that political democracy is not a near-future possibility, and that goals such as justice or individual freedom are necessary intermediate steps toward the longer range goal of democracy. Based on the available data, though, there is no way to tell. We hope to consider this possibility in future Beijing area studies.

The fact that younger people are more likely to select *individual freedom* as their most important value would suggest that their will be greater pressure in the future for a more open society and perhaps even democratization. It is difficult to argue, however, that this *necessarily* implies greater pressure for democratization. It is conceivable that respondents could merely be expressing a desire for less government control over their day-to-day existence and family decisions.

The fact that increasing education leads to a decreasing probability of selecting *individual freedom* as the most important value has multiple interpretations. First, it is likely that, at least to some extent, the education system is effectively socializing people to downgrade the importance of values such as freedom. It is also possible that more educated people are more concerned about the *fair administration of justice,* a pattern we observed earlier (see table 9.3). In the final analysis, though, the available data cannot disaggregate these potential causal mechanisms. We hope to take this issue up as well in future Beijing area studies, if conditions permit.

Arguably the most important finding of this paper is the total irrelevance of income as a predictor of either *political democracy* or *individual freedom* as the most important value. This finding flies directly in the face of modernization theory. In addition, it seems to suggest that, at least from a political value standpoint, China remains a largely classless society. We suspect that this is because, even in China's most developed cities such as Beijing, the level of income is still so low that for the vast majority of people there has not yet been an income-based divergence of political opinions.

The fact that being dependent on the state for one's income makes one significantly less likely to have selected *individual freedom* as the most important values bears out our original hypothesis about this variable. While economic interests are certainly a concern, we also suspect that there is a socialization component to this as well. Most of these respondents are currently employed by the state or spent their working lives employed by the state. It seems reasonable to expect that a lifelong work environment that stresses the group over the individual has an impact on one's attitudes. At some level, this result also suggests that in the future China will also have increased public opinion pressure for some political opening because we expect many fewer people in the future to be dependent on the state for their income.

Conclusion

It is time to reiterate that results of an opinion survey in Beijing do not necessarily reflect the opinions in the country at large. In fact, it is safe to say that there are major differences between the residents of Beijing and the eight hundred million or so agricultural peasants who would very much like to live in a place with as much economic opportunity as Beijing. Other cities that are less developed or culturally distinct from Beijing would also, no doubt, exhibit important differences as well. This is to say nothing of the fact that sometimes seemingly similar areas exhibit very different attitudes.

Despite the limitations, though, several important conclusions come out of this paper. The first is that any future discussions of the prospects for opening or democratization in China ought to employ a survey-based public-opinion perspective, an elite-based "change-from-the-top" approach, or an empirical analysis of the existence or lack of existence of civil society and the implications this may have for future openings. We think all of these approaches are useful for understanding developments in China; we do *not* believe that further normatively driven speculation without empirical evidence is useful or worthwhile.

Another important point is that while we find no apparent pressure for democratization in Beijing, and only some hope of longer term pressure for liberalization, this should not be interpreted to mean that the residents of Beijing are fundamentally content with their lives or their polity. Other aspects of our data set (the topic of another paper) indicate that economic confidence in Beijing is quite high. Given the rate of Chinese economic growth, this is not surprising. At the same time, respondents to this survey expressed, in overwhelming majorities, deep resentment toward other political issues. Ultimately, however, these data do not address those important questions and nothing herein should be interpreted to suggest one or another conclusion concerning the attitudes of the residents of Beijing toward regime legitimacy. It is important to note that our data cannot predict, and we have no comment on the likelihood of, a near-term violent revolution in the People's Republic of China.

If the reader were to take only one point away from this article, we would hope that it would be the recognition that it is time to focus more explicitly and systematically on Chinese public opinion than we have in the past. There are certainly difficulties involved in such an undertaking. Yet given the enormity of the task at hand, small beginnings now, when we might establish baselines for attitudes during the very early stages of the development process, are time, money, and effort well spent.

Appendix 1: Details of the Beijing Area Study, 1995

This study targeted adults between the ages of eighteen and seventy years old who were dwelling in a formally registered, nonagricultural family household in one of the four urban districts of Beijing (Dongcheng, Xicheng, Chongwen, or Xuanwu), or one of the four "suburban" districts of Beijing (Chaoyang, Fengtai, Shijingshan, or Haidian). The sampling design was a two-stage systematic selection scheme with "probabilities proportional to the size" (PPS) measures. The primary sampling units were neighborhood committees (*junmin weiyuanhui*); households were the secondary sampling units. The sample is self-weighting because it employed a proportionate stratification based on socioeconomic variables. The final sample selection consisted of 1,189 households. In the event that the respondent wasn't home, the interviewer was required to make at least three return visits. In total, 916 interviews were completed, yielding a response rate of 77 percent.* A copy of the complete sampling report is available from the authors upon request.

*All of the information in this section, including some of the exact wording, comes from the sampling report by Hao Hongsheng of the Research Center for Contemporary China and People's University in Beijing.

Notes

1. We define *political liberalization* as a movement away from a totalitarian or authoritarian political structure toward one that entails greater personal freedom, autonomy, and rights, yet is not necessarily similar to a Western liberal democracy with a political system based on a one man, one vote electoral system. This type of change in nondemocratic systems has also been labeled *opening,* and *the emergence of civil society,* but it is not the same as democratization.

2. For a debate over these issues see Gordon White, "Democratization and Economic Reform in China," *Australian Journal of Chinese Affairs* 31 (1994), 73–93; and Barrett McCormick, "Democracy or Dictatorship: A Response to Gordon White," *Australian Journal of Chinese Affairs* 31 (1994), 94–110.

3. Giuseppe DiPalma, "Legitimation from the Top to Civil Society: Politic-Social Change in Eastern Europe," *World Politics* 44 (1991), 49–80.

4. See Kenneth G. Lieberthal and Michel Oksenberg, *Policy Making in China* (Princeton, N.J.: Princeton University Press, 1988); and Harry Harding, *China's Second Revolution: Reform After Mao* (Chicago: University of Chicago Press, 1987).

5. See Edward Friedman, *National Identity and Democratic Prospects in Socialist China* (Armonk, N.Y.: M. E. Sharpe, 1995); Minxin Pei, *From Reform to Revolution* (Cambridge, Mass.: Harvard University Press, 1994); and Stephen Young, "Post-Tiananmen Chinese Politics and the Prospects for Democratization," *Asian Survey* 35 (1994), 652–67.

6. Friedman, *National Identity,* 340.

7. Young, "Post-Tiananmen Politics," 664.

8. Barrett McCormick and David Kelly, "The Limits of Anti-Liberalism," *Journal of Asian Studies* 53 (1994), 805.

9. Dorothy J. Solinger, *China's Transition from Socialism* (Armonk, N.Y.: M. E. Sharpe, 1993); Mark Blecher and Vivienne Shue, *Tethered Deer: Government and Economy in a Chinese County* (Stanford, Calif.: Stanford University Press, 1996); Andrew Walder, "The Quiet Revolution from Within: Economic Reform as a Source of Political Decline" in Walder, ed., *The Waning of the Communist State* (Berkeley and Los Angeles: University of California Press, 1995).

10. Andrew J. Nathan and Tianjian Shi, "Cultural Requisites for Democracy in China: Findings from a Survey," *Daedalus* 122 (1993), 95–124; Alfred Chan and Paul Nesbitt-Larking, "Critical Citizenship and Civil Society in Contemporary China," *Canadian Journal of Political Science* 28 (1995), 293–310; Yongnian Zheng, "Development and Democracy: Are They Compatible in China?" *Political Science Quarterly* 109 (1994), 235–60; and Jie Chen et al., "The Level and Sources of Popular Support for China's Current Political Regime," *Communist and Post-Communist Societies* 30 (1997), 45–64.

11. See the appendix for a description of the data.

12. The question and choices in Mandarin: "*Xiamian you gezhong jiazhi, nin renwei na yi yang zui zhong yao?*" *Geren ziyou, gonggong zhixu, sifa gongzheng, shi hui ping deng, zhengi minzhu, fanrong anding, bu zhidao.*

13. While it would be ideal to have a nationally representative survey of mainland China, none are available that directly address these issues. While we avoid overgeneralizing beyond the sample, there are good reasons to believe that the trends that manifest themselves in Beijing *may* also portend changes nationally. First, pressure for democratization has, historically, come from urban areas and the China of the future will be more urbanized than the China of today. Further, Beijing is one of the most economically advanced Chinese cities. If the strength and size of the middle class is a relevant predictor of democratization, the China of the future, particularly urban areas, will look a great deal like the Beijing of today with respect to income characteristics and distribution. In addition, to the extent that education is relevant to the desire for democratization, the level and quality of education in Beijing today is also similar to the future of other urban areas of China.

    None of these comments diminish our appreciation of the extraordinary economic, cultural, linguistic, geographic, and political differences that exist in China today and will certainly remain for generations to come. There can be no doubt that a survey of Beijing, just like a survey of Washington D.C. or Paris, will exhibit important differences from the larger nation in which they exist. We conceptualize this as a first step towards a much broader and deeper understanding of public opinion regarding liberalization and, perhaps, democratization in the People's Republic of China.

14. Phillip Converse, "Of Time and Partisan Stability" *Comparative Political Studies* 2 (1969), 139–71; Angus Campbell et al., *The American Voter* (New York: John Wiley and Sons, 1960); Donald Green and Bradley Palmquist, "Of Artifacts and Partisan Instability," *American Journal of Political Science* 34 (1990), 872–902.

15. As with any survey-based analysis, one ought to be concerned about the sources of error in the variables of interest. In particular, in the People's Republic of China it is tempting to think that respondents may have been afraid to provide certain answers. We were concerned about this possibility as well until we analyzed other data that is not available for publication. Respondents were overwhelmingly willing to specifically state that they thought cadres were "corrupt." This leads us to believe that respondents felt quite comfortable speaking their minds to the interviewer.

16. We considered treating the *fair administration of justice* option as a response that was inherently democratic but rejected this possibility. Our thought was that one could favor a repressive, illiberal regime that fairly administered the law. Fair administration of justice, though, may be conceptualized as a step toward democracy. Certainly, the democracy movement in Hong Kong seems as much concerned about the rule of law as it is about elections. As such, any analysis of this variable would be ambiguous.

17. Approximately $120–$180 U.S. at the exchange rates at the time of the survey.

18. Approximately $180–$240 U.S. per month.

19. This variable is scored 1 if the respondent said they were employed by the government or a state-owned industry or is retired and 0 otherwise. As such, respondents who are unemployed, in school, doing housework, etc., are all considered "not dependent on the state." This definition was chosen because our theoretical concern is with the effect of being, quite literally, dependent on the state for one's income and what effect this might have on preferences for their most important value.

20. Note that this survey was conducted in December of 1995 and early January of 1996. We chose to not subtract the year of birth of those interviewed in 1996 from that year because that decision assumes that the respondent's birthday was in the first few weeks of January. It introduces less error to subtract all of the respondents' birth years from 1995.

21. For a discussion of this technique, see Tim Futing Liao, *Interpreting Probability Models Logit Probit and other Generalized Linear Models* (Thousand Oaks, Calif.: Sage Publications, 1994); or Scott Menard, *Applied Logistic Regression Analysis* (Thousand Oaks, Calif.: Sage Publications, 1995). For a broader discussion of the employment of maximum likelihood techniques, see Gary King, *Unifying Political Methodology* (Cambridge: Cambridge University Press, 1989). For a more technical discussion, see G. G. Judge et al., *Introduction to the Theory and Practice of Econometrics* (New York: John Wiley and Sons, 1988).

10

The Political Pragmatism of Chinese University Students at the Dawn of the Twenty-First Century

CHE-PO CHAN

Chinese university students were politically active in the 1980s, and their cohort was one growing up in a period of rapid change. The result of a decade's reform and exposure to the outside world had a major impact on them. The gap between their expectations and reality was great. They intended to change the society, which they viewed as unjust, and to accelerate the pace of reform through student movements. The movements of 1983, 1986, and 1989 were prominent examples of this phenomenon.

Various Western studies have shown that Chinese youths were discontented with their social and political systems and were skeptical of the official ideology in the 1980s.[1] The 1989 movement was the climax of the eighties cohort's political activism. In it Chinese students saw themselves inheriting the Chinese intellectuals' tradition as spokesmen for the society. They gathered around Tiananmen Square to fight against the regime's corruption, bureaucratism, and political control. They demanded, among other things, a democratic system with greater participation, rule of law, freedom of the press, freedom of organization, and political reform. Nevertheless, the movement was suppressed and students were "purged" by the authorities. The role of the students in the 1989 movement exemplified an orientation of political idealism, and the 1989 movement was a process of putting their idealism to the test in reality. Setbacks in the movement, however, induced them and the later cohorts to move away from idealism.

Chinese society has gone through a decade of tranquillity and stability since the 1989 movement. Students are inert and restrict their activities on campus; they keep a distance from real politics. This is no doubt partly due to the re-education campaigns and behavioral controls by authority.[2] Since 1989, instead of politics, economics has become the students' major concern. They care about national economic development and relate their personal interests to that development.

This chapter will investigate the political orientation of Chinese university students after the 1989 incident and will show that there is actually no major change in their beliefs; yet what happened after the incident has changed their viewpoints on how to achieve their beliefs as goals. The change is from idealism to pragmatism. The nature and process of the change will also be examined.

Pragmatism here means a down-to-earth approach to problems and affairs. The meaning of ideas is to be sought in their practical result, and truth is preeminently to be tested by the practical consequences of belief. Whether reality fits with the guiding political principles is not the ultimate consideration. Rather, whether the principles can solve existing problems is the main concern. Any principle is conditional. It may be doubted and judged by rationality.[3] Under pragmatism, political truth and authority are separated. Authority is denied if it is not effective or efficient in solving practical problems. Inquiry is initiated in conditions of doubt.[4] Utility, efficiency, and feasibility are some major considerations of a pragmatic attitude. Skepticism, experimentation, and reform are the pragmatic keys to social progress.[5] Pragmatism is sometimes indistinct from cynicism if one finds oneself becoming too skeptical and disillusioned to get involved.

Pragmatism among the Chinese student population originates from two sources. One has been a continuing trend of secularization since economic reform and opening up to the outside world started in the late 1970s. The Chinese people's disastrous experiences in the Cultural Revolution made them disbelieve the utopian socialist principles and disdain the once charismatic supreme leaders. They were tired of Mao Zedong's hollow slogans and were only interested in the actual effect of policies and in genuine improvement to their lives. They were concerned for their own freedom and welfare and how soon these individual benefits could be achieved. They moved away from collectivism and toward individualism, which was once a taboo in the period of Mao. The new phenomenon of reform and openness paved the way for secularization in Chinese society. With the continuation of reform, people's social status has depended less on political achievement, which has been judged solely by the Chinese Communist Party (CCP), and more on academic and economic successes that are a result of personal effort. The impact of secularization on university students has been especially strong, so that students deny authority and become self-centered. They only believe in and achieve for themselves. We witnessed an intensifying secularization among students in the 1990s.

Another source of pragmatism among students has emerged only since the 1989 movement. Throughout the 1980s, political participation was a major channel through which university students could express themselves. With their setbacks in the 1989 movement and political channels blocked by authority, students conformed with the reality. Political apathy became a general trend on campus, as students avoided political activity. They did not care for political achievement and they had no interest in acquiring political knowledge and information. In the 1990s, if there was any political participation, it was either under government control or was undertaken exclusively within small circles.[6]

Students were diverted primarily to the economic sphere to seek independence and achievement.

A major portion of the data for this study comes from surveys conducted by Chinese academies or research institutes. Some of these surveys are sponsored by the CCP. Results of these surveys have been published in various Chinese academic and professional journals. Surveys in China sometimes are used for political or propaganda purposes, such as to evaluate the effects of the party's youth policy and ideological education. Problems of validity and reliability thus exist in the Chinese surveys.[7] Nevertheless, a careful use of the raw data can still provide a general picture of how university students think about Chinese society and politics today.[8]

The Ideological Crisis of Chinese Youth

The aim, content, and methods of official moral and ideological education have remained the same since the establishment of the Communist regime, and not much has been improved as a result of the reforms starting in the late 1970s. Marxist and Maoist thought are still the guidelines for the school curriculum.

In schools, Chinese youths learn how the CCP cadres work wholeheartedly for the people as well as abide by party rule and law. In society, they witness degenerated "party work style" such as bureaucratism, corruption, extravagance, lawlessness, and power abuse. Likewise, they are taught socialist morals such as self-sacrifice and working for the collective good. At the same time, they witness selfishness and profiteering. The discrepancy between school and reality makes youths feel discontented with the social and political systems. They are also puzzled over the Four Cardinal Principles (i.e., upholding the socialist road, the people's democratic dictatorship, the leadership of the Communist Party, and Marxism-Leninism and Maoist thought). This gives rise to a "crisis of confidence" among Chinese youths toward the communist ideology, system, and authority.

A survey of Beijing students in several universities before the 1989 movement found that 45 percent of respondents either doubted or rejected Marxism[9]; 53 percent supported a multiparty system as well as a separation of powers among government institutions; 57 percent disapproved of upholding the Four Cardinal Principles and the Anti–Bourgeois Liberalization Campaign; and 79 percent saw no difference between socialism and capitalism.[10] The survey showed that on the eve of the 1989 movement, university students (at least those in the Beijing area) were either negative or skeptical of official ideology and inclined to accept some Western alternatives.

Chinese youths did not share a common political belief or rational pursuit in the 1989 movement. In the decade after Mao Zedong died, old beliefs were questioned and abandoned, and new ones sought. Exposure to the outside world introduced some Western ideas into China, ideas that were new and stimulating to students. On campus, Jean-Paul Sartre's existentialism, Friedrich Nietzsche's superman concept, Sigmund Freud's psychoanalysis, Alvin Toffler's "third wave" approach, John Keynes's economic theory, and Abraham Maslow's psychology were some examples of hot topics for self-learning and peer discussion at different periods. Other Western political theories such as those of the balance of power and social contract were also among the students' favorite subjects of inquiry.[11]

To the students, there was a strong contrast between Western ideas and official Chinese ideology. The Western ideas influenced them, and thus they were upset with the socialist doctrine of collectivism. Instead, they pursued freedom of mind, pluralistic thinking, and self-fulfillment—in short, individualism. Wishing to avoid being controlled by the state in most of its important decision making, students stood for "personal choice, individual planning, and self-fulfillment."[12]

According to a panel survey carried out in a university, in 1986, students who approved of "individual planning" constituted 25.8 percent. A year later, the figure rose to 48.5 percent. Those who disapproved of "individual planning because of its nature of individualism" constituted 4.1 percent in 1986. A year later, the figure had dropped to only 2.4 percent. In the same survey, as shown in table 10.1, there was an increasing trend among Chinese students who approved of "individual struggle."[13] Another study also confirmed that "control over one's life was more salient to the students than the realization of communism."[14] On the whole, we could conclude that on the eve of the 1989 movement, Chinese students had moved away from collectivism and became more self-centered in their orientation.

The growing self-consciousness of Chinese youth during the previous decade contributed to the occurrence of the 1989 movement. Students in the movement were mainly against the regime's monopoly of power and ideology and the evils it generated. They fought to change the society into one in which they could have more freedom to pursue their own needs.

The trend of individualism has not weakened since 1989. A survey conducted in September 1995 showed that, as indicated in table 10.2, a sum of 67.8 percent (for responses to items 1 and 2 combined) of students approved of individualism. When students were asked for their purpose of study, 18.7 per-

Table 10.1. Question: What Is Your Opinion on "Individual Struggle"?

	It will lead to individualism and should not be encouraged.	It is the basic factor leading to success and should be strongly encouraged.
1985	6.1%	20.4%
1986	3.5%	32.1%
1987	1.4%	42.5%

Source: Zhang Yuanlong, "Xifang xueshu sichao yu dangdai daxuesheng xingtai" (Western Academic Thoughts and Contemporary University Student Thinking), *Sixiang lilun jiaoyu* (*Education in Ideology and Theory*), February 1990, 61.

Table 10.2.   Question: What Is Your View on "Individualism"?

1. We should not object to it because it drives personal and social progress.	12.8%
2. Under a socialist market economy, it is rational to have it.	55.0%
3. It should be objected to because it is the major value of the bourgeois class.	32.2%

Source: Min Yongxin, "Daxuesheng qunti shenghuo jiazhiguan de zhuanbian yu sikao" (The Change of and Reflection on the Value of University Students' Group Life), *Qingnian tansuo* (*Youth Exploration*) 65 (1996), 38.

cent replied it was for their motherland, and the other 81.3 percent said it was for various self-interests and personal considerations.[15] In a more updated survey conducted in a technical university, students were asked to identify their purpose in life; 33.8 percent wanted to contribute to the society and country, 51.3 percent strove for a successful personal career, 9.7 percent for a happy family, and 3.3 percent for earning a lot of money, and the remaining 1.9 percent had no answer.[16]

We should not interpret the individualism of Chinese youth as the extreme opposite of the wholehearted dedication to collectivity and sacrifice of oneself as exemplified by the spirit of Lei Feng. In Mao Zedong's time, pursuing individual interests was against the social norm. Today, Chinese youths aim at pursuing individual interests and at the same time contributing to societal interests, working, as they describe it, "subjectively for oneself and objectively for others." They expect respect and opportunities for fulfillment from society, while a sense of social obligation still lingers in their minds.[17]

The Impact of the 1989 Movement on Chinese Youth: Frustration and Depression

The 1989 movement was a setback for both Chinese youth and the CCP. It was a setback for youths because the consequence of their movement was the opposite of their expectations; it was a setback for the CCP because Chinese youths had openly challenged the official ideology, showing that the official ideological education had lost some of its validity.

However, the CCP authorities did not revise their ideological education as a result. Both the content and approach of the education remained the same as before the 1989 movement. Some old political campaigns such as the Emulation of Lei Feng Movement, the Patriotism Education Movement, and the study of Marxist activities were still carried out on a large scale. Some of the new campaigns were just "old wine in a new bottle"; these include Anti–Peaceful

Evolution Education and the Anti–Bourgeois Liberalization Campaign. Students
were forced to participate even though they were repelled by these activities.

Moreover, the government revised a series of policies for university students,
such as introducing military training, centralized job allocation after graduation, emphasizing political standards in the recruitment of graduate students,
and setting constraints on self-financed overseas study. These policies aimed at
achieving a tougher control over the students, who generally felt suspicious and
resentful. They regarded these measures as showing the government's mistrust
of them, and as a punishment for their participation in the 1989 movement.

After the 1989 movement, the first political campaign publicized by the CCP
was the Emulation of Lei Feng Movement. Chinese youth were urged to learn
from Lei Feng his self-sacrifice, altruism, firm class standpoint, and how to be
the CCP's "rust-free screw." Did youth learn from the model of the 1960s? The
individualistic orientation among Chinese youths since the 1980s provided a
force of resistance. Youth criticized the official endorsed role models for stressing only duties, not rights.[18] A study found that among different sources of
influence such as family (39.5 percent), social trends (20.3 percent), classmates
and friends (19.5 percent), and school and teachers (14.7 percent), the role
model had the least influence (i.e., 6.2 percent) on students' values and behavior.[19] The influence of Lei Feng is minimal on 1990s students; whether they
learn from 1960s models can be further answered by a survey conducted in
Dalian in 1997. When students were asked of their values in life when faced
with the choice between personal and societal interests, 60.6 percent approved
the moderate orientation, "both giving (to society) and taking (from society)."
The second largest majority, 35.2 percent, endorsed the more altruistic orientation, "giving to society." Only 2.1 percent favored "caring for (personal) status
and money"; another 2.1 percent favored "taking (from society) only."[20] The
absolute altruism displayed by Lei Feng is no longer accepted by contemporary
Chinese students; they would rather support a middle-road position between
selfishness and altruism.

For a time after June 1989, Chinese students still felt shocked, confused,
upset, and helpless.[21] Chinese campuses were surrounded with political pessimism. Students were inactive and apathetic to politics. They found channels
to relieve their energy and frustration: mass culture and hedonism quickly
became popular on campus. Students played mah-jongg, listened to rock and
roll music, drank alcohol, danced, and developed love affairs. To directly relieve
their political frustration, on consecutive June Fourth anniversaries, students
smashed small bottles on campus as a form of protest.[22]

Since 1991, "classroom desk literature" has become widespread on the
Beijing campuses. Students write their feelings down on classroom desks, and
sometimes echoes or comments from classmates appear next to the originals.[23]
According to a study, about 30 percent of the total writings reflected students'
disappointment, frustration, and confusion, especially about their futures.[24]
One of such themes is a strong wish to go abroad as an escape. The following
stanza is an example:

Tianya wuchu rong woshen
Weiyou fuxi bi huairen

Nowhere could I hide
Only leaving for the West could evade the bad guys

Another 20 percent of the writings are attacks on social evils and criticism of different social phenomena. There is discontent about degenerated "party work style" and on the leftists returning to power. An example is as follows:

Xue hao shu-li-hua
Buru youge hao-baba
Buru dangge pipan-jia
Zhou pian tianxin dou bupa

Studying mathematics, science, and chemistry well
Is incomparable to having a good father[25]
Is incomparable to working as a political critic[26]
Which enables one to achieve well anywhere

Students were also dissatisfied with the low income of intellectuals, and society's lack of respect for knowledge. About 15 percent of the desk literature writings belong to this category. The following is an example of students mocking themselves:

Xueshi cheng kegui
Shuoshi jia geng gao
Ruo wei chaopiao gu
Liangzhe jie kepao

A bachelor's degree is valuable
A master's degree is even better
For the sake of money
Both can be given up

Other desk literature writings, which constitute the remaining 35 percent, include love themes, personal grievances, and complaints with school curricula, especially such things as the ideological-political courses.

The negative and perplexed emotions of students are also exemplified in other respects. After the 1989 movement, many students became passive with their lives; they lived as if without any purpose. A popular self-portrait among the students goes as follows:

Da majiang
Yiye erye bushui
Tiaowu
Shanbu sibu quanhui

Hejiu
Wuliang liuliang buzhui

Playing mah-jongg
Can stay awake for one night two nights
Dancing
Is good at three steps four steps
Drinking
Won't get drunk with five liang, six liang[27]

Moreover, Chinese university students have been in a low mood in their studies since 1989. A common study attitude was to get only sixty marks (a passing grade); to get an extra mark was considered a waste. According to a survey at a Shanghai university, 72 percent of the respondents approved of this study attitude, and only 22.7 percent of students studied outside class.[28]

Unchanged Political Attitudes before and after 1989

After the 1989 movement and under the tight control of the government, Chinese youth have avoided involvement in politics. Behavioral alienation does not necessarily entail losing one's faith in previous beliefs, however. As one way to find out whether Chinese students still hold their pre-1989 political attitudes and whether they try to approach them differently today, we examine their present interpretations of the major themes of the 1989 movement.

Most students believe in the correct direction of the economic reforms initiated by Deng Xiaoping, and their beliefs have been the same both before and after 1989. Table 10.3 shows that a great majority, 95.7 percent of students from Wuhan University, approved of the policy of reform and opening to the outside world; not a single student from the sample disapproved of the policy. A

Table 10.3. What Is Your Attitude to the Policy of Reform and Opening to the Outside World?[29]

Completely approve	56.4%
Approve	39.3%
Disapprove	0%
Completely disapprove	0%
No response	4.3%

Source: Yu Shuanghao and Lee Binxiong, "Daxuesheng zhengzhi xing zhouxiang" (The New Political Direction of University Students), *Qingnian yanjiu (Youth Studies)* 7 (1994), 34.

Table 10.4.   Survey of Shanghai Area University Students in April 1992

Reform of large and medium-sized enterprises could be judged successful as long as it benefits economic development; no constraint should be set on the enterprises.	86%
I am concerned most with economic development, and experiments in share-holding systems and labor contractual systems.	78%
Political structural reform will not work well if it is not backed up by strong economic capacity.	81%
This is the right time to put great effort into developing the economy.	86%
I am not interested in the debate on whether the enterprise reform is named *socialism* or *capitalism*.	87%

Source: Shanghai Gaojiao Yanjiusuo (Shanghai Research Institute on Higher Education), "Da zhong xing qiye gaige yu jiushi niandai daxuesheng" (Reform of Large and Medium-Sized Enterprises and 1990s University Students), *Qingnian tansuo* (*Youth Exploration*) 43, no. 5 (1992), 44.

---

small number, 4.3 percent of respondents, appeared to be too apathetic to answer the question. The broad picture is that Chinese students have no objection to the general direction of economic reforms carried out in China. If there is disagreement, it is most likely on the intensity and speed of the economic reforms. Also, students prefer having political reforms carried out together with economic reforms.[30]

The spirit of reform is to get into the right course through experimentation, as is testified in Deng's own words, "crossing the river by touching stones" (*mo zhe shitou guo he*); and students today follow Deng's pragmatism. As shown in table 10.4, 86 percent of the respondents did not accept any restriction on enterprise reform, and 78 percent were concerned about different experimental programs within the reforms, some of which were highly controversial. Students were concerned about the usefulness rather than the philosophic nature of these programs. Among the Shanghai students, 87 percent were so bold as to point out that, to them, whether the reform was socialist or capitalist in nature did not make any difference.

Chinese students adopted a peaceful approach in the 1989 movement. They did not aim to replace the Communist regime. Instead, they asked the CCP to release some of its powers and to undertake more reforms. In the 1990s, the CCP focused on economic reform, but still would not allow significant political change, though pushing for political reform was the intention of students in the

1989 movement. After the failure of the movement, students realized that if grassroots mobilization could not bring change, more economic development might be an alternative way to induce political reform.

From Table 10.4, it is interesting to note that as high as 81 percent of students acknowledged the importance of economic strength in pushing for political structural reform. From the above analysis, students today have obviously moved away from radicalism and are more pragmatic and utilitarian in their evaluation of the Chinese reform. They treat reform more as a process involving constant trying and changing than as a goal with fixed ideals.

One of the major themes in the 1989 movement was the fight against the cadres' corruption and power abuse. Two surveys showed that students in recent years still viewed corruption as a very serious political problem. One survey was conducted in ten Shanghai universities in 1996[31]; as illustrated in table 10.5, among the nine factors influencing social stability, 81.46 percent of students thought the CCP cadres' degenerated work style and widespread corruption was the greatest of the nine factors, much in need of government attention. Among the other eight factors, problems directly arising from economic reform such as inflation, income inequality, and state enterprise reform were also major student concerns. Corruption was likewise seen as a problem arising from economic reform. The CCP government's legitimacy has relied heavily on economic reform, and students focused their attention on exactly that.

The other survey was conducted in ten universities in the cities of Henan province[32]; from table 10.6 it can be seen that students perceived that a government without corruption should be a priority on the political reform agenda.

Table 10.5.   What Are the Factors Influencing Stability?
(Choose Three Answers)

Serious inflation	46.08%
Degenerated party work style and widespread corruption	81.46%
Worsening public security	27.82%
Influence of bourgeois liberalization values	11.96%
Separatist movements of nationalities	11.06%
Intervention from foreign enemies	22.61%
Enlarging the gap between rich and poor	48.19%
Agricultural problems	15.45%
Difficulties of the state enterprise reform	29.93%

Source: The Party Unit of the Shanghai City Educational Commission, Propaganda Department, 'Shanghai shi gaoxiao sixiang zhengzhi qingkuang diaocha' (The Investigation on the Condition of Political Thinking in Shanghai Universities), *Sixiang lilun jiaoyu (Education in Ideology and Theory)*, August 1996, 10–19.

Table 10.6.   Which Is the Most Important Issue That Needs to Be
Handled in the Area of Political Reform?

To have a clean government	47%
To eliminate bureaucracy	20%
To establish a socialist political system with Chinese characteristics	17%
To have civil liberty and rights	6%

Source: Xu Keheng, "Daxuesheng suzhi xianzhuang de diaocha yanjiu" (The Investigation and Study on University Students' Existing Qualities), *Qingnian tansuo* (*Youth Exploration*) 70 (1997), 16.

Several years after the 1989 movement, the CCP cadres' corruption and negative work style still have not improved in students' perceptions. To have a clean political culture without corruption and abuse of power has been a political goal that Chinese students have looked forward to since the start of economic reforms. It is interesting to note that *to have civil liberty and rights* was once a political goal of the 1989 movement, and today is of comparatively less concern among the four issues. *To have a clean government* and *to eliminate bureaucracy* are two orientations that now have to be handled more on the policy level. *To establish a socialist political system with Chinese characteristics* is more a review of the fundamental structure. An issue of structure should be more important than an issue of policy. Yet students care more about policy than structure; this reveals that they are politically pragmatic. They would rather have an immediate political problem solved than have the fundamental political structure changed in a direction that might be accompanied by uncertainty and instability.

The CCP also realizes the urgency of eliminating the widespread corruption, and has carried out periodic anticorruption campaigns. Yet, no significant result has been achieved and the bad trend cannot be curbed. Surveys throughout the 1990s have pointed out that most students think that the government has not done enough to solve the problem, and that they are pessimistic about having the problem solved.[33] As shown in table 10.7, more than half (51.4 percent) of the respondents had no faith in government action. Less than one-fifth (19 percent) of the interviewees were skeptical and would rather let time decide. The other one fifth (22.6 percent) were of conditional optimism.

In Mao Zedong's time, the CCP was proud of its honorable "party work style." The CCP cadres were characterized as working wholeheartedly and enthusiastically for the people, and as strictly following party rules. Since the reform began, the party work style has degenerated, and eventually became a focus of one of the major protests of the 1989 movement. After 1989, when students were asked whether cadres should be supervised by law, the people, the CCP, or the executive chief, 41.31 percent of respondents thought that cadres

Table 10.7.   What Do You Think about the Prospect of the Recent
              Anticorruption Struggle?

The anticorruption activity is temporary and cannot solve the nature of the problem.	51.4%
It is difficult to judge right now and needs time for more observation.	19.0%
If the struggle continues in a serious way, hopefully it will fundamentally solve the corruption problem.	22.6%

Source: Wei Shusong, "Guanyu zai xiang shichang jingji guodu shiqi xuesheng sixiang zhengzhi zhuangkuang de diaocha baogao" (Regarding the Report of Investigation on the Students' Political Situation and Thinking in the Transition to Market Economy), *Beijing jingji liaowang* (*Beijing Economic Outlook*), April 1994, 47.

Table 10.8.   What Is the Best Method to Increase
              Administrative Efficiency?

The activities of the cadres of state organs should be within legal boundaries.	41.31%
The activities of the cadres should be under supervision of the people because people are the master of the state; only if the cadres' work is in accordance with people's wishes can administrative efficiency be increased.	42.79%
The Chinese Communist Party is the leading party and the work of the government should be under its supervision.	10.97%
The executive chief should have total control of power and should not be checked by other organs; then administrative efficiency can be increased.	2.96%

Source: Fei Guangfa, "Muqian da-xue-sheng zhengzhi xingtai tanxi" (Analysis of the Present Political Thinking of University Students) *Qingnian xue yanjiu* (*Research and Youth Study*), April 1990, 47–48.

should abide by the law (see table 10.8). Although the question did not directly address the cadres' work style, the answer still reflected the serious lawlessness of the cadres. Another 42.79 percent of respondents preferred cadres supervised by people and comparatively fewer respondents preferred cadres supervised by the CCP (10.97 percent) or by the executive chief (2.96 percent). Although the

CCP and its leaders have been in actual control of the government, students chose a greater role to be played by the people in the supervision of the government. Democracy was a major theme in the 1989 movement, and is still a major concern of students since then.

Another question in the same survey examined more directly students' evaluation of the practice of democracy in China. As revealed in table 10.9, only 25.06 percent of the respondents were satisfied with China's practice of democracy, while 71.40 percent of them were unhappy with the democratic progress, among which about one-fifth of the respondents thought that Chinese democracy needs major improvement. From the survey, we may understand in part the reason behind so many students' participation in the 1989 movement, and their fight for democracy in an unconventional way.

Half a decade after the 1989 movement, most students still identified with the norm of democracy. In a survey conducted in October 1995 among 1128 students from universities in the Wuhan area, when asked whether they identified democracy as the best political system, 71.6 percent agreed, 18.5 percent disagreed, and 9.1 percent had no preference.[34] To another question—"Do you think that university students could more or less influence the progress of democracy?"—59.1 percent of respondents answered yes, 29.8 percent thought that the "influence is insignificant," and 9.6 percent answered with "not at all."[35] We could interpret the results as showing that democracy has been an important political goal for Chinese university students and they have not given up pursuing it, though many are not too optimistic about its future.

Though students endorse the norm of democracy, they have reservations and pragmatic concerns in their consideration of its application to Chinese society. The survey results shown in table 10.10 reflect such an ambivalent attitude. The majority of respondents who approved of the first statement (a combined 85.9 percent agreed and strongly agreed) showed that students understood and endorsed the independent values of economic development and democracy. China's pursuit for economic reform should not be an excuse for sacrificing the

---

Table 10.9.   What Is Your Opinion of the Practice of Democracy in China?

Very good	11.44%
Fairly good	13.62%
Needs improvement	51.74%
Needs major improvement	19.66%

Source: Fei Guangfa, "Muqian da-xue-sheng zhengzhi xingtai tanxi" (Analysis of the Present Political Thinking of University Students) *Qingnian xue yanjiu* (*Research and Youth Study*), April 1990, 47–48.

long-term development of democracy. On the other hand, the transformation to market economy, an important goal of Chinese economic development, has grown rapidly since the last decade while the development of democracy has lagged. The political authority endorses a market economy but not democracy. Although the two coexist in Western capitalist society, there is no consequential link between them in China. Students' responses to the fourth item in table 10.10 showed diverse opinions on the linkage between democracy and market economy. The distributions were almost the same (40.8 percent versus 40.7 percent) for those who approved (agreed and strongly agreed) and disapproved (disagreed and strongly disagreed) of the fourth statement; 16.9 percent of the respondents had no particular preference. Their answers reflect their uncertainty as to whether the two pursued objectives can be achieved at the same time when reflecting on Chinese reality.

The majority of students (a combined 73.5 percent for agreed and strongly agreed) endorsed democracy as the best political system to protect civil rights, as shown by their responses to the third item in table 10.10.[36] Nevertheless, as high as 63.8 percent of respondents (agreeing and strongly agreeing) expected that democracy would lead to social chaos. This perception is probably a reaction to the "big democracy" that came about during the Cultural Revolution,

Table 10.10.   What Is Your Opinion on the Following Statements about Democracy?

	Strongly Agree	Agree	Hard to Say	Disagree	Strongly Disagree
Economic modernization should not sacrifice democracy.	56.9%	29.0%	4.4%	3.2%	5.4%
Democracy lacks efficacy; it easily leads to social chaos.	25.1%	38.7%	9.6%	15.2%	10.1%
Democracy is the best political system in terms of protecting civil rights.	32.5%	41.0%	12.0%	4.3%	8.5%
Democracy is a political system which guarantees market economy.	39.2%	1.6%	16.9%	32.3%	8.4%

Source: Lee Binxiong, "Wuhan diqu gaoxiao xuesheng minzhu yishi xin zhouxiang" (The New Orientation on Democracy among the University Students of the Wuhan Area), *Qingnian yanjiu (Youth Studies)* 2 (1996), 11.

and to the various social and student movements of the 1980s. Today's university students hold pragmatic attitudes toward the social effects of democracy.

Diversion to Economic Activities

Reform and opening since the 1980s have provided university students with three channels to success: through the "black (cap and gown) road," by studying postgraduate degrees, preferably abroad; through the "red road," by joining the Chinese Communist Party and working up to being a leading official, and through the "golden road," by becoming an entrepreneur and getting rich. For a period after the suppression of the 1989 movement, the government set up different obstacles for all three channels. Ideological purity was stressed in the recruitment of graduate students and government officials, and a minimum of five years after graduation had to elapse with an undergraduate degree before one could go abroad to undertake postgraduate study. Students were actually worried about the future of opening and reform.

After the Tiananmen incident, China once again emphasized orthodox ideology and was immersed in a political atmosphere of "leftism." The mass media stressed the need to fight against "peaceful evolution" (*heping yianbian*). In 1991, there was an ideological debate on whether opening and reform should be named *socialism* or *capitalism*. China's reform architect, Deng Xiaoping, was concerned that the rising leftism would hamper his reform. He toured south China in early 1992 and used the tour as a platform to defend his economic reform program and the opening up of policies while attacking the emerging leftist thinking. Deng called for the emancipation of the mind and an increase of the pace of reform and opening.[37]

Deng's southern tour changed students' pessimism. They knew that another cycle of emphasizing economics and deemphasizing politics had come. This in turn raised their economic consciousness.[38] Having been denied political participation for three years, students needed other means to divert their energies and express their concerns. Pursuing economic success was a process in which students could exercise their own free will and fulfill their sense of achievement, without much control from authority.[39] Deng's declaration assured students of the future of reform and opening and incited them to participate with enthusiasm in economic activities.

The "golden road" became the most popular channel among students after Deng's southern tour.[40] Their interests focused on earning money, both on and off campus.[41] Classrooms teaching economics, finance, accounting, international trade, computer science, and English were filled with students. Books on economics and business were the most popular extracurricular reading, and economic theories took the place of political theories as hot subjects of discussion on campus.[42] Incoming freshmen also chose economics and business-related majors as their first priority.[43] The choice of what to study was mainly from a career consideration. In terms of choosing a career, in the past graduating students had three "choices": going to the frontier of the country, going to where one could experience harsh life, and going to where the motherland needed one most. Today, upon graduation, students have three new choices: going to where one could fulfill oneself, going to work where one could earn the most, and going to work in a comfortable environment.[44] Even before graduation, students usually work part-time jobs or start their own small businesses in order to earn quick money. A survey at Beijing University (Beida) showed that 75.4 percent of students already had or wanted to have part-time jobs; 54.5 percent already had or wanted to start their own businesses.[45] As shown in table 10.11, high income was one of the two most important considerations in career hunting among students, as expected. This was especially true among students who majored in economics and business-related fields. The other consideration was making use of professional expertise. The deepening of the market economy and the trend of secularization in Chinese society lead youths to realize the importance of competition and professionalism. Students learn that their economic success depends on their aggressiveness and professional competence.[46] The trend of apathy toward study has abated.[47] Students are prepared to develop a skill or expertise before graduation in order to achieve better things in the market economy.

The trend toward earning money reflects students' utilitarian orientation, part of the now widespread commercial culture in China. Commercial culture

Table 10.11. **What Is the Major Factor You Would Consider in Choosing Your Career?**

	All Students	**Economics and Finance Students**	**Business and Trade Students**
It should be related to my study; then I can use my expertise to contribute more to the society.	43.9%	37.2%	32.4%
High social status	9%	10.5%	8.6%
High income	28.4%	38.4%	45.9%
The chance to go abroad	1.1%	1.6%	1.4%
A light workload	4.6%	2.8%	4.1%
A stable job	11.9%	8.8%	7.2%

Source: Wang Xushan, "Shichang jingji xia daxuesheng de xuyao tanwei" (Investigation into the Needs of University Students under the Market Economy), *Xuzhou shifan xueyuan xuebao: zheshe ban* (*The Academic Journal of Xuzhou Normal College: Philosophy and Social Science Edition*), January 1994, 116–19.

has been especially strong in the 1990s, and has had a great impact on the campus culture. With more and more students interested in commercial activities, the pragmatic and utilitarian elements embedded therein have made university students' idealistic pursuit of truth, concern for the fate of their fellow citizens, and rebellion against the establishment secondary in their pursuits. Students do not expect any radical change to upset the reforms and create hindrances on their way to achievement. They have become more secular and accommodative. This partly explains the lessening concern or apathetic attitude towards politics among students since 1989.[48]

Political Pragmatism

Pragmatism has been directly reflected in students' political behavior; if political concern and involvement do not bring any reward and have even caused trouble, keeping a distance from real politics would be the safest approach. As in the 1980s, in the early years immediately following the 1989 movement students were generally not interested in applying for membership in or attending activities of the Chinese Communist Party (CCP) and the Communist Youth League (CYL).[49] In one Beijing university, 90.7 percent of students had no intention of applying for CCP membership, and 66.5 percent of students had no interest in any CCP or CYL activities.[50] Since the mid-1990s, students have gradually changed their perceptions and recognized that joining the CCP was a channel to career success and individual interests; they could get better jobs after graduation if they were CCP members. The application for CCP membership among university students has increased since then. According to one study in the Wuhan area, the application rate has now increased to 30 to 40 percent among the student population. This study revealed that the majority of students joined the CCP due to pragmatic and self-interest considerations.[51] As shown in table 10.12, a majority (54.9 percent) chose the third item in 1995 and the third and fourth items combined (27.5 percent + 27 percent = 54.5 percent) in 1996. That explains why students "join the organization but do not necessarily believe in the (communist) ideology."[52]

If university students were divided into different hometown origins and their motivations for applying for CCP membership were examined, we found that those with city backgrounds had more pragmatic considerations than those with village backgrounds. Students from villages tended to join the CCP with moralistic and idealistic intentions while students from cities (especially larger cities) tended to do the same out of pragmatic and self-interest considerations.[53] This finding is consistent with our secularization thesis. Chinese cities have more information about reform and more exposure to the outside world than villages. Students from cities should have been more influenced by the secularization process and hence, more pragmatic than students from villages. Students from the more senior classes also tended to be more pragmatic and in favor of self-interest than their underclass peers in their motivations for joining the

Table 10.12.   *Why Do You Think Your Classmates Apply for CCP Membership?*[54]

	1995	1996
To follow their beliefs in communism	18%	17%
To pursue a virtuous personality	5.7%	17%
For practical interest considerations	54.9%	27.5%
To create a good condition for one's study and career	———	27%
Because of pressure from the surrounding environment	3.6%	2.9%
Other	14.8%	8%

Source: Hao Shuang, "Dangdai daxuesheng ru dang dongji de xin zhouxiang" (The New Orientation of the Motivation of Contemporary University Students for Their Joining the Party), *Qingnian Tansuo* (*Youth Exploration*) 67 (1996), 33.

CCP.[55] This is possibly due to a longer exposure to the pragmatic and utilitarian campus culture and its influence.

Students also retreated from their previous political concerns; that is, they showed decreasing interest in Western political theories and ideologies. Before 1989, students had common concerns about major national problems and a common interest in the discussion and fulfillment of political principles such as democracy, human rights, and political reform. After 1989, if students still showed any concern and interest, the issues discussed were practical ones, such as issues of anticorruption, unequal distribution, social morale, and public security. There was a lack of a significant political topic that could become the focus of debate among university students. One survey also showed that from the early to mid-1990s, students had increasingly preferred their people's congress representative to vote for the interests of their locality rather than for national interests if conflict arose between the two.[56] Obviously, students' political orientation was becoming more utilitarian and in favor of self-interest.

Students' retreat from political concerns has also been a result of increasing neutrality towards ideology. Socialism is the official ideology, and capitalism is the official enemy. Mao Zedong–era socialism is perceived as a total failure; the economic reform of the Deng Xiaoping era has been welcomed. Students are told that economic reform still follows a socialist approach. This official interpretation has been doubted, and it is suspected that Chinese economic reform is on its way to capitalism. Students have ambivalent conceptions of the official ideology; staying neutral is one way out of this ambivalence.[57] The mixed understandings of the official ideology among Shanghai students are shown in table 10.13. To all three statements, less than half of the respondents endorsed the official position (47.95 percent, 40.46 percent, and 38.39 percent).[57] The other respondents were either against the official position or hesitant to give their answers. If students did not contest the official ideology, they simply avoided judging the meaning of it.

Democracy requires citizens' attention and participation, or in other words, a minimum level of self-awareness and self-initiation in political affairs. According to the Chinese constitution, citizens' voices are represented by the various levels of the people's congress. University students, as the elite group in China, should be concerned about the election of county-level people's congress members because that is the only election in which they can vote for their delegates. When students were asked whether they were willing to vote in such an election, only 50.5 percent had a positive response and the others were either unwilling or did not care.[59]

The National People's Congress (NPC) is usually in session for about two weeks annually. In the Wuhan survey, when students were asked if they were interested in what has happened during sessions of the NPC, 40.9 percent expressed some or strong interest, 32.7 percent had minimal interest, and 24.3 percent were apathetic about the meetings.

The rate of political participation has been low among students. Obviously, students identify more with democratic norms than with actual practice. The reason for the low political participation rate is probably due to a mixture of

Table 10.13.   Do You Agree with the Following Statements?

	Agree	Don't Agree	Hard to Judge Now	Never Think about It
Socialism will eventually win over capitalism.	47.95%	11.39%	33.79%	5.00%
Socialism and capitalism will merge and eventually become one.	29.16%	40.46%	20.25%	7.97%
As long as people are rich and the country is strong, it does not matter what system we practice.	47.91%	38.39%	8.54%	2.97%

Source: The Party Unit of the Shanghai City Educational Commission, Propaganda Department, "Shanghai shi gaoxiao sixiang zhengzhi qingkuang diaocha" (The Investigation on the Condition of Political Thinking in Shanghai Universities), *Sixiang lilun jiaoyu* (*Education in Ideology and Theory*), August 1996, 17.

low efficacy and low trust in the system. Among the Wuhan students, 23.1 percent anticipated that "their own participation would not influence the election result;" 11.6 percent supposed that without their participation, the election would "go on in due process anyway;" and 45.7 percent said that "election is only a formality."[60]

Students' low efficacy and low trust in the system are also reflected in another type of political participation. Surveys confirmed that students feel indignant over the cadres' corruption and bribery. How would they respond if they encountered such a case? A similar question was asked to the students in a survey: "If you find out that personnel in charge of business activity extorts money from a small businessman (getihu), what would you do?" A total of 51 percent of students answered, "I'd be outraged but I would not do anything"; another 29 percent said they would "report it to newspaper or broadcasting station." Only 7 percent said they would "report it to the supervisor of personnel." Some 5 percent of the students said they would "pretend not to have seen anything."[61] The survey results indicated a gap between students' cognition and behavior. They did not approve what they saw, but were unwilling to put in any effort to remedy the wrongdoing. The survey revealed the low political efficacy among students. Even among those who were willing to do something, more would do it through unofficial channels. This indicated a low trust in the established system; students considered that the unofficial channel was more effective in solving the problem.

Students' apathetic and practical orientation has not just been reflected in their participation in real politics. It is also manifested in their participation in student affairs on campus. In a general survey at the Beijing University (Beida), 56.3 percent of undergraduate students were willing to "participate actively" in their class-organized activities. Nevertheless, only 26.9 percent of them were willing to be organizers and "actively help out"; 42.5 percent expressed no interest or willingness to help out. Moreover, among those who were willing to be organizers, 44.3 percent would do the job "with consideration to pragmatic interests."[62]

In 1996 and afterwards, there was a limited and temporary phenomenon of the reappearance of students' political activism. In the summer of 1996, a book named *The China That Can Say No*, which advocated Chinese nationalism, was published,[63] and had a great influence on campus. Sino-American and Sino-Japanese relationships were hot topics of discussion among students. Before 1996, surveys already showed that university students had a high level of nationalism.[64] For example, according to a survey of ten universities in the Wuhan area in 1995, when students were asked if they agreed with the statement, "There should be no conditions set on loving your motherland," 56.2 percent strongly agreed, 24.0 percent agreed, 8.3 percent had no particular opinion, 6.9 percent disagreed, and 4.1 percent strongly disagreed.[65] Over 80 percent of students set a high standard for themselves in loving their country, and it indicated a strong nationalistic feeling among the student population.

In the fall of 1996, the sovereignty of the Diaoyu Islands was an issue of controversy in the Sino-Japanese relationship. Students in Beijing, Shanghai, and Shenzhen protested Japan's occupation of the Diaoyu Islands. They put up posters on campus, convened seminars to discuss the "national shame," petitioned the government, and boycotted Japanese products. Plans for anti-Japanese demonstrations were rejected by the government, however.[66] The students' response to the Diaoyu Islands case reflects their orientation of political pragmatism. The nature of protest has its legitimacy: patriotism is part of the official ideology and the political authority has no right to ban protests. Students understood the feasibility of their action and they limited their activities mainly to the campuses. In fact, the political authorities exercised self-restraint in using means of repression. When some students wanted to demonstrate on the street and were forbidden to do so by the authorities, they complied without resort to further extreme action. The protests came to an end in a short time when the students realized that their appeals could not go any further.

Conclusion

The 1989 movement had a great impact on Chinese youth. The failure of the movement was a tremendous shock and upset to its participants. Thus, it took a long time for their emotions to quiet. Though the students did have to consider the consequences of their political actions, before 1989 the political atmosphere still left a little space for them to air their discontent and grievances; after 1989, that space was taken away. However, strict controls on the students only led them to be more skeptical of official ideology, apathetic to CCP-sponsored political activities, and negative toward their own lives.

Significantly, the negative effects of the 1989 movement have not changed much of Chinese students' political attitudes thus far. Survey results point to the fact that the political attitudes of Chinese youth have remained the same before and after the 1989 movement. Today, they are still for reform, democracy, and legality, and still against the CCP's "work style," corruption, and collectivism. Also, the trend of self-centeredness among Chinese youths has remained the same now as it was before 1989. The CCP's reeducation campaigns have therefore not proved effective.

What *has* clearly changed is that the opportunity structure on Chinese campuses in recent years is different from that of the 1980s.[67] Before 1989, the general underdevelopment of China had channeled student interests almost exclusively to the political arena. In the last decade, the campuses have been under close political surveillance. All official channels of political participation have legally or practically been abolished. It is difficult for students to mobilize resources for another movement, as any challenge to the political authority may result in great sacrifice. On the other hand, on campuses economic possibilities abound. Such opportunities provide an alternative way for students to enjoy independence and to pursue achievement. The restricted opportunity structure and the opening up of economic channels have enabled Chinese university students to pursue nonpolitical careers and crystallize their goals in life. Political goals are no longer such a priority; the "golden road" is more important. In this context, Chinese students today clearly separate the real from the ideal, as students do in all economically developed countries.

With the deepening of Chinese economic reform, there has also been new emphasis on the political leadership's qualifications. In the last decade, we have seen a new elite profile emerge. Leaders are predominantly university graduates with degrees in technology, management, or science, or technocrats who have the ability to handle economic affairs. These new leaders put less stress on ideology and more on the actual results of policies. Both their career paths and their orientations provide new role models for Chinese students. In addition to the restricted opportunity structure for political expression and the pluralization and crystallization of life goals, the new elite is probably another source of political pragmatism for university students.

According to traditional Chinese thinking, intellectuals should have the ideals of moral integrity, and those of serving and improving society. Undoubtedly, university students see themselves as intellectuals and believe that they should also possess such ideals. Stanley Rosen correctly points out that Chinese students believe in the necessity of having ideals but their ideals are not very firm.[68] This is not a matter of whether or not to have ideals but a matter of the intensity of the ideals. Students were mobilized to fight for democracy and against corruption in the 1989 movement. Since their commitment to action was not strong enough, setbacks in the movement made them put aside the quest and return to a more down-to-earth political outlook. Contemporary university students, on the one hand, still show concern for the future of their country and have a strong sense of responsibility for contributing to its progress; on the other hand, they now pursue professional careers and their own advancement in China's booming economy.

Notes

1. See Ruth Cherrington, *China's Students: the Struggle for Democracy* (New York: Routledge, 1991); Corinna-Barbara Francis, "The Progress of Protest in China: the Spring of 1989," *Asian Survey* 29 (1989), 898–915; Stanley Rosen, "Youth and Social Change in the PRC," in Ramon H. Myers, ed., *Two Societies in Opposition: The Republic of China and the People's Republic of China after Forty Years* (Stanford, Calif.: Hoover Institution Press, 1991); Stanley Rosen, "Students and the State in China: the Crisis in Ideology and Organization," in Arthur Lewis Rosenbaum, ed., *State and Society in China: the Consequences of Reform* (Boulder, Colo.: Westview Press, 1992); and Yan Sun, "The Chinese Protests of 1989: the Issue of Corruption," *Asian Survey* 31 (1991), 762–82.
2. Stanley Rosen, "The Effect of Post-4 June Re-education Campaigns on Chinese Students," *China Quarterly* 134 (1993), 310–34. Ming Hua, "Zhonggong dui xuesheng shetuan mimi modi" (The CCP's Secret Investigation into Student Organizations), *Hong Kong: The Nineties*, April 1995, 44–45.
3. William James, *Pragmatism and Four Essays from the Meaning of Truth* (Cleveland: Meridian Books, 1963).

4. John Dewey, *Logic: the Theory of Inquiry* (New York: Henry Holt, 1938).

5. H. S. Thayer, "Pragmatism," in Paul Edwards, ed., *The Encyclopedia of Philosophy* (New York: Macmillan, 1967), 6, 430–36.

6. In the early 1990s, there were sporadic sensitive political activities among small groups of students. Examples such as holding seminars on topics of human rights, reflection on the June Fourth incident, comparison between Eastern and Western culture, and publishing sensitive political articles in student journals did all take place on campus, but these activities were closely observed and banned if necessary by authorities. See Fang Gang, "Beijing yuanxiao liusi hou de shetuan he kanwu" (Student Organizations and Journals of the Beijing Universities after the June Fourth), *Hong Kong: The Nineties*, October 1994, 46–48.

7. See Stanley Rosen and David Chu, *Survey Research in the People's Republic of China* (Washington, D.C.: U.S. Information Agency, 1987); and Jian-hua Zhu, "'I Don't Know' in Public Opinion Surveys in China: Individual and Contextual Causes of Item Non-Response," *Journal of Contemporary China* 5, no. 12 (1996), 223–44.

8. This study avoids using data that is obviously for propaganda purposes and uses only information bearing at least some description of data-gathering process that enables one to judge its validity. In terms of reliability, statistics of the samples provided in this paper come from major Chinese cities. They do not claim to represent the actual distribution of the whole Chinese population but only indicate a trend or general picture in student populations with similar backgrounds. In the case of comparison among descriptive statistics, readers should pay attention to the order of priority and relative difference among categories of answers rather than absolute statistics for a single answer. Observations from Western academics and outside reports are also used for another source of information and for validation against the Chinese surveys.

9. A separate survey carried out in Beijing in 1988 found that 32.7 percent of students approved that "Marxism is only one of the many theories and should not be elevated (by the CCP) as the guiding principle." In May 1990, one year after the 1989 movement, the same statement was approved by 58.26 percent of students in Shanghai. See Issue Group, Educational Commission, Central Propaganda Department, Chinese Communist Party, eds., "Guowai shehui wenhua sixiang dui woguo qingnian xuesheng de yingxiang he women de duice" (Impact of Foreign Social and Cultural Ideas on Our Young Students and Our Strategy), *Gaoxiao lilun shijian* (*University and Theory in Practice*), April 1992, 54–64 (hereafter cited as CPD).

10. Zhang Yuanlong, "Xifang xueshu sichao yu dangdai daxuesheng xingtai" (Western Academic Thought and Contemporary University Student Thinking), *Sixiang lilun jiaoyu* (*Education in ideology and theory*), February 1990, 61–63.

11. See Guo Xiaocong, "Cong xifang sichao dui daxuesheng de yingxiang fansi gaoxiao sixiang zhengzhi gongzhuo" (With the Influence of Western Ideas Toward University Students, We Should Reflect on the Ideological-Political Work on Campus), *Gaojiao Tanshuo* (*Investigation on University Education*), January 1990, 34–39; see also CPD.

12. Zhang Yuanlong, 61.

13. Ibid.

14. Rosen, *The Effect,* 170.

15. Min Yongxin, "Daxuesheng qunti shenghuo jiazhiguan de zhuanbian yu sikao" (The Change of and Reflection on the Value of University Students' Group Life), *Qingnian tansuo* (*Youth Exploration*) 65 (1996), 38.

16. Duan Xinxin et.al., "Daxuesheng sixiang daode zhuangkuang de diaocha fenxi" (Investigation and Analysis on University Students' Thinking and Ethics), *Zhongguo Qingnian Zhengzhi Xueyuan Xuebao* (*Academic Journal of the Chinese Youth Political Academy*) 2 (1998), 13.

17. The Investigating Team of the Wuhan University Student Affairs Department on Freshmen's Attitudes and Educational Response, "Gaoxiao xinsheng sixiang bianhua tedian ji jiaoyu duiche" (The Specialty of Freshmen's Changing Attitudes and Educational

Response in Higher Education), *Qingnian Tansuo* (*Youth Exploration*) 66 (1996), 4–7.

18. See Jing Lin, *The Opening of the Chinese Mind: Democratic Changes in China since 1978* (Westport, Conn.: Praeger, 1993), 155.

19. Ye Chongqing, "Daxuesheng de guannian xianzhuang pingxi" (Evaluation and Analysis on University Students' Existing Ideas), *Qingnian yanjiu* (*Youth Studies*) 1 (1996), 9.

20. Shi Yanling, "Dalian shi daxuesheng zheye guan de diaocha yu fenxi" (Investigation and Analysis on Dalian University Students' Ideas for Choosing a Career), *Qingnian yanjiu* (*Youth Studies*) 2 (1997), 9.

21. Fu Youmin, "Dongluan hou de daxuesheng zhengzhi xingtai yu jiaoyu" (Political Thinking and Education of University Students after the Upheaval), *Hunan: Yunmeng xuekan* (*Yunmeng Academic Journal: Social Science Edition*), January 1990, 26–29.

22. *Small bottle* in Chinese, is read as "*xiao-ping*," which is same as the first name of Deng Xiaoping. Smashing a small bottle symbolizes an act of disrespect to Deng.

23. Duan Jianxing and Meng Lingdong, "Daxuesheng kezhuo wenhua de diaocha yu fenxi" (Investigation and Analysis on University Students' Desk Culture), *Qingnian yanjiu* (*Youth Studies*) 12 (1996), 32–35.

24. *Ming Pao*, 4 November, 1991, 9.

25. Children of high-level CCP cadres enjoy privileges and good opportunities everywhere.

26. Leftists are perceived by Chinese students as only good in empty words, and having no ability in policy making.

27. Dong Jianjiang, "Dangdai daxuesheng ren-sheng-guan diaocha tanxi" (Investigation and Analysis on Contemporary University Students' Value of Life), *Qingshaonian tantao* (*Youth and Adolescence Inquiry*), January 1991, 15. *Liang* is a Chinese liquid measure.

28. Shanghai Colloquium (A Colloquium Report on the Ideology and Theory Education of the Shanghai Universities), *Sixiang lilun jiaoyu* (*Education in Ideology and Theory*), January 1990, 1–7.

29. The sample size is small because the survey was done only at one university. According to the description of the sampling procedure in the report, the sample size is acceptable. See Yu Shuanghao and Lee Binxiong, "Daxuesheng zhengzhi xing zhouxiang" (The New Political Direction of University Students), *Qingnian yanjiu* (*Youth Studies*) 7 (1994), 33–34.

30. One piece of evidence for students' favoring a political reform could be detected in a survey in which students were asked to evaluate the anticorruption job carried out by the government; 46.6 percent of them replied that "corruption could not be curbed without reforming the political system." See Liu Qingleng and Yuan Hengbing, "Tuxianzhong de daxuesheng jingji jiazhiguan toushi" (Analysis on the Emerging Economic Values of the University Students), *Qingnian yanjiu* (*Youth Studies*) 7 (1995), 33.

31. See The Party Unit of the Shanghai City Educational Commission, Propaganda Department, "Shanghai shi gaoxiao sixiang zhengzhi qingkuang diaocha" (The Investigation on the Condition of Political Thinking in Shanghai Universities), *Sixiang lilun jiaoyu* (*Education in Ideology and Theory*), August 1996, 16.

32. Xu Keheng, "Daxuesheng suzhi xianzhuang de diaocha yanjiu" (The Investigation and Study on University Students' Existing Qualities), *Qingnian tansuo* (*Youth Exploration*) 70 (1997), 15–19.

33. See, for example, Wei Shusong, "Guanyu zai xiang shichang jingji guodu shiqi xuesheng sixiang zhengzhi zhuangkuang de diaocha baogao" (Regarding the Report of Investigation into the Students' Political Situation and Thinking in the Transition to Market Economy), *Beijing jingji liaowang* (*Beijing Economic Outlook*), April 1994, 47; and The Party Unit of the Shanghai City Educational Commission, Propaganda Dept., 16.

34. Lee Binxiong, "Wuhan diqu gaoxiao xuesheng minzhu yishi xin zhouxiang" (The New Orientation on Democracy among the University Students of the Wuhan Area), *Qingnian yanjiu* (*Youth Studies*) 2 (1996), 10–16.

35. Ibid., 14.
36. In the same survey, 78.1 percent disagreed (7.6 percent agreed, and 13.2 percent chose "hard to say") that police could arrest students if they publicly endorsed freedom of speech. See Lee Binxiong, 13.
37. See Suisheng Zhao, "Deng Xiaoping's Southern Tour: Elite Politics in Post-Tiananmen China," *Asian Survey* 33, no. 8 (1993), 739–56.
38. Yang Xiong, "Xinshiqi zhongguo qingnian shehui chanyu de shan da bianhua" (The Three Big Changes in Social Participation among Chinese Youths in the New Era), *Dangdai qingnian yanjiu (Contemporary Youth Studies)* 5–6 (1994), 23–25.
39. The Chinese government has carried out a reform of job assignment for university students. Implemented in different stages, different numbers of students are allowed to choose their own jobs. It is expected that by 2001, all graduate students in China will have free choice in their careers. See *South China Morning Post* (Hong Kong), December 6, 1997, 8.
40. Before 1989, the "black road" was the most popular among university students. See Stanley Rosen, "The Chinese Communist Party and Chinese Society: Popular Attitudes toward Party Membership and the Party's Image," *The Australian Journal of Chinese Affairs* 24 (1990), 63–64.
41. According to a survey of various universities in the Beijing area, ways to earn money included giving private tutoring (21.3 percent), engaging in various kinds of employment (16.7 percent), peddling (10.1 percent), running businesses (7.1 percent), working as broker (6.7 percent), working part-time (6.2 percent), selling bonds and securities (2.4 percent), and "others" (10.1 percent). See Liu Qingleng and Yuan Hengbing, 26–34.
42. Qiu Shuiping, "Shichang jingji tizhi xia daxuesheng zhuangkuang de bianhua ji xuesheng gongzhuo de tiaoshi" (Under the Market Economy System, the Change of Situation among University Students and the Adaptation of Work on Student Affairs), *Re dian Yan Jiu (Investigation on Hot Topics)* 3 (1993), 7–9.
43. Wang Xushan, "Shichang jingji tiaojian xia daxuesheng de xuyao tanwei" (Investigation into the Needs of University Students under the Market Economy), *Xuzhou shifan xueyuan xuebao: zheshe ban (The Academic Journal of Xuzhou Normal College: Philosophy and Social Science Edition)* (January 1994), 116–19.
44. Duan Xinxin, et al., 16.
45. The Sociological Association of Beijing University, "Miandui shichang jingji de beida ren" (The Peking University People Facing the Market Economy), *Shehuixue yu shehui diaocha (Sociology and Sociological Investigation)* 5 (1993), 61.
46. Lu Jianhua, "Qingnian fazhan de hengliang biaozhun wenti" (The Issue of Measuring the Development of Youth), *Qingnian yanjiu (Youth Studies)* 10 (1995), 26–29.
47. See Liu Qingleng and Yuan Hengbing.
48. See Tan Jianguang, "Shangye wenhua yu qingnian wenhua de hudong fenxi" (Analysis on the Interaction between Commercial Culture and Youth Culture), *Qingnian yanjiu (Youth Studies)* 3 (1994), 4–8.
49. See Qiu Shuiping, 7. On the trend toward disinterest in the CCP and the CYL that already existed before 1989, see Rosen, "The Chinese Communist Party," 62–67.
50. Wei Shusong, 47.
51. Surveys in Shanghai also revealed the same orientation among Shanghai students. In those surveys, separate questions were asked for the reasons they did or did not join (or want to join) the CCP. Joining or not was a strategic calculation. See The Party Unit of the Shanghai City Educational Commission, Propaganda Department, August 1996, 16, and the same study for 1995, 3.
52. See Hao Shuang, "Dangdai daxuesheng ru dang dongji de xin zhouxiang" (The New Orientation of the Motivation of Contemporary University Students for Their Joining the Party), *Qingnian Tansuo (Youth Exploration)* 67 (1996), 34.
53. See Yu Shuanghao, "Dangdai daxuesheng ru dang dongji tan mi" (Investigation into the Motivation of Contemporary University Students for Their Joining the Party), *Qingnian*

yanjiu (*Youth Studies*) 7 (1996), 12–18. It should be noted that Yu's and Hao's are two different studies but examine the same data set.

54. In the same study (Hao, 33), the students' own motivations for joining the CCP were also investigated and data were also presented. As the author of the study confessed, problems of both overreporting and underreporting existed. Students tended to evaluate themselves with more idealistic orientations and less practical reasons. It would be more accurate to rely on the data in which students evaluated their classmates rather than themselves. In fact, those who admitted that they applied for the CCP membership with pragmatic reasons constituted 48.5 percent in 1995 and 34.1 percent in 1996, both less than the same evaluations on their classmates. Another survey could be used here as a reference. In Duan Jianxing and Meng Lingdong, 32–35, students were asked directly why they joined the CCP. The first ranking was "to get a better job and to be more able to compete" (35.6 percent); the second ranking was "to have a better chance to work at my ability" (25.5 percent); a few chose the reason, "I believe in communism" (9.7 percent).

55 Duan Jianxing and Meng Lingdong, 32–35.

56. See Lee Binxiong, 14–15.

57. See Yu Shuangxiang and Liu Yuanzhang, "Dangdai daxuesheng zhengzhi guan zhongli xianxiang de chengying" (The Reason for Contemporary University Students' Political Neutrality), *Qingnian yanjiu* (*Youth Studies*) 5 (1992), 42–44.

58. It should be noted that since this survey was carried out by a CCP department, out of prudence respondents were likely overreporting in answering such questions. We suspect that the figures of endorsement here skew toward the higher side.

59. Hao, 13.

60. Ibid., 14.

61. Xu Keheng, 16.

62. The Sociological Association of Beijing University, 62.

63. Song Qian, Zhang Zangzang, and Qiao Bian, *Zhonnguo Keyi Shuo Bu* (*The China That Can Say No*) (Beijing: Zhonghua Gongshang Lianhe Chubanshe, 1996).

64. See, for example, Yu Shuanghao et al., "Daxuesheng aiguo zhuyi sixiang guannian de diaocha yu fenxi" (Investigation and Analysis on University Students' Patriotism), *Gaodeng jiaoyu yanjiu* (*Study of Higher Education*) 2 (1995), 50–54; and Yu Zhen and Guo Zhenglin, "Diwudai zhongguo qingnian de aiguo qingjie" (The Patriotic Disposition of Chinese Youth of the Fifth Generation), *Qingnian yanjiu* (*Youth Studies*) 11 (1996), 18–23.

65. Yu Shuanghao et al., 52.

66. Refer to the series of 1996 reports in *Ming Pao* (*Hong Kong Daily News*): (September 6, 1996), A1; (September 10, 1996), A4; (September 14, 1996), A7; (September 17, 1996), A4; (September 18, 1996), A9; and (September 19, 1996), A4.

67. The discussion on the importance of opportunity structure for various Chinese dissident groups including students can be found in Alan P. L. Liu, *Mass Politics in the People's Republic: State and Society in Contemporary China* (Boulder, Colo.: Westview Press, 1996), esp. ch. 1.

68. Rosen, *The Effect,* 333.

11

Economic Development and Village Elections in Rural China

TIANJIAN SHI

Observers of political development in China usually suggest that there are certain crucial relationships between economic development and village elections. Kevin O'Brien, for example, argues that village elections are more likely to succeed in rich villages.[1] Jean C. Oi proposes that "there may be an inverse relationship between level of economic development and progress in the implementation of democratic village rule."[2] Amy Epstein, however, contends that "provinces that are at the middle level of economic development with relatively strong agricultural and industrial sectors have developed their elections most aggressively and with the most success."[3]

Although these debates touch on an important issue—whether economic development will eventually bring democracy to Chinese society—they fail, unfortunately, to provide a valid answer to this question.[4] This is because all arguments on the relationship between economic development and village elections are based on case studies that on the one hand can help researchers to pinpoint political dynamics in different localities but on the other hand do not allow researchers to make a reliable enough assessment of that relationship to be generalized for the whole country. This study is designed to fill this gap, by using empirical data gathered from a 1993 nationwide survey to examine the relationship between economic development and village elections in rural China. The sample represents all eligible voters residing in family households at the time of the survey, excluding those living in the Tibetan Autonomous Region. The description of the sample is found in appendix 1.

I begin this chapter with a review of the theoretical argument on the relationship between economic development and democracy. This is followed by an assessment of (1) how many peasants in rural China had a chance to vote in village elections, (2) how many peasants had a chance to vote in semicompetitive elections, and (3) how many elections were semicompetitive. I conclude with a statistical analysis of the relationship between economic development and village elections in rural China.

Theoretical Arguments

Social mobilization theory has been criticized as deterministic and has been buried again and again, but it is still used in various forms by students of Chinese politics.[5] According to the theory, economic development increases the desire and capability of people to participate in decision-making processes, and this in turn facilitates democratic transition. The theory proposes that three areas of social and political life vary with the level of economic development and also increase political participation. First, economic development increases the interaction between individuals and states; in turn, increases in this interaction stimulate people to influence governmental decision making.[6] Second, economic development changes the composition of the population. As a nation develops economically, the shape of its social stratification structure is altered. That is, as greater numbers of citizens become members of the educated, white-collar class, the middle stratum expands and eventually becomes the majority class.[7] Finally, economic development transforms people's orientation toward political objects.[8] When people become more interested in politics, have more political knowledge, and feel more efficacious, they expect to have more input in the decision-making process in their society.

The theory in its original form, however, can hardly explain electoral reform in rural China.[9] Besides the fact that the pressure from the general populace has played only a limited role in electoral reform in rural China, other difficulties also prevent us from applying social mobilization theory to explain political reform in Chinese villages.[10] First, the per capita gross domestic product (GDP) in China is still far below the threshold for change. Empirical studies demonstrate that the transition to democracy usually happens when the per capita GDP reaches the equivalent of U.S. $5,000–$6000.[11] The per capita GDP in China in 1994, even using the figures adjusted for purchasing power parity, is only about U.S. $2,500.[12] Moreover, the theory predicts that democratic change should occur in urban areas, but electoral reform in China has taken place in rural areas. Finally, according to the theory, increased wealth contributes to democracy by increasing the size of the middle class. Contrary to such a claim, electoral reforms in China happened among peasants.

Responding to an overemphasis on the role of ordinary people in the transitional process, students of Latin-American politics proposed that elites usually play a crucial role in this process. Guillermo O'Donnell, Philippe Schmitter, and Lawrence Whitehead argue that political elites can significantly influence democratic transitions.[13] They forcefully demonstrate that soft-liners in those countries played a crucial role in the opening up of authoritarian systems.

Although the elite approach represents a major advance in our understanding of the process of democratic transition, it still leaves some critical questions unanswered: Why do some people in government perceive their options differently from others? More specifically, do changes in the demographic composition, attitudes, and perceptions of a population undergoing economic development influence the choices made by decision makers? If so, how do changes in popular attitudes influence political elites?

Despite the fact that few scholars have tried to deal with these issues in a systematic way, students of Chinese politics tend to combine these two approaches in their study of electoral reform in rural areas. For example, O'Brien's analysis of the impacts of economic development on electoral reform focuses on both masses and elites, especially incumbent village leaders. According to him, economic development has positive effects on the successful implementation of Organic Law. Incumbent leaders who have brought prosperity to their villages have (1) fewer fears of electoral defeat; (2) greater incentive to retain their position; and (3) enough money to co-opt villagers. Ordinary villagers also play an important role in this process. A profitable *collective* economy in the village may heighten villagers' interest in public affairs because they want to ensure that public funds are not misused or squandered.[14]

Differing from O'Brien, Susan V. Lawrence and Jean C. Oi argue that economic development is negatively associated with elections. And whereas Lawrence also emphasizes the role of elites, Oi focuses on township leaders. According to Lawrence, "It was precisely because the village is so unmanageable, and performing so poorly economically, that local authorities felt the need to experiment with new forms of village governance."[15] Ordinary peasants play no role in the process of electoral reform.

Oi observes that some of the most economically advanced areas lagged behind in carrying out political reform.[16] High levels of economic development, she believes, do not necessarily arouse enthusiasm for democratic reform among local officials. The key economic decisions in the wealthier places in rural China are usually made by a nondemocratically elected official—the party secretary. Because party officials adapted well to the economic reforms and led local development, they control the economic organizations and have more say on economic issues in the villages. Even if elections make village committees accountable to peasants, there is no systematic arrangement that subjects a party secretary to the periodic scrutiny of peasants. Thus, although the current institutional arrangement may result in a stronger village economy, it reduces the power of the village committee.

Election experts in the International Republican Institute (IRI) argue that the provinces that are at the middle level of economic development with relatively strong agricultural *and* industrial sections are the ones that tend to succeed in village elections. As they see it, "the development of local elections is dependent on support from local and provincial officials.[17] Indeed, they argue, the poorest and richest provinces have proceeded most slowly with the development of village elections and also generally with the most resistance.

In poor provinces, one might expect that frustration and lack of resources would lead ordinary villagers to make demands for improvements. Yet officials in those provinces usually do not see the value of village elections and pay little attention to improving transparency or competitiveness. And villagers tend to be concerned primarily with securing adequate food and shelter, not on improving local governance. In wealthier provinces, where one could argue that prosperity would lend itself to increased demands for popular control and autonomy, powerful local bosses have inhibited the development of competitive elections. A village committee chairman's economic success generally secures his reelection, giving rise to the development of "boss" politics. In recent years, local bosses have been cropping up in wealthy Chinese villages. Their success at building factories, increasing prosperity, and implementing social programs such as kindergartens and housing developments helps ensure their continued reelection.

Rather than adopting the traditional deterministic approach to their study of the relationship between economic development and electoral reform, students of Chinese politics now focus on the interaction between elites and peasants and argue that this complicated relationship determines the consequences of electoral reform in rural China. They also argue that economic development has certain impacts on the interaction between state and society. In the next section, we use survey data to test the relationship between economic development and village elections.[18]

The Current State of Affairs in Rural China

From the previous discussion, we learned that different scholars use different dependent variables in the study of the relationship between economic development and electoral reform in rural China. Our inquiry will be limited to the success or failure to introduce semicompetitive elections for local leaders in Chinese villages. This is not to say that other aspects of political reform, such as accountability of the party secretary or the supervision of the village assembly, are not important. But we do argue that introducing semicompetitive election into Chinese villages is the critical first step in political reform in rural China.

How Many People in Rural China Voted for Village Leaders?

We asked respondents in the 1993 survey to report whether their village had held elections for people to choose their leaders. If respondents gave a positive answer to this question, we asked them to report whether the election provided them with candidate choices. In table 11.1, we report the frequency distribution of the answers to these questions given by respondents holding rural household registration.[19]

We learned that more than 75 percent of the respondents residing in rural China reported that their villages had held elections. Of the respondents, 16.7 percent reported that their villages failed to hold elections, and 7.5 percent of rural residents either reported that they forgot whether their villages had held elections or refused to answer the question.

Table 11.1.   *Percentage of People Who Reported That Their Villages Had Elections*

If the village held any elections: *"During the past five years, were elections held in your village for people to choose their leaders?"*

Answers	Percentage (N)	
No	16.7	(433)
Yes	75.8	(1,961)
Not in the village	1.6	(42)
Do not remember	5.9	(152)
Total	100.0	(2,588)

Nature of elections: *"What kind of elections were they? Were they elections with or without a choice of candidates (deng'e xuanju haishi cha'e xuanju)?"*

Answers	Percentage (N)	
No elections	24.2	(627)
Plebiscitary elections	12.5	(325)
Semicompetitive elections	51.6	(1,336)
Do not know	11.6	(300)
Total	100.0	(2,588)

Source: 1993–94 Nationwide Survey on Political Culture and Political Participation in China.

The next question asked whether the elections provided them with candidate choice. In responses, 50.6 percent of peasants reported that elections in their villages were semicompetitive, and 12.5 percent of people reported that elections were plebiscitary. Among respondents from rural China, 24.2 percent stated that their village did not hold any election for them to choose village leaders, and 11.6 percent claimed that they did not know whether elections were plebiscitary or semicompetitive. In other words, only slightly more than 50 percent of the people in rural China voted in semicompetitive elections for village leaders.

From Individual Voters to Villages

Knowing the percentage of people who voted in semicompetitive elections is important. For our purposes, though, even more important is how many villages in rural China held elections for villagers to choose their leaders and how many of those elections were semicompetitive. There are usually two ways for researchers to get such data. First, they can rely on official reports and official statistics. Unfortunately, official reports on village elections were not available until 1996. Even when official statistics are available, however, it is not clear how reliable they are. The government does not provide information on how the data are collected, how different kinds of elections are categorized, and the distribution of different elections across different geographic regions. Experiences in both the Soviet Union and China have demonstrated that official data were usually contaminated by local bureaucrats.[20]

The second approach is using data on individual voters from a sample survey to deduce the figures. Although this method can avoid the contamination by government officials, it has two other problems: (1) since villages are required by the authorities to hold elections for peasants to choose their leaders and the elections are required to be semicompetitive, peasants from villages that fail to hold elections or from the villages where elections fail to provide voters with candidate choice may lie to interviewers to avoid political trouble, and (2) reports of respondents in surveys can be inaccurate. This problem is more serious when respondents are asked to report on something that happened in the past.[21]

To avoid the first problem, we instructed our interviewers not to contact any local officials, including county, township, and village leaders before interviewing designated respondents in villages. The central office of the survey provided interviewers with a name list of respondents in the village and instructed them to contact those respondents directly when entering the locality. These measures worked, and our interviewers reported that respondents were usually candid in expressing their opinions during interviews.[22]

Fortunately, certain statistical techniques can be used to test the validity of the questions and provide a reliable assessment of the scope of political contamination. The survey included two questions designed to tap the scope of political fear in China. The first asks if respondents fear criticizing the government and the other asks if respondents fear criticizing national leaders. Table 11.2 reports the distribution of these two questions. The data show that substantial numbers of people in China still fear criticizing the government and/or national leaders: about half of the respondents reported that they are at least a little concerned about possible political repercussion for any criticism they might level.

A more careful examination of the data shows that the problem may not be as serious as it appears to be. Among people claiming that they were concerned when criticizing the government, the majority were only "a little concerned." Less than 5 percent of respondents claimed that they were very concerned about possible persecution when criticizing the government or national leaders.

It should be pointed out that even if a respondent is very concerned about political persecution when criticizing the government, such a concern may not necessarily lead him to lie to interviewers about the nature of elections in his vil-

Table 11.2.   Political Fear of Respondents in Rural China

Fear of Criticizing the Government: *If you criticized the government in conversations where you live or work, would you be concerned that someone would report you to the authorities?*

Answers	Percentage	(N)
Completely unconcerned	1.2	(35)
Unconcerned	47.2	(1,223)
A little concerned	39.0	(1,008)
Very concerned	3.6	(94)
Do not know	8.0	(207)
No answer	0.9	(22)
Total	100	(2,588)

Fear of Criticizing Leaders of the Country: *If you criticized the party and state leaders in conversations where you live or work, would you be concerned that someone would report you to the authorities?*

Answers	Percentage	(N)
Completely unconcerned	1.2	(33)
Unconcerned	43.9	(1,137)
A little concerned	40.0	(1,034)
Very concerned	4.6	(120)
Do not know	9.0	(233)
No answer	1.2	(31)
Total	100	(2,588)

Source: 1993–94 Nationwide Survey on Political Culture and Political Participation in China.

lage. Whether the answers of respondents to questions inquiring about elections are contaminated by political fear is an empirical question that can be tested by examining the correlation between political fear and the report of the presence of village elections. If political fear contaminates respondents' answers, we should find that fear of political persecution is positively correlated with (1) the answers that the village held elections and (2) the election was semicompetitive. If the fear of political persecution is not correlated with the answers to these

Table 11.3.   *Zero-Order Correlation of Political Fear and Elections in Rural China*

Variables	Report on Elections	Report on Nature of Election
Fear of criticizing government	−.028 (.185)	−.023 (.263)
Fear of criticizing country leaders	−.023 (.362)	.040 (.106)

Source: 1993–94 Nationwide Survey on Political Culture and Political Participation in China.

Note: Data in parentheses are level of significance (two-tailed test).

Table 11.4.   *Number of Villages That Hold Semicompetitive Elections for Villagers to Choose Their Leaders*

	Majority Rule	Majority Plus 1	Absolute Rule
No elections	19.1 (62)	19.1 (62)	19.1 (62)
Noncompetitive elections	26.8 (87)	31.1 (101)	53.2 (173)
Semicompetitive elections	54.2 (176)	49.8 (162)	27.7 (90)

Source: 1993 Nationwide Survey on Political Culture and Political Participation in China.

two questions, we will be able to conclude that political fear does not influence the way our respondents answered these questions.

Table 11.3 reports the results of the tests. The analyses show that political fear does not significantly correlate with respondents' reportage about the presence and the nature of elections. These findings clearly reveal that political fear did not make respondents in rural China lie to interviewers in the survey.

Ruling out that survey questions are contaminated by political fear is relatively easy. More difficult is identifying misreporting for nonpolitical reasons.[23] Note that we used the *probability proportional to size* (PPS) technique to draw the sample. Such design required us to interview two to seventeen respondents from each village.[24] That allowed us to use different methods based on the answers of different respondents in the same village to calculate whether a village held elections and the nature of those elections. The results are summarized in table 11.4.

First, we tried to find whether a particular village held elections. The question has four response categories: *yes, no, do not know*, or *refusal*. We first coded all the *do not know* answers and *refusals* as no elections.[25] Then, we examined the answers of respondents from each village and found that people from the same village gave different answers to our interviewers: whereas some respondents reported that there had been elections in their village, others reported that no elections had been held.[26]

We then used two standards to deduce from answers of respondents from each village whether a particular village had in fact held elections for peasants to choose their leaders. The first one is majority rule: if the number of respondents in a village telling us that their village held election exceeds (1) the number of respondents telling us that their village failed to hold elections, plus (2) the number of respondents telling us they do not know if their village held elections, plus (3) the number of respondents who refused to answer the question, we categorize the village as having held elections for people to choose their leaders. Using this rule, we found that 267 villages had held elections, which represents 82.2 percent of the villages included in our sample.

Next, we used a more stringent standard—the *majority-plus-one* rule—to determine whether the village had held elections. According to this rule, for us to categorize a village having held elections, the number of respondents in a particular village who gave positive answers to this question must be two more than the people who gave all other answers. Using this method, we found that 244 villages, which represents 75.1 percent of the 325 villages included in our rural sample, had held elections for people to choose their leaders.

Finding out how many villages in rural China held elections for people to choose their leaders is important, but an even more important question is how many elections were semicompetitive: Were voters provided with candidate choices? To find out, we coded all villages that failed to meet the standard of majority rule as having had no elections. We then used three different methods to determine how many villages in rural China had actually held semicompetitive elections.

First we used the majority rule. The number of the peasants in a particular village who reported that elections in their village were semicompetitive must be at least one more than the number of peasants who reported that elections were noncompetitive for us to categorize elections in that village as semicompetitive. Using this rule, we found that elections in 54.2 percent of villages in rural China were in fact semicompetitive.

Next, we applied the majority-plus-one rule. To meet this standard, the number of peasants in a village who reported that elections were semicompetitive must be two more than the number of peasants who claimed that elections were noncompetitive, plus the number of people telling us they did not know the nature of elections, plus the number of people who refused to answer the question. Based on this rule, we found that elections in 49.8 percent of villages included in the sample were semicompetitive.

Finally, we used the most stringent standard—the *consensus* rule—to determine the nature of elections in those villages. To categorize elections in a village as semicompetitive, all respondents from that village had to report that the election in their village was semicompetitive. Using this method, we found that elections in 27.7 percent of villages were semicompetitive.

Of these three methods, we believe the majority-plus-one rule provides us with a reasonable balance. On average, we interviewed five to seven persons from each village. In reality, the majority-plus-one rule allows only one of the five respondents or two of the seven respondents from a village to either report that elections in their village were noncompetitive and/or to give *don't know* or *refusal* answers. In other words, most respondents must claim that elections in their village were semicompetitive for us to characterize elections in that village as semicompetitive. We therefore decided to use data deduced from this rule in the following analysis.

Economic Development and Village Elections: An Empirical Test

In this section we use multivariate techniques to study the relationship between economic development and semicompetitive elections in rural China. We chose *logistic regression* for our test. The dependent variable is whether a village has held semicompetitive elections. Three variables are used to predict the presence of semicompetitive elections in rural China. The first one is the level of economic development measured by the per capita gross domestic product (GDP) of the county in which the village is located. We used county-level data to measure economic development because the changes specified by social mobilization theory are unlikely to be brought about by economic development in a single village. We divided all the counties in the nation into three categories: poor counties whose per capita GDP ranged from 1,025 to 2,714 RMB, middle-developed counties whose per capita GDP ranged from 2,715 to 4,327 RMB, and rich counties whose per capita GDP ranged from 4,328 to 48,035 GDP. The poor counties are coded 1, middle-developed counties coded 2, and the rich counties coded 3.

The second predictor is the speed of economic development, measured by the ratio of per capita GDP of the sampling county between 1982 and 1993. The figure ranges from .75 to 27.73. We again divided our sampling counties into three categories: low-speed development counties (.75 to 4.2), middle-speed development counties (4.21 to 6.69), and high-speed development counties (6.70 to 27.73). The low-speed development counties are coded as 1, middle-speed development counties as 2, and high-speed development counties as 3.

Finally, included in the model are the distances in kilometers between a village and its county seat. This variable tests the role of local officials. Some scholars argue that local officials played a major role in introducing semicompetitive elections in rural China; others believe that incumbent village officials played the more crucial role. If the success of village elections is deter-

Table 11.5.   Logistic Regression Model for the Relationship between Economic Development and the Presence of Semicompetitive Elections in Chinese Villages

Dependent Variable	Model 1	Model 2
Intercept	−.359 (.420)	−1.322 (1.008)
Per capita GDP (1993)	.019 (.144)	2.508 (1.034)*
Speed of development from 1982 to 1993	.008 (.123)	−1.213 (.508)*
Distance to major cities or county seats	.010 (.006)	.015 (.006)**
Per capita GDP squared		−.590 (.251)*
Speed of development squared		.231 (.109)*
−2 log likelihood	446.787	433.752
Model chi-square	3.608	16.643
Degree of freedom	3	5
Significance	.307	.005

Source: 1993 Nationwide Survey on Political Culture and Political Participation in China.

Note: The dependent variable is the presence of semicompetitive elections.

mined by county officials, we should expect to find the distances between the village and the county seat negatively correlated with the presence of semicompetitive village elections. On the contrary, if incumbent village officials played a critical role, the distances between villages and county seats should have no significant impact on the presence of semicompetitive elections in rural China. We present the model on the left side of table 11.5. The result is simple and straightforward: economic development is not correlated in a linear way either positively or negatively with village elections.

On the right side of the table, we test the theory proposed by Amy Epstein, who argues that the relationship between economic development and the success of village elections is curvilinear. For such a purpose, we add two new variables to the model: the levels of economic development squared and the speed of economic development squared. If the relationship between economic development and village elections is curvilinear, we should find that when the new variables are added to the model, the original variables and the squared ones should both have significant impacts on village elections.

When the two new variables are entered into the model, each pair of variables has a significant impact on elections. While the per capita GDP has a positive impact on village elections, the per capita GDP squared has a negative impact. This result clearly indicates that the relationship between economic development and village elections appears to be a concave curve. To state the finding in a nontechnical way, economic wealth increases the likelihood that a village will hold semicompetitive elections for people to choose their leaders, but its impact diminishes as economic wealth increases. This finding confirms Epstein's argument that the middle-developed counties in rural China are most likely to hold semicompetitive elections for people to choose their leaders.[27]

The relationship between the speed of economic development and village elections is also curvilinear, but the shape of the curve is different from the previous one. The relationship between the speed of economic development and village elections appears to be a convex curve: a higher rate of economic development reduces the likelihood that Chinese villages will hold semicompetitive elections in an accelerated manner; that is, the higher the rate of economic development in a county, the less likely that elections in the villages located in that county will be semicompetitive. Finally, the distance between a village and county seat also influences village elections: the farther a village is from a county seat, the better the chance that elections in that village will be semicompetitive.

Discussion

My analysis reveals that certain kinds of relationships do exist between economic development and political change in rural China, although such relationships are somewhat different from that suggested by social mobilization theorists. Rather than being linearly associated with economic development, the relationship between electoral reform and economic development appears to be a curvilinear one, which seems to be in conflict with social mobilization theory.

Several reasons may help explain the "deviation" of the Chinese case. First, a number of empirical studies show that the transition to democracy usually occurs when the mean income of a country reaches between $5,000 and $6,000, and it becomes impregnable at the $7,000 level.[28] At the time of the survey, the mean per capita GDP in China was far below these figures. The level of development therefore has yet to reach the threshold at which the above political dynamic begins to operate.

Second, social mobilization theorists ignore the role of political elites in the process of transition. Recent studies have shown that political elites are important actors in this process.[29] Research on electoral reform in China has demonstrated that bureaucrats in the Ministry of Civil Affairs (MCA) and local officials played a key role in introducing semicompetitive elections into rural China. To understand the electoral reform in China, we need to analyze the impacts of economic development not only on the general populace but also on the interaction between state and society. While modernization theorists limit their inquiry to the changes brought about by economic development on demands, intentions, and resources for the general populace to participate in politics, it is also necessary to pay attention to the changes brought about by the economic development on the attitudes and policy preferences of political elites in a society.

All political entities—whether state, town, or village—rest on some mixture of coercion and consent. The consent of peasants used to be based on history and on tradition. Economic development has significant influence over the legitimacy of various political organizations. Before the reforms, peasants worked collectively for the people's communes to produce food, vegetables, housing, and other commodity goods. Although those materials were produced by peasants themselves, the communes controlled all of them and represented the state in distributing them to peasants. Such an arrangement blurred the nature of the relationship between individuals and the state, and many peasants believed it was the state that gave them those resources.

The de facto privatization in rural China after 1978 fundamentally changed the relationship in the villages between individuals and the state. Production is now organized by individuals, and peasants have regained control of the resources that they produced. Grassroots administration now depends on farmers to provide it with resources for its own operations, and public projects now usually rely on "donations" for funding. As peasants changed roles from "recipients" of resources to "providers" of resources for local administration, they naturally demanded inputs into the decision-making process. A crucial but usually neglected consequence of this change is that the basis of the legitimacy of the grassroots organizations has gradually been altered. Legitimacy of village authorities is now heavily dependent on the performance of local officials. Economic development is not only testament to the previous performance of incumbent officials, but it also influences their ability to extract political support from both their superiors and subordinates.

In rich villages, there are usually collective enterprises, many of which were established by incumbent leaders.[30] These enterprises can provide leaders with money to spend for various purposes. Even in places where development is largely based on private enterprise as distinct from collective enterprises, village leaders can extract money from those enterprises. First, since economic resources can increase the ability of incumbent leaders to accomplish various governmental projects, local officials are usually reluctant to replace them with other people. Second, incumbent leaders can use those resources to co-opt their protégés and persuade them either to ignore the requirements of higher authorities to hold elections or to tolerate them to turn the required semicompetitive elections into noncompetitive ones. Third, villagers in those places usually have little incentive to replace incumbent leaders because village leaders can use the newly acquired economic resources to trade for political support to offset the impacts of economic development on peasants. In 1996, I visited a village in Zhaoyuan County in Shangdong Province. More than 90 percent of the people in that village voted for the incumbent leader, who has been the head of the village for more than forty years. When asked why they voted for that person, the peasants in the village said that they did not need to pay anything to the government; the village used the profits earned by the collective enterprises to pay agricultural taxes on behalf of all peasants. In addition, each resident also received about 3,600 yuan per year from the village.[31] This might be an extreme case, but it is not unique, as similar situations can be found in many other villages. In 1997, I observed the elections in a rich village in Hebei Province. Afterward, the incumbent leader who was reelected told me privately that in order to attract popular votes he had spent more than 200,000 yuan before the election to build roads and a primary school.

The political dynamics in poor areas is different. First, local officials may not be able to collect money for agricultural taxes and public projects. If the county is characterized as *qiongkunxian* (an officially impoverished county), not only will the government waive agricultural taxes, but it will also provide peasants with various means of subsistence. Second, peasants in poor areas are concerned more about securing adequate food and shelter, especially to find a proper way to put their "body and soul together," than about public affairs. Finally, people in poor areas may adopt different ways to pursue wealth. Because the opportunity in those areas is limited, those who want a better life tend to go to rich coastal regions in search of higher paying jobs, rather than trying to improve the governance in their own village.

The situation in middle-developed areas is different from both the rich and the poor areas. First, village authorities need to collect money from peasants to support the administration and to run public projects. When authorities ask for money from peasants, the latter will ask for the right to participate in the decision-making process. Second, it is not new to students of politics that rather than being generated by absolute poverty, the desire for change is more likely to be the product of a sense of "relative deprivation."[32] Such feelings are more likely to occur among people residing in semideveloped areas than in either rich or poor areas. People are more likely to ask such why people in other places are wealthier than themselves, whether incumbent leaders are responsible for the economic stagnation, and, more important, whether replacing incumbent leaders can improve the economic situation in the village.[33] Because incumbent village leaders do not have the resources to co-opt villagers, they are less likely to be able to defend themselves against pressure from peasants to hold elections for them to choose their leaders. Third, village officials do not have sufficient resources to co-opt their superiors to resist change either. This explains why officials in counties of midlevel development have developed their elections most aggressively and with most success.

Conclusion

The findings of this chapter demonstrate that a fundamental change has occurred in rural China. After the authoritarian regime was opened up in the late 1980s, the changes in society brought about by privatization and economic development began to play a critical role in the process of political development in rural China. As occurred in other developing countries, changes brought about by economic development not only significantly influenced the attitudes of elements of the political elites toward political reform, but also increased the peasants' resources and skills and enhanced their desire to get involved in decision-making processes in their villages.

Nonetheless, economic development is not linearly correlated with political reform, as the social mobilization theorists suggest. Rapid economic development may even delay the process of political development. Rather than simply freeing people from political control, economic development in some places may help to consolidate the power of incumbent leaders by (1) making people in those places more dependent on the village authority, (2) providing incumbent leaders with economic resources to co-opt peasants, and (3) providing incumbent leaders with economic resources to bribe their superiors into ignoring the decisions of the central government to introduce competitive elections into Chinese villages.

Of course, these findings should not be interpreted as indicating that increases in wealth will not benefit political development in China. Political reform is a product of, among other things, interactions between elites and the general populace. Despite the fact that newly acquired economic resources may help incumbent village leaders consolidate their power at the current stage of economic development, economic growth may eventually break this equilibrium. For example, generational replacement of local officials will make it more difficult for village leaders to persuade them to resist required political reforms. Increases in the level of education of peasants will eventually change their expectations about power and authority. Thus, further economic development may make it difficult, if not impossible, for village officials to co-opt their constituencies in the future. Although we do not know when the current equilibrium will be broken by changes brought about by economic development, we know for sure that economic development increases both the ability for ordinary people to participate in politics and the difficulties of incumbent officials in co-opting constituencies: it also changes the attitudes of local officials toward elections. We are therefore confident that the dynamic interaction of these factors will have significant influences over the future of political development in rural China.

Appendix: Sample Design

The data in this study come from a survey conducted in China from September 1993 to June 1994 in cooperation with the Center for Social Survey of the People's University of China. The sample represents the adult population over eighteen years of age residing in family households at the time of the survey, excluding those living in the Tibetan Autonomous Region. A stratified multistage area sampling procedure with probability proportional to size (PPS) measures was employed to select the sample.

The primary sampling units (PSUs) employed in the sample design are counties (*xian*) in rural area and cities (*shi*) for urban areas. Before selection, counties were stratified by region and geographical characteristics, and cities by region and size. A total of forty-nine counties and eighty-five cities were selected as the primary sampling units. The secondary sampling units (SSUs) were townships (*xiang*) and districts (*qu*) or streets (*jiedao*). The third stage of selection was geared to villages in rural areas, and neighborhood committees (*juweihui*) in urban areas; a total of 551 villages and neighborhood committees were selected. Households were used at the fourth stage of sampling. Data analyzed in this paper include all villages in the sample, as well as neighborhood committees in urban areas with more than 50 percent of residents holding rural household registration.

In the selection of PSUs, the national population databook was used as the basic material to construct the sampling frame.* The number of family households for each county or city was taken as the measure of size in the PPS selection process. For the successive stages of sampling, population data were obtained either from the public security bureaus of the regions or from the statistical bureaus of local governments. At village and neighborhood committee levels, lists of household registrations (*hukou*) were obtained from police stations in urban areas and villagers' committees in rural areas.

Retired high school teachers were employed as interviewers for most surveys. Although most people in China read and write standard Chinese, people in many provinces in the South speak varying dialects, some of which are extremely difficult for Mandarin speakers to understand. To deal with this problem, professional interviewers from the National General Team for Rural Surveys (*guojia nongcun diaocha zongdui*) who speak local dialects were hired to interview in seven southern, largely dialect-speaking provinces. Interviewers were given formal training before the fieldwork.

Before the interview began, we sent letters to all the sampling spots to check whether there were any changes of address. We then removed all invalid addresses from our sampling frame and thereby eliminated the majority of noncontacts. The project scheduled interviews with 3,425 people and 3,287 of the prospective respondents contacted by interviewers answered our questions, for a response rate of 94.5 percent.

---

* Ministry of Public Security, *Zhongguo Chengxian Renko Tongji* (*Population Statistics by City and County of the People's Republic of China*), (Beijing: Map Publishing House of China, 1987).

Notes

1. See Kevin J. O'Brien, "Implementing Political Reform in China's Villages," *Australian Journal of Chinese Affairs* 32 (1994).

2. Jean C. Oi, "Economic Development, Stability and Democratic Village Self-Governance," in Maurice Brosseau, Suzanne Pepper, and Tsang Shu-ki, eds., *China Review 1996* (Hong Kong: Chinese University of Hong Kong, 1996), 140.

3. Amy Epstein, "Village Elections in China: Experimenting with Democracy," in Joint Economic Committee, Congress of the United States, eds., *China's Economic Future* (Armonk, N.Y.: M. E. Sharpe 1997), 419.

4. For such debates, see, among others, Gordon White, "Democratization and Economic Reform in China," *Australian Journal of Chinese Affairs* 31 (1994); White, *Riding the Tiger: The Politics of Economic Reform in Post-Mao China* (Stanford, Calif.: Stanford University Press, 1993); Barrett L. McCormick, "Democracy or Dictatorship?: A Response to Gordon White," *Australian Journal of Chinese Affairs* 31 (1994); and McCormick, *Political Reform in Post-Mao China: Democracy and Bureaucracy in a Leninist State* (Berkeley and Los Angeles: University of California Press, 1990).

5. For a recent reevaluation of the thesis, see Ross E. Burkhart and Michael S. Lewis-Beck, "Comparative Democracy: The Economic Development Thesis," *American Political Science Review* 88, no. 4 (1994), 903–10.

6. As a nation develops, its government usually becomes responsible for more regulation and redistribution. Individuals' relationships with the nation-state now become critical. If taxes are collected and regulations to control the economy are imposed, individuals are very likely to respond by defending themselves against the state. For discussion, see Myron Weiner, "Political Participation: Crisis of the Political Process," in Leonard Binder et al., eds., *Crisis and Sequences in Political Development* (Princeton, N.J.: Princeton University Press, 1971), 173–75.

7. Norman H. Nie, Bingham G. Powell, and Kenneth Prewitt, "Social Structure and Political Participation: Developmental Relationships, Part I," *American Political Science Review* 63, no. 2 (1969), 362–78.

8. Among different aspects of psychological orientation toward social objects, some, such as cognition and feeling, are relatively easily influenced by changes in the social environment, while others, especially deep-seated norms, are more difficult to change.

9. Tianjian Shi, "Village Committee Elections in China: Institutionalist Tactics for Democracy," *World Politics* 51, no. 3 (1999), 385–90.

10. All empirical research in China shows that electoral reform was both introduced and sponsored by midlevel officials in the central government. See O'Brien, "Implementing Political Reform in China's Villages"; Daniel Kelliher, "The Chinese Debate over Village Self-Government," *China Journal* 37 (1997); Epstein, "Village Elections in China: Experimenting with Democracy"; Lawrence, "Democracy, Chinese Style"; Shi, "Village Committee Elections in China"; Lianjiang Li, "The Two-Ballot System in Shanxi: Subjecting Village Party Secretaries to a Popular Vote," *China Journal*, forthcoming; Lianjiang Li and Kevin J. O'Brien, "The Struggle over Village Elections," in Roderick MacFarquhar and Merle Goldman, eds., *The Paradox of China's Reforms* (Cambridge, Mass.: Harvard University Press, 1999), 129–44.

11. For the comparative study of the relationship between levels of economic development and democracy, see, among others, Bingham G. Powell Jr., *Contemporary Democracies: Participation, Stability, and Violence* (Cambridge, Mass.: Harvard University Press 1982). For recent literature on the relationship between economic development and political change, see, among others, Adam Przeworski and Fernando Limongi, "Modernization: Theories and Facts," *World Politics* 49, no. 2 (1997) 155–83; Burkhart and Lewis-Beck, "Comparative Democracy: The Economic Development Thesis," 903–10. Przeworski found that above a level of about $6,000 in per capita GDP (in 1992 purchasing-power-parity U.S. dollars) there is not a single case of a democracy reverting to authoritarian rule.

12. World Bank, *From Plan to Market: World Development Report 1996* (New York: Oxford University Press, 1996).

13. Guillermo O'Donnell, Philippe C. Schmitter, and Lawrence Whitehead, *Transitions from Authoritarian Rule* (Baltimore: Johns Hopkins University Press, 1986), 3.

14. O'Brien, "Implementing Political Reform in China's Villages," 47–48.

15. Susan V. Lawrence, "Democracy, Chinese Style," *Australia Journal of Chinese Affairs* 32 (1994), 67.

16. It should be pointed out that the dependent variable used by Oi is not identical to the one used by O'Brien and Lawrence. Whereas the research of the latter two scholars tries to explain the emergence of semicompetitive village elections, Oi tries to explain the establishment of the democratic governing process. For her, election itself is important, but more important is whether institutional transformation provides villagers with a real opportunity to voice their opinions on the key issues facing them. Thus, her dependent variable is the "*democratic accountability* of local officials to peasants," Oi, "Economic Development, Stability and Democratic Village Self-Governance," 143.

17. Epstein, "Village Elections in China," 418–19.

18. This paper does not intend to test the hypotheses proposed by the scholars cited above. First, none of them tried to make generalizations on the relationship between economic development and village elections in China. Second, the dependent variables in their studies are somewhat different from the one used in this study. For example, O'Brien uses *up-to-standard* (*dabiaocun*) of the Ministry of Civil Affairs in the implementation process of organic law as a dependent variable, of which having good elections is only one part. Oi's dependent variable is the establishment of the democratic governing process. Finally, the timing of their studies is different. While O'Brien tries to explain what happened in the first stage of the implementation process, Oi and Epstein explain what happened in the second stage of the implementation process.

19. *Rural population* in Chinese has two meanings. The first refers to those who hold rural household registration (*Chi nongcun huko deren*), and the second refers to people living in a rural area. Note that those who hold rural household registration may not live in rural area (a typical case for people belonging to this category are those living in the suburbs of big cities) and that those who live in rural areas may not hold rural household registration (especially retirees). We chose the type of household registration to differentiate the rural population from the urban one. The rationale for the choice is that only people who hold rural household registration have the right to vote for members of village committees.

20. Students of political participation in communist societies have long noticed the flaw in official records of voter turnout. For example, Theodore H. Friedgut reported that more than one million voters in Moscow—close to one-fifth of the eligible population—were absent in the 1970 election although official records report voter turnout of more than 95 percent. See Friedgut, *Political Participation in the USSR* (Princeton, N.J.: Princeton University Press, 1979). Studies based on emigré informants on political participation in the Soviet Union revealed the actual turnout rate there was much lower than the 99 percent figure claimed by the authorities. See Rasma Karklins, "Soviet Elections Revisited: Voter Abstention in Noncompetitive Voting," *American Political Science Review* 80, no. 2 (1986) 449–69. A more recent study reports that the "Soviet scholars now admit privately that the turnout data may have been exaggerated." See Donna Bahry and Brian D. Silver, "Soviet Citizen Participation on the Eve of Democratization," *American Political Science Review* 84, no. 3 (1990), 821–41. According to their report, much of the well-accepted 99 percent voter turnout in communist societies was "achieved" not by the ability of the regime to mobilize its citizens to vote, but by its own bureaucrats cheating at various levels. Failing to mobilize private citizens to vote, bureaucrats in the Soviet Union, in an attempt to shift the burden of blame to please their superiors, helped ordinary people bypass existing rules and regulations. I have found that officials in China engaged in the same technique to shield themselves from being blamed by higher authorities for failing to

mobilize citizens under their jurisdiction to vote. See Tianjian Shi, *Political Participation in Beijing* (Cambridge, Mass.: Harvard University Press, 1997).

21. John Zaller, *The Nature and Origins of Mass Opinion* (Cambridge: Cambridge University Press, 1992).

22. We do have independent evidence to show that respondents were cooperative and outspoken. For example, when we conducted the pretest in 1990, many respondents asked our interviewers to bring the complaints to Beijing. After the actual fieldwork, our central office in Beijing received more than three hundred letters from people in different areas to report corruption or power abuse by local officials. More important, very few of those letters were anonymous. Had people been fearful of expressing their opinions, they would not have asked our interviewers to bring the complaints to Beijing, nor would they have written to our central office after the survey. Tianjian Shi, "Survey Research in China," in Michael X. Delli Carpini, Leonie Huddy, and Robert Y. Shapiro, eds., *Research in Micropolitics: Rethinking Rationality*, vol 5 (Greenwich, Conn.: JAL Press, 1996), 213–50.

23. In fact, survey researchers even debate the meaning of conflicting reports by the same respondents in the survey. See Zaller, *The Nature and Origins of Mass Opinion* .

24. For PPS sample design, see Leslie Kish, *Survey Sampling* (New York: John Wiley and Sons, 1965).

25. The real situation could be much more complicated. While refusals might reflect the reluctance of respondents to reveal the truth that there had been no election in the village, the *don't know*s may simply reflect respondents who really did not know whether there had been an election in their village.

26. Several reasons can make people in the same village give different answers to this question: (1) the respondent was not at home during election time and thus knew nothing about the elections; (2) the person was at home but had no interest in the elections; (3) the person knew about elections but forgot them; (4) there were no elections, but some respondents dared not tell the truth to interviewers; and (5) there were no elections and respondents reported it faithfully to our interviewers.

Figure 1

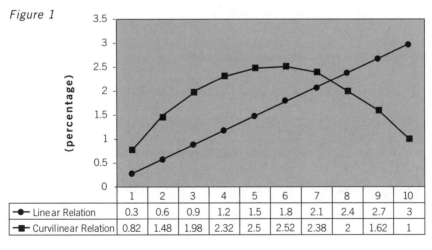

	1	2	3	4	5	6	7	8	9	10
Linear Relation	0.3	0.6	0.9	1.2	1.5	1.8	2.1	2.4	2.7	3
Curvilinear Relation	0.82	1.48	1.98	2.32	2.5	2.52	2.38	2	1.62	1

27. In figure 1, we present two curves. The curve that represents the linear relationship assumes only one variable in the model. In OLS model, $Y_i = a + ßx_i$. For simplicity, we assume a equals 0. We then assume that the values of x_i ranges from 1 to 10, if ß equals .3. If the value of x (that is, per capita GDP) equals 1, Y will be $0.3*1$. If the value of x equals 3, Y will be $0.3*3 = 0.9$, etc. When GDP squared is added to the model, we will have $Y = a + ßx_1 + ßx_2$. Suppose ß for x_1, that is, the per capita GDP in the new model equals 0.9 and

ß for x_2 or the GDP^2 equals $-.08$. If GDP equal 1, we will have $1*0.9+(-.08*1) = 0.82$; if GDP equals 3, we will have $3*0.9 = (-.08*3^2) = 1.98$. If GDP equals 6, we will have $6*0.9+(-.08*6^2) = 2.52$. If GDP equals 10, we will have $10*.09+(-.08*10^2) = 1$. In the figure we also plot the data for this model. The value of Y in the second model first increases and then declines.

28. Przeworski and Limongi, "Modernization: Theories and Facts"; Burkhart and Lewis-Beck, "Comparative Democracy: The Economic Development Thesis."

29. O'Donnell, Schmitter, and Whitehead, *Transitions from Authoritarian Rule.*

30. Jean C. Oi, "Communism and Clientelism: Rural Politics in China," *World Politics* 37, no. 1 (1984), 238–66 .

31. Interview with villagers in Zhaoyuan county, Shangdong Province, July 1996.

32. Ted Gurr, "Causal Model of Civil Strife: A Comparative Analysis Using New Indices," *American Political Science Review* 62, no. 4 (1968), 1104. See also Joseph Greenblum and Leonard Pearlin, "Vertical Mobility and Prejudice: A Socio-Psychological Analysis," in Reinhard Bendix and Seymour M. Lipset, eds., *Class, Status, and Power: A Reader in Social Stratification,* (Glencoe, Ill.: Free Press, 1953), 480–91.

33. In fact, these questions are usually raised by villagers in semideveloped areas. Interviews of people from seven villages in Shangxi, Hebei, and Fujian Provinces, 1996–97.

12

Chinese Nationalism and Authoritarianism in the 1990s

SUISHENG ZHAO

A prominent scholar of nationalism, Ernst B. Haas, has observed that "the 1990s are the decade of nationalism."[1] Over the years there indeed has existed a growing trend of nationalism in the post–Cold War world, including China. Although the rise of nationalism is not necessarily in contradiction to democratization and may even reenforce the development of democratic institutions in a liberal society, it may also become a competing value system, particularly when nationalism is associated with authoritarianism. That is why Liah Greenfeld made a distinction between two types of nationalism: "individualistic-liberatarian nationalism and collectivistic-authoritarian nationalism,"[2] or put simply, *liberal* versus *authoritarian* nationalism. While liberal nationalism may promote democracy with the idea that the state is the property of its citizens, authoritarian nationalism may be a barrier to democracy with the demand that citizens subordinate their individual interests to those of the state.

The rise of Chinese nationalism in the 1990s was promoted by the authoritarian state and associated with a neo-authoritarian intellectual currency. It began after the Tiananmen crackdown on the democratic movement in the spring of 1989. Because the democratic movement was developed under the influence of Western liberal ideas, the Communist government took nationalism as an instrument to block Western influences and shore up its waning legitimacy in the post-Tiananmen era. These nationalistic sentiments and anti-Western rhetoric gained wide currency among Chinese intellectuals in spite of the fact that popular nationalism emerged, to an extent, independent of official propaganda. Intellectuals advocated nationalism out of their concern that China faced a crisis of national disintegration comparable to those faced by the former Soviet Union and Yugoslavia after the sudden collapse of communism in those states. Under these circumstances, Chinese intellectuals who once snatched ideas from the West and totally negated their own traditions rediscovered the value of their own past and became suspicious of the Western mind-set. Based on China's economic achievements as a result of successful reforms, many, particularly young, intellectuals began to develop a new sense of national pride and self-confidence. In this case, a shared objective of holding a nation together during the turbulent transitional period brought the government and intellectuals together under the banner of nationalism. Chinese nationalism is thus a result of a volatile mix of rising pride and lingering insecurity in response to profound domestic crises. The rising Chinese nationalism is characterized by pragmatic concerns of both the Chinese government and intellectual elite about overriding domestic problems and represents an aggregation of varied political forces. Chinese nationalism is invoked in at least partial explanation of a remarkable range of phenomena such as aversion to foreign ideas and celebration of national traditions in China of the 1990s.

This chapter explores the rise of Chinese nationalism and its association with authoritarianism. The first section discusses the relationship between Chinese nationalism and the authoritarian state. The second section goes on to analyze the intellectual connections of Chinese nationalism, particularly its connection with neo-authoritarianism in the reform years. The conclusion highlights the major argument that the rise of Chinese nationalism in the 1990s was associated largely with authoritarianism rather than liberalism. This situation raises a serious question about if Chinese nationalism could be compatible with the worldwide trend of democratization.

Chinese Nationalism and the Authoritarian State

Although nationalism is not totally new in China it is an ideological artifact of relatively recent historical provenance. As a modern concept, it consists of doctrines or a set of ideas that dictate political action or movement. Hans Kohn sees nationalism as a "political creed" that "centers the supreme loyalty of the overwhelming majority of the people upon the nation-state, either existing or desired."[3]

Chinese people were not imbued with an abiding sense of nationalism before the nineteenth century. James Harrison observed that the traditional Chinese self-image was generally "defined as culturalism, based on a common historical heritage and acceptance of shared beliefs, not as nationalism, based on the modern concept of nation-state."[4] Joseph Levenson's writings also indicate that, because of "Chinese culture as the focus of loyalty," nationalism did not exist in traditional China and culturalism permeated traditional Chinese thought.[5] The concept of the Chinese nation was a relatively recent creation influenced by foreign intellectual discourses. There was not even a serviceable word for the historical and ethical community of "China" before the nineteenth century. As John Fitzgerald points out, "the Chinese custom of referring to their historical community by dynasty (*chaodai*) rather than by country (*guojia*) implied that there was in fact no Chinese nation at all."[6] *Zhonghua minzu* (the Chinese nation) is a rather modern concept that emerged only at the turn of the twentieth century. *Minzu* began to appear in Chinese revolutionary journals in 1895, adopted from the writings of the Japanese Meiji period. The term *zhonghua minzu* was first used by intellectuals during the early republic period and often associated with nationalistic writings warning the Chinese people of the danger of annihilation under Western invasion.[7]

Unlike the formation of nationalism in Europe as an indigenous process driven by a combined force of mercantilism and liberalism, nationalist consciousness in China first emerged not in association with liberal or democratic ideas, but was triggered as a painful reaction to foreign invasions. Andrew Nathan and Robert Ross state that "while European ideologies had their roots in European culture, China's ferment was reactive in motives as well as in content."[8] Most Chinese scholars hold the view that modern Chinese nationalism has arisen largely in response to threats from foreign imperialism. Xiao Gongqin calls it "*yingji-zhiwei xing*" (reactive-defensive type) nationalism, which is "derived from the reaction to the challenges from the West."[9] A reactive sentiment to foreign incursions was a starting point for Chinese nationalism. The vast, powerful, and wealthy Chinese empire stagnated and was ruthlessly humiliated by Western powers in the long century starting from its defeat in the Opium Wars of 1840 to 1842. During the century of humiliation, foreign imperialists carved out spheres of influence, sold opium to the Chinese masses, and enjoyed the protection of the extraterritoriality in their enclaves on Chinese soil. Nationalism held a powerful appeal in China's struggle to rid itself of foreign imperial powers. In the early days of the People's Republic of China (PRC), its leaders brought with them traumatic memories of China's inability to determine its own fate in the preceding hundred years. China viewed itself as the victim of foreign imperialism. Nationalism as much as Marxism-Leninism drove China's vision of its right place in the world in the years following 1949.

Indeed, the communist leadership always played upon nationalism to its advantage, although Marxism-Leninism overshadowed nationalism in some years of the PRC history. Nationalism was seen by the communist leaders as an instrument to counter the challenge of liberal democratic ideas when the internal legitimacy crisis became a grave concern of the regime after the serious decay of communist ideology in the post-Mao reform years. Beginning in the 1980s, the regime was deeply troubled by "three spiritual crises" (*sanxin weiji*), namely, a "crisis of faith" in socialism; a crisis of confidence in the future of the country; and a crisis of trust in the party. When Communist official ideology lost credibility, the Communist regime became incapable of enlisting popular support for a vision of the future. Under these circumstances, some intellectuals turned to Western liberal ideas and called for democratic reform. The "three spiritual crises" led to a prodemocracy movement and the large-scale Tiananmen Square demonstrations in Spring 1989. How to restore the legitimacy and build a broad-based national support became the most serious challenge to the post-Tiananmen leadership.

At first, the government concentrated all its efforts on stabilizing the nation. Order was established through the persecution of those who were involved in the democratic movement and through the administration of draconian penalties for the agitators. After the government forcefully reasserted its authority and democratic voices were virtually silenced, extreme conservative leaders tried to turn the clock back by initiating repeated attacks on market-oriented reform policies and by attempting to resuscitate Maoist ideology.[10] The conservatives, however, were not successful. They encountered strong resistance from Deng and other reform leaders who were not willing to abandon lucrative economic reforms. The nation endured a period of political and intellectual stagnation while the party searched for a means of reversing the decline of faith and confidence among the Chinese people. One lesson that the party leaders, reformers and conservatives alike, learned from the Tiananmen incident was that the political indoctrination of the younger generation was an urgent need. They all saw the Tiananmen incident as a fatal consequence of losing "spiritual pillars" (*jingsheng zhizhu*), which had been incarnated as Marxism-Leninism and Maoist thought and had guided the Chinese people to support the communist regime and sacrifice themselves for the regime under Mao. For the reformist leaders, an added lesson was that nothing now in the communist arsenal could garner mass support, that resorting to old Communist ideology was ineffective for indoctrination. They rejected efforts made by conservatives to restore Maoist ideology and looked for something else that could replace Marxism-Leninism dogma as a cohesive ideology.

The utility of nationalism was thus rediscovered. The Communist regime moved quickly to use nationalism to fill the spiritual vacuum left by the diminishing Communist ideology. Deng Xiaoping and his successor, Jiang Zemin, began to wrap themselves in the banner of nationalism, which, they found, remained the one bedrock of political belief shared by most Chinese people across political and ideological lines. In fact, the prodemocracy demonstrators in Tiananmen Square, while confronting the government, had claimed that patriotism drove them to take to the streets in the spring of 1989. Most people involved in the demonstration, both the students and their supporters, equated democracy with patriotism; urging the government to start political reform was considered a most patriotic action. With the renewed discovery of the power of nationalism, Chinese Communist leaders began to place emphasis on the party's role as the paramount patriotic force and guardian of national pride.

Nationalism is a powerful instrument for the Chinese regime. The power of nationalism comes from the fact that it "locates the source of individual identity within a 'people,' which is seen as the bearer of sovereignty, the central object of loyalty, and the basis of collective solidarity."[11] In modern world history, "nationalism proved to be stronger than socialism when it came to bonding working classes together, and stronger than capitalism that bound bankers together."[12] Nationalism proved its persistent power in modern Chinese history. After the Chinese political elite embraced modern nationalist doctrines in the late nineteenth century, while other movements and ideologies waxed and waned, nationalism permeated them all.

Nationalism in the PRC was often associated with and in fact used by the authoritarian government. As a political instrument, the Chinese Communist Party (CCP) regime preferred the term *aiguozhuyi* (patriotism) to refer to nationalism because *aiguozhuyi* means "loving the communist state" while *minzuzhui* (nationalism) has a strong ethnic dimension in Chinese language. In fact, the PRC government never officially endorsed a term for nationalism. The sentiments of the Chinese people were not described as nationalistic but *aiguo*, or patriotic, which in Chinese literally means "loving the state." CCP general secretary Jiang Zemin emphasized in 1990 that "the patriotism we advocate is by no means a parochial nationalism."[13] In the PRC official discourse, the terms *nationalism* and *chauvinism* referred to parochial and reactionary attachments to nationalities, whereas *patriotism* was love and support for China, always indistinguishable from the Chinese state and the Communist Party. From this perspective Chinese patriotism can be understood as a state-centric conception of nationalism or, in Charles Tilly's term, a "state-led nationalism." With state-led nationalism, "rulers who spoke in a nation's name successfully demanded that citizens identify themselves with that nation and subordinate other interests to those of the state."[14] This was exactly what patriotism demanded in China. As Michael Hunt observed, "by professing *aiguo*, Chinese usually expressed loyalty to and a desire to serve the state, either as it was or as it would be in its renovated form."[15] As a conception of state-led nationalism in the PRC, patriotism portrays the communist state as the embodiment of the nation's will. A *People's Daily* editorial on the 1996 National Day stated, "Patriotism is specific. . . . Patriotism requires us to love the socialist system and the road chosen by all nationalities in China under the leadership of the Communist Party."[16] By identifying the party with the nation, the regime would make criticism of the party and its policy an unpatriotic act.

To fully make use of nationalism, the CCP government launched a patriotic education campaign in the early 1990s. The main target of the patriotic education campaign was youth, a group most vulnerable to the influence of Western liberal ideas. As a state-led campaign, the government took full advantage of the state machine to mobilize support. In January 1993, the State Education Commission issued a document, "Program for China's Education Reform and Development," which laid out patriotism as a guiding principle for China's educational reform. In November of the same year, the CCP Central Propaganda Department, the State Education Commission, the Ministry of Broadcast, Film, and Television, and the Ministry of Culture jointly issued a "Circular on Carrying Out Education in Patriotism in Primary and Secondary Schools throughout the Country by Films and Television." In implementing the document, more than 95 percent of primary and middle school students in Beijing were urged, by May 1994, to watch patriotic films recommended by the State Education Commission. Beijing cinemas and television stations aired the films and some projection teams were sent to the mountainous areas to show films. Television stations copied videotapes for schools in the suburban mountainous areas. Beijing's students wrote more than 1.5 million papers about what they learned from the heroes in the films.[17] A national on-the-spot meeting (*xianchanghui*) on patriotic education in primary and middle schools was held in Shanghai on May 18–21, 1994, jointly hosted by the Central Propaganda Department, the State Education Commission, the Ministry of Radio, Film, and Television, the Ministry of Culture, and the Central Committee of the Communist Youth League.[18] In June 1994, a national conference on education adopted a document, "Guidelines for Patriotic Education," which embraced the patriotic themes of the 1993 program and was passed down to all educational institutions from kindergartens to universities. The patriotic education campaign reached a climax when the Central Committee published a document, "The Outline for Conducting Patriotic Education," drafted by the Central Propaganda Department and carried in *Renmin Ribao* on September 6, 1994. The goal of education in patriotism was "to boost the nation's spirit, enhance its cohesion, foster its self-esteem and sense of pride, consolidate and develop a patriotic united front to the broadest extent, and direct and rally the masses' patriotic passions to the great cause of building socialism with Chinese characteristics." The outline particularly singled out youth as a targeted group and called for incorporating education in patriotism into teaching from kindergarten all the way through to the universities.[19]

The patriotic education campaign represented a state-led effort to rebuild the legitimacy of the post-Tiananmen leadership in a way that would permit the Communist Party's rule to continue on the basis of a noncommunist ideology. Although the essence of the patriotic education campaign was to make the Chinese people support the leadership of the Communist Party, the content of the patriotic education was not totally communist. Marxism-Leninism and Maoist thought were abandoned in all but name in the campaign. In a way, the campaign deliberately blurred the lines that separated patriotism, nationalism, socialism, and communism. For example, for the first time since university entrance examinations were reinstated in the late 1970s, high school students applying for science subjects at colleges were exempted from taking Marxist study courses, which had been widely resented by students. Instead, patriotic education courses were added to the curricula of high schools and colleges. By getting rid of the Marxist courses the government removed one source of tension between the students and the authorities, as students had complained about and rebelled against the study of Marxist doctrine and Communist Party propaganda.[20] In abolishing the examination, the authorities were not easing up on the student population; they merely switched to the softer approach of patriotic education. While abolishing the political dogma examination, the authorities launched an "I am Chinese" program in universities, which taught students to be proud of being Chinese by concentrating on the "great achievements" of the Chinese people and especially the Communist Party. The aim was to win more respect for the party by demonstrating what it had done for the people of China. By appealing to the students' sense of patriotism rather than trying to convert them to Marxism, the Communist regime hoped to reassert the legitimacy of the party.

The contents of the patriotic education were designed to induce the Chinese youth toward a national consciousness in contrast with Western liberal ideas. The long history of China and of Chinese cultural achievements held a prominent place in education. Special emphasis was given to efforts to improve China's position in the world, and to struggle against foreign aggression and oppression after repeated setbacks. The CCP tried to discover a noncommunist past for the PRC and defined patriotism in terms that had everything to do with Chinese history and culture and almost nothing to do with Marxist doctrine. After the "Outline for Conducting Patriotic Education" was published in 1994, Li Ruihuan, the chairman of China's People's Political Consultant Conference, broke a long-standing Communist taboo against ancestor worship by laying flowers and planting a pine tree by the mausoleum of China's Yellow Emperor, the legendary ancestor of the Chinese people. (The legend was spun by nobles in 450 B.C.E. who transformed a local agrarian god into a common ancestor to legitimize their claim to power.) As a historical site, the mausoleum drew many visitors during the patriotic education campaign.[21] The Great Wall was also celebrated as a patriotic symbol of Chinese history.[22] The celebration of the Chinese tradition was accompanied by the revival of Confucianism and other Chinese cultural activities. Icons in Tiananmen Square, itself symbolic of the mandate of heaven in imperial times, were reshuffled. National Day celebrations no longer included large portraits of the communist philosophers Karl Marx and Friedrich Engels. Instead, a giant portrait of the noncommunist Chinese nationalist Sun Yat-sen stood alone in the square. In the official statement on the patriotic education campaign, "Chinese people's patriotism and brave patriotic deeds" rather than the CCP's socialist experiments became "the greatest epics ever written in the Chinese history, and they represent a glorious page in world history."[23] The leadership of the CCP was claimed because of its patriotism in China's long struggle for national independence and prosperity, not because of its communist ideals. Patriotism rather than communism thus became the basis of the CCP's legitimacy.[24]

Another emphasis of the patriotic education campaign was on China's national essence or national conditions (*guoqing*). The purpose was to help the Chinese people understand where China was strong, where it lagged behind, and what its favorable and unfavorable conditions were so as to enhance a sense of historical mission and responsibility. Patriotism was used as a national call, while the peculiarity of the "national essence" offered a rationale for that call. The communist government that would otherwise be hardly acceptable to the Chinese people after the end of the Cold War was justified by the national essence. Liberal democracy was also rejected based on national conditions. As a result, some intellectuals, including those who had sharply criticized the government during the spring 1989 prodemocracy movement, changed their attitudes. They accepted the themes of the patriotic education campaign about China's special conditions, that is, the argument that sudden democratization in China would result in rapid social disintegration, as witnessed in the former Soviet Union and Eastern European countries. The fear of total disintegration in China was thus used as a lever to boost nationalism and to alleviate the crisis of legitimacy faced by the regime. It is revealing that, while Chinese students demonstrated in Tiananmen Square urging for democracy in confrontation with the People's Liberation Army (PLA) in May 1989, these same young people showed enthusiastic support for the PLA's launching missiles just off the shores of Taiwan in defending what it claimed as China's territorial integrity and national unity in 1995 and 1996. When nationalistic books such as *The China That Can Say No* became instant bestsellers in the summer of 1996,[25] one Chinese scholar found that although most Chinese intellectuals would not say that democracy was less appealing to them, many of them would emphasize that they were patriots first and democrats second. Talking about democracy seemed to be becoming taboo among Chinese students and scholars in the 1990s. Among some academic circles such talk might be regarded as unpatriotic. As nationalism came to dominate the thoughts of Chinese people, it became "hard for democracy to take root." [26]

Chinese Nationalism and Neo-Authoritarianism

It is important to indicate that the communist regime was not the only driving force of nationalist sentiment in China of the 1990s. Chinese intellectuals also contributed to a nationalistic discourse, which was linked to neo-authoritarianism. Although this intellectual discourse overlapped, to a certain extent, with patriotic rhetoric of the Chinese government, its emergence was largely independent of official propaganda. Those who contributed to the intellectual discourse on nationalism were from various political backgrounds, including liberal intellectuals who supported the 1989 democratic movement, established scholars of neo-authoritarianism, and extremely conservative intellectuals who were against any form of Westernization. The important common denominator that brought about the coming together of intellectuals with such different political views under the banner of nationalism was the concern over the threat of social disorder and even disintegration, following the course of the former Soviet Union and Eastern European nations. These intellectuals deemed it necessary to promote nationalism as a new force of unity in order to find a Chinese path toward modernization and to realize their shared *qiangguomeng* (dream of a strong China). National greatness was an agreed-upon objective and historical mission of Chinese intellectuals, notwithstanding their other differences. Far from being detached scholars observing the rapid sociopolitical changes from the sidelines, Chinese intellectuals were active participants in the process and their embrace of nationalism was a result of a soul-searching for their nation's destiny.

China was a major world power, built on a superior culture extending back for millennia. Many Chinese intellectuals pointed to the lack of modernization as the reason why China fell prey to imperialism in the nineteenth century. Recollections of ancient grandeur, combined with outrage at China's humiliation, provided the starting point for modern Chinese nationalism. To revive China, many had adopted a hostile view toward their own past, calling for the complete rejection of Chinese tradition and boundless adoption of Western culture. From the May Fourth Movement, to the Maoist years, to Deng's reform era, there have been repeated attacks on China's cultural heritage. During the early reform years of the 1980s, there was a rise of "cultural fever" (*wenhua re*) among Chinese intellectuals.[27] There were two basic themes in the cultural fever: "criticism of traditional Chinese culture," and "criticism of Chinese national character."[28] Many Chinese intellectuals blamed China's "feudal culture" for the country's absolutism, narrow-mindedness, and love of orthodoxy, even calling Chinese people "the ugly Chinese." Although this antitraditionalism (*fanchuantong zhuyi*) never totally dominated Chinese intellectual discourse, it became widespread and highly influential. Modernization was confused with Westernization. In the minds of many Chinese intellectuals, the West represented material wealth, rationality, freedom and democracy, and modernity.

The excessive trend of Westernization, however, quickly vanished after the 1989 Tiananmen tragedy. To the surprise of some observers at the time, many Chinese intellectuals developed an anti-Western sentiment along with a positive appreciation of their own cultural tradition. One study of Chinese intellectual discourse revealed a "strong criticism of the national traitor mentality, leveled at those accused of losing their backbone and surrendering their independence and destiny to others."[29] This new development resulted largely from the discovery by Chinese intellectuals that the post–Cold War transformation in Eastern Europe and the former Soviet Union was not as positive as expected. The West, its values and systems, did not make much difference to post-communist countries. Although Russia took a big-band approach to adopt a democratic system, the Western countries, as Chinese saw it, still tried to weaken Russia's standing in the international affairs by expanding the North Atlantic Treaty Organization (NATO) to Eastern Europe as it struggled internally with its reform program. Even those who supported the 1989 student movement concluded that if China were to initiate the dramatic democratic reform promoted by the West, the nation could well have suffered a similar disorder to what Russia had. In contrast to the former Soviet Union, China's incremental economic reform without democratization brought about rapid economic growth in the 1990s.

The comparison between Russia's failure and China's economic success transformed the nation's intellectual discourse and built up Chinese intellectuals' self-confidence in their tradition and awakened national pride and cultural identities. Many social scientists and humanities scholars called for a "paradigm shift." A conservative, nationalistic intellectual discourse emerged. This discourse supported neo-authoritarianism by arguing that a centralized power structure must be strengthened in order to maintain social stability and economic development. It also vocally promoted cultural nationalism, or an anti-Westernism movement (*fan xifangzhuyi yundong*) that gave top priority to the revival of national and cultural identity as well as state authority.

Neo-authoritarianism that was called for by nationalist discourse was not necessarily associated with either Marxism or Maoism. It was a less Marxist-colored but nondemocratic intellectual discourse that began to emerge in the late 1980s, one that supported a strong and authoritarian state to enforce modernization programs and an "enlightened autocracy" for economic development.[30] Neo-authoritarianism argued that the economic miracle of the four "little dragons" in East Asia was created because they all shared Confucian collectivism, family loyalty, and frugality, as well as patriarchal power structure. Before the Tiananmen incident, neo-authoritarianism was only a heatedly debated topic.[31] It was advocated mainly by some personal aides to Zhao Ziyang, then the CCP general secretary, and by a few scholars such as Shanghai-based Xiao Gongqin and Wang Huning.[32] Many liberal scholars, especially antitraditionalist scholars, argued strongly against neo-authoritarianism by questioning the validity of the alleged causal relationship between Confucianist authoritarianism and economic success.[33] After the Tiananmen incident, when the government enforced official ideological control, non-Marxist voices, even those of neo-authoritarianism, were silenced. Deng Xiaoping's southern China tour in 1992 undermined the extreme rigidity of the conservative ideological control, setting the stage for some less communist ideas, including some neo-authoritarian arguments under a new name, neoconservatism, to reemerge. Neoconservatism emphasized political and economic stability and control while restoring moral values based on the conservative elements of Confucianism.[34]

Immediately after the Tiananmen incident, He Xin, a conservative scholar at the Chinese Academy of Social Science, was the most visible symbol of neoconservatism. He vigorously supported official slogans such as "stability above everything" to defend government action suppressing student demonstrations.[35] But He Xin was quickly rejected by most intellectuals because he was seen as merely saying what the most conservative authorities wanted him to say. In 1992, a group of politically ambitious intellectuals published a widely circulated article, "Realistic Responses and Strategic Choices for China after the Disintegration of the Soviet Union," which became a banner of neoconservatism.[36] The group argued that Marxism-Leninism was no longer effective in mobilizing loyalty and legitimating the state. It was necessary to develop a new ideological vision that drew selectively from China's culture; the CCP should base itself firmly on Chinese nationalism.

Some prominent scholars also joined the chorus of neoconservatism in arguing for strong state power to ward off the possible breakup of the country and economy. In 1994, Xiao Gongqin issued warnings about the dangers of weakening ideological control. Xiao saw no solutions in Western nostrums or in communist ideology but only in nationalism. Xiao's view was elucidated in two articles, "Nationalism and Ideology in China in the Transitional Era" and "History and Prospect of Nationalism in China."[37] Xiao worried about the possible disintegration of Chinese society resulting from the decline of the official ideology and argued that "the central political task of modernization is to prevent the problems of desubstantiation (*kongdonghua*) and povertization (*pinkunhua*) of the ideology due to the lack of ideological resources. Therefore, the overriding issue of China's modernization is how, under new historical circumstances, to find new resources of legitimacy so as to achieve social and moral integration in the process of social transition."[38] According to Xiao, nationalism could play "the function of political integration (*zhengzhi zhenhe*) and cohesion (*ningju*)" in the post–Cold War era.[39] Commenting on South Korean experiences, another scholar, Yi Baoyun, states, "For nations lagging behind, the appropriate choice is not a renunciation of nationalism, but a revitalization of it so as to integrate and elevate people's loyalty on the national level. . . . Nationalism insures national integration so that through a change of the system, the nation can be led to the road of self-strengthening and peaceful competition."[40]

How to understand the changing nature of international conflict in the post–Cold War world is a central concern of the discourse on nationalism. Chinese intellectuals especially noted two views from the West. Francis Fukuyama portrays the end of the Cold War as a triumph of capitalism and Western liberalism and believes that it is not just "the passing of a particular period of postwar history, but the end of history: that is, the end point of mankind's ideological evolution and the universalization of Western liberal democracy as the final form of human government."[41] Samuel P. Huntington, on the other hand, foresees "the clash of civilizations" and argues that geopolitical struggles in the post–Cold War world are not ideologically motivated but defined by different civilizations.[42] In response to these views, Chinese intellectuals are convinced that after the end of the Cold War, nations and countries that used to be confined by ideology have come to realize their own national identity, interests, and values. As a result, a confrontation between different nation-states, understood as cultures, but under the banner of nationalism, is going to replace the opposition between communism and capitalism. The vacuum left by the end of political-ideological confrontation has been filled by nationalism.

Chinese intellectuals paid special attention to Huntington's argument that the biggest threat to Western civilization is Islamic and Confucian culture, thus the West should be alert to a Confucian and Islamic alliance. This argument faced vociferous attacks from Chinese intellectuals. Wang Jisi, director of the American Studies Institute of the Chinese Academy of Social Science, put together a group of Chinese scholars' articles on Huntington's clash of civilizations into a book entitled *Civilization and International Politics*.[43] Wang Xiaodong (using a pen name, Shi Zhong), one of the editors of *Zhanlue yu Guanli*, published an article in the first issue of the journal to rebuff Huntington. He argued that there was no desire on the part of the Chinese to Confucianize the rest of the world and that useful Western values were generally welcomed by the Chinese apart from the instances where their transmission involved economic and other forms of imperialism. According to Wang, any future conflicts would depend on economic interests; the thesis of a clash of civilizations was little more than a guise for the clash of national interests. China could come into conflict with other powers because of its growing economic strength.[44] In another article, Wang criticized the overly optimistic view of globalization on the grounds that the real power of this globalization process was singularly beneficial to the West. That is, interdependence and liberal internationalism were seen as myths hiding the continuing reality of neomercantilist nationalism. Under these circumstances, nationalism is indispensable and a rational choice for advancing the interests of China.[45]

Due to the rise of nationalism, Chinese intellectuals took more critical attitudes toward Western mainstream scholarship. In the 1980s, Chinese intellectuals became familiar with the West mostly by reading a large number of Western scholarly works, which were translated into Chinese. Many of these books were printed in runs of hundreds of thousands, outnumbering the printing in their native languages. Frequent and wide international exchange, especially with the United States, allowed many Chinese intellectuals to take a closer look at Western societies and their academic world, which helped remove the myth of Western modernization models and gave Chinese the courage and ammunition to criticize Western theories. Previously the West was a remote object of admiration and imitation, convincing Chinese scholars that all nations would converge on the model of modernization found in Western industrialized countries. When Chinese scholars traveled to the West and obtained a deeper understanding, they saw the inherent problems in the West and came to believe that the so-called universal theories and principles of modernization were only unique products of Western history and culture. There was a huge gap between the Western model and Chinese reality. This led these intellectuals to doubt the worth of modern Western values to Chinese society and the utility of mainstream Western theories for building strong China. Therefore, some Chinese intellectuals turned to critical theories of the West, such as postcolonialism and post-Marxism, in an attempt to find intellectual inspiration for a new path of modernization that would fit the Chinese essence (*guoqing*). Some other scholars looked toward non-Western civilizations, including the Chinese, to discover a new path that can resolve the problems that arose in the process of China's modernization. An increasing number of young intellectuals began to realize that China had to modernize itself according to its own national and historical conditions.

As a result, Chinese intellectuals rediscovered the value of the Chinese cultural legacy, which the party had so relentlessly attacked for so long. Aware of the incompatibility of the orthodox official doctrines with the needs of modernization, many intellectuals argued that old-style communist indoctrination would not be effective, that a new way of thinking must be found. This new way was an embrace of Chinese culture and a negating of the so-called Western value system. A new awareness arose of a need to articulate a more vivid sense of Chinese collective identity. The authors of *The China That Can Say No* confessed that back at colleges they craved Western culture and things, but they began to think differently after Beijing's defeat in the Olympic site competition and after U.S. aircraft carriers were sent to defend Taiwan in March 1996. Before the Chinese could say no to the Americans, they had to say no first to their own lack of nationalistic spirit and to their blind worship of the United States.[46] This feeling gave rise to cultural nationalism, which took Chinese culture as a symbol against Western cultural hegemony (or cultural colonialism). Only Chinese culture could serve the positive function of maintaining political order. Opposition to Western cultural hegemony and cultural colonialism was a central concern of cultural nationalism. As a result of the upsurge of cultural nationalism, the "Western learning fever" (*xixue re*) was replaced by a "Chinese/Confucius learning fever" (*guoxue re*) among intellectuals, especially humanities scholars. Intellectual debates were redefined in terms of "Chinese-ness." Some scholars called for an academic nativism (*xueshu bentuhua*)— namely, extracting a brand-new set of concepts and theories from ancient Chinese thoughts and experiences. Liu Kang and Li Xiguang, two leading advocates of cultural nationalism, stated that "in the 1990s, Chinese intellectuals ought to ... liberate themselves from 'modern' Western speech and thought patterns, and acquire a new understanding of modern nationalism and nativism, to form a genuinely humane spirit (*renwen jingsheng*) and rebuild their 'academic lineage' and 'ethical traditions' with Chinese culture."[47] In this intellectual discourse, Chinese culture not only counteracted the invasion of Western culture, but also replaced the unwelcome official ideological doctrines. *Fayang chuantong* (getting back to tradition) became a call of cultural nationalism. In this way, Chinese intellectual discourse concurred with the central theme of state-led nationalism advocated in patriotic education by the communist government. Yet it arrived at this point largely independent of government indoctrination. Because it discarded official ideological rhetoric, its arguments seemed more influential and persuasive to many Chinese.[48]

Conclusion

The rallying under the banner of nationalism in the 1990s occurred after the crackdown on the prodemocracy movement in 1989. This revival of Chinese nationalism represented a great aggregation of various political and intellectual forces with different motivations and agendas. Besides the government propaganda campaign in fanning nationalistic flames, the intellectual undercurrent moved almost simultaneously in the same direction. As Wang Xiaodong (Shi Zhong) observed, "among those under the banner of nationalism, there is a full array of people, some of whom advocate authoritarianism, others who support expansionism; while some people believe in more state controls, others uphold the total freedom of a market economy. There are also those who propose a return to tradition and others opposing this restoration."[49] Nationalism addressed pragmatic concerns of both the Chinese government and the intellectual elite about establishing domestic order and stability for modernization. The Communist regime used nationalism as an instrument to strengthen its authority and to create a sense of commonalty among citizens when the regime faced a threat to its legitimacy. The Communist state, therefore, stressed the pragmatic or instrumental aspect of nationalism rather than its intrinsic value. The Chinese government promoted nationalist sentiment to hold the nation together during a period of rapid and turbulent transition toward the post–Cold War era and to reduce the threat of liberalism and democracy to Communist authoritarian legitimacy. Nationalism also helped Chinese intellectuals to participate in the modernization process by identifying with the Chinese nation. Many Chinese intellectuals were afraid of the serious danger of national integration and suspected the West of using the issues of democracy and human rights to obstruct and delay China's modernization. Patriotic intellectuals indicate that "backward is apt to be beaten" and called upon the Chinese people to work hard and to build a prosperous China and strong Chinese state. Following some elites of other East Asian countries, they rejected liberal democracy on the basis that "democracies can . . . prevent rapid economic development."[50]

From this perspective, it is clear that Chinese nationalism in the 1990s was closely related to a conservative or authoritarian political and intellectual tendency. It is similar to Liah Greenfeld's collectivistic-authoritarian nationalism. Although the rise of nationalism was not totally detached from the Chinese intellectual search for and affirmation of individual subjectivity and dignity, the notion of the collectivity and even the authoritarian state was taken as a starting point of nationalist discourse. The individuality had to be sacrificed in the collectivity and totality of the nation and state.

Associated with authoritarianism, Chinese nationalism lacked a cosmopolitan outlook to reach out to the best of the world's civilization. As a matter of fact, the resurgence of the Chinese nationalist discourse was particularly concerned with the fate of the Chinese culture, as well as on how Chinese culture could contribute to the solution of many problems of modernity. Some Chinese scholars argued that Asians in general and Chinese in particular have their own set of values, different from those of the West. Some even suggest that Asian values are superior and should therefore be the criteria of the values of the world in the next century. Sheng Hong, a controversial economist in Beijing, launched a fierce attack on Western civilization in an article published in a 1994 issue of *Zhanlie yu Guanli.* According to Sheng, Western civilizations developed out of monotheistic religions. Because each religion worshipped only one god, war and competition were inevitable. In the context of religious conflict and competition, social Darwinism developed. Sheng claimed that Western culture thus would neither be able to save China nor the world but would lead humanity into catastrophe. Only Chinese civilization could save China, and eventually the world, because it was not developed from a monotheistic religious form. Confucian respect for universal harmony and collectivism in Chinese culture are instrumental for world peace and development.[51] Following the lead of prime minister Mahatier of Malaysia and Shintaro Ishihara of Japan in their books, *The Asia That Can Say No* and *The Japan That Can Say No,* Chinese nationalists published a series of "Say No" books, such as *The China That Can Say No,*[52] *The China That Still Can Say No,*[53] and *How Can China Say No.*[54]

This type of Chinese nationalism was particularly hostile toward the United States, because the United States represents an opposing value system—that is, liberalism and individualism. Deep-rooted nationalist sentiments among Chinese people were also directed against Japan, due mainly to the humiliation and injustices the Chinese people suffered at the hands of Japanese imperialists during World War II. The animosity toward Japan did not have a cultural value dimension. Thus, the United States was treated in a very different way in nationalistic sentiments. The 1996 bestseller, *The China That Can Say No*, stated, "The moral decay inside the United States for the past several centuries has formed evil results," and the United States will "inevitably face a fin-de-siècle-type general squaring of accounts." As a comparison, the book asserted that "the power of Chinese thought and Chinese managerial ability will deeply affect the world, and become the only force leading the future human ideological trend."[55] This type of Chinese nationalism raises a serious question about how Chinese nationalism could be compatible with the worldwide trend of democratization when China is further incorporated into the modern world system.

Notes

1. Ernst B. Haas, *Nationalism, Liberalism, and Progress: The Rise and Decline of Nationalism* (Ithaca, N.Y.: Cornell University Press, 1997), vii.
2. Liah Greenfeld, *Nationalism: Five Roads to Modernity* (Cambridge, Mass.: Harvard University Press, 1992), 11.
3. Hans Kohn, "Nationalism," *International Encyclopedia of the Social Sciences,* vol. 11 (1968), 63.
4. James Harrison, *Modern Chinese Nationalism* (New York: Hunter College Research Institute on Modern Asia, 1969), 2.
5. Joseph Levenson, *Liang Ch'i-ch'ao and the Mind of Modern China* (Berkeley and Los Angeles: University of California Press, 1967), 108.
6. John Fitzgerald, "The Nationless State: The Search for a Nation in Modern Chinese Nationalism," in Jonathan Unger, ed., *Chinese Nationalism* (Armonk, N.Y.: M. E. Sharpe, 1996), 67.
7. Han Jinchun and Li Yifu, "Hanwen 'minzu' yi ci de chuxian jiqi chuqi shiyong qingkuang" (The Emergence of the Term "Minzu" in Chinese Language and Usage), *Minzu yanjiu* 2 (1984), 36–43.
8. Andrew J. Nathan and Robert S. Ross, *The Great Wall and the Empty Fortress: China's Search for Security* (New York: W. W. Norton, 1997), 32–33.
9. Xiao Gongqin, "Zhongguo Minzu Zhuyi de Lishi yu Qianjing" (The History and Prospect of Chinese Nationalism), *Zhanlie yu Guanli* 2 (1996), 59.
10. For one study of the struggle between the conservatives and reformers in the ideological arena after the Tiananmen incident, see Suisheng Zhao, "Deng Xiaoping's Southern Tour: Elite Politics in Post-Tiananmen China," *Asian Survey* 33, no. 8 (1993), 739–56.
11. Liah Greenfeld, *Nationalism*, 3.
12. Joseph S. Nye Jr., *Understanding International Conflicts* (New York: Harper Collins, 1993), 61.
13. Jiang Zemin, "Patriotism and the Mission of Chinese Intellectuals," *Xinhua*, May 3, 1990 (electronic edition).
14. Charles Tilly, "States and Nationalism in Europe, 1492–1992," in John L. Comaroff and Paul C. Stern, eds., *Perspectives on Nationalism and War* (Amsterdam, the Netherlands: Gordon and Breach, 1995), 190.

15. Because of its state-centric nature, Michael Hunt argues against reducing Chinese patriotism to the Western term *nationalism.* Hunt, "Chinese National Identity and the Strong State: The Late Qing-Republican Crisis," in Lowell Dittmer and Samuel S. Kim, eds., *China's Quest for National Identity* (Ithaca, N.Y.: Cornell University Press, 1994), 63.

16. "To Construct the Motherland More Beautiful and Better," *Renmin Ribao,* October 1, 1996, 1.

17. "Beijing Students Watch Patriotic Films," *Xinhua,* May 16, 1994 (electronic edition).

18. "Ding Guangen, Li Lanqing" (Patriotic Education Meeting), Beijing Central Television program, May 21, 1994, translated in Foreign Broadcast and Information Service (FBIS)-CHI-94-102, May 26, 1994, 18.

19. *Renmin Ribao,* September 6, 1994, 1.

20 Geoffrey Crothall, "China: Patriotic Patter Winning Students," *South China Morning Post,* July 10, 1994, 8.

21. Steven Mufson, "Maoism, Confucianism Blur into Nationalism," *Washington Post,* March 19, 1996, A1.

22. For one excellent description on how the CCP used the Great Wall for patriotic education purposes, see Arthur Waldron, "Scholarship and Patriotic Education: The Great War Conference, 1994," *China Quarterly* 143 (1995), 844–50.

23. "Beijing Radio Commentator on Party's Patriotic Education Document," *Reuters Textline,* September 7, 1994 (electronic edition).

24. "Gaoju Aiguozhuyi Qizhi" (Hold High the Banner of Patriotism), *Renmin Ribao,* November 28, 1993, 1.

25. Song Qiang, Zhang Zangzang, and Qiao Bian, *Zhongguo Keyi Shuo Bu (The China That Can Say No)* (Beijing: Zhonghua Gongshang Lianhe Chubanshe, 1996).

26. Samuel Wang, "Teaching Patriotism in China," *China Strategic Review* 1, no. 4 (1996), 13.

27. For one systematic description of the cultural fever, see Wu Xiuyi, *Zhongguo Wenhua Re* (*China's Cultural Fever*) (Shanghai: Shanghai Renmin Chuban She, 1988). Chen Kuide, the former chief editor of *Sixiangjia (Thinker)* in Shanghai and one of the active participants in the cultural fever, wrote an excellent article to reflect cultural fever, "Wenhua Re: Beijing, Shichao ji Liangzhong Qinxiang" (The Cultural Fever: Background, Ideology, and Two Tendencies), in Chen Kuide, ed., *Zhongguo Dalu Dangdai Wenhua Bianqian (Contemporary Cultural Changes in Mainland China)* (Taipei: Guigan Chuban She, 1991).

28. Merle Goldman, Perry Link, and Su Wei, "China's Intellectuals in the Deng Era: Loss of Identity with the State," in Dittmer and Kim, eds., *China's Quest for National Identity,* 143.

29. Min Lin with Maria Galikowski, *The Search for Modernity: Chinese Intellectuals and Cultural Discourse in the Post-Mao Era* (New York: St. Martin's Press, 1999), 161.

30. Liu Zaiping, "Summary of a Seminar on New Authoritarianism," *Guangmin Ribao,* March 24, 1996.

31. For a collection of debate articles, see Qi Me, ed., *Qing Quanwei Zhuyi: Dui Zhongguo Dalu Weilai Mingyun de Lunzheng* (New Authoritarianism: A Debate for the Future of Mainland China) (Taipei: Tangshan Chuban She, 1991). For a collection of English translation articles on this debate, see Stanley Rosen and Gary Zou, eds., "The Chinese Debate on the New Authoritarianism," *Chinese Sociology and Anthropology,* Winter 1990–91.

32. For some representative titles, See Xiao Gongqin, "Quanwei yu minzhu: he fazhan guojia de lianglan xuanzhe" (Authority and Democracy: The Dilemma for Late-Developing Countries), "Lun guodu xing quanwei zhengzhi de xiandaihua yiyi" (On the Significance of Transitional Authoritarian Politics), "Dongyia quanwei zhengzhi yu xiandaihua" (Authoritarian Politics and Modernization in East Asia), all in *Xiao Gongqin Ji (Collected Works of Xiao Gongqin)* (Harbin: Helongjiang Jiaoyu Chuban She, 1995).

33. See, for example, Huang Wansheng, "Questions and Answers on the Criticism of New Authoritarianism," *Wenhui Bao*, February 22, 1989; Bao Zunxin, "Confucian Ethics and the Four Little Dragons of Asia," *Wenhui Bao*, May 12, 1988.

34. For one systematical analysis of neoconservatism, see Joseph Fewsmith, "Neoconservatism and the End of the Dengist Era," *Asian Survey* 35, no. 7 (1995), 635–51.

35. He Xin's articles are collected in *Zhonghua Fuxing yi Shijie Weilai* (*Renovation of China and the Future of the World*), two vols., (Chengdou: Shichuan Renmin Chuban She, 1996), and *Wei Zhongguo Shengbian* (*Defending China*) (Jinan: Shandong Youyi Chuban She, 1996).

36. This article was first published in the name of the Ideology and Theory Department of the *Zhongguo Qingnian Bao* (*China Youth Daily*) as an internal circulating article in September 1991. It quickly leaked abroad and was reprinted in the *Zhongguo Zhichun* (*China Spring*) in New York City. I interviewed one of the authors of this article in Beijing in the summer of 1994. He confirmed the above speculation that it was written based on the proceedings of a meeting held in *Zhongguo Qingnian Bao* and the participants were a group of party and government officials active in policy analysis and consulting for the post-Tiananmen leadership.

37. Xiao Gongqin, "Minzuzhuyi yu Zhongguo Zhungxing Shiqide Yishi Xingtai" (Nationalism and Ideology in China in the Transitional Era), *Zhanlue yu Guanli* 4 (1994), 21–25, and "Zhongguo Minzuzhuyi de Lishi yu Qianjing" (History and Prospect of Nationalism in China), *Zhanlue yu Guanli* 2 (1996), 58–62.

38. Xiao Gongqin, "Minzuzhuyi yu Zhongguo Zhungxing Shiqide Yishi Xingtai" (Nationalism and Ideology in China in the Transitional Era), *Zhanlue yu Guanli*, no. 4, 1994, 23.

39. Xiao Gongqin, "History and Prospect of Nationalism in China," 62.

40. Yi Baoyun, "Minzu Zhuyi yu xiandai jingji fazhan" (Nationalism and Modern Economic Development), *Zhanlie yu Guanli* 3 (1994), 32.

41. Ibid., 4.

42. Samuel B. Huntington, "The Clash of Civilizations," *Foreign Affairs* 72, no. 3 (1993); and *The Clash of Civilizations and the Remaking of World Order* (New York: Simon and Schuster, 1996).

43. Wang Jishi, ed., *Wenmin yu Guoji Zhengzhi: Zhongguo Xuezhe Ping Huntington de Wenmin Chongtulun* (Civilization and International Politics: Chinese Scholars on Huntington's Clash of Civilizations) (Shanghai: Shanghai Renmin Chuban She, 1995).

44. Shi Zhong (Wang Xiaodong), "Weilai de Chongtu" (Future Conflicts), *Zhanlie yu Guanli* 1 (1993), 46–50.

45. Shi Zhong, "Zhongguo xiandaihua mianlin de tiaozhan" (The Challenges to China's Modernization), *Zhanlie yu Guanli* 1 (1994), 9.

46. Song Qiang, Zhang Zangzang, and Qiao Bian, *Zhongguo Keyi Shuo Bu* (*The China That Can Say No*) (Beijing: Zhonghua Gongshang Lianhe Chubanshe, 1996), 3–15.

47. Li Xiguang and Liu Kang, "Kan meiguo zhuliu meiti dui zhonggao de baodao" (A Look at the Coverage of China by the Mainstream US Media) *Zhongguo Jizhe* (*The Chinese Journalist*), May 15, 1996, p, 19. For an English translation of this article, see FBIS-CHI-96-147, July 30, 1996, 4–8.

48. Some parts of discussion in this section are adapted from my article, "Chinese Intellectuals' Quest for National Greatness and Nationalist Writing in the 1990s," *China Quarterly* 152 (1997), 725–45.

49. Shi Zhong, "Zhongguo de minzu Zhuyi yu zhongguo de weilai" (Chinese Nationalism and China's Future), *Huaxia Wenzhai* (China Digest), an Internet electronic magazine, 1996, n.p.

50. Kisbore Mahbubani, "The Pacific Way," *Foreign Affairs* 74, no. 1 (1995), 103.

51. Sheng Hong, "Shenme shi wenmin" (What Is Civilization?), *Zhanlue yu Guanli* 5 (1995); "Chong minzuzhuyi dao tianxiazhuyi" (From Nationalism to Cosmopolitanism), *Zhanlue yu Guanli* 1 (1996); and "Jingjixue tiaozhan xifang" (Economics Challenges the West), *Dongfang* 1 (1996).

52. Song Qiang, Zhang Zangzang, and Qiao Bian, *The China That Can Say No.*
53. Song Qiang, Zhang Zangzang, Qiao Bian, Tang Zhengyu, and Gu Qingsheng, *Zhongguo haishi neng shuo bu* (The China That Still Can Say No) (Beijing: Zhongguo Wenlian Chuban She, 1996).
54. Zhang Xueli, *Zhongguo heyi shuo bu* (How Can China Say No) (Beijing: Hualin Chuban She, 1996).
55. Song Qiang, Zhang Zangzang, Qiao Bian, *The China That Can Say No,* 49, 50, 51, 230.

About the Editor
and Contributors

The Editor

Suisheng Zhao is 1999–2000 Campbell National Fellow at the Hoover Institution of Stanford University; associate professor in the department of government at Colby College and the department of political science at Washington College; research associate at the Fairbank Center for East Asian Research, Harvard University; and founder and editor of the *Journal of Contemporary China*. He received a Ph.D. degree in political science from the University of California–San Diego, and is the author of *Power by Design: Constitution-Making in Nationalist China* (University of Hawaii Press, 1995) and others. His most recent book is *Across the Taiwan Strait: Mainland China, Taiwan, and the 1995–96 Crisis* (Routledge, 1999). His articles have appeared in *Political Science Quarterly*, *China Quarterly*, *World Affairs*, *Asian Survey*, *Journal of Northeast Asian Studies*, *Asian Affairs*, *Journal of Democracy*, *Communism and Post-Communism Studies*, *Brown Journal of World Affairs*, *Problems of Post-Communism*, *Journal of East Asian Affairs*, *Issues and Studies*, *Journal of Contemporary China*, and elsewhere.

The Contributors

Allen Carlson received his Ph.D. from the department of political science at Yale University and is assistant professor at the department of government, Cornell University.

Che-po Chan is an assistant professor of political science at Lingnan University, Hong Kong.

271

Larry Diamond is a senior research fellow at the Hoover Institution of Stanford University, co-editor of the *Journal of Democracy,* and co-director of the National Endowment for Democracy's International Forum for Democratic Studies. He is the author of *Developing Democracy: Toward Consolidation,* and has edited numerous books on democracy, including *The Global Resurgence of Democracy* (Johns Hopkins University Press, 1996) and *Democracy in East Asia* (Johns Hopkins University Press, 1996) (both with Marc F. Plattner), and *Consolidating the Third Wave Democracies* (Johns Hopkins University Press, 1996) (with Marc F. Plattner, Yun-han Chu, and Hung-mao Tien). He is also co-editor, with Ramon H. Myers of a special issue of *China Quarterly* on "Elections and Democracy in Greater China," which is also forthcoming as a book from Oxford University Press. Currently he is writing about democratic development and consolidation in Taiwan.

Yijiang Ding received his Ph.D. in political Science from the University of Calgary in Canada. He was a research associate at the Asian Pacific Foundation of Canada in 1998 and 1999 and is currently assistant professor in the department of political science, Okanagan University College, Canada.

Daniel V. Dowd is a doctoral candidate in the department of political science at Yale University.

Dawn Einwalter received her Ph.D. in sociocultural anthropology at the University of Washington and is currently teaching at the University of Nevada–Reno.

Edward X. Gu received his Ph.D. from the Sinological Institute of Leiden University in the Netherlands and is currently a research fellow at the East Asian Institute at the National University of Singapore.

Baogang He received his Ph.D. from the department of political science, Research School of Social Science, Australian National University, in 1993 and an M.A. from the People's University of China in Beijing in 1986. He is currently an associate professor in the department of political science, University of Tasmania in Australia. He is the author of *The Democratization of China* (New York: Routledge, 1996), *The Democratic Implications of Civil Society in China* (London: Macmillan, 1997), and *Nationalism, National Identity and Democratization in China* (London: Ashgate, 1999, co-authored with Yingjie Guo). He has co-authored and co-translated several books in Chinese (including John Rawls's *A Theory of Justice*), and has published more than twenty articles in English in *Journal of Communist Studies, Modern China, Journal of Democratization, the Australian Journal of Political Science, Social Philosophy and Policies*, and elsewhere. Presently, he is working on a book on democracy and the boundary problem in East Asia, to be published by Routledge in 2000.

Shaohua Hu is currently a visiting assistant professor at Colgate University's department of political science. He received his Ph.D. from the American University's School of International Service, and his B.A. and M.A. from Beijing University's department of international politics. A former research fellow at the Institute of World Economy and Politics of the Chinese Academy of Social Sciences, he is the author of *Explaining Chinese Democratization* (Westport, Conn.: Praeger, 2000).

Andrew J. Nathan is professor of political science and former director of the East Asian Institute, Columbia University. He is co-author of *The Great Wall and the Empty Fortress* (New York: W. W. Norton, 1997) and author of *China's Transition* (New York: Columbia University Press, 1997).

Mingming Shen received his Ph.D. from the department of political science, University of Michigan, and is currently the director of the Research Center for Contemporary China and an associate professor of political science at Beijing University, China.

Tianjian Shi received his Ph.D. degree in political science from Columbia University. He is associate professor of political science at Duke University and the author of *Political Participation in Beijing* (Cambridge, Mass.: Harvard University Press, 1997).

Regina F. Titunik is an assistant professor of political science at the University of Hawaii–Hilo. She received her Ph.D. from the University of Chicago in 1991. She is the author of "The Continuation of History: Max Weber and the Advent of a New Aristocracy," in the *Journal of Politics* 59 (1997).

Enbao Wang is an assistant professor of political science at the University of Hawaii–Hilo. He received his Ph.D. from the University of Alabama in 1993. He is the author of *Hong Kong, 1997: The Politics of Transition* (Boulder, Colo.: Lynne Riener, 1995).

Index